E3

CW01672898

ROT
CONCIS
TO LONDON

Rothmans

Rothmans Publications Limited

First published 1981 by Portman Publishing Limited.

While every effort has been made to ensure the accuracy of all entries in this Guide, the publishers cannot accept any liability under any circumstances should any description be found inaccurate. It is important to note that the prices shown are those given to us by the proprietors at the time of going to press. Similarly the reported standards and facilities are as known to us at the date of publication. We would appreciate it if any inaccuracies were drawn to our attention.

All rights reserved. No part of this publication may be reproduced, stored in a retrieval system, or transmitted in any form or by any means, electrical, mechanical, photocopied, recorded or otherwise, without the prior permission of the publisher.

Editor
Joy Leslie Gibson
Assistant Editor/Research
Pat King

Research
Mary Lynsky
Mary Lewis

Contributors:
William Forrester
Nicholas Goodison
Nanette Newman

Design
Dennis Fairey & Associates Ltd.
Title Page Illustrations
Dexter Brown
Photography & Illustrations
Marina Palmer

Acknowledgements
The London Tourist Board
City of London Information Centre
Daily Telegraph Information Bureau
London Transport
British Rail

© Rothmans Publications Ltd. PO Box 100, Oxford Road, Aylesbury, Bucks. *ISBN 0 907574 21 1*

Printed & Bound by A Wheaton & Company Limited, Exeter.

Typesetting by Citype Limited, Leicester.

As Lord Mayor of London I welcome you to this great city. I hope that the information in this guide will help to make your visit both interesting and enjoyable.

The Lord Mayor of London
Sir Anthony Jolliffe

Rothmans
of Pall Mall

Contents

London Transport Underground Map Registered User Number 83/065.

Introduction

Welcome to London and to this guide book. With its help you will be able to discover some of the rich variety of our capital city and meet some of the people who make London a special place.
History, pageantry, museum and art galleries are some of the reasons why people come to London — and they are not disappointed. All through the year the pageantry of British life is on view. The Changing of the Guard at Buckingham Palace, Horseguards Parade, Windsor Castle and the Ceremony of the Keys at the Tower of London continue today as they have for many hundreds of years in various guises. Colourful processions for the Trooping the Colour, the State Opening of Parliament, the Lord Mayor's Show, not to mention other royal occasions such as weddings, are not mere rituals of traditions but play a real part in the affairs of City and State.
Our free museums and galleries offer a choice of works of art from around the world and artefacts covering every period of history. The exploration of London's own history would ideally start at the Museum of London where the living history of London is recorded and where the City's busy archaelogical team is based.
The London of today is just as exciting with shops and stores from the elegance of Bond Street and Knightsbridge to the lively informality of Covent Garden Market. Theatres, concerts, cinemas and the great variety of restaurants complete the picture, making a good comprehensive guide book such as this a necessity.
Enjoy London and come back again soon.

Mrs Mary Baker
Chairman, London Tourist Board

Helpful information about London

A B C D E F G H I J K L
1 2 3 4 5 6
Kensal Green
KILBURN LANE
HARROW ROAD
FERNHEAD RD.
ELGIN AVENUE
CASTELLAIN RD.
Maida Vale
MAIDA VALE
ST. JOHNS WOOD RD.
WELLINGTON ROAD
REGENT'S PARK
ALBANY STREET
EUSTON STATION
EUSTON ROAD
GRAYS INN ROAD
KING'S CROSS ROAD
ROSEBERRY AVENUE
GOSWELL ROAD
CITY ROAD
OLD STREET
Old Street
GREAT EASTERN ST.
HACKNEY ROAD
LADBROKE GROVE
Ladbroke Grove
Westbourne Park
GREAT WESTERN RD
WESTBOURNE PARK
TALBOT ROAD
CHEPSTOW RD.
COLVILLE TER.
BISHOPS BRIDGE ROAD
WESTBOURNE GROVE
CLIFTON GDNS
Warwick Avenue
LISSON GROVE
EDGWARE ROAD
Edgware Road
Marylebone
MARYLEBONE ROAD
Baker Street
Regent's Park
Great Portland Street
Warren Street
Goodge Street
TOTTENHAM COURT RD.
GOWER STREET
SOUTHAMPTON ROW
GUILFORD ST.
THEOBALDS RD.
CLERKEN WELL ROAD
FARRINGDON ST.
Chancery Lane
ALDERSGATE ST.
CITY ROAD
Moorgate
MOORGATE
Bank
LIVERPOOL ST. STATION
BISHOPSGATE
COMMERCIAL ST.
WHITECHAPEL
PADDINGTON STATION
WESTBOURNE TER
SEYMOUR PLACE
PORTMAN SQUARE
BAKER STREET
MARYLEBONE HIGH ST.
PORTLAND PL.
REGENT ST.
Oxford Circus
OXFORD STREET
GOODGE ST.
Tottenham Court Rd.
NEW OXFORD STREET
HOLBORN
Holborn
HOLBORN VIA
CHANCERY LANE
FLEET ST.
St Paul's
CHEAPSIDE
HOUNDSDITCH
Aldgate
LEMAN ST.
Marble Arch
Marble Arch
GROSVENOR SQUARE
Bond Street
NEW BOND ST.
OLD BOND ST.
POLAND ST.
WARDOUR ST.
CHARING CROSS ROAD
SHAFTESBURY AV.
DRURY LANE
LONG ACRE
Covent Garden
Aldwych
STRAND
Somerset House
Temple
EMBANKMENT
LUDGATE HILL
QUEEN VICTORIA ST.
Blackfriars
Mansion House
LEADENHALL ST.
FENCHURCH ST.
Monument
Tower Hill
MINORIES
EAST SMITHFIELD
Lancaster Gate
Bayswater
PEMBRIDGE RD
QUEENSWAY
Queensway
BAYSWATER ROAD
Notting Hill Gate
NOTTING HILL GATE
PORTLAND ROAD
ELGIN CRES.
BLENHEIM CRES.
CLARENDON RD.
KENSINGTON GARDENS
HYDE PARK
SERPENTINE
ROTTEN ROW
PARK LANE
BERKELEY SQUARE
CURZON ST.
PICCADILLY
Piccadilly Circus
Leicester Square
CHARING CROSS STATION
WATERLOO BRIDGE
BLACKFRIARS BRIDGE
RIVER THAMES
SOUTHWARK BRIDGE
LONDON BRIDGE
Monument
TOWER HILL
TOWER BRIDGE
HOLLAND PARK AVENUE
Holland Park
KENSINGTON CHURCH ST
Hyde Park Corner
Green Park
GREEN PARK
PALL MALL
THE MALL
ST. JAMES'S PARK
VICTORIA
STAMFORD ST.
SOUTHWARK STREET
TOOLEY STREET
ST. THOMAS ST.
Borough
HOLLAND PARK
CAMPDEN HILL RD
KENSINGTON HIGH STREET
KENSINGTON RD.
KNIGHTSBRIDGE
Knightsbridge
BELGRAVE SQUARE
GROSVENOR PL.
BIRDCAGE WALK
St James's Park
Westminster
WESTMINSTER BRIDGE
YORK ROAD
WATERLOO ROAD
WATERLOO STATION
Lambeth North
BLACKFRIARS RD.
SOUTHWARK BRIDGE RD.
BOROUGH HIGH ST.
LONDON BRI. STATION
LONG LANE
HOLLAND ROAD
High Street Kensington
QUEEN'S GATE
EXHIBITION ROAD
South Kensington
BROMPTON ROAD
BEAUCHAMP PLACE
WALTON RD.
CADOGAN GDNS
SLOANE STREET
VICTORIA STREET
VAUXHALL BRIDGE ROAD
HORSE FERRY ROAD
LAMBETH BRIDGE
LAMBETH PALACE RD.
WESTMINSTER BRIDGE RD.
LAMBETH ROAD
BOROUGH RD.
CAUSEWAY
NEWINGTON
LONDON RD.
ST. GEORGE'S RD.
GREAT DOVER ST.
HAMMERSMITH ROAD
EARLS COURT ROAD
CROMWELL ROAD
Gloucester Road
OLD BROMPTON ROAD
SYDNEY ST.
KING'S ROAD
Sloane Square
BUCKINGHAM PALACE ROAD
VICTORIA STATION
MILL BANK
THAMES
ALBERT EMBANKMENT
KENNINGTON ROAD
Elephant and Castle
NEW KENT RD
WALWORTH ROAD
OLD KENT ROAD
ABBEY STREET
SHEPHERD'S BUSH RD
WARWICK ROAD
WEST CROMWELL ROAD
NORTH END ROAD
Earls Court
TALGARTH ROAD
FULHAM PALACE ROAD
LILLIE ROAD
West Brompton
REDCLIFF GARDENS
FULHAM ROAD
ROYAL HOSPITAL ROAD
CHELSEA BRIDGE RD
Pimlico
CHELSEA EMBANKMENT
CHELSEA BRIDGE
GROSVENOR ROAD
VAUXHALL BRIDGE
Vauxhall
HARLEYFORD RD
KENNINGTON PARK ROAD
Kennington Park
ALBANY ROAD
KING'S ROAD
ALBERT BRIDGE
BATTERSEA PARK
NINE ELMS LANE
FENTIMAN RD
Oval

HELPFUL INFORMATION ABOUT LONDON

CURRENCY

The currency is based on The *(£)* Pound Sterling and is a decimal system with 100 pence making one Pound. Bank notes are in values of £50, £20, £10, £5 and £1. The coins are 50p, 20p, 10p and 5p, all cupro-nickel *(silver)* and 2p, 1p and ½p in bronze *(copper)*. Often £1 notes are called *quids*, £5 notes, *fivers* and £10 notes *tenners*. A £1 coin is to be issued in 1983. Most hotels and many stores accept American dollars but with a lower exchange rate than banks.

Banks London is famous for the number of international banking houses so there is never a problem exchanging money or travellers cheques.

Exchange Rate Due to the frequent fluctuations of rates it is best to check at any bank where a list of all the major currencies and the equivalent rate of exchange is displayed. The major newspapers also give this information.

TIPPING

Most restaurants and hotels in London automatically add a 10% to 15% service charge on your final bill. When this occurs you do *not* have to give any more remuneration as a tip. If however you feel that the service you have received has been exceptional then you can if you wish add an amount to the bill.

Hotels If no service charge has been added then it is normal to add 10% to 15%, depending upon the service received, to the bill. In hotels you can either give the individual staff members i.e. chambermaids, housekeepers, cash remuneration or when paying the bill mention to the receptionist that you are adding something. Porters usually receive 10p per bag.

Restaurants It is usual to tip 10% to 15% of the final bill.

Taxis Taxi drivers can be paid 10% to 15% on the final metered figure.

Hairdressers It is usual to tip 20% of the bill.

Shops No tipping.

Bars and Cocktail Lounges No tipping when standing at the bar and 10% if you receive waiter service.

TELEPHONES

Telephone kiosks are plentiful in the streets — they are at present red in colour, but are being changed to yellow — and in Post Offices.

Instructions on how to telephone are clearly fixed inside the kiosk.

Telephones are on a timed calling system and the coins required are 5p *(approximately 3 minutes)* and 10p *(approximately 6 minutes)*.

Various telephone numbers and services are as follows:-

EMERGENCY	999
OPERATOR	100
DIRECTORY ENQUIRIES *(London area)*	142
DIRECTORY ENQUIRIES *(Great Britain)*	192
WEATHER FORECAST	01-246 8091
TIME	123
BED TIME STORIES	01-246 8000
CHILDRENS LONDON	01-246 8007
TEST MATCH	154

DAILY EVENTS IN LONDON

(In English)	01-246 8041
(In French)	01-246 8043
(In German)	01-246 8045
ALARM CALLS	Dial 100 and book call through Operator.

Check the cost of any long distance call if you make it from your Hotel room.

MAIL

Post Boxes are usually sited on street corners and there are plenty in London.
Like the Telephone Kiosks they are also red. Collection times are clearly stated on the front of each box. There are two rates of postage, slow and fast, for inland letters and cards up to 60 grams. If you have a bulky letter or a parcel you should check it into the nearest Post Office for weighing.

TELEGRAMS

These can be sent from any Post Office or direct by telephone by dialling 190 for Great Britain or 193 for Overseas. If you send from a coin box you must have the exact money in 5p or 10p coins.

POST OFFICES

Open: 9.00am-5.00pm, Monday to Friday.
9.00am-12.30pm on Saturday.
Map Ref. 3H

Some central Post Offices:

43 Albemarle Street, W.1.
Tel: 01-493 5620
Map Ref. 3G

111 Baker Street, W.1.
Tel: 01-935 3701
Map Ref. 3G

15 Broadwick Street, W.1.
Tel: 01-437 6842
Map Ref. 2G

10 Parkway, N.W.1.
Tel: 01-485 3550
Map Ref. 1G

33 Cannon Street, E.C.4.
Tel: 01-248 1576
Map Ref. 3K

78 Chancery Lane, W.C.2.
Tel: 01-242 8600
Map Ref. 2I

232 Kings Road, S.W.3.
Tel: 01-352 1565
Map Ref. 5F

185 Earls Court Road, S.W.5.
Tel: 01-370 2841
Map Ref. 5B

1 Star Street, W.2.
Tel: 01-723 7522
Map Ref. 2E

165 Euston Road, N.W.1.
Tel: 01-387 3121
Map Ref. 1G

60 Fenchurch Street, E.C.3.
Tel: 01-488 3936
Map Ref. 3K

40 Fleet Street, E.C.4.
Tel: 01-353 7101
Map Ref. 2I

7 Gt Portland Street, W.1.
Tel: 01-636 2205
Map Ref. 2G

52 High Holborn, W.C.1.
Tel: 01-242 8676
Map Ref. 2I

257 Kensington High Street, W.8.
Tel: 01-602 6651
Map Ref. 4C

13 Euston Road, N.W.1.
Tel: 01-278 5077
Map Ref. 1H

55 Knightsbridge, S.W.1.
Tel: 01-235 2385
Map Ref. 4F

43 Seymour Street, W.1.
Tel: 01-723 0867
Map Ref. 2E

28 Marylebone High Street, W.1.
Tel: 01-935 7838
Map Ref. 2F

22 Queen Street, W.1.
Tel: 01-499 3522
Map Ref. 3F

South Place, E.C.2.
Tel: 01-606 7641
Map Ref. 2L

New Fetter Lane, E.C.4.
Tel: 01-353 1345
Map Ref. 2I

41 Spring Street, W.2.
Tel: 01-723 0279
Map Ref. 3D

132 Wigmore Street, W.1.
Tel: 01-935 6357
Map Ref. 2F

11 Regent Street, S.W.1.
Tel: 01-930 9538
Map Ref. 2G

3 Heddon Street, W.1.
Tel: 01-734 5556
Map Ref. 2G

9 Kings Road, S.W.1.
Tel: 01-730 1832
Map Ref. 5F

87 Charterhouse Street, E.C.1.
Tel: 01-253 5980
Map Ref. 2I

13 Soho Street, W.1.
Tel: 01-437 3235
Map Ref. 2G

25 Exhibition Road, S.W.7.
Tel: 01-589 2018
Map Ref. 4D

28 Circus Road, N.W.8.
Tel: 01-722 0996
Map Ref. 1D

24 William IV Street, W.C.2.
Tel: 01-930 9580
Map Ref. 3H

110 Victoria Street, S.W.1.
Tel: 01-834 0509
Map Ref. 4G

57 Waterloo Road, S.E.1.
Tel: 01-928 6785
Map Ref. 4I

125 Westminster Bridge Road, S.E.1.
Tel: 01-928 5504
Map Ref. 4I

ELECTRICITY

The supply is 200-250 volts AC and 50 cycles so be careful if you have brought your own hairdryers, irons or shavers etc, as they may be on 120 volts 60 cycles. Most hotels will supply you with a transformer but, if not, a good electrical supply shop can sell you one. Some hotels also have special sockets which can take both voltages and it is wise to check with the Porter.

BANKING

London is considered to be the Banking centre of the world and although this refers to the City where the international trade is conducted, nevertheless, all the major Banks have branches scattered throughout London and you will find one in every major street.

Travellers cheques can be cashed, but take your passport. You can also obtain money on the production of certain credit cards. Any Bank will tell you which card they accept.

If you have a particular Bank in your own country and wish to use the same one in London, the chances are that there will be a branch somewhere. To obtain the address or telephone number it is best to look in a telephone directory.

Besides the Banks, there are many Bureaux de Change facilities in large hotels and stations but you will usually find that the Banks give the best rates of exchange.

Here are some central branches of the four main banks:

BARCLAYS BANK LTD
Head Office:
54 Lombard Street, E.C.3.
Tel: 01-626 1567
Map Ref. 2E
2 Victoria Street, S.W.1.
Tel: 01-222 2651
Map Ref. 4G
235 Baker Street, N.W.1.
Tel: 01-486 8191
Map Ref. 2F
93 Baker Street, W.1.
Tel: 01-486 8191
Map Ref. 2F
23 Grosvenor Gardens, S.W.1.
Tel: 01-828 4671
Map Ref. 4F
2 Bloomsbury Way, W.C.1.
Tel: 01-831 6082
Map Ref. 2H
25 Charing Cross Road, W.C.2.
Tel: 01-839 1422
Map Ref. 2H
56 Great Portland Street, W.1.
Tel: 01-637 9812
Map Ref. 2G
23 Euston Road, N.W.1.
Tel: 01-278 9552
Map Ref. 1G
5 Oxford Street, W.1.
Tel: 01-734 6642
Map Ref. 2G
451 Oxford Street, W.1.
Tel: 01-629 9701
Map Ref. 2G

NATIONAL WESTMINSTER BANK LTD
Head Office:
41 Lothbury, E.C.2.
Tel: 01-606 6060
Map Ref. 2K
Baker Street Station, 133 Baker Street, W.1.
Tel: 01-487 4563
Map Ref. 1F
10 St. Martin Place, W.C.2.
Tel: 01-836 0401
Map Ref. 3H
320 Euston Road, N.W.1.
Tel: 01-387 0221
Map Ref. 1G
82 Fleet Street, E.C.4.
Tel: 01-353 9065
Map Ref. 2I
94 Kensington High Street, W.8.
Tel: 01-938 1701
Map Ref. 4C
1 Connaught Street, W.2.
Tel: 01-402 0971
Map Ref. 2E
40 Oxford Street, W.1.
Tel: 01-637 4555
Map Ref. 2G
250 Regent Street, W.1.
Tel: 01-439 4161
Map Ref. 3G
140 Victoria Street, S.W.1.
Tel: 01-828 2884
Map Ref. 4G

MIDLAND BANK LTD
Head Office:
Poultry, E.C.2.
Tel: 01-606 9911
Map Ref. 2F
90 Baker Street, W.1.
Tel: 01-935 8226
Map Ref. 2F
337 Kings Road, S.W.3.
Tel: 01-821 1344
Map Ref. 5E
154 Fleet Street, E.C.4.
Tel: 01-353 0511
Map Ref. 2I
92 Kensington High Street, W.8.
Tel: 01-821 1344
Map Ref. 4C
76 Edgware Road, W.2.
Tel: 01-723 0064
Map Ref. 2E
196 Oxford Street, W.1.
Tel: 01-637 4044
Map Ref. 2G

LLOYDS BANK LTD
Head Office
71 Lombard Street, E.C.3.
Tel: 01-626 1500
Map Ref. 2K

185 Baker Street, N.W.1.
Tel: 01-935 1477
Map Ref. 2F

179 Earls Court Road, S.W.5.
Tel: 01-370 2155
Map Ref. 5B

7 Great Cumberland Place, W.1.
Tel: 01-237 4247
Map Ref. 2F

20 Soho Square, W.1.
Tel: 01-439 6911
Map Ref. 2G

EXCHANGE RATES

These can vary daily and it is essential to check either with the National Newspapers or in the window of a Bank.

BANKING HOURS

Normally 9.30am-3.30pm Monday to Friday, closed Saturday and Sunday.

BANKING AFTER NORMAL HOURS

Harrods, Knightsbridge, S.W.1.
Tel: 01-730 1234
Open: 9.30am-5.00pm, Monday to Saturday.
9.30am-6.00pm on Wednesday.
Map Ref. 4E

Erskine Bureaux which exchange Foreign Currency are found at:
15 Shaftesbury Avenue, W.1.
Tel: 01-734 1400
Open: 7.30am to 11.30pm Mondays to Thursdays and Sundays.
9am to 12 Midnight Fridays and Saturdays.
Map Ref. 3G

152a Cromwell Road, S.W.7.
Tel: 01-370 6848
Open: 8.30am to 6.30pm Mondays to Sundays.
Map Ref. 5C

237 Oxford Street, W.1.
Tel: 01-437 2689
Open: 9am to 8pm Mondays to Fridays.
8.30am to 8.30pm Saturdays
10am to 4pm Sundays.
Map Ref. 2G

22 Leinster Terrace, W.2.
Tel: 01-402 6305
Open: 7.45am to 8.30pm Mondays to Sundays.
Map Ref. 3D

2 London Street, W.2.
Tel: 01-723 9964
Open: 8am to 8pm Mondays to Sundays.
Map Ref. 2E

Bureau de Change
Platform 15, Victoria Station, S.W.1.
Tel: 01-828 2012
Open twenty four hours every day.
Map Ref. 5G

Cheque Point
130 King's Road, S.W.3.
Tel: 01-589 7466
Open: 8.30am to 12 midnight Mondays to Sundays.
Map Ref. 5F

89 Gloucester Road, S.W.7.
Tel: 01-370 5137
Open: 8am to midnight Mondays to Sundays.
Map Ref. 5C

LOST PROPERTY

Lost anywhere Check at the nearest Police Station as that is where found property is taken.
Lost on Taxis Apply 15 Penton St., N.1.
Tel: 01-278 1744 Map Ref. 1G

Railway-Southern Region Check at the stations or at Waterloo Station. York Road, S.W.1. Tel: 01-928 5151

Lost Children Check at the nearest police station.

Air Travel Held by each individual airline, or if lost in main airport buildings, enquire at the British Airport Police, Lost Property Office, London Airport Heathrow. Tel: 01-759-4321.

Buses or Underground Check at the Lost Property Office, 200 Baker St., W.1.

Map Ref. 1F

POLICE

The London Policeman often referred to as a 'Bobby', is world famous for his help and understanding to visitors who need assistance. Policemen can usually be found walking through the streets of London with their familiar helmets and if you need advice or directions they are happy for you to ask.

MAIN POLICE STATIONS IN LONDON. When telephoning ask for Police Station by name.

Bow Street, 28 Bow Street, W.C.2. Tel: 01-434 5212 Map Ref. 3H

Cannon Row, 1 Cannon Row, S.W.1. Tel: 01-434 5212 Map Ref. 4H

Chelsea, 2 Lucan Place, S.W.3. Tel: 01-741 6212 Map Ref. 5E

Fulham, Heckfield Place, S.W.6. Tel: 01-741 6212 Map Ref. 6B

Hammersmith, 226 Shepherds Bush Road, W.6. Tel: 01-741 6212 Map Ref. 5A

Hyde Park, North of the Serpentine, W.2. Tel: 01-434 5212 Map Ref. 3E

Kensington, 72 Earls Court Road, W.8. Tel: 01-741 6212 Map Ref. 5B

Marylebone, 1, Seymour Street, W.1. Tel: 01-725 4212 Map Ref. 2E

Rochester Row, 63 Rochester Row. S.W.1. Tel: 01-434 5212 Map Ref. 5G

Vine Street 10 Vine Street, W.1. Tel: 01-434 5212 Map Ref. 3G

PUBLIC HOLIDAYS

1983	**1984**	
3rd Jan.	2nd Jan.	New Year
1st Apr.	20th Apr.	Good Friday
4th Apr.	23rd Apr.	Easter Monday
2nd May	7th May	May Day
30th May	28th May	Spring B/Holiday
29th Aug.	27th Aug.	Summer B/Holiday
25th Dec.	25th Dec.	Christmas Day
26th Dec.	26th Dec.	Boxing Day

BRITISH TOURIST AUTHORITY

64 St. James Street, S.W.1.
Open: 9.00am-6.00pm, Monday to Friday.
9.00am-1.00pm, Saturday.
Closed Sunday.
Provides information about Gt. Britain.
Tel: 01-499 9325

Map Ref. 3G

LONDON TOURIST BOARD INFORMATION BUREAU

Victoria Station
26 Grosvenor Gardens, S.W.1.
Open: 9.00am-9.30pm Summer.
9.00am-6.00pm Winter.
Provides a complete London advisory and booking service. Numerous leaflets and tourist guides are freely available.
Tel: 01-730 0791 or 01-730 3400.

also London Tourist Board maintain Information Desks in:
Harrods, S.W.1.
and **Selfridges,** Oxford Street, W.1.

DAILY TELEGRAPH INFORMATION BUREAU

Telephone only — 01-353 4242
Open: 9.30am-5.30pm, Monday to Friday.
Provides information about general topics.

GUILDHALL LIBRARY

King Street — off Gresham Street, E.C.2. Entrance in Aldermanbury.
Open: 9.30am-5.00pm, Monday to Saturday.
Closed Sunday.
Information about anything historical in London.
Tel: 01-606 3030.

CITY OF LONDON INFORMATION CENTRE

St. Paul's Churchyard, E.C.4.
Open: 9.30am-5.00pm, Monday to Friday.
10.00am-4.00pm, Saturday.
Closed Sunday.
Information and advice with specific reference to the City of London. Free Literature.
Tel: 01-606 3030

HEALTH SERVICE

Most Embassies have a list of Doctors and Dentists, as do Hotels, Local Libraries, and main Post Offices. The National Health Service is available to visitors only in emergencies such as car accidents or heart attacks. Visitors staying for more than three months are however entitled to register with a National Health Service Doctor. Ambulance services are free.

HOSPITALS

The following are main hospitals which are open 24 hours. In case of emergency Dial 999 and ask for the ambulance service or go to the casualty section.

Middlesex Hospital
Mortimer Street, W.1.
Tel: 01-636 8333
Map Ref. 2G

St. Mary's Hospital
Praed Street, W.2.
Tel: 01-262 1280
Map Ref. 2E

Moorfields Eye Hospital
High Holborn W.C.1.
Tel: 01-836 6611
Map Ref. 1H

Childrens Hospital
Great Ormond Street, W.C.1.
Tel: 01-405 9200
Map Ref. 1H

Charing Cross Hospital
Fulham Palace Road, W.6.
Tel: 01-748 2040
Map Ref. 6A

Guy's Hospital
St. Thomas Street, S.E.1.
Tel: 01-407 7600
Map Ref. 4J

Royal Free Hospital
Pond Street, N.W.3.
Tel: 01-794 0500
No Map Ref.

University College Hospital
Gower Street, W.C.1.
Tel: 01-387 9300
Map Ref. 1G

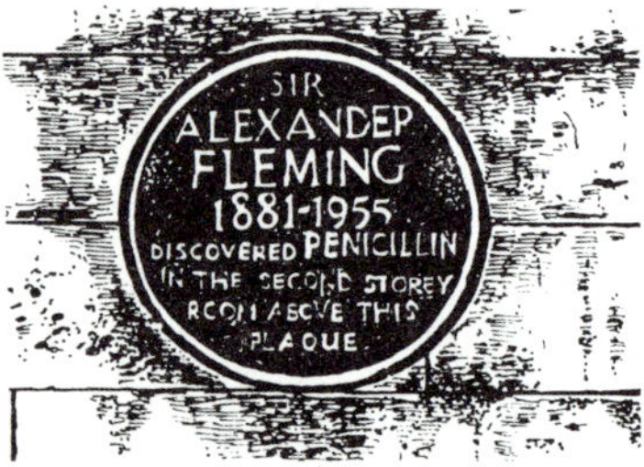

PRIVATE CLINICS

Harley Street Clinic
35 Weymouth Street, W.1.
Tel: 01-935 7700
Map Ref. 2F

Wellington Hospital
7a Wellington Place, N.W.8.
Tel: 01-586 5959
Map Ref. 1D

The Allan Clinic
3 Vincent Court, Seymour Place, W.1.
Tel: 01-262 9306
Map Ref. 2E

Bowley Private Clinic
12 Ladbroke Terrace, W.11.
Tel: 01-727 2661
Map Ref. 2A

British School of Osteopathy
1-4 Suffolk Street, S.W.1.
Tel: 01-930 9254
Map Ref. 4G

The London Clinic
20 Devonshire Place, W.1.
Tel: 01-935 4444
Map Ref. 2F

CHEMISTS / DRUG STORES

There are numerous chemists in London most of which have a Pharmacy section. It is also possible to purchase cosmetics and associated household products.

Some central chemists:

Underwoods
96 Baker Street, W.1.
Map Ref. 2F
174 Kensington High Street, W.8.
Map Ref. 4C
60 Kings Road, S.W.3.
Map Ref. 5E
120 Tottenham Court Road, W.1.
Map Ref. 2G

Boots
316 Edgware Road, W.2.
Tel: 01-723 5556
Map Ref. 2E

1/3 Marble Arch, W.1
Tel: 01-723 4011
Map Ref. 2E

73 Brompton Road, S.W.3.
Tel: 01-589 3911
Map Ref. 4E

Clan Drug Store
5 Liverpool Street, E.C.2.
Tel: 01-283 6231
Map Ref. 2L

Regent Street Pharmacy
283a Regent Street, W.1.
Tel: 01-493 4660
Map Ref. 2G

LATE NIGHT CHEMISTS

H D Bliss
54 Willesden Lane, N.W.6.
Tel: 01-624 8000
Open: 24 hours.
No Map Ref.

Boots
Piccadilly Circus, W.1.
Tel: 01-734 6126
Open: Mon-Fri. 8.30am-8.00pm.
Saturday 9.00am-8.00pm.
Map Ref. 3G

W W Brunton
240 Earls Court Road, S.W.5.
Tel: 01-373 5078
Open: 8.30am-10.30pm, Monday to Saturday.
10.00am-10.00pm, Sunday.
Map Ref. 5B

VACCINATION CENTRES

West London Vaccination Clinic
53 Great Cumberland Place, W.1.
Tel: 01-262 6456
Map Ref. 2E

Thomas Cook
45 Berkeley Street, W.1.
Tel: 01-499 4900
Map Ref. 3F

British Airways
75 Regent Street, W.1.
Tel: 01-439 9584/5
Map Ref. 5F

GUIDE INTERPRETER

If you require the services of a guide who speaks your language contact:

Guide Booking Service
Tel: 01-736 7572
01-731 2574

Guild of Guide Lecturers
Tel: 01-589 0531

CITIZENS ADVICE BUREAU

You can obtain free confidential advice on any subject including personal, family consumer, legal etc. Hours vary so telephone first. They are listed under 'C' in the London Telephone Book and as there are many of them you are sure to find one near your location.

Some main addresses:

Paddington
439 Harrow Road, W.10.
Tel: 01-960 4481
Map Ref. 1B

Marylebone
Marylebone Road, N.W.1.
Tel: 01-486 6425
Map Ref. 1E

Chelsea
Old Town Hall, Kings Road, S.W.3
Tel: 01-351 2114
Map Ref. 5F

Westminster
33 Charing Cross Road, W.C.2.
Tel: 01-839 2825
Map Ref. 2H

DOMESTIC STAFF

Universal Aunts
36 Walpole Street, S.W.3.
Tel: 01-730 9834
A well known agency that will help with almost everything. Supplies nannies, housekeepers, babysitters. They will do your shopping, collect and deliver parcels and book anything.
Map Ref. 5E

Belgravia Bureau
35 Brompton Road, S.W.3.
Tel: 01-589 1941
Supplies cooks, housekeepers, cleaners, nannies, secretaries and mother's helps.
Map Ref. 4E

Babysitters Unlimited
313 Brompton Road, S.W.3.
Tel: 01-584 1046
Supply carefully selected babysitters, mother's helps, nannies and cleaners.
Map Ref. 5E

Babycare Childminders
67 Marylebone High Street, W.1.
Tel: 01-935 2049/4386
Supplies referenced and experienced babysitters, day nannies and temporary nannies.
Map Ref. 2F

Albemarle Nannies
138 New Bond Street, W.1.
Tel: 01-493 2441
A specialist agency for trained and experienced nannies.
Map Ref. 2F

NEWSPAPERS AND MAGAZINES

The major London and National daily newspapers are the *Daily Telegraph, Financial Times* and *The Times* which give comprehensive coverage of world affairs, sport and finance. Others are the *Daily Express, Daily Mail, The Guardian, The Mirror, The Sun* and *The Star* all of which cover to a greater or lesser degree topical and news items. The National Sunday Papers are the *Sunday Times, Sunday Telegraph, The Observer, Sunday Mirror, Sunday Express, Sunday People* and *News of the World*. London also has a daily 'evening' paper, *The New Standard*, which comes out at fixed times during the day and evening, and gives good coverage of local and international and sporting events.
Whats On In London, Where To Go and *Time Out* are useful weekly publications which are sold at bookstalls. They supply latest information on theatres, cinemas, night clubs and dining clubs. *London Week* and *Diary of Events*, both free from the London Tourist Board, are also very useful.

Foreign Newspapers
Most Foreign Newspapers are obtainable in London — large Hotels generally have bookstalls which stock the papers that would be read by their overseas clientele. For European papers go to OLD COMPTON STREET where two newsagents stock continental papers and magazines. In SHAFTESBURY AVENUE you will find Oriental newspapers. Round EARLS COURT STATION and KENSINGTON HIGH STREET there will be Arabic papers. If you are staying sometimes your hotel porter or the local newsagent will be able to order your paper for you.

How to get around London

A B C D E F G H I J K L
1 2 3 4 5 6
EUSTON STATION
PADDINGTON STATION
CHARING CROSS STATION
WATERLOO STATION
VICTORIA STATION
LIVERPOOL ST. STATION
LONDON BRI. STATION
REGENT'S PARK
KENSINGTON GARDENS
HYDE PARK
SERPENTINE
GREEN PARK
ST. JAMES'S PARK
HOLLAND PARK
BATTERSEA PARK
Kennington Park
Kensal Green
RIVER THAMES
Marble Arch
Somerset House
Monument
PORTMAN SQUARE
GROSVENOR SQUARE
BERKELEY SQUARE
BELGRAVE SQUARE
Maida Vale
Warwick Avenue
Marylebone
Baker Street
Great Portland Street
Regent's Park
Warren Street
Goodge Street
Edgeware Road
Westbourne Park
Ladbroke Grove
Tottenham Court Rd.
Oxford Circus
Marble Arch
Lancaster Gate
Bond Street
Bayswater
Queensway
Notting Hill Gate
Holland Park
Hyde Park Corner
Green Park
Piccadilly Circus
Leicester Square
Covent Garden
Holborn
Chancery Lane
Aldwych
Temple
Blackfriars
Mansion House
St Paul's
Moorgate
Bank
Monument
Tower Hill
Aldgate
Old Street
Westminster
St James's Park
Knightsbridge
South Kensington
High Street Kensington
Gloucester Road
Earls Court
West Brompton
Sloane Square
Pimlico
Vauxhall
Lambeth North
Borough
Elephant and Castle
Oval
KILBURN LANE
HARROW ROAD
ELGIN AVENUE
CASTELLAIN RD
MAIDA VALE
ST. JOHN'S WOOD RD.
LISSON GROVE
WELLINGTON ROAD
ALBANY STREET
EUSTON ROAD
GRAYS INN ROAD
KING'S CROSS ROAD
ROSEBERRY AVENUE
GOSWELL ROAD
CITY ROAD
OLD STREET
GREAT EASTERN ST.
HACKNEY ROAD
FERNHEAD RD.
GREAT WESTERN RD
CLIFTON GDNS
EDGWARE ROAD
MARYLEBONE ROAD
TOTTENHAM COURT RD.
GOWER STREET
SOUTHAMPTON ROW
GUILFORD ST.
THEOBALDS RD.
CLERKEN WELL ROAD
FARRINGDON ST.
ALDERSGATE ST.
BISHOPSGATE
COMMERCIAL ST.
WHITECHAPEL
LADBROKE GROVE
WESTBOURNE PARK
TALBOT ROAD
CHEPSTOW RD.
COLVILLE TER.
BISHOPS BRIDGE ROAD
WESTBOURNE TER
SEYMOUR PLACE
BAKER STREET
MARYLEBONE HIGH ST.
PORTLAND PL.
GOODGE ST.
NEW OXFORD STREET
HOLBORN
HOLBORN VIA.
CHANCERY LANE
FLEET ST.
LUDGATE HILL
CHEAPSIDE
MOORGATE
HOUNDSDITCH
LEMAN ST.
ALDGATE
CLARENDON RD
BLENHEIM CRES.
WESTBOURNE GROVE
OXFORD STREET
REGENT ST.
NEW BOND ST.
OLD BOND ST.
POLAND ST.
WARDOUR ST.
CHARING CROSS ROAD
DRURY LANE
LONG ACRE
STRAND
QUEEN VICTORIA ST.
LEADENHALL ST.
FENCHURCH ST.
MINORIES
EAST SMITHFIELD
ELGIN CRES.
PEMBRIDGE RD
QUEENSWAY
BAYSWATER ROAD
PARK LANE
SHAFTESBURY AV.
EMBANKMENT
TOWER HILL
PORTLAND ROAD
NOTTING HILL GATE
KENSINGTON CHURCH ST
CURZON ST.
PICCADILLY
PALL MALL
THE MALL
WATERLOO BRIDGE
BLACKFRIARS BRIDGE
SOUTHWARK BRIDGE
LONDON BRIDGE
TOWER BRIDGE
STAMFORD ST.
SOUTHWARK STREET
TOOLEY STREET
ROTTEN ROW
KENSINGTON RD.
KNIGHTSBRIDGE
VICTORIA
WATERLOO ROAD
BLACKFRIARS RD.
SOUTH WARK BRIDGE RD
BOROUGH HIGH ST.
ST. THOMAS ST.
HOLLAND PARK AVENUE
CAMPDEN HILL RD
KENSINGTON HIGH STREET
QUEEN'S GATE
EXHIBITION ROAD
GROSVENOR PL.
BIRDCAGE WALK
WESTMINSTER BRIDGE
YORK ROAD
PALACE RD
WESTMINSTER BRIDGE RD
BOROUGH RD.
CAUSEWAY
LONG LANE
HOLLAND ROAD
BEAUCHAMP PLACE
CADOGAN GDNS
SLOANE STREET
VICTORIA STREET
HORSE FERRY ROAD
LAMBETH PALACE RD
LAMBETH ROAD
ST GEORGE'S RD
LONDON RD
NEWINGTON CAUSEWAY
GREAT DOVER ST.
ABBEY STREET
EARLS COURT ROAD
CROMWELL ROAD
BROMPTON ROAD
WALTON RD.
KING'S ROAD
BUCKINGHAM PALACE ROAD
VAUXHALL BRIDGE ROAD
LAMBETH BRIDGE
MILLBANK
KENNINGTON ROAD
NEW KENT RD
HAMMERSMITH ROAD
WARWICK ROAD
OLD BROMPTON ROAD
SYDNEY ST.
CHELSEA BRIDGE RD.
ALBERT EMBANKMENT
WALWORTH ROAD
OLD KENT ROAD
SHEPHERD'S BUSH RD
TALGARTH ROAD
NORTH END ROAD
WEST CROMWELL ROAD
REDCLIFF GARDENS
LILLIE ROAD
FULHAM ROAD
ROYAL HOSPITAL ROAD
CHELSEA EMBANKMENT
CHELSEA BRIDGE
GROSVENOR ROAD
VAUXHALL BRIDGE
HARLEYFORD RD
KENNINGTON PARK ROAD
ALBANY ROAD
FULHAM PALACE ROAD
KING'S ROAD
ALBERT BRIDGE
NINE ELMS LANE
FENTIMAN RD

HOW TO GET AROUND LONDON

TOURS BY COACH

One of the best ways to see London if you are a first time visitor is to take a guided coach tour. All the main tourist attractions are visited and commentaries given en route. There is a choice of half-day, all day and also 'London by Night' tours.
The following companies can arrange coach tours.

London Transport Tours,
Victoria Coach Station S.W.1.
Tel: 01-730 0202
Bright yellow open-topped buses leaving every hour from Buckingham Palace Road, and Piccadilly Circus.
Map Ref. 5F

Around London Sightseeing Tour
This covers the West End and the City and last about 2 hours. The tours set out from Victoria Coach Station (Buckingham Palace Road) and Piccadilly Circus. Seats not bookable.

Vintage Bus Service
An original 1930 bus which leaves hourly from Horse Guards Parade.
Map Ref. 4H

TOURS BY PRIVATE GUIDES

If you want to see London in a limited time and you don't want to travel by coach then the tours by limousine are very suitable. In many cases driver/guides speaking most languages can be arranged. The tours are arranged to suit your schedule.

British Tours Limited
6 South Molton Street, W.1.
Tel: 01-629 5267
Map Ref. 3F

Thomas Cook
45 Berkeley Street, W.1.
Tel: 01-499 4000
Thomas Cook arrange a number of different tours of the West End, the City and also Evening Drives.
Map Ref. 3F

Frames
11 Herbrand Street, W.C.1.
Tel: 01-837 3111/6311
Map Ref. 2H

Evan Evans Tours Ltd
1a Alfred Place, W.C.1.
Tel: 01-637 4171
Map Ref. 2H

Autoguide (London) Ltd
93 Knightsbridge, London, S.W.1.
Tel: 01-235 0806
Private car tours by qualified London Tourist Board guides, for parties of 1-6.
Map Ref. 4F

UNDERGROUND

London has the best Underground train system (called *Subway* or *Tube)* of any city in the world. It is possible to reach almost any area with trains running frequently. It is easy for a visitor to comprehend and is usually the quickest way to move around London. The various lines are clearly marked by colour coding in the stations and simple maps are found on the platforms and in the trains themselves. You just follow the colour of the line you want to the platform and check to see on the front of the incoming train or indicator if it is the one you require.

TAXIS

Like London's red buses, the distinctive black taxi cabs are world famous. They can be waved down on any street and it is easy to tell by the yellow illuminated sign whether one is vacant or not. No one knows London better than a taxi driver. All taxis have meters and as mentioned earlier the tip is usually 10%.
You can also telephone for a taxi to collect you.

TAXI RANKS

Islington High Street, N.1.
Tel: 01-837 2394
Kensington Close, W.8.
Tel: 01-937 0736
Moorgate, E.C.2.
Tel: 01-606 4526
St. Georges Square, S.W.1.
Tel: 01-834 1014
Sloane Square, S.W.1.
Tel: 01-730 2664
South Kensington Stations S.W.7.
Tel: 01-589 5242

All London Radio Taxis
Tel: 01-286 4848

Yellow Cars
Tel: 01-607 7779
Tel: 01-609 1400
Tel: 01-609 3001
Tel: 01-609 3003
24-hour service.

Taxi Service Ltd
Tel: 01-286 6010/01-289 2947

Radio Taxis
Tel: 01-272 3030
24-hour service.

LONDON TRANSPORT ENQUIRY OFFICES

Victoria Underground Station
8.30am-6pm.
Victoria BR Station
8.30am-9.30pm.
King's Cross BR Station
8.30am-6pm.
Oxford Circus Underground
8.30am-6pm (Thursdays 9.30pm).
Piccadilly Underground
8.30am-6pm.
St. James's Underground
8.30am-6.30pm.
Euston Station
8.30am-6pm.

Also: See British Railways Advertisement in the Telephone Directory A-D Section which lists Telephone Information available.

BUSES

There are hundreds of the familiar red double-decker buses, which serve a complex number of routes, and outside the 'rush hours' (*usually 8.30am-10.00am* and *4.30pm-6.30pm)* they are an easy way to travel. If you sit on the top deck it is good for sightseeing.
Information about special cheap fares can be obtained from any London Transport Enquiry Offices.
The buses have their route number and destination clearly visible on window panels and at each bus stop there is also a route number and list of route stops.

BRITISH RAIL

London is very well served for Railway Stations which are part of the national British Rail network. Trains are very useful if you want to visit the suburbs which are not covered by the Underground but, like the buses, stay clear of the 'Rush hours'. For train information telephone the following stations; expect to wait some time for an answer as calls are taken in rotation.

Charing Cross Station
Charing Cross, W.C.2.
Tel: 01-928 5100
South and South East.
Map Ref. 3H

Victoria Station
Victoria Street, S.W.1.
Tel: 01-928 5100
South and South East.
Map Ref. 5G

Waterloo Station
York Road, S.E.1.
Tel: 01-928 5100
South and South West.
Map Ref. 4I

Paddington Station
Praed Street, W.2.
Tel: 01-262 6767
Wales, South Wales.
Map Ref. 2E

Cannon Street Station
Cannon Street, E.C.4.
Tel: 01-928 5100
South and South East.
Map Ref. 3J

Euston Station
Euston Road, N.W.1.
Tel: 01-387 7070
North West and Scotland.
Map Ref. 1G

Kings Cross Station
Euston Road, N.W.1.
Tel: 01-278 2477
North East and Scotland.
Map Ref. 1H

Liverpool Street Station
Liverpool Street, E.C.2.
Tel: 01-283 7171
East.
Map Ref. 2L

CAR HIRE

There are many firms specialising in the hire of self-drive cars by the hour, day, week or month. Unless you have a recognised credit card most firms will require a deposit. The price of car rental varies according to the size of car and length of hire.

Avis Rent-a-Car
35 Headfort Place, S.W.1.
Tel: 01-245 9862
Map Ref. 4F

141-145 Warwick Road, W.14.
Tel: 01-581 2252
Map Ref. 5B

68 North Row, W.1.
Tel: 01-629 7811
Map Ref. 2E

Hertz Rent-a-Car
35 Edgware Road, W.2.
Tel: 01-402 4242
Map Ref. 2E

Kenning Car Hire
84-90 Holland Park Avenue, W.11.
Tel: 01-727 0123
Map Ref. 4A

Godfrey Davis
Davis House, 129 Wilton Road, S.W.1.
Tel: 01-834 8484
Map Ref. 4F

J. Davy
7 Logan Place, W.8.
Tel: 01-373 9738
Map Ref. 5B

Sportshire
6 Kendrick Place, Reece Mews, S.W.7.
Tel: 01-589 8309
Specialists in hiring sports cars.
Map Ref. 5D

Horseless Carriage Hire
59 Eccleston Square Mews, S.W.1.
Tel: 01-736 9229
For sports and vintage cars.
Map Ref. 5G

Central Rent-a-car
48/56 Ebury Bridge Road, S.W.1.
Tel: 01-730 9130
Map Ref. 6F

28 Queensway, W.2.
Tel: 01-229 7211
Map Ref. 3C

Guy Salmon
7-23 Bryanston Street, Marble Arch, W.1.
Tel: 01-408 1255
All major credit cards accepted.
Free delivery and collection within Greater London and to Heathrow and Gatwick airports.
Map Ref. 2E

Swan National Car Rental
305 Chiswick High Road, W.4.
Tel: 01-995 9465
No Map Ref.

International Car Rental
31 Notting Hill Gate, W.11.
Tel: 01-727 1467
Map Ref. 3B

Travelwise Rent-a-car
77 Pavilion Road, S.W.1.
Tel: 01-235 0751
Map Ref. 4E

CHAUFFEUR DRIVE CAR HIRE

Victor Briton Avis
Kingston House North, Prince of Wales Gate, S.W.7.
Tel: 01-262 3134
Most types of luxury cars.
Map Ref. 5D

Berry Hurst Car Hire
37 Harlyford Road, S.E.11.
Tel: 01-582 0244
Map Ref.

Patrick Barthropp
1 Dorset Mews, Wilston Street, S.W.1.
Tel: 01-245 9171
Rolls Royces and other luxury cars.
Map Ref. 4F

Belvedere Car Service Ltd
116 Brompton Road, S.W.3.
Tel: 01-581 0071
Luxury saloons, limousines and Rolls Royces, 24-hour service for airport transfers, sightseeing tours, restaurants, theatres.
Map Ref. 5E

Rollhand Ltd
Sara Lane Court, L.G. Garage,
London N.1.
Tel: 01-739 1705
No Map Ref.

Top Cars
3 Coventry Close, N.W.6.
Tel: 01-624 5090
No Map Ref.

ALL NIGHT PETROL

Chelsea Cloisters Garage
Sloane Avenue, S.W.3.
Tel: 01-589 1226
Map Ref. 5E

Station Supreme
63 Fortune Road Green, N.W.6.
Tel: 01-435 2211
No Map Ref.

Maida Vale Service Station
115-117 Maida Vale, W.9.
Tel: 01-286 7321
Map Ref. 1D

BREAKDOWN SERVICES – 24 HOURS

Cavendish Motors
Cavendish Road, N.W.3.
Tel: 01-459 0046
No Map Ref

BOAT TRIPS

One of the best ways of seeing London is via the famous River Thames; besides the regular sightseeing boats there are also water buses. They operate from April to September approximately every half hour and can be boarded at the following piers.

Greenwich	Tel: 01-858 3996
Tower Pier	Tel: 01-488 0344
Charing Cross	Tel: 01-930 0970
Westminster	Tel: 01-930 4097
Putney	Tel: 01-788 5104
Kew	Tel: 01-940 3891
Richmond	Tel: 01-940 2244
Hampton Court	Tel: 01-977 5702

It is wise to telephone first to check times as they fluctuate according to weather and tides.

CYCLING

A very good way to see London is by bicycle. They can be hired by the day, week or month. The following lists the places where bicycles can be hired. A deposit is usually required with identification.

Savile's Cycle Store
97 Battersea Rise, S.W.11.
Tel: 01-228 4279
No Map Ref

Bicycle Revival
28 North End Parade, North End Road, W.14.
Tel: 01-602 4499
Map Ref. 6C

19 Elizabeth Street, S.W.1.
Tel: 01-730 6716
Map Ref. 5F

Bell Street Bikes
73 Bell Street, N.W.1.
Tel: 01-724 0456
No Map Ref

What to wear

WHAT TO WEAR

Fashion writer, Joy Leslie Gibson takes you through the mode of British Fashion. LE STYLE ANGLAIS is now famed throughout the world — it is sold in smart Paris, brilliant Italy, conservative Spain and charming Greece as one of the most desirable fashions ever created. The English, for long considered by the rest of Europe as lacking in chic are now smiling to themselves for they have long discovered the virtues of pleated skirts, luscious "woollies" and sensible shoes. It may not have the flair and brilliance of continental styles but it is enduring, smart and always right in appearance. It is based on the English virtues of understatement, good taste and never being noticeable except for being entirely at ease. Although it is called LE STYLE ANGLAIS it owes a lot to Scotland as the kilt, velvet jackets and lovely knitwear play their part in creating these styles.

It is, too, an off-spring of the variable English (British) climate. One never knows from one day to the next what the weather will bring — snow in the height of summer; hotter days in Autumn than in Summer; Spring Showers all the year round — these are the symptoms of British weather, so we tend to dress in clothes that are adaptable, that can be discarded or replaced as temperatures soar or chill. And when you visit our shores you can do no better than to stock up on our natural style to ensure that you will be comfortably clad throughout the vagaries of weather.

The basic requirement is a raincoat — a Burberry is top style. If a trench coat does not suit your shape, and to be frank, you need to be thin for it to do so, then there is a feel for romantic clothes in the air and you can buy a cloak at BORN & BRED in BOURNE STREET with a matching skirt which will be useful to you throughout your visit. A BURBERRY, of course, you buy at BURBERRY'S themselves in the HAYMARKET. AQUASCUTUM is the other place to get a really good raincoat for both men and women — they sell both the classic and more frivolous versions of this must. And both BURBERRY'S and AQUASCUTUM do up-market versions of LE STYLE ANGLAIS beautifully. And one of the great virtues of this style of dressing is that it

lasts so that it pays to buy the best. No English gentlewoman thinks twice about donning a skirt that she has had for years, because it is made in a classic style out of very good fabric, it improves with age. And aristocratic men pass their clothes on to each other so good and long-lasting is English tailoring! AUSTIN REED in Regent Street is another good store for these clothes. If you want something good, but a little less expensive (though very top class) then go to JAEGAR (Regent Street, Knightsbridge, and all over London) where you will find classic English style interpreted with a modern glint and alongside some very smart, less classic clothes. And for good clothes in this style in fabrics that are probably man-made rather than expensive natural fibres (or in blends of both) then go to COUNTY CASUALS, or NEXT, both of which sell beautiful clothes at reasonable prices.

GOING ABOUT

As you will see when you walk around, the British nowadays, tend to dress for comfort when shopping, sight-seeing or travelling and the blue jean syndrome is still with us, though lessening, I am glad to say. But casual skirts or trousers, with silk or cotton skirts, blouson jacket or cardigans (plus your raincoat) will take care of most problems during a sight-seeing day. It is LE STYLE ANGLAIS brought down to casual, less expensive, dimensions. And low-heeled lace shoes for women are sensible to wear. The stylish Princess of Wales has set her imprint on low-heeled shoes and these are especially good for walking round London streets, for they are both smart and comfortable. Head-scarves are less worn than of late, while smart caps and berets are becoming more worn, though most people go hatless except in the coldest weather. If you are having lunch anywhere at all, smart men must wear a jacket and tie, and women will not be admitted in trousers unless the outfit is a very smart trouser suit. And jeans are not generally allowed in the smartest hotels and restaurants. Good casual clothes are now just permitted, but it is better to put on a good suit for a man, and an elegant shirt and skirt or dress for a woman.

EVENING WEAR

In the evening people tend not to dress up too much for the Theatre unless it is a Gala Performance. At these there is generally a Royal Visitor so black tie (or for the young the trendy equivalent) is de rigueur for men, while women will be expected to wear a long dress with jewellery and beautifully done hair. At ordinary evenings it is still considered a good thing to wear a suit or good co-ordinates if a man and a pretty dress if a woman, though there is no hard and fast rule. And with more and more theatres selling off any unsold tickets to students at the last moment, people are, regretably becoming less smart at theatres. At first nights, though, you do find smart audiences, even some long dresses. At concerts, people wear similar clothes to at the theatre.

Restaurants — again a good suit and a pretty dress generally suffices, though at Gala Occasions you would find most people wearing evening dress, and at Charity Balls, if you get asked to one, then you put on everything you've got — long dress, best jewels, the lot. Men can wear black or white tie — ask your host. If you are in London without evening dress then you can easily hire one at MOSS BROTHERS in COVENT GARDEN who have evening clothes for both men and women in an extraordinary range of sizes for you to hire by the day.

This also goes for the curiously named MORNING DRESS which the Brits wear to formal daytime occasions such as Royal Ascot, Weddings and upper class funerals. Again Moss Bros. (as it is affectionately known) is the place to go to get kitted out. The cost of made-to-measure Morning clothes is so much nowadays that only the upper classes have their own and even this may be handed down from the family! However, it is a distinguished dress and looks marvellous on most men. Ladies for these formal occasions wear a pretty dress covered with a matching or co-ordinating coat, a dress and jacket, preferably in silk or something similar, with a beautiful hat. The Queen has this idiom nicely judged. If you have a national costume then this is allowed on such occasions and, indeed, saries, African dress, and the tunics and trousers of Pakistan ladies add much to the colour of the English Social scene.

For Henley you dress much the

same, if female, as for Ascot, though your dress or suit could be in cotton, while men go for a more casual sporting look. While for Wimbledon, unless you are in the Royal Box you can dress comfortably and casually. Cricket, Football matches and Athletics Meetings need comfortable clothes which are well weatherproof as you will be in the open and not able to get under shelter if the rains descend.

TRENDY CLOTHES

You may want to see what the young and trendy are wearing — it's often good for a laugh anyway and the place to do this is THE KING'S ROAD, CHELSEA. Carnaby Street, nowadays, is just full of tourists snapping other tourists — the trendy dress shops having now moved on. But the King's Road, especially the part furthest from Sloane Square, still has shops which reflect the current young idea, as well as the young parading up and down in the latest gear.

THE LONDON FASHION SCENE

Nowadays there is really no such thing as FASHION — at one time a style or line, often dictated by Paris, later on in the sixties by a band of brilliant British Designers, led by Mary Quant, was worn by anyone who had pretensions to be in fashion. But now the choice is very bewildering and no one has the authority to impose a style. So we can all choose the clothes we like to wear best of all to suit our physique, personality, or, even, the personality we wish to put over! London is full of shops that invite you to make a choice from the clothes they sell to build up your individual style. You may go for the sporty or the traditional; the fancy dress look of another age or very casual clothes. But if you are going to invest in clothes while you stay here, then we suggest that you cannot do better than to choose what we have long been good at — tweeds, woollen goods, smart skirts, trousers and shirts. They are the best we have, made from our finest materials.

Where to stay

WHERE TO STAY

London has hundreds of fine hotels most of them of a high international standard and it would not of course be possible to list them all within this section. What we have therefore done is to select those hotels which give the visitor a choice between the famous luxury ones to the more moderate but nevertheless good hotels. We also include in this section some guest houses and very small hotels which offer extremely reasonable accommodation. Because a number of visitors like to stay in a particular area of London which they like, we have described hotels as they are situated in each of those areas. This will enable you to identify quickly the type of hotel which is likely to meet your requirement in the area of your choice. As we explained at the beginning of the guide we are against using confusing and obscure symbols so each entry has a full explanation without reference to a glossary of explanation in another part of the book.
The hotels are listed as Luxury consisting of the very best and famous hotels known for their legendary grandeur, First Class all of which provide excellent accommodation and service, Medium offering good value, and Small for those visitors who are on restricted budgets. The catering arrangements in small hotels usually refer to cooked breakfast and Continental breakfast, unless otherwise stated. We strongly advise you to check prices at the time of making the reservation.
Credit Cards: Where Major Credit Cards are mentioned these refer to American Express, Diners, Access and Visa, unless otherwise stated.

BAYSWATER AND PADDINGTON W.2.

FIRST CLASS HOTELS

London Metropole
Edgware Road, W.2.
Tel: 01-402 4141
Telex: 23711
Rooms: 590 all with bath/shower, T.V., telephone and radio.
Major Credit Cards.
A large modern building situated within ten minutes' walk of Marble Arch and Paddington Station. Bedrooms, which are functional and modern, have air-conditioning. Good conference facilities. In-house movies.
Map Ref. 2E

Royal Lancaster
Lancaster Terrace, W.2.
Tel: 01-262 6737
Telex: 24822
Rooms: 434 all with bath. 17 suites, 15 studio suites.
Major Credit Cards.
A modern hotel in a tower block with telephone, radio and good views over Hyde Park. Well appointed bedrooms. Colour television. Excellent conference facilities. Good restaurant. In-house movies.
Map Ref. 2D

Whites
Lancaster Gate, W.2.
Tel: 01-262 2711
Telex: 23922
Rooms: 61 all with bath/shower, T.V., radio and telephone.
Major Credit Cards.
A charming Victorian but well modernised building overlooking Hyde Park. Gay balconies and white paint give the hotel a cheerful character. Mini bars in all rooms.
The interior has been tastefully modernised and the bedrooms are attractively decorated. Car park.
Map Ref. 3D

A
B
C
D
E
F
G
H
I
J
K
L
1
2
3
4
5
6
Kensal Green
KILBURN LANE
HARROW ROAD
FERNHEAD RD.
ELGIN AVENUE
GREAT WESTERN RD
CASTELLAIN RD.
Maida Vale
MAIDA VALE
CLIFTON GDNS.
Warwick Avenue
ST. JOHN'S WOOD RD
LISSON GROVE
WELLINGTON ROAD
EDGWARE ROAD
Marylebone
REGENT'S PARK
EUSTON STATION
ALBANY STREET
Great Portland Street
EUSTON ROAD
Baker Street
Regent's Park
Warren Street
MARYLEBONE ROAD
TOTTENHAM COURT RD
GOWER STREET
SOUTHAMPTON ROW
GRAYS INN ROAD
GUILFORD ST.
KING'S CROSS ROAD
ROSEBERRY AVENUE
GOSWELL ROAD
CITY ROAD
OLD STREET
Old Street
GREAT EASTERN ST.
HACKNEY ROAD
LADBROKE GROVE
Ladbroke Grove
Westbourne Park
WESTBOURNE PARK
TALBOT ROAD
CHEPSTOW RD
HARROW ROAD
Edgeware Road
Goodge Street
THEOBALDS RD.
CLERKEN WELL ROAD
FARRINGDON ST
ALDERSGATE ST.
LIVERPOOL ST. STATION
CLARENDON RD
BLENHEIM CRES.
COLVILLE TER.
BISHOPS BRIDGE ROAD
PADDINGTON STATION
WESTBOURNE TER
SEYMOUR PLACE
PORTMAN SQUARE
BAKER STREET
MARYLEBONE HIGH ST.
PORTLAND PL.
GOODGE ST.
Tottenham Court Rd.
NEW OXFORD STREET
HOLBORN
Holborn
Chancery Lane
HOLBORN VIA
CHANCERY LANE
Moorgate
MOORGATE
BISHOPSGATE
HOUNDSDITCH
COMMERCIAL ST.
WHITECHAPEL
Aldgate
Bank
St Paul's
CHEAPSIDE
WESTBOURNE GROVE
Oxford Circus
OXFORD STREET
REGENT ST.
Marble Arch
FLEET ST.
LUDGATE HILL
LEADENHALL ST.
LEMAN ST.
MINORIES
ELGIN CRES.
PEMBRIDGE RD.
Bayswater
QUEENSWAY
Lancaster Gate
GROSVENOR SQUARE
Bond Street
NEW BOND ST.
POLAND ST.
WARDOUR ST.
CHARING CROSS ROAD
DRURY LANE
Covent Garden
LONG ACRE
Aldwych
STRAND
Somerset House
QUEEN VICTORIA ST.
Mansion House
FENCHURCH ST.
Monument
Blackfriars
Temple
EMBANKMENT
BAYSWATER ROAD
Queensway
KENSINGTON GARDENS
HYDE PARK
PARK LANE
BERKELEY SQUARE
OLD BOND ST.
SHAFTESBURY AV.
Piccadilly Circus
Leicester Square
RIVER THAMES
BLACKFRIARS BRIDGE
SOUTHWARK BRIDGE
LONDON BRIDGE
Monument
Tower Hill
TOWER HILL
EAST SMITHFIELD
PORTLAND ROAD
Notting Hill Gate
NOTTING HILL GATE
KENSINGTON CHURCH ST.
SERPENTINE
CURZON ST.
PICCADILLY
PALL MALL
CHARING CROSS STATION
WATERLOO BRIDGE
STAMFORD ST.
SOUTHWARK STREET
TOOLEY STREET
TOWER BRIDGE
HOLLAND PARK AVENUE
Holland Park
ROTTEN ROW
Hyde Park Corner
Green Park
GREEN PARK
THE MALL
ST. JAMES'S PARK
Westminster
VICTORIA
WATERLOO ROAD
Borough
ST. THOMAS
HOLLAND PARK
CAMPDEN HILL RD.
KENSINGTON HIGH STREET
KENSINGTON RD.
KNIGHTSBRIDGE
BELGRAVE SQUARE
GROSVENOR PL.
BIRDCAGE WALK
WESTMINSTER BRIDGE
YORK ROAD
WATERLOO STATION
SOUTH WARK BRIDGE RD
BOROUGH HIGH ST.
LONDON BRI. STATION
QUEEN'S GATE
EXHIBITION ROAD
Knightsbridge
SLOANE STREET
St James's Park
PALACE RD.
WESTMINSTER BRIDGE RD
Lambeth North
BOROUGH RD.
CAUSEWAY
LONG LANE
HOLLAND ROAD
High Street Kensington
BEAUCHAMP PLACE
CADOGAN GDNS
WALTON RD.
BROMPTON ROAD
South Kensington
VICTORIA STREET
HORSE FERRY ROAD
LAMBETH BRIDGE
LAMBETH ROAD
LONDON RD
NEWINGTON
ST GEORGE'S RD
GREAT DOVER ST.
ABBEY STREET
EARLS COURT ROAD
CROMWELL ROAD
KING'S ROAD
VAUXHALL
Elephant and Castle
NEW KENT RD.
HAMMERSMITH ROAD
WARWICK ROAD
Gloucester Road
OLD BROMPTON ROAD
SYDNEY ST.
Sloane Square
BUCKINGHAM PALACE ROAD
VICTORIA STATION
BRIDGE ROAD
MILL BANK
KENNINGTON ROAD
WALWORTH ROAD
OLD KENT ROAD
SHEPHERD'S BUSH RD
TALGARTH ROAD
NORTH END ROAD
WEST CROMWELL ROAD
Earls Court
FULHAM ROAD
CHELSEA BRIDGE RD.
Pimlico
ALBERT EMBANKMENT
VAUXHALL BRIDGE
KENNINGTON PARK ROAD
LILLIE ROAD
REDCLIFF GARDENS
ROYAL HOSPITAL ROAD
CHELSEA EMBANKMENT
CHELSEA BRIDGE
GROSVENOR ROAD
Vauxhall
HARLEYFORD RD.
Kennington Park
FULHAM PALACE ROAD
West Brompton
KING'S ROAD
ALBERT BRIDGE
BATTERSEA PARK
NINE ELMS LANE
FENTIMAN RD
Oval
ALBANY ROAD

MEDIUM HOTELS

Clarendon Court
Edgware Road, W.9.
Tel: 01-286 8080
Telex: 27374
Rooms: 155 all with T.V. and telephone, 144 with bath/shower.
Major Credit Cards.
Famous for visiting cricketing sides being close to the Lords Cricket Ground. This is a friendly hotel with a good restaurant. Recently modernised, the bedrooms and bathrooms are comfortably furnished and well equipped. Amenities include a small health centre and a sauna.
Map Ref. 1D

Coburg Hotel
129 Bayswater Road, W.2.
Tel: 01-229 3654
Telex: 268235
Rooms: 125 all with T.V. and telephone, 70 with bath/shower.
Major Credit Cards.
An imposing Edwardian Hotel overlooking Kensington Gardens. Public rooms are in elegant taste blending the old with the new. Bedrooms are individually styled and bathrooms spacious.
Map Ref. 3C

Central Park
49 Queensborough Terrace, W.2.
Tel: 01-229 2424
Telex: 27342
Rooms: 291 all with bath/shower, T.V., telephone and radio.
Major Credit Cards.
This modern hotel off the Bayswater Road has a spacious, bustling foyer and is popular with businessmen. Bedrooms are bright and well appointed with very modern bathrooms. The hotel has a sauna.
Map Ref. 3C

London Embassy
150 Bayswater Road, W.2.
Tel: 01-229 1212
Telex: 27727
Rooms: 193 all with bath/shower, T.V., telephone and radio.
Major Credit Cards.
Overlooking Hyde Park, this is a modern hotel with a pleasant cocktail bar and outdoor patio for summer drinking. Bedrooms are comfortable and bright with tiled bathrooms. Friendly service. Car Park.
Map Ref. 3C

Great Western Royal
Praed Street, W.2.
Tel: 01-723 8064
Telex: 263972

Rooms: 164 all with T.V. and telephone, 150 with bath/shower.
Major Credit Cards.
Old-fashioned in the grand Victorian manner, this station hotel has a dignified grace. Both the public rooms and most of the bedrooms are large with comfortable modern furnishings. The restaurant and coffee shop are cheerful. Very friendly staff.
Map Ref. 2D

Leinster Towers
25-31 Leinster Gardens, W.2.
Tel: 01-262 4591
Telex: 267465
Rooms: 160 all with bath/shower, telephone, T.V. and radio.
Major Credit Cards.
A modernised hotel in an historic house, which was once the house of the Duke of Leinster. Bedrooms are cheerfully decorated and the staff efficient and attentive.
Map Ref. 3C

Post House
104 Bayswater Road, W.2.
Tel: 01-262 4461
Telex: 22667
Rooms: 175 all with bath, T.V., telephone and radio.
Major Credit Cards.
A ten storey hotel overlooking Kensington Gardens. Within easy reach of West End. There is a split level restaurant offering a good menu. Bedrooms are cheerful and well equipped. Free car park.
Map Ref. 3C

SMALL HOTELS

Parkwood
4 Stanhope Place, W.2.
Tel: 01-402 2241
Telex 8812714
Rooms: 18 all with T.V., 12 with bathroom.
Major Credit Cards.
Two minutes from Marble Arch in a select and quiet residential street. Regency style town house recently refurbished and modernised. Pleasant atmosphere. Breakfast only.
Map Ref. 2D

Grosvenor Court Hotel
144 Praed Street, W.2.
Tel: 01-262 3464
Telex: 25971
Rooms: 93 all with bath/shower, telephone, T.V. and radio.
Major Credit Cards.
Very well equipped small hotel close to Paddington Station and within 15 minutes walk of Oxford Street.
Map Ref. 2D

Lancaster Court
202 Sussex Gardens, W.2.
Tel: 01-402 8438
Telex: 21879/25247 LANCO.
Rooms: 43 all with T.V., 39 with bath/shower.
Major Credit Cards.
Ten minutes from Marble Arch this nice little hotel is clean and modern inside. There is a small dining room which serves Continental breakfast only.
Map Ref. 2E

Pembridge Court Hotel
34 Pembridge Gardens, W.2.
Tel: 01-229 9977
Telex: 298363
Rooms: 35 all with bath/shower, T.V., telephone and radio.
Major Credit Cards.
This is a very pleasant little hotel with attractive bedrooms and nice tiled bathrooms. There is a comfortable lounge, a small bar and friendly staff.
Map Ref. 3C

Royal Park Hotel
5 Westbourne Terrace, W.2.
Tel: 01-402 6187
Rooms: 60 all with T.V., telephone and radio, 46 with bath/shower.
Credit Cards: American Express and Diners.
Converted Victorian town houses form this welcoming hotel. All the bedrooms are nicely decorated and the bathrooms tiled and modern. There are two lounges and a small bar. Cooked breakfast only.
Map Ref. 2D

Apollo Hotel
64 Queensborough Terrace, W.2.
Tel: 01-229 6251
Rooms: 18 all with bath/shower, T.V. and telephone.
Credit Cards: Visa, Access.
A pleasant family-run hotel with clean, modern bedrooms and bathrooms. Very friendly staff and a good hearty cooked breakfast.
Map Ref. 3D

West Two Hotel
22 Kensington Gardens Square, W.2.
Tel: 01-229 7938
Rooms: 31.
No Credit Cards.
Situated in a quiet square, these two converted terrace houses have been turned into a good small hotel.

Although there are no private bathrooms or televisions, the bedrooms are pleasant. Cooked breakfast only.

Map Ref. 3C

BLOOMSBURY AND HOLBORN W.C.1.

FIRST CLASS HOTELS

Bloomsbury Crest
Coram Street, W.C.1.
Tel: 01-837 1200
Telex: 22113
Rooms: 250 all with bath, T.V., telephone and radio.
Major Credit Cards.
A stylish modern hotel, all bedrooms comfortably furnished with films shown free on the T.V. set. Restaurants, two bars, good food.

Map Ref. 1H

Russell
Russell Square, W.C.1.
Tel: 01-837 6470
Telex 24615
Rooms: 318 all with bath/shower, T.V. and telephone.
Major Credit Cards.
This is a beautiful building which is without doubt one of the finest examples of Victorian magnificence and opulence. It has been skillfully modernised and the public rooms are a delight. Bedrooms and bathrooms are modernised with nice fittings.

Map Ref. 1H

President
Russell Square, W.C.1.
Tel: 01-837 8844
Telex: 263951/21822
Rooms: 447 all with bath/shower, T.V., telephone and radio.
Major Credit Cards.
This large modern hotel is well situated for easy access to both the West End and the City. The Cocktail bar is attractively furnished and the Day and Night Grill Bar is open until the early hours. Within the hotel there are shops and a bank.

Map Ref. 1H

Imperial
Russell Square, W.C.1.
Tel: 01-837 3655
Telex: 21822/263951
Rooms: 458 all with bath/shower, T.V., telephone and radio.
Major Credit Cards.
An excellent modern hotel with well furnished bedrooms and bathrooms. A la Carte Restaurant. In-house movies.

Map Ref. 1H

Royal Scot
100 Kings Cross Road, W.C.1.
Tel: 01-278 2434
Telex: 27657
Rooms: 349 all with bath/shower, T.V., telephone and radio.
Major Credit Cards.
Conveniently placed for both Kings Cross and Euston stations. The bedrooms, some of which have four poster beds, have modern facilities such as drinks dispensers, tea and coffee making facilities.

Map Ref. 1I

Tavistock
Tavistock Square, W.C.1.
Tel: 01-636 8383
Telex: 21822
Rooms: 300 all with bath/shower, T.V., telephone and radio.
Major Credit Cards.
Overlooking the delightful Tavistock Square. The Genevieve Bar and Tavlin Snack Bar provide a wide range of refreshments, whilst the main dining hall provides excellent varied table fare. Bedrooms are modern and tastefully decorated.
Map Ref. 1H

MEDIUM HOTELS

Bonnington Hotel
92 Southampton Row, W.C.1.
Tel: 01-242 2828
Telex: 261591
Rooms: 261 all with T.V., radio and telephone, 102 with bath.
Major Credit Cards.
Functional, modern hotel situated within easy reach of theatres, and usefully located for businessmen and tourists. Bedrooms are well equipped and double glazed against noise. Pleasant bar and restaurant.
Map Ref. 2H

Bedford Corner Hotel
Bayley Street, W.C.1.
Tel: 01-580 7766
Telex: 296464
Rooms: 85 all with radio, T.V. and telephone, 45 with bath.
Major Credit Cards.
An established, comfortable hotel close to Tottenham Court Road and Oxford Street. An attractive restaurant and bar and modern styled bedrooms.
Map Ref. 2H

Bedford
Southampton Row, W.C.1.
Tel: 01-636 7822
Telex: 21822
Rooms: 180 all with bath/shower, T.V., telephone and radio.
Major Credit Cards.
This modern hotel is situated close to the Piccadilly Tube and central bus routes. There is a pleasant lounge and dining room overlooking small gardens and a sun terrace. Staff are friendly and helpful. Car Park.
Map Ref. 1H

Kingsley
Bloomsbury Way, W.C.1.
Tel: 01-242 5881
Telex: 21157
Rooms: 169 all with T.V. and telephone, 123 with bath/shower.
Major Credit Cards.
A Victorian building which has been modernised without losing its charm. This is a pleasant hotel with a unique quiet charm providing a personal and friendly service. Bedrooms are attractive and bathrooms well appointed. There is a delightful little bar and a carvery in the restaurant.
Map Ref. 2H

Cora
Upper Woburn Place, W.C.1.
Tel: 01-387 5111
Telex: 261591
Rooms: 150 all with T.V., radio and telephone, 52 with bath/shower.
Major Credit Cards.
Situated close to Euston and Kings Cross stations, the Cora Hotel is within the vicinity of many places of historical interest. The bedrooms are furnished in attractive style. Efficient and friendly staff.
Map Ref. 2H

SMALL HOTELS

Bloomsbury
Bloomsbury Square, W.C.1.
Tel: 01-242 5401
Rooms: 57 all with radio and telephone.
Major Credit Cards.
A comfortable, well furnished hotel which caters particularly for those guests who appreciate individual attention. It has a pleasant Cocktail Bar and an excellent restaurant. Situated close to British Museum and Covent Garden.
Map Ref. 2H

George Hotel
58-60 Cartwright Gardens, W.C.1.
Tel: 01-387 1528/6789
Rooms: 42, 5 with shower.
Major Credit Cards (not Visa).
Situated in a lovely crescent of Georgian houses, this homely little hotel is well run with friendly service. Bedrooms are bright and cheerful. Breakfast only.
Map Ref. 1H

Jenkins Hotel
45 Cartwright Gardens, W.C.1.
Tel: 01-387 2067
Rooms: 12.
No Credit Cards.
This is very much like staying in a private house, which is what it originally was. Everything about it is designed to make you feel at home, from the fresh flowers to the charming bedrooms. A cooked breakfast only, but a good one.
Map Ref. 1H

Ruskin Hotel
23 Montague Street, W.C.1.
Tel: 01-636 7388
Rooms: 35, 3 with shower.
Credit Cards: American Express, Barclaycard, Access and Diners.
A pleasant small hotel, family-run with comfortable bedrooms. A nice lounge and a breakfast room in the basement. Cooked breakfast only.
Map Ref. 2H

Wansbeck
Bedford Place, W.C.1.
Tel: 01-636 6232
Telex: 261591
Rooms: 34.
Credit Cards: Visa, Access.
Situated in a quiet tree-lined street in Bloomsbury, this Georgian House has been turned into a quiet, small functional hotel. Although bedrooms do not have private bathrooms or television they are otherwise well appointed and there is a T.V. lounge

and the dining room operates for the service of full English breakfast only.
Map Ref. 1H

CHELSEA, BELGRAVIA, & KNIGHTSBRIDGE

LUXURY HOTELS

Hyatt Carlton Tower
Cadogan Place, S.W.1.
Tel: 01-235 5411
Telex: 21944
Rooms: 228 all with bath/shower, T.V., telephone and radio.
Major Credit Cards.
This exclusive hotel overlooking Cadogan Gardens has been one of the top hotels for many years. Bedrooms are beautifully appointed and the bathrooms modern and spotless. There are two fine restaurants, one serving excellent French cuisine and the other magnificent beef and steaks. There are 47 suites, eight of which are really luxurious. Free videos. Awarded Michelin Star.
Map Ref. 4F

Berkeley Hotel
Wilton Place, S.W.1.
Tel: 01-235 6000
Telex: 919252
Rooms: 152 all with bath/shower, T.V., telephone and radio.
Credit Cards: Access and Visa.
Modern luxury hotel with comfort and quality of a very high order. Marvellous services and very efficient staff. Public rooms are reminiscent of a private house. There is a swimming pool and a bar area on the roof. Bedrooms and bathrooms are superb and there is a wide choice of suites. Excellent cuisine in a delightful dining room.
Map Ref. 4F

Hyde Park Hotel
Knightsbridge, S.W.1.
Tel: 01-235 2000
Telex: 262057
Rooms: 179 all with bath/shower, T.V., telephone and radio.
Major Credit Cards.
Standards are still maintained at this old established hotel. There is a stately grandeur about the public rooms, with marble and chandeliers blending with mouldings in gold leaf. Bedrooms are elegant with antiques, paintings, mixing with modern amenities. There are 19 suites with views across Hyde Park, all of which reflect the grandeur of the Edwardian days. The two restaurants have a pleasant atmosphere, with good food.
Map Ref. 4F

Sheraton Park Tower
101 Knightsbridge, S.W.1.
Tel: 01-235 8050
Telex: 917222
Rooms: 295 all with bath/shower, T.V., telephone and radio.
Major Credit Cards.

A circular 17 storey building with all bedrooms having outward views. The decor is elegant and the bathrooms have gold and marble fittings. The public areas are smart with contemporary furnishings and the bar area has nice styling. There are 23 suites, with six luxury penthouses looking over London. Video films.
Map Ref. 4F

FIRST CLASS HOTELS

Capital Hotel
22 Basil Street, S.W.1.
Tel: 01-589 5171
Telex: 919042
Rooms: 60 all with bath/shower, T.V., telephone and radio.
Major Credit Cards.
Very close to Harrods, this small, elegant and modern hotel offers a very high standard of service and amenities. Good sized bedrooms with very well-fitted bathrooms. The restaurant although small, offers exceptional cuisine and wines, has Michelin Star.
Map Ref. 4E

Lowndes Hotel
21 Lowndes Street, S.W.1.
Tel: 01-235 6020
Telex: 919065
Rooms: 80 all with bath/shower, T.V., telephone and radio.
Major Credit Cards.
A small hotel which has lovely 18th Century style decor and offers luxury and elegance. The bedrooms are compact and attractively decorated with very well appointed bathrooms and mini bars.
Map Ref. 4F

London Belgravia
20 Chesham Place, S.W.1.
Tel: 01-235 6040
Telex: 919020
Rooms: 107 all with bath/shower, T.V., telephone and radio.
Major Credit Cards.
A pleasant. modern hotel near Belgravia Square. Bedrooms are spacious and well equipped including air-conditioning and have warm wood decor. There is a smart foyer, public areas and a bar with lots of atmosphere.
Map Ref. 4F

Holiday Inn, Chelsea
Sloane Street, S.W.1.
Tel: 01-235 4377
Telex: 919111
Rooms: 217 all with bath/shower, T.V., telephone and radio.
Major Credit Cards.
Crystal chandeliers, marble floors and leather and velvet furnishings make the setting for this hotel. Bedrooms are excellent with well designed bathrooms. There is a good restaurant with an outside/indoor swimming pool.
Map Ref. 4E

Cadogan Hotel
75 Sloane Street, S.W.1.
Tel: 01-235 7141
Telex: 267893
Rooms: 70 all with bath/shower, T.V., telephone and radio.
Major Credit Cards.
This old established hotel has a lovely Edwardian atmosphere about it. Recently refurbished bedrooms and bathrooms are comfortable. There is a nice bar and a good restaurant.
Map Ref. 4E

MEDIUM HOTELS

Wilbraham Hotel
Wilbraham Place, S.W.1.
Tel: 01-730 8296
Rooms: 57 with telephone, 34 with bath/shower. T.V. in some rooms.
No Credit Cards.
A Victorian town house with an informal atmosphere. This is a charming hotel with two pleasant lounges and a nice bar. Bedrooms are pretty and the bathrooms spotless.
Map Ref. 5F

Basil Street Hotel
Basil Street, S.W.3.
Tel: 01-730 3411
Telex: 28379
Rooms: 103 all with telephone, 68 with bath/shower, radio, some T.V.
Major Credit Cards.
A traditional English hotel where old-fashioned comforts still prevail. Antiques and paintings in the public rooms lend an air of dignity and grace. Comfortable bedrooms are nicely decorated. Coffee shop. Ladies club.
Map Ref. 4E

Royal Court Hotel
Sloane Square, S.W.1.
Tel: 01-730 9191
Telex: 23241
Rooms: 98 all with bath/shower, T.V., telephone and radio.
Major Credit Cards.
Personal supervision by efficient staff reflects the elegance of this hotel. It has a comfortable lounge, restaurant and cocktail bar together with a real ale bar, the Tavern. Bedrooms are tastefully decorated.

Map Ref. 5F

SMALL HOTELS

Eden House Hotel
111 Old Church Street, S.W.3.
Tel: 01-352 3403
Telex: 291446
Rooms: 14, 7 with bath/shower.
Major Credit Cards.
Centrally located for Kings Road and Fulham Road. Friendly and efficient service and ideal for short stays as the facilities for children are good. Cooked breakfast.

Map Ref. 5E

Campden Court Hotel
28 Basil Street, W.3.
Tel: 01-589 6286

Rooms: 18, all with T.V. and telephone, 10 with bath/shower.
Credit Cards: American Express and Visa.
Only one minute's walk from Harrods, this little hotel has comfortable bedrooms and a pleasant little breakfast room.

Map Ref. 4E

Culford House
9 Culford Gardens, S.W.3.
Tel: 01-581 3255
Rooms: 22 all with T.V. and telephone, 10 with bath/shower.
Credit Cards: Access, American Express, Diners and Visa.
There are no public rooms, but the bedrooms are compact and nicely decorated. Continental breakfast only, served in your bedroom.

Map Ref. 5E

Diplomat
2 Chesham Street, S.W.1.
Tel: 01-235 1544/01-263 2500
Rooms: 26 all with bath/shower, T.V., telephone and radio.
Credit Cards: American Express, Access, Eurocard and Visa.
Old established hotel which still has an air of Edwardian tranquility. The bedrooms are pleasantly decorated and, as there are no public rooms, a cooked breakfast is served in the bedroom.

Map Ref. 5F

Knightsbridge Green Hotel
159 Knightsbridge, S.W.1.
Tel: 01-584 6274
Rooms: 20 all with T.V. and telephone, 16 with bath/shower.
Credit Cards: American Express, Visa.
This is an unusual little hotel in so far as the double bedrooms have sitting rooms as well as a bathroom. Very comfortably furnished with pleasant and polite staff. No public rooms so breakfast is served in the bedroom.

Map Ref. 4F

Willett Hotel
32 Sloane Gardens, S.W.1.
Tel: 01-730 0634
Rooms: 17 all with T.V., 14 with bath/shower.
No Credit Cards.
Charming little hotel with pleasant fresh bedrooms and bathrooms. There is a breakfast room where a cooked breakfast is served and a small garden.
Map Ref. 5F

Executive Hotel
57 Pont Street, S.W.1.
Tel: 01-581 2424
Telex: 263250
Rooms: 29 all with bath/shower, T.V. and telephone.
Credit Cards: American Express, Diners, Visa and Access.
Very handy for Harrods, this hotel has attractive features, with small modern bedrooms, a little bar and restaurant.
Map Ref. 4F

CITY E.C.1., E.C.2., E.C.4., E.1.

FIRST CLASS HOTELS

Tower Hotel
St. Katherine's Way, E.1.
Tel: 01-481 2575
Telex: 885934
Rooms: 826 all with bath/shower, T.V., telephone and radio.
Major Credit Cards.
Located next door to the Tower of London and London Bridge, facing the Thames on one side and St. Katherine's Dock and the many yachts on the other, it has a spectacular location. It is a very efficient hotel with excellent bedrooms and suites and cuisine of a very high standard.
Map Ref. 3L

Great Eastern Hotel
Liverpool Street, E.C.2.
Tel: 01-283 4363
Telex: 886812

Rooms: 153 all with T.V., radio and telephone, 126 with bath/shower.
Major Credit Cards.
Like many railway hotels, the Great Eastern has an atmosphere of bygone years but with the spaciousness which the Victorians demanded. The service is polite and helpful, the bedrooms and bathrooms well appointed and the food of a very good standard.
Tea and coffee making facilities. 2 restaurants.
Map Ref. 2L

EARLS COURT AND SOUTH KENSINGTON S.W.5 and S.W.7.

FIRST CLASS

The Gloucester
Harrington Gardens, S.W.7.
Tel: 01-373 6030
Telex: 917505
Rooms: 550 all with bath/shower, T.V., telephone and radio.
Major Credit Cards.
This is a modern hotel with very comfortable bedrooms and good room service. There is a pleasant wine bar within the hotel, a Carvery and a real ale Tavern.
Map Ref. 5D

Blakes Hotel
33 Roland Gardens, S.W.7.
Tel: 01-370 6701
Telex: 8813500
Rooms: 50 all with bath/shower, T.V., telephone and radio.
Major Credit Cards.
Although small, this is really a lovely little hotel with beautiful decor in the various public rooms and the bar. The bedrooms are individually styled and all are quite charming. Pleasant dining room.
Map Ref. 5D

John Howard Hotel
4 Queens Gate, S.W.7.
Tel: 01-581 3011
Telex: 8813397
Rooms: 32 all with bath/shower, T.V. and telephone.
Major Credit Cards.
An exclusive small hotel with a marble floored entrance hall and lovely furnishings. Very attractive bedrooms with air conditioning and well equipped bathrooms and mini bars. There is a nice cocktail bar. No children under twelve.
Map Ref. 4D

Rembrandt Hotel
11 Thurloe Place, S.W.7.
Tel: 01-589 8100
Telex: 295828
Rooms: 200 all with T.V., radio and telephone, most with bath/shower.
Major Credit Cards.
Opposite the Victoria and Albert Museum, this hotel has spacious public rooms, a nice bar and restaurant and roomy individually decorated bedrooms.
Map Ref. 5D

Penta Hotel
97 Cromwell Road, S.W.7.
Tel: 01-370 5757
Telex: 919663
Rooms: 914 all with bath/shower, T.V., telephone and radio.
Major Credit Cards.
This towering modern block of 27 floors is reminiscent of many American hotels of the type, which cater for large masses of people at any one time. Everything is clean, quick and functional and there is an English Pub and a coffee shop.
Map Ref. 5C

MEDIUM HOTELS

Barkston Hotel
Barkston Gardens, S.W.5.
Tel: 01-373 7851
Telex: 8953154
Rooms: 72 all with bath/shower, T.V., telephone and radio.
Major Credit Cards.
Overlooking a garden square, the Barkstone is a quiet, spacious hotel with comfortable modern bedrooms and bathrooms. There is a good restaurant which offers a Grill menu and a friendly bar. Tea and coffee making facilities.
Map Ref. 5C

Elizabetta Hotel
162 Cromwell Road, S.W.5.
Tel: 01-370 4282
Telex: 918978
Rooms: 84 all with bath/shower, T.V. and telephone.
Major Credit Cards.
The inside of this modern hotel is surprisingly elegant with marble floors, ornate wallpaper and a generally sumptuous feeling in the dining room and bar. Fully tiled bathrooms and tasteful bedrooms with air conditioning. Friendly and courteous staff. Video films.
Map Ref. 5C

Hogarth Hotel
Hogarth Road, S.W.5.
Tel: 01-370 6831
Telex: 8951994
Rooms: 86 all with bath/shower, T.V. and telephone.
Major Credit Cards.
A quiet hotel, well situated for Earls Court Exhibition Centre and the Air Terminal. Modern in every detail, it still

offers personal service and care has been taken in the decor of the public rooms and the bedrooms. There is a small cocktail bar.
Map Ref. 5C

Eden Plaza
68 Queens Gate, S.W.7.
Tel: 01-370 6111
Telex: 916228
Rooms: 66 all with bath/shower, T.V., telephone and radio.
Major Credit Cards.
Quietly elegant, this hotel has well equipped bedrooms and modern functional bathrooms. There is a nice dining room which serves very good French food. Hairdryers in all rooms.
Map Ref. 5D

Embassy House Hotel
31 Queen's Gate, S.W.7.
Tel: 01-584 7222
Telex: 881 3387
Rooms: 70 all with bath/shower, T.V., telephone and radio.
Major Credit Cards.
A new hotel inside old facades of a row of houses. Modern and bright decor in all the public rooms. The bedrooms and bathrooms are very well equipped. Restaurant and bar.
Map Ref. 4D

Norfolk Hotel
2 Harrington Road, S.W.7.
Tel: 01-589 8191
Rooms: 95 all with bath/shower, T.V. and telephone.
Major Credit Cards.
A solid Victorian hotel with spacious public rooms and functional modern bedrooms. Friendly and efficient staff. Real ale bar, wine bar and restaurant.
Map Ref. 4D

SMALL HOTELS

The Alexander
9 Sumner Place, S.W.7.
Tel: 01-581 1591
Telex 917133
Rooms: 36 all with telephone, 34 with bath/shower, 25 with T.V.
Major Credit Cards.
Behind the graceful 19th Century façia is a hotel with restful decor in the public rooms. The bedrooms are modern, the bathrooms clean, and the hotel is noted for its high standards of service. Dinner and breakfast.
Map Ref. 5D

Kensington Court Hotel
33 Nevern Place, S.W.5.
Tel: 01-370 5151
Telex 8814451
Rooms: 35 all with bath/shower, T.V. telephone and radio.
Major Credit Cards.
A new modern hotel located in a quiet residential area. Each bedroom is tastefully decorated, and there are nice family rooms. There is a cocktail bar, and a small dining room which serves cooked breakfast only.
Map Ref. 5B

Burns Hotel
18 Barkston Gardens, S.W.5.
Tel: 01-373 3151
Telex 27885
Rooms: 104 all with T.V. and telephone, 97 with bath/shower.
Major Credit Cards.
This modern hotel rooms which are very functional and clean, as are the bathrooms. There is a restaurant, a bar and a nice lounge. Cooked breakfast only.
Map Ref. 5B

Concord Hotel
155 Cromwell Road, S.W.5.
Tel: 01-370 4151
Rooms: 40 all with telephone, 16 with bath/shower.
Credit Cards: American Express.
This hotel has been converted from two terraced houses and has elegant decor in the public rooms, with comfortable bedrooms and modern bathrooms. Cooked breakfast only.
Map Ref. 5B

Mowbray Court Hotel
28 Penywern Road, S.W.5.
Tel: 01-373 8285
Rooms: 85 all with telephone, 60 with T.V., 20 with bath/shower.
Credit Cards: American Express, Access.
Formed from three converted houses, the bedrooms are bright and cosy and the bathrooms compact. There is a cheerful breakfast room where cooked breakfast is served.
Map Ref. 5B

Number Sixteen
16 Sumner Place, S.W.7.
Tel: 01-589 5232
Rooms: 24 all with bath/shower and telephone.
Credit Cards: American Express, Diners.
This is a gorgeous little hotel which is just like staying in a lovely London town house. There are antiques and oil paintings in the public rooms and the charming bedrooms are beautifully decorated with well equipped bathrooms. Breakfasts are served in the bedrooms.
Map Ref. 5D

FULHAM, S.W.6.

MEDIUM HOTELS

West Centre Hotel
47 Lillie Road, S.W.6.
Tel: 01-385 1255
Telex: 917728
Rooms: 499 all with bath/shower, T.V., telephone and radio.
Major Credit Cards.
Situated next to Earls Court Exhibition Centre, this tall hotel has extensive conference facilities. The lounge and bar is large and all the bedrooms and bathrooms are spacious and modern. In-house movies.
Map Ref. 6B

SMALL HOTELS

Hotel Lily
23 Lillie Road, S.W.6.
Tel: 01-381 1881
Telex: 918922
Rooms: 99 all with bath/shower, T.V., telephone and radio.
Major Credit Cards.
Modern hotel popular with businessmen being close to Earls Court Exhibition Centre. There is an open plan restaurant and bar, the bedrooms are well equipped and the bathrooms tiled. Cooked breakfast only.
Map Ref. 6B

Lindsay Hotel
422 Fulham Road, S.W.6.
Tel: 01-385 8561
Rooms: 58 all with telephone, 30 with bath/shower.
Major Credit Cards, Not Barclaycard.
An attractive old terrace of houses converted into a cheerful hotel with tiles, pot plants and bamboo furniture. Bedrooms are bright and modern. Restaurant.
Map Ref. 6C

ST. JAMES, STRAND AND CHARING CROSS, S.W.1. AND W.C.2.

LUXURY HOTELS

Savoy Hotel
Strand, W.C.2.
Tel: 01-836 4343
Telex: 24234/5
Rooms: 200 all with bath/shower, T.V., telephone and radio.
Credit Cards: Access, American Express, Visa and Diners.
Every word of praise has been written about this hotel over the years and they were as true then as they are now. The Savoy is one of the great London institutions, with magnificent service, two superb restaurants, and bedrooms and suites of which some are the finest in the world. It is simply — THE Hotel.
Map Ref. 3H

Howard Hotel
Temple Place, W.C.2.
Tel: 01-836 3556
Telex: 268047
Rooms: 137 all with bath/shower, T.V., telephone and radio.
Major Credit Cards.
A modern hotel overlooking the Thames. The interior is very opulent and luxurious, with glittering chandeliers, marble columns and French furniture. Bedrooms are equally luxurious and the suites facing the river are exceptional. Garage parking.
Map Ref. 3I

FIRST CLASS HOTELS

Dukes Hotel
35 St. James's Place, S.W.1.
Tel: 01-491 4840
Telex 28283
Rooms: 44 all with bath/shower, T.V., telephone and radio.
Major Credit Cards.
Situated in a quiet courtyard off St. James's Street, this little hotel epitomises the serenity of the area. The public rooms are elegantly furnished, the bedrooms very comfortable and the service friendly with particular attention to detail.
Map Ref. 3G

Stafford Hotel
St. James's Place, S.W.1.
Tel: 01-493 0111
Telex: 28602
Rooms: 60 all with bath/shower, T.V., telephone, and radio.
Credit Cards: American Express.
Hidden away in a little street, the Stafford is a haven of tranquility and yet only minutes away from Bond Street and the West End. Public rooms are beautifully decorated and elegant, as are the bedrooms. Staff are very polite and helpful.
Map Ref. 3G

Royal Horseguards Hotel
2 Whitehall Court, S.W.1.
Tel: 01-839 3400
Telex: 917096
Rooms: 280 all with bath/shower, T.V., telephone and radio.
Major Credit Cards.
Situated within a Victorian building and smartly modernised, with comfortable public rooms including a garden terrace facing the Embankment. Bedrooms are elegantly decorated and have a relaxing calm.
Map Ref. 4H

Cavendish Hotel
Jermyn Street, S.W.1.
Tel: 01-930 2111
Telex: 263187
Rooms: 253 all with bath/shower, T.V., telephone and radio.
Major Credit Cards.
A modern hotel with dark wood panelling and a plush, relaxing bar. Bedrooms are spacious and very well equipped, bathrooms modern, and there are four lovely penthouse suites.
Map Ref. 3G

Charing Cross Hotel
Strand, W.C.2.
Tel: 01-839 7282
Telex: 261101
Rooms: 210 all with bath/shower, T.V., telephone and radio.
Major Credit Cards.
One of the grand old station hotels which has been nicely modernised but still retaining the opulence and dignity of the Victorian era. Bedrooms are comfortable and bathrooms spacious. There is a sauna and an all night bar for residents.
Map Ref. 3H

Waldorf Hotel
Aldwych, W.C.2.
Tel: 01-836 2400
Telex: 24574
Rooms: 310 all with bath/shower, T.V., telephone and radio.
Major Credit Cards.
There is a world of Edwardian splendour within this hotel. Elegant public rooms provide an ambience that is serene. The bedrooms combine tradition with convenience and there are also some lovely suites. Afternoon tea, dances on Fridays.
Map Ref. 3H

Drury Lane Hotel
10 Drury Lane, W.C.2.
Tel: 01-836 6666
Telex: 8811395
Rooms: 130 all with bath/shower, T.V., telephone and radio.
Major Credit Cards.
A modern hotel situated within an office complex. The decor inside is plush and the bedrooms and bathrooms are well equipped and comfortable.
Map Ref. 2H

Strand Palace Hotel
Strand, W.C.2.
Tel: 01-836 8080
Telex: 24208
Rooms: 786 all with bath/shower, T.V., telephone and radio.
Major Credit Cards.
Continuous modernisation of this large hotel means that the bedrooms are all well equipped and comfortable. Popular with both tourists and businessmen, there is a good restaurant, a carvery, coffee shop and two bars.
Map Ref. 3H

MEDIUM HOTELS

Pastoria Hotel
St. Martins Street, W.C.2.
Tel: 01-930 8641
Telex: 25538
Rooms: 54 all with T.V. and telephone, 40 with bath/shower.
Major Credit Cards.
Well sited little hotel handy for the West End. Public areas are brightly decorated, bedrooms modern and bathrooms functional.
Map Ref. 3H

SMALL HOTELS

Devereux Hotel
20 Devereux Court, W.C.2.
Tel: 01-583 4562
Rooms: 5.

Major Credit Cards.
Hidden in a tiny alley by the Middle Temple and close to the Royal Courts of Justice, this former coffee house has simple accommodation. At night it is very quiet and the food is good. There is a bar and a restaurant for lunches — Monday-Friday.

Map Ref. 3I

VICTORIA, S.W.1.

FIRST CLASS HOTELS

Goring Hotel
15 Beeston Place, Grosvenor Gardens, S.W.1.
Tel: 01-834 8211
Telex: 919166
Rooms: 100 all with bath/shower, T.V., telephone and radio.
Major Credit Cards.
A dignified Edwardian styled hotel, which prides itself on first class and courteous service. Bedrooms have been decorated to blend elegant styling with modern amenities and the bathrooms are well equipped. The public rooms are spacious and comfortable.

Map Ref. 4F

Royal Westminster Hotel
Buckingham Palace Road, S.W.1.
Tel: 01-834 1302
Telex: 916821
Rooms: 135 all with bath/shower, T.V., telephone and radio.
Major Credit Cards.
There is an attractive foyer bar and a modern restaurant in this hotel, which is convenient for Victoria Station. Bedrooms are tastefully decorated and there are also eighteen superb suites in a variety of styles.

Map Ref. 4G

St. Ermin's Hotel
Caxton Street, S.W.1.
Tel: 01-222 7888
Telex: 917731
Rooms: 246 all with bath/shower, T.V., telephone and radio.
Major Credit Cards.
Set back from the street, this hotel has an impressive entrance hall and the bar and lounge area are comfortable. Bedrooms are modern and bathrooms tiled.

Map Ref. 4G

St. James Hotel
Buckingham Gate, S.W.1.
Tel: 01-834 2360
Telex: 919557
Rooms: 470 all with bath/shower, T.V., telephone and radio.
Major Credit Cards.
A large hotel which has been re-modernised. Free in-house movies. Cocktail bar and coffee shop.

Map Ref. 4G

Grosvenor Hotel
101 Buckingham Palace Road, S.W.1.
Tel: 01-834 9494
Telex: 916006
Rooms: 356 all with bath/shower, T.V. and telephone.
Major Credit Cards.
Outside, a splendid example of Victorian architecture, inside, a blend of the old with the new. The bedrooms are modern and the bathrooms well equipped.
Map Ref. 5F

MEDIUM HOTELS

Rubens Hotel
Buckingham Palace Road, S.W.1.
Tel: 01-834 6600
Telex: 916577
Rooms: 175 all with bath/shower, T.V., telephone and radio.
Major Credit Cards.
Bedrooms are well equipped, spacious and comfortable, and the Grill room and Cocktail Bar comfortable. Just re-decorated.
Map Ref. 4G

Ebury Court
26 Ebury Street, S.W.7.
Tel: 01-730 8147
Rooms: 40 all with telephone, 3 with bath/shower. T.V. for hire.
Credit Cards: Access, Visa.
Privately owned, this is a cosy little hotel which goes out of its way to make guests happy and comfortable. Bedrooms are neat and prettily decorated and four of the rooms have four-poster beds.
Map Ref. 5F

SMALL HOTELS

Alison House Hotel
82 Ebury Street, S.W.1.
Tel: 01-730 9529
Rooms: 15 all with T.V., 2 with bath/shower.
No Credit Cards.
Excellent service including helpful information over breakfast about travel or sightseeing. Compact modern bedrooms and cheerful basement room serving cooked breakfast only.
Map Ref. 5F

Belgrave House Hotel
30 Belgrave Road, S.W.1.
Tel: 01-828 1563
Rooms: 40.
No Credit Cards.
A simple, bright and comfortable little hotel ideal for overnight accommodation. Bedrooms are modern and nicely decorated, as is the T.V. lounge. There is a little breakfast room which serves cooked breakfast.
Map Ref. 5F

Elizabeth Hotel
37 Eccleston Square, S.W.1.
Tel: 01-828 6812
Rooms: 24, 3 with bath/shower.
No Credit Cards.
Overlooking the square, this neat terrace house has a comfortable lounge, a pleasant breakfast room and simply furnished bedrooms. Cooked breakfast.
Map Ref. 5F

KENSINGTON, W.8., W.14., AND W.6.

FIRST CLASS HOTELS

Royal Garden Hotel
Kensington High Street, W.8.
Tel: 01-937 8000
Telex 263151

Rooms: 434 all with bath/shower, T.V., telephone and radio.
Major Credit Cards.
Overlooking Hyde Park Corner and Kensington Gardens, most of the bedrooms have lovely views. All are luxuriously appointed together with the bathrooms. There are three bars and restaurants including The Royal Roof, where there is nightly dancing. Good food.

Map Ref. 4C

Kensington Palace Hotel
De Vere Gardens, W.8.
Tel: 01-937 8121
Telex: 262422
Rooms: 320 all with bath/shower, T.V., telephone and radio.
Major Credit Cards.
Overlooking Kensington Gardens and within easy reach of good shopping, the public rooms are nicely decorated and attractive. Bedrooms and bathrooms, which are tiled, are modern and well equipped.

Map Ref. 4C

Kensington Close Hotel
Wrights Lane, W.8.
Tel: 01-937 8170
Telex: 23914
Rooms: 530 all with bath/shower, T.V., telephone and radio.
Major Credit Cards.
Besides being a modern hotel in a quiet oasis, there is an amazing number of facilities including a swimming pool and squash courts. Bedrooms and bathrooms are compact and decorated in contemporary style. Charcoal Grill Restaurant.

Map Ref. 4C

London Tara
Scarsdale Place, Wrights Lane, W.8.
Tel: 01-937 7211
Telex: 918835/4

Rooms: 840 all with bath/shower, T.V., telephone and radio.
Major Credit Cards.
A large modern hotel with a relaxed style. Being an Irish hotel the colours in the public rooms, are a pleasant green and the theme is carried through to some of the bedrooms, all of which are modern and well equipped. There is a choice of restaurants and a new nightspot.

Map Ref. 4C

Cunard International
Shortlands, Hammersmith, W.6.
Tel: 01-741 1555
Telex: 934539
Rooms: 640 all with bath/shower, T.V., telephone and radio.
Major Credit Cards.
Basically a conference hotel and geared for the businessman, there is easy access to London Airport. The interior is modern but pleasant and the bedrooms and bathrooms well equipped.

Map Ref. 5A

MEDIUM HOTELS

De Vere Hotel
60 Hyde Park Gate, W.8.
Tel: 01-584 0051
Telex: 8953644
Rooms: 84 all with bath/shower, T.V., telephone and radio.
Major Credit Cards.
Overlooking Kensington Gardens and close to the Royal Albert Hall and good shopping, this hotel has recently been redecorated and has nicely styled bedrooms and modern bathrooms. Pleasant and spacious public rooms.
Map Ref. 4C

SMALL HOTELS

Hotel Atlas
24 Lexham Gardens, W.8.
Tel: 01-373 7873.
Telex: 264189
Rooms: 70 all with telephone, 20 with bath/shower.
Major Credit Cards.
Modernised inside, this is an attractive hotel with nice public rooms, including a bar, and prettily decorated bedrooms. Cooked breakfast only.
Map Ref. 5C

Suncourt Hotel
57 Lexham Gardens, W.8.
Tel: 01-373 7242
Rooms: 112 all with telephone, 27 with bath/shower.
Major Credit Cards.
One of a chain of hotels noted for their efficiency, this modern hotel has spacious public rooms and comfortable, well equipped bedrooms. There is a snack bar, as well as a breakfast room which serves cooked breakfast.
Map Ref. 5C

Hotel One Two Eight
128 Holland Road, W.14.
Tel: 01-602 3395
Rooms: 28 all with telephone, 7 with bath/shower.
No Credit Cards.
A nice small hotel with attractive public rooms decorated with plants and cane furniture. The bedrooms are comfortable and modernised. Cooked breakfast.
Map Ref. 4A

Hotel Lexham
32 Lexham Gardens, W.8.
Tel: 01-373 6471
Rooms: 64 all with telephone, 15 with bath/shower.
Credit Cards: Visa.
Four adjacent private houses converted into a friendly hotel. The bedrooms are nicely decorated and the bathrooms modern and functional. The public rooms are pleasant and airy. Cooked breakfast only.
Map Ref. 5C

REGENTS'S PARK, MARYLEBONE AND KINGS CROSS. N.W.1., N.W.8., N.1.

FIRST CLASS HOTELS

The White House
Albany Street, N.W.1.
Tel: 01-387 1200
Telex: 24111
Rooms: 589 all with bath/shower, T.V., telephone and radio.
Major Credit Cards.
Formerly a block of self-contained flats, now converted into a smart hotel. Bedrooms are modern and comfortable, there is a nice cocktail bar, a wine bar and an excellent restaurant offering French styled cuisine.
Map Ref. 1G

Kennedy Hotel
43 Cardington Street, N.W.1.
Tel: 01-387 4400
Telex: 28250
Rooms: 325 all with bath/shower, T.V., telephone and radio.
Major Credit Cards.
Ideal for Euston Station and used extensively by businessmen, this modern hotel has very pleasantly decorated bedrooms, well equipped bathrooms and bright and busy public rooms.
Map Ref. 1G

Westmoreland Hotel
Lodge Road, N.W.8.
Tel: 01-722 7722
Telex: 23101
Rooms: 350 all with bath/shower, T.V., telephone and radio.
Major Credit Cards.
If you are a cricket enthusiast then remember to reserve a bedroom on the top where you get a splendid view of Lords. Bedrooms are elegantly decorated and the public rooms spacious and comfortable. Carvery Restaurant and Coffee Shop.
Map Ref. 1E

MEDIUM HOTELS

Harewood Hotel
Harewood Row, N.W.1.
Tel: 01-262 2707
Telex: 291855
Rooms: 95 all with bath/shower, T.V., telephone and radio.
Major Credit Cards.
Close to Marylebone Station, this red brick modern hotel has very well decorated bedrooms and well equipped bathrooms, some with small patios. There is a nice little bar and a fast food restaurant.
Map Ref. 1E

Great Northern Hotel
Kings Cross, N.1.
Tel: 01-837 5454
Telex: 299041
Rooms: 71 all with T.V. and telephone, 40 with bath/shower.
Major Credit Cards.
Spacious and solid and, like most of the railway hotels, reflecting the age of the 19th Century. Bedrooms are functional and comfortable and the public rooms spacious. Friendly staff.
Map Ref. 1H

MAYFAIR AND WEST END, W.1.

LUXURY HOTELS

Claridges
Brook Street, W.1.
Tel: 01-629 8860
Telex: 21872
Rooms: 205 all with bath/shower, T.V., telephone and radio.
Credit Cards: Access, Eurocard and Visa.
The hotel at which Kings, Queens and Prime Ministers stay. This is one of the great hotels of the world and to step inside is to enter an elegance and atmosphere difficult to find in these times. The personal service throughout, the spacious and beautiful bedrooms, the magnificent suites, and the cuisine, all make this hotel an unforgettable experience.
Map Ref. 3F

Connaught
Carlos Place, W.1.
Tel: 01-499 7070
Rooms: 90 all with bath/shower, T.V., telephone and radio.
Credit Cards: Access and Eurocard.
Similar to entering a private club or house, the Connaught offers the very best of luxury and service. The public areas are gracious, the bedrooms decorated in traditional and elegant style. The Connaught also has one of the finest restaurants in London. Formal dress only — no jeans.
Map Ref. 3F

Dorchester
Park Lane, W.1.
Tel: 01-629 8888
Telex: 887704
Rooms: 285 all with bath/shower, T.V., telephone and radio.
Major Credit Cards.
The world-wide reputation of this hotel is upheld in a worthy manner. Superb service, magnificent public rooms and bedrooms have a timeless elegance. The suites are sumptuous with antiques and enormous bathrooms. The cuisine in the restaurant is exceptional. New cocktail bar. Terrace restaurant superb.
Map Ref. 3F

Grosvenor House
Park Lane, W.1.
Tel: 01-499 6363
Telex: 24871
Rooms: 478 all with bath/shower, T.V., telephone and radio.
Major Credit Cards.
Overlooking Hyde Park, this luxury hotel provides impeccable service and great comfort in a serene atmosphere. There is however a swimming pool and a gymnasium should one feel active. Bedrooms and suites are superbly maintained and the cuisine is excellent.
Map Ref. 3F

Inn on the Park
Hamilton Place, Park Lane, W.1.
Tel: 01-499 0888
Telex: 22771
Rooms: 228 all with bath/shower, T.V., telephone and radio.
Major Credit Cards.
There is an atmosphere of gracious luxury, usually given to hotels of longer standing, about the Inn on the Park. The furnishings and decor are tasteful and extend to the bedrooms and

bathrooms, all of them having every modern amenity. There is a garden and an excellent restaurant.
Map Ref. 3F

Inter-Continental Hotel
1 Hamilton Place, Park Lane, W.1.
Tel: 01-409 3131
Telex: 25853
Rooms: 497 all with bath/shower, T.V., telephone and radio.
Major Credit Cards.
Modern styled hotel in a prestige location, this hotel justifies luxury status with its elegant and impressive furnishings and decor. Bedrooms and suites are opulent and fitted out with all modern amenities including air conditioning. 7th floor discotheque and cocktail bar.
Map Ref. 3F

Ritz
Piccadilly, W.1.
Tel: 01-493 8181
Telex: 267200
Rooms: 142 all with bath/shower, T.V., telephone and radio.
Major Credit Cards.
Completely renovated, the Ritz is now back to its old grandeur, with breathtaking decor of elegant surroundings. Bedrooms are spacious and luxuriously furnished with modern bathrooms. Staff are very helpful and the service is impeccable. Dining in the restaurant is a memorable experience.
Map Ref. 3G

FIRST CLASS HOTELS

Athenaeum
Piccadilly, W.1.
Tel: 01-499 3464
Telex: 261589

Rooms: 112 all with bath/shower, T.V., telephone and radio.
Major Credit Cards.
Facing Green Park, this hotel prides itself on the service which the staff give. The decor is luxurious in the public rooms and bar and the bedrooms are charming and the bathrooms superb. The food in the elegant restaurant is good.
Map Ref. 3G

Bristol
3 Berkeley Street, W.1.
Tel: 01-493 8282
Telex: 24561
Rooms: 197 all with bath/shower, T.V., telephone and radio.
Major Credit Cards.
Modern comfort combined with old French decor make this a very pleasant ideally situated hotel. The bedrooms are also tastefully furnished with well equipped bathrooms. Air conditioned.
Map Ref. 3G

Britannia
Grosvenor Square, W.1.
Tel: 01-629 9400
Telex: 23941
Rooms: 434 all with bath/shower, T.V., telephone and radio.
Major Credit Cards.
Situated in the middle of a terrace of Georgian buildings, the public rooms are grandly furnished and beautifully decorated. There is a nice bar, a shopping arcade and smart bedrooms and bathrooms.
Map Ref. 3F

Brown's Hotel
Dover Street, W.1.
Tel: 01-493 6020
Telex: 28686
Rooms: 132 all with bath/shower, T.V., telephone and radio.
Major Credit Cards.
There has always been an air of traditional comfort in this old hotel. The individual reception area and the habit of afternoon tea in the lounge make this a haven of tranquility. Bedrooms are pretty and bathrooms modern.
Map Ref. 3G

Chesterfield Hotel
34 Charles Street, W.1.
Tel: 01-491 2622
Telex: 269394
Rooms: 82 all with bath/shower, T.V., telephone and radio.
Major Credit Cards.
A converted Georgian town house, this elegant, small hotel has a lovely foyer, comfortable lounge and luxurious

cocktail bar. Buttery and French Restaurant.
Map Ref. 3F

Churchill Hotel
Portman Square, W.1.
Tel: 01-486 5800
Telex: 264831
Rooms: 489 all with bath/shower, T.V., telephone and radio.
Major Credit Cards.
The decor of this hotel is basically Regency and furnishings and pictures have been created by international artists. The bedrooms and suites are delightful, the bar and restaurant extremely comfortable and the cuisine excellent.
Map Ref. 2F

Cumberland Hotel
Marble Arch, W.1.
Tel: 01-262 1234
Telex: 22215
Rooms: 898 all with bath/shower, T.V., telephone and radio.
Major Credit Cards.
A large hotel popular with businessmen and tourists. There are

five restaurants including a good Carvery and modern, nicely decorated bedrooms and bathrooms.

Map Ref. 2F

Curzon Hotel
Stanhope Row, Park Lane, W.1.
Tel: 01-493 7222
Telex: 291855
Rooms: 70 all with bath/shower, T.V., telephone and radio.
Major Credit Cards.
Although of modern design, this is a peaceful hotel with an opulent feeling about it. There is a marbled foyer and a luxurious bar. Bedrooms are well designed and bathrooms have every modern amenity. Garage parking.
Map Ref. 3F

Europa Hotel
Grosvenor Square, W.1.
Tel: 01-493 1232
Telex: 268101
Rooms: 275 all with bath/shower, T.V., telephone and radio.
Major Credit Cards.
A well-situated hotel for Oxford Street, with nice public rooms and bright spacious bedrooms and tiled bathrooms. 24 hour room service.
Map Ref. 3F

Hilton International Hotel
Park Lane, W.1.
Tel: 01-493 8000
Telex: 24873
Rooms: 509 all with bath/shower, T.V., telephone and radio.
Major Credit Cards.
One of the first towering blocks of hotels to be built in London, and still the tallest, the Hilton bedrooms on the upper levels have an incomparable view over the city and Hyde Park and are well equipped and well decorated. There is a lovely roof restaurant and a Polynesian one in the basement.
Map Ref. 3F

Holiday Inn
134 George Street, W.1.
Tel: 01-723 1277
Telex: 27983
Rooms: 243 all with bath/shower, T.V., telephone and radio.
Major Credit Cards.
This is a smart modern hotel with extremely well-appointed bedrooms and excellent bathrooms. The decor of the public areas is pleasantly relaxing. Free car park. Heated swimming pool.
Map Ref. 2E

Londonderry Hotel
19 Park Lane, W.1.
Tel: 01-493 7292
Telex: 263292
Rooms: 140 all with bath/shower, T.V., telephone and radio.
Major Credit Cards.
Elegant decor from the marbled foyer to the leather furnishings give this hotel an intimate and relaxing air. Bedrooms are comfortable and there are many suites. Air conditioning.
Map Ref. 3F

Mayfair Hotel
Berkeley Street, W.1.
Tel: 01-629 7777
Telex: 262526
Rooms: 391 all with bath/shower, T.V., telephone and radio.
Major Credit Cards.
Public areas are ornate and plush and the bedrooms spacious and elegant. There is a well-known night club within the hotel, a nice bar and restaurant and a general feeling of luxury.
Map Ref. 3G

Montcalm Hotel
Great Cumberland Place, W.1.
Tel: 01-402 4288
Telex 28710

Rooms: 116 all with bath/shower, T.V., telephone and radio.
Major Credit Cards.
This is a small hotel which offers comfort and personal service in elegant surroundings. All the bedrooms are beautifully decorated and the suites are designed on two levels with a spiral staircase leading to the bedrooms. There is a popular cocktail bar and an excellent restaurant.
Map Ref. 2F

Park Lane Hotel
Piccadilly, W.1.
Tel: 01-499 6321
Telex: 21533
Rooms: 325 all with bath/shower, T.V., telephone and radio.
Major Credit Cards.
Overlooking Green Park, this old and favourite hotel has recently been completely refurbished. The public areas are now luxurious and the bedrooms individually decorated. There is a friendly air about the hotel and the service is efficient and courteous.
Map Ref. 3G

Piccadilly Hotel
Piccadilly, W.1.
Tel: 01-734 8000
Telex: 25795
Rooms: 290 all with bath/shower, T.V., telephone and radio.
Major Credit Cards.
There is still a nice Edwardian splendour about this hotel with its wood panelling, leather Chesterfields and elegant decor. Bedrooms are furnished with reproduction antiques and bathrooms are modern and well equipped. Air conditioned. Cocktail bar.
Map Ref. 3G

Portman Inter-Continental Hotel
22 Portman Square, W.1.
Tel: 01-486 5844
Telex: 261526
Rooms: 275 all with bath/shower, T.V. and telephone.
Major Credit Cards.
This is a streamlined hotel with excellent service throughout. Bedrooms are restful with all amenities and there is an air of total efficiency. There is an excellent restaurant. Free in-house movies.
Map Ref. 2F

Saint George's Hotel
Langham Place, W.1.
Tel: 01-580 0111
Telex: 27274
Rooms: 85 all with bath/shower, T.V., telephone and radio.
Major Credit Cards.
This hotel occupies the top six floors of a 14 storey tower block, thereby giving marvellous views over London. There is an open plan lounge with large picture windows, a circular bar and well designed, modern bedrooms and bathrooms. Mini bars and tea/coffee making facilities in all rooms. In-house movies.
Map Ref. 2G

Selfridge Hotel
Orchard Street, W.1.
Tel: 01-408 2080
Telex: 22361
Rooms: 298 all with bath/shower. T.V., telephone and radio.
Major Credit Cards.
This is a stylish hotel with staff who are eager to please. The public rooms all have character, the bar is quaint and the bedrooms and bathrooms cleverly planned. 24 hour room service. Air conditioned.
Map Ref. 2F

Westbury Hotel
New Bond Street, W.1.
Tel: 01-629 7755
Telex: 24378
Rooms: 272 all with bath/shower, T.V., telephone and radio.
Major Credit Cards.
This long established hotel gives an air of comfort and tranquility situated as it is, so centrally. There is nice wood panelling and decor in the public rooms, the bedrooms are spacious and there are seventeen luxurious suites.
Map Ref. 3G

MEDIUM HOTELS

Clifton-Ford Hotel
Welbeck Street, W.1.
Tel: 01-486 6600
Telex 22569
Rooms: 229 all with bath/shower, T.V. and radio.
Major Credit Cards.
A quiet modern hotel with a spacious foyer and a comfortable lounge. Bedrooms and bathrooms are well equipped and smart in appearance.
Map Ref. 2F

Flemings Hotel
Half Moon Street, W.1.
Tel: 01-499 2964
Rooms: 133 all with bath/shower, T.V., telephone and radio.
Major Credit Cards.
Traditional hotel situated close to Green Park. The interior is modern and the bedrooms and bathrooms nicely decorated with modern amenities.
Map Ref. 3G

Green Park Hotel
Half Moon Street, W.1.
Tel: 01-629 7522
Telex: 28856
Rooms: 175 all with T.V., radio and telephone, 88 with bath/shower.
Major Credit Cards.
A functional hotel with modern decor in the public areas, a small bar and a sauna. Bedrooms and bathrooms clean and modern.
Map Ref. 3G

Londoner
Welbeck Street, W.1.
Tel: 01-935 4442
Telex: 894630
Rooms: 143 all with bath/shower, T.V., telephone and radio.
Major Credit Cards.
Popular with tourists, with comfortable public areas, compact bedrooms and tiled bathrooms, it is centrally placed for the Oxford Street shops.
Map Ref. 2F

Mostyn Hotel
Bryanston Street, W.1.
Tel: 01-935 2361
Telex: 27656
Rooms: 123 all with bath/shower, T.V., telephone and radio.
Major Credit Cards.

Recently refurbished, this is a cosy hotel with modern decor in the public areas and smart bedrooms and bathrooms.

Map Ref. 2F

Mount Royal
Bryanston Street, W.1.
Tel: 01-629 8040
Telex: 23355
Rooms: 702 all with bath/shower, T.V., telephone and radio.
Major Credit Cards.
Large modern hotel very popular with tourists. There is a pleasant restaurant and bar; bedrooms and bathrooms are functional with good amenities.

Map Ref. 2F

Rathbone Hotel
Rathbone Street, W.1.
Tel: 01-636 2001
Telex: 28728
Rooms: 64 all with bath/shower, T.V., telephone and radio.
Major Credit Cards.
There is a nice lounge and bar in this bright modern hotel. Pleasant bedrooms with clean compact bathrooms. Mini bars in all rooms.

Map Ref. 2G

Regent Crest Hotel
Carburton Street, W.1.
Tel: 01-388 2300
Telex: 22453
Rooms: 330 all with bath/shower, T.V., telephone and radio.
Major Credit Cards.
A modern hotel which caters well for tourists with nice public rooms, including bar. Bedrooms are well designed with tiled bathrooms and modern amenities.

Map Ref. 2G

Regent Palace Hotel
Piccadilly Circus, W.1.
Tel: 01-734 7000
Telex 23740
Rooms: 1002 all with T.V., radio and telephone. None with bath/shower.
Major Credit Cards.
This old established hotel is still the largest in terms of rooms. It is very busy, but very comfortable, and there is a good variety of bars and restaurants. Tea and coffee making facilities in each room.

Map Ref. 3G

Sherlock Holmes
108 Baker Street, W.1.
Tel: 01-486 6161
Telex: 8954837
Rooms: 150 all with bath/shower, T.V., telephone and radio.
Major Credit Cards.
An elegant hotel with a club-like atmosphere offering traditional comfort. Bedrooms are smart and well equipped.

Map Ref. 2F

Washington Hotel
Curzon Street, W.1.
Tel: 01-499 7030
Telex: 24540
Rooms: 163 all with bath/shower, T.V., telephone and radio.
Major Credit Cards.
The hotel is efficiently run by courteous and welcoming staff. There is a comfortable lounge, a nice bar and bright cheery bedrooms with compact bathrooms.
Map Ref. 3F

SMALL HOTELS

Stratford Court Hotel
350 Oxford Street, W.1.
Tel: 01-629 7474
Telex: 22270
Rooms: 137 all with bath/shower, T.V., telephone and radio.
Major Credit Cards.
This is a modern hotel with a pleasant little lounge and bar. Bedrooms are neat and bathrooms compact. There is a coffee shop where breakfast is served. Free in-house movies.
Map Ref. 2F

Durrants Hotel
26 George Street, W.1.
Tel: 01-935 8131
Telex: 894919
Rooms: 104 all with T.V. and telephone, 84 with bath/shower.
Major Credit Cards (not Visa).
This family-owned hotel is a gem. The Regency decor, both inside and out, create a dignified atmosphere. The lounges are comfortable and some bedrooms decorated in Edwardian style. There is a good restaurant.
Map Ref. 2F

Little Mayfair
7 Down Street, W.1.
Tel: 01-499 1853
Telex: 858875
Rooms: 12 all with T.V.
None with bath/shower.
Major Credit Cards.
Bedrooms are spacious and clean and the Victorian style decor lends itself to lots of atmosphere. There is a restaurant with good grills in the evening and a cooked breakfast in the morning. Tea and coffee making facilities in each room.
Map Ref. 3F

Merryfield House
42 York Street, W.1.
Tel: 01-935 8326
Rooms: 8 all with bath/shower.
No Credit Cards.
This little hotel is spotless and run very efficiently. Breakfast is served in the

bedrooms which are prettily decorated with nice functional bathrooms.
Map Ref. 2E

Milford House
31 York Street, W.1.
Tel: 01-935 1935
Rooms: 7 all with bath/shower.
No Credit Cards.
A nice little hotel that is well looked after and reflects the service that is offered. Bedrooms are airy and pleasant and there is a T.V. lounge and small breakfast room serving cooked breakfast.
Map Ref. 2E

Rose Court Hotel
35 Great Cumberland Place, W.1.
Tel: 01-262 7241
Telex: 24939
Rooms: 45 all with bath/shower, T.V., telephone and radio.
Major Credit Cards.
Smart hotel with a comfortable little lounge and breakfast room. There is also a small bar. Bedrooms are functional and bathrooms spotless.
Map Ref. 2E

HOLLAND PARK AND NOTTING HILL. W.11.

FIRST CLASS HOTELS

Hilton International Kensington
Holland Park Avenue, W.11.
Tel: 01-603 3355
Telex: 919763
Rooms: 611 all with bath/shower, T.V., telephone and radio.
Major Credit Cards.
Large modern hotel run on the efficient Hilton Hotel lines. Bedrooms are tastefully decorated containing individual vending machines and bathrooms are compact and well appointed. The public rooms are attractively decorated and the restaurants, one of which is Japanese, offer quick service and good food. Excellent breakfast.

Map Ref. 4A

SMALL HOTELS

Park Avenue Hotel
Holland Park, W.11.
Tel: 01-727 3562
Telex: 23374
Rooms: 88 all with bath/shower, T.V., telephone and radio.
Major Credit Cards (not Diners).
Situated in a peaceful area, this lovely old house has been converted into a very nice hotel. There is a bar and coffee shop, as well as two attractive breakfast rooms. The bedrooms are nicely furnished with simple decor and the atmosphere is friendly and relaxed. Cooked breakfast.

Map Ref. 4A

APARTMENTS

There are of course a large number of visitors, particularly those with families, who prefer the independence of catering for themselves and find it easier to stay in an apartment rather than a hotel. London has a large selection of this type of accommodation and listed below are some useful addresses. There are also agents who specialise in the letting of short term accommodation and these are listed as well.

BAYSWATER, HOLLAND PARK, W.2. AND W.11.

Craven Hill Lodge
5 Craven Hill, W.2.
Tel: 01-402 7768
From £55 per week.
No Credit Cards and no Cheques.
Small, compact and handy for Marble Arch and shops.

Map Ref. 3C

22 Pembridge Crescent
22 Pembridge Crescent, W.11.
Tel: 01-221 5759
From £160.00 per week.
No Credit Cards.
Very nicely decorated apartments in an old Victorian house. Very clean and homely.

Map Ref. 3C

Around Town Flats Ltd
120 Holland Park Avenue, W.11.
Tel: 01-229 0033
From £35.00 per week.
No Credit Cards.
Specialists in furnished apartments or houses for long or short stays.

Map Ref. 4A

BELGRAVIA, CHELSEA, KNIGHTSBRIDGE AND SOUTH KENSINGTON. S.W.1., S.W.3., S.W.7.

Lambs Service Flats
21 Egerton Gardens, S.W.3.
Tel: 01-589 6297
From £29.00 per day.
No Credit Cards.
Delightful decor in old French style with nice paintings and a good atmosphere in this apartment house. Nice rooms have all modern amenities. No Children.

Map Ref. 5E

55 Sloane Gardens
55 Sloane Gardens, S.W.1.
Tel: 01-730 9400
From £112.00 per week.
No Credit Cards.
Because there are only four apartments in this house they are of a very high standard with very well equipped kitchens and nice bathrooms.

Map Ref. 5F

Aston Studio Apartments
39 Rosary Gardens, S.W.7.
Tel: 01-352 2221/730 1100
From £30.00 per week.
No Credit Cards.
Stylish studios in a quiet area. Fully equipped and well fitted out. Ideal for holiday stay.

Map Ref. 5D

Emperor's Lodge
41 Emperor's Gate, S.W.7.
Tel: 01-373 6492
Telex: 897712
From £109.00 per week.
No Credit Cards.
Luxury serviced studio flats which are all elegantly furnished with nice decor and well equipped.

Map Ref. 5C

45 Ennismore Gardens
45 Ennismore Gardens, S.W.7.
Tel: 01-584 4123
From £100.00 per week.
No Credit Cards.
Self-contained service flats situated in a nice area, each with modern decor, well equipped kitchens and entry phone. Private telephone.
Map Ref. 4D

Normandie Suites
165 Knightsbridge, S.W.1.
Tel: 01-589 2900
From £300.00 per week.
No Credit Cards.
New and modern and very tastefully decorated, these apartments have everything that a visitor to London requires in accommodation.
Map Ref. 4E

Holiday Flat Services
51 Kensington Court, W.8.
Tel: 01-937 9886
Telex: 916223
From £100.00 per week.
No Credit Cards.
Large number of flats particularly in Kensington, Chelsea and Knightsbridge areas. Immediate and advance reservations.
Map Ref. 4E

Regency Suites
130 Queens Gate, S.W.7.
Tel: 01-370 4242
From £230.00 per week.
No Credit Cards.
Very elegant and plush, these apartments are superb in every respect right down to the security T.V. door monitor.
Map Ref. 4D

Nell Gwynne House
Sloane Avenue, S.W.3.
Tel: 01-584 8317
From £110.00 per week.
No Credit Cards.
Some of the most luxurious pied-à-terre apartments in London, decorated by experts with modern kitchens and luxurious bathrooms.
Map Ref. 5E

Draycott House
10 Draycott Avenue, S.W.5.
Tel: 01-584 4659
Telex: 916266
From £225.00 per week.
No Credit Cards.
Individually designed with elegant furnishings and balconies, these are beautiful apartments. Two penthouse apartments each have a roof garden. First class facilities available.
Map Ref. 5E

Sue Richardson Properties
15 Richards Place, S.W.3.
Tel: 01-581 3355
From £100.00 per week.
Specialists in dealing with luxury rented accommodation of all sizes.
Map Ref. 5E

ST. JAMES AND VICTORIA. S.W.1.

Dolphin Square
Dolphin Square, S.W.1.
Tel: 01-834 9134
From £30.00 per night.
Credit Cards: Mastercharge and Eurocard.
This is one of the largest blocks in Europe and there is a large choice of accommodation available. Apartments are bright and cheery and well equipped. There is a swimming pool, tennis and squash courts.
Map Ref. 6G

64 Buckingham Gate
64 Buckingham Gate, S.W.1.
Tel: 01-222 6677
Telex: 8954926
From £200.00 per week.
No Credit Cards.
These are very modern apartments on the top floors of a tower block. The views are therefore excellent. Decor is bright and kitchens and bathrooms spotless. Washing machines and dryers.
Map Ref. 4G

These are very modern apartments on the top floors of a tower block. The views are therefore excellent. Decor is bright and kitchens and bathrooms spotless.

Map Ref. 4G

Service Apartments

Dukes Hotel
St. James's Place, S.W.1.
Tel: 01-491 4840
From £135.00 per night.
Major Credit Cards.
Very elegant and fully serviced, these apartments are ideally situated in a quiet backwater in St. James's but only minutes away from Piccadilly and Bond Street. The facilities of the hotel are also available.

Map Ref. 3G

MAYFAIR AND THE WEST END. W.1.

One Carlos Place
1 Carlos Place, W.1.
Tel: 01-491 4165
Telex: 28604
From £80.00 per night.
Major Credit Cards.
These apartments are the ultimate in luxury with everything from magnificent furnishings to the most modern kitchens and bathrooms.

Map Ref. 3F

Grosvenor House
Park Lane, W.1.
Tel: 01-499 6363
From £90.00 per night.
Major Credit Cards.
Although one normally thinks of this as a hotel, there are also a number of excellent service apartments available. Ideal for frequent business visitors as all the amenities of the hotel can be used.

Map Ref. 3F

Ten Lees Place
10 Lees Place, W.1.
Tel: 01-491 7055
Telex: 8953400
From £385.00 per week.
Credit Cards: American Express and Diners.
Elegantly furnished with modern, fully equipped kitchens and bathrooms, these apartments are charming and very comfortable. 7 day week maid service and porterage.

Map Ref. 3F

47 Park Street
47 Park Street, W.1.
Tel: 01-491 7282
Telex: 22116.
From £95.00 per night.
Major Credit Cards.
Lovely apartments which are spacious and well-designed with all amenities and comfort. Daily maid service, 24 hour porterage and reception. Safety deposit boxes.

Map Ref. 3F

Keith Cardale Groves
43 North Audley Street, W.1.
Tel: 01-629 6604
Telex: 27839
From £90.00 per week.
No Credit Cards.
Specialists in obtaining temporary rented accommodation. Specialise in long stays.

Map Ref. 3F

KENSINGTON AND EARLS COURT. W.8. AND S.W.5.

Central London Luxury Flats
51 Kensington Court, W.8.
Tel: 01-937 9886
From £130.00 per week.
No Credit Cards.
Large selection of good quality holiday flats ideal for short stays. Principally in Kensington, Chelsea and Mayfair.

Map Ref. 4C

The Courtlands
13 Marloes Road, W.8.
Tel: 01-229 0724
From £140.00 per week.
No Credit Cards.
Very good value, nicely decorated and clean serviced flats.

Map Ref. 5C

Collingham Apartments
27 Collingham Gardens, S.W.5.
Tel: 01-373 6306
From £140.00 per week.
No Credit Cards.
Modern decor with all amenities and very well equipped kitchens. No Children.

Map Ref. 4C

Shopping in London

A B C D E F G H I J K L
1 2 3 4 5 6
REGENT'S PARK
EUSTON STATION
PADDINGTON STATION
LIVERPOOL ST. STATION
KENSINGTON GARDENS
HYDE PARK
SERPENTINE
ROTTEN ROW
GREEN PARK
ST. JAMES'S PARK
HOLLAND PARK
Kensal Green
BATTERSEA PARK
Kennington Park
RIVER THAMES
CHARING CROSS STATION
WATERLOO STATION
VICTORIA STATION
LONDON BRI. STATION
Marble Arch
Somerset House
Monument
OXFORD STREET
REGENT ST.
PICCADILLY
THE MALL
EMBANKMENT
WESTMINSTER BRIDGE
WATERLOO BRIDGE
BLACKFRIARS BRIDGE
SOUTHWARK BRIDGE
LONDON BRIDGE
TOWER BRIDGE
LAMBETH BRIDGE
VAUXHALL BRIDGE
CHELSEA BRIDGE
ALBERT BRIDGE
PORTMAN SQUARE
GROSVENOR SQUARE
BERKELEY SQUARE
BELGRAVE SQUARE
HARROW ROAD
EUSTON ROAD
MARYLEBONE ROAD
BAYSWATER ROAD
KENSINGTON RD
KNIGHTSBRIDGE
CROMWELL ROAD
KING'S ROAD
Maida Vale
Warwick Avenue
Marylebone
Baker Street
Regent's Park
Great Portland Street
Warren Street
Goodge Street
Tottenham Court Rd.
Oxford Circus
Bond Street
Marble Arch
Lancaster Gate
Queensway
Bayswater
Notting Hill Gate
Holland Park
Ladbroke Grove
Westbourne Park
Edgware Road
Hyde Park Corner
Green Park
Piccadilly Circus
Leicester Square
Covent Garden
Holborn
Chancery Lane
Aldwych
Temple
Blackfriars
Mansion House
St Paul's
Moorgate
Bank
Monument
Tower Hill
Aldgate
Old Street
Westminster
St James's Park
Knightsbridge
South Kensington
Gloucester Road
High Street Kensington
Earls Court
West Brompton
Sloane Square
Pimlico
Vauxhall
Oval
Lambeth North
Elephant and Castle
Borough

SHOPPING IN LONDON

When you visit London the chances are that you will want to buy something for yourself or to take back with you to your home. Because there is such a bewildering selection of shops the wisest course to adopt is to spend at least one day just looking and browsing and try to decide beforehand which particular shops you want to visit, as the success of any shopping expedition lies in knowing where to go for what. The other point we make is also important and that is that in London prices can differ from one area to another and it is sensible to 'shop' around before making a purchase. Many of London's most interesting shops are not in the main thoroughfares but are hidden in back streets away from the main areas. This is why you will find this section so useful as it will introduce you to many of these.

If you are an overseas visitor, carry your passport as you will have the benefit of not having to pay Value Added Tax (VAT). By showing your passport and filling out a form you can take advantage of the Over-the-Counter Export scheme. Most large stores and the luxury goods shops operate this and any of the sales personnel will be happy to advise you. Most London shops are open from 9.30am-5.30pm Monday-Saturday. West End shops stay open until 7.30pm on Thursday and in Knightsbridge on Wednesday. Some of the big stores close at lunchtime on Saturday.
One other word of advice. Always keep the receipt for goods you buy and if you are not satisfied or they are faulty, take them back to the shop. You do not have to accept a credit note which some shops will try to give you. You can ask for a cash refund.
The shops we have listed are a selection which we believe will give you a good choice and help you to find your way around in a more relaxed way.

ANTIQUES

Basically the sale of antiques in London is divided into 4 categories: the SPECIALITY ANTIQUE SHOPS, the AUCTION HOUSES, the HYPER or SUPERMARKETS and the STREET MARKET STALLS.
It really depends what you want and as London is probably the antique city of the world the chances are that you will find it.

ANTIQUE SPECIALITY SHOPS

These are not where you would pick up bargains but they are reliable and the antiques are genuine.

ARCHITECTURAL PIECES

T Crowther
282 North End Road, S.W.6.
Tel: 01-385 1375
Specialists in 17th and 18th Century carved chimney pieces, grates and oak panelled rooms and doors.
Map Ref. 6B

J Crotty
74 New Kings Road, S.W.6.
Tel: 01-385 1789
Period chimney pieces, grates, fenders, hearths, chandeliers and lanterns.
Map Ref. 6D

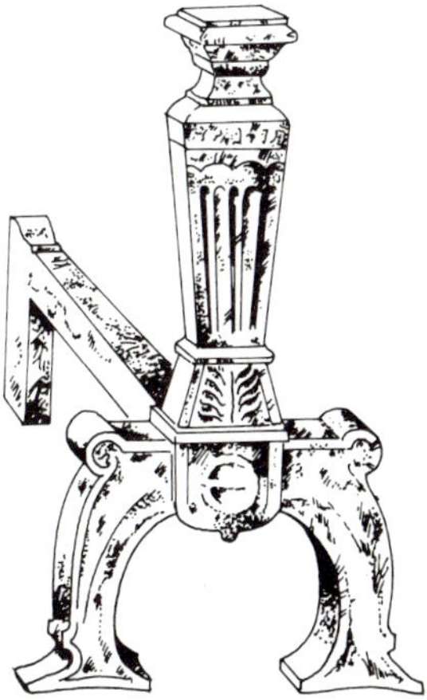

ANTIQUITIES

Charles Ede
37 Brook Street, W.1.
Tel: 01-493 4944
For the enthusiast this is an ideal gallery as the range of Roman and Cypriot items are the best in London.
Map Ref. 3F.

Jonathan Mankowitz
By appointment only.
Tel: 01-603 7424
Very high quality, Egyptian, African and classical works of art.
Map Ref. 2F

Robin Symes
3 Ormond Yard, Duke of York Street, S.W.1.
Tel: 01-938 9856
The most famous and probably the most expensive dealer. If you want to see the finest works of antiquity then this is the gallery. Closed on Saturday.
Map Ref. 3G

AUTOGRAPHS

Winifred Myers
Suite 91, St. Martins Lane, W.C.2.
Tel: 01-836 1940
Large and valued stock.
Map Ref. 3H

BOOKS

Bell, Book and Radmell
80 Longacre, W.C.2.
Tel: 01-240 2161
First editions of early twentieth century and contemporary literature.
Map Ref. 2H

Maggs
50 Berkeley Square, W.1.
Tel: 01-499 2051
Books, manuscripts, autographs and oriental miniatures.
Map Ref. 3F

Peter Eaton
80 Holland Park Avenue, W.11.
Tel: 01-727 5211
A very modern looking shop with an interesting selection of books. Lovely to browse in at leisure and real knowledge behind the buying.
Map Ref. 4A

Quaritch
5 Lower John Street, Golden Square, W.1.
Tel: 01-734 0562
Specialising in natural history and English literature, they are leading dealers in old and rare books.
Map Ref. 2G

Piccadilly Rare Books Ltd
30 Sackville Street, W.1.
Tel: 01-437 2135
Good books and staff who are very helpful in trying to get what you want. Often a selection of more modern books knocked down in price. Interesting stock.
Map Ref. 3G

E Joseph
49a Charing Cross Road, W.C.2.
Tel: 01-836 4111
Tel: 01-836 9366
In this road, which is a mecca for all book lovers, E. Joseph has a shop where you can browse away an hour or two among the interesting collection of books. Give yourself an hour or two extra to explore this street.
Map Ref. 2H

E P Goldschmidt
64 Drayton Gardens, S.W.10.
Tel: 01-373 2266
Architectural books of 16th and 17th Century.
Map Ref. 6C

BOXES

S J Phillips
139 Bond Street, W.1.
Tel: 01-629 6261
Old spice, snuff and money boxes in gold, silver and enamel. Antique jewellery and silver.
Map Ref. 3G

Keith Harding
93 Hornsey Road, N.7.
Tel: 01-607 6181
One of the largest dealers in musical boxes in the world.
No Map Ref.

Park Antiques
62 New Kings Road, S.W.6.
Tel: 01-736 6222
An unusual collection of snuff boxes.
Map Ref. 5E

CARPETS AND RUGS

David Black
96 Portland Road, W.11.
Tel: 01-727 2566
Antique tribal and village rugs from Turkey, the Caucasus and Persia. Crisp and authorative knowledge offered along with your purchase.
Map Ref. 3A

Alexander Juran and Co.
74 New Bond Street, W.1.
Tel: 01-629 2550
Browse among these carpets and you won't be disappointed. Some very pretty rugs and carpets that will grace a room now and become an investment for the future.
Map Ref. 3G

Anglo Persian Carpet Centre
6 South Kensington Station, S.W.7.
Tel: 01-589 5457
What the name implies, a centre for good carpets from the Middle East and the Orient. Good stock and advice when buying characterises this charming shop.
Map Ref. 5D

Vigo Carpet Gallery
6a Vigo Street, W.1.
Tel: 01-439 6971
Very good carpets are found here, mostly antique or second hand. Aubussons, Eastern carpets of wonderful quality.
Map Ref. 3G

Mayor Cas
38 Jermyn Street, W.1.
Tel: 01-629 4195
Antique tapestries, textiles, needlework and vestments along with a lovely collection of carpets can be found in this shop.
Map Ref. 3G

Benardout & Benardout
7 Thurloe Place, S.W.7.
Tel: 01-584 7658
All types of antique carpets and rugs.
Map Ref. 5D

C John
70 South Audley Street, W.1.
Tel: 01-493 5288
Specialists in old European as well as oriental rugs and carpets.
Map Ref. 3F

CHANDELIERS AND LIGHTS

Christopher Wray
600 Kings Road, S.W.6.
Tel: 01-736 8008
One of the largest selections of Victorian and Edwardian light fixtures.
Map Ref. 6D

Crick
166 Kensington Church Street, S.W.3.
Tel: 01-229 1338
Antique cut glass and ormolu chandeliers.
Map Ref. 4B

W G Burne
11 Elystan Street, S.W.3.
Tel: 01-589 6074
Specialists in 18th and early 19th Century crystal chandeliers. Beautiful selection. Table glass and antique wine glasses.
Map Ref. 5E

H W Poulter & Sons
279 Fulham Road, S.W.10.
Tel: 01-352 7268
17th and 18th Century brass lanterns and chandeliers.
Map Ref. 6D

Mr. Light
279 King's Road, S.W.3.
Tel: 01-806 7076
For classic and modern lamps and fittings.
Map Ref. 6D

John Cullen
Smith Street, S.W.3.
Tel: 01-352 3566
Lighting designer with imaginative ideas.
Map Ref. 5H

Thomas Goode
South Audley Street, W.1.
Tel: 01-499 2823
Very good for chandeliers, both antique and modern.
Map Ref. 3F

Department stores with good Lighting Departments include:
Harrods
John Lewis
Peter Jones

CLOCKS, WATCHES AND BAROMETERS

A Lee
122 St. John Street, E.C.1.
Tel: 01-253 6901
Repairs and restores antique watches and clocks.
Map Ref. 1I

Camerer Cuss
32 Sloane Square, S.W.1.
Tel: 01-730 7046
All modern stock including a range of carriage clocks that are very superior.
Map Ref. 5F

Hollander
80 Fulham Road, S.W.3.
Tel: 01-589 7239
English clocks and good selection of barometers of 1750-1825 period.
Map Ref. 5D

Strike One
51 Camden Passage, N.1.
Tel: 01-226 9709
Specialising in Longcase and bracket clocks along with Act of Parliament Clocks, antique carriage clocks, watches and barometers. All antiques. Very knowledgeable staff.
No Map Ref.

Aubrey Brocklehurst
124 Cromwell Road, S.W.7.
Tel: 01-373 0319
Early period clocks and barometers.
Map Ref. 5C

Philip & Bernard Dombey
174 Kensington Church Street, W.8.
Tel: 01-229 7100
Specialists in 18th and 19th Century French clocks.
Map Ref. 4C

Graus
125 New Bond Street, W.1.
Tel: 01-629 6680
Antique enamel watches and 16th Century pocket and chatelaine watches.
Map Ref. 3G

COINS AND MEDALS

B A Seaby
11 Margaret Street, W.1.
Tel: 01-580 3677
The largest dealers of old coins in the world. They also specialise in publishing reference books on coins.
Map Ref. 2G

Spink
5 King Street, S.W.1.
Tel: 01-930 7888
They probably have one of the best selections of antiques and modern coins and medals in the world, ranging from Greek and Roman to modern collectors items.
Map Ref. 3G

A H Baldwin
11 Adelphi Terrace, W.C.2.
Tel: 01-930 6879
Specialists in ancient, medieval and modern coins and medals.
Map Ref. 3H

DOLLS

Kay Desmonde
17 Kensington Church Walk, W.8.
Tel: 01-937 2602
Possibly the largest selection of antique dolls and doll's houses in the world. By appointment only.
Map Ref. 4C

Pat Walker
Antiquarius Market
139 Kings Road, S.W.3.
Tel: 01-937 2602
Victorian, Edwardian, French and German dolls, doll's houses and clothes.
Map Ref. 6E

FURNITURE

Partridge Fine Art Ltd
144-146 New Bond Street, W.1.
Tel: 01-629 0834
Magnificent 18th Century French and English furniture, silver, paintings and objets d'art.
Map Ref. 3G

Mallett
40 New Bond Street, W.1.
Tel: 01-499 7411
Beautiful and unusually high quality English furniture mainly of the 18th and early 19th Century.
Map Ref. 3G

William Bedford
327 Upper Street, N.1.
Tel: 01-226 9648
An antique gallery with an interesting stock that is well-worth looking through. Specialises in Georgian period.
No Map Ref.

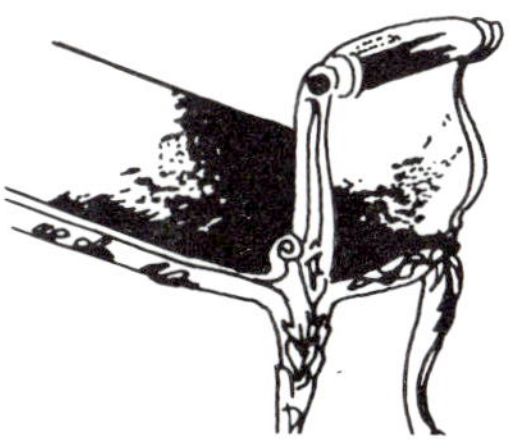

Mallett
Bourdon House, Davies Street, W.1.
Tel: 01-629 2444
Very good high class antiques — a pleasure to visit.
Map Ref. 3F

Harrods
Knightsbridge, S.W.1.
Tel: 01-730 1234
A very good selection of both antique and Victorian furniture in this store nicely set out on the third floor.
Map Ref. 4E

Church Street Galleries
77 Kensington Church Street, W.8.
Tel: 01-937 9175
Specialising in furniture from 1700 to 1800 this shop is for the specialist who really understands his period, or for those who want to learn!
Map Ref. 4C

Redford
9 Mount Street, W.1.
Tel: 01-629 1165
Small shop with interesting stock that is well worth a visit. Early 18th Century furniture.
Map Ref. 3F

Dark and Rendlesham
498 Kings Road, S.W.10.
Tel: 01-351 1442
A lovely eclectic stock including furniture and objets d'art of all periods.
Map Ref. 6D

Pelham Galleries
163 Fulham Road, S.W.3.
Tel: 01-589 2686
Old English Furniture mainly 18th Century along with some Continental pieces. Tapestries and objets d'art are also included in this shop with a helpful staff.
Map Ref. 5D

Asprey's
165 New Bond Street, W.1.
Tel: 01-493 6767
A luxurious stock of exquisite furniture and objets d'art.
Map Ref. 3G

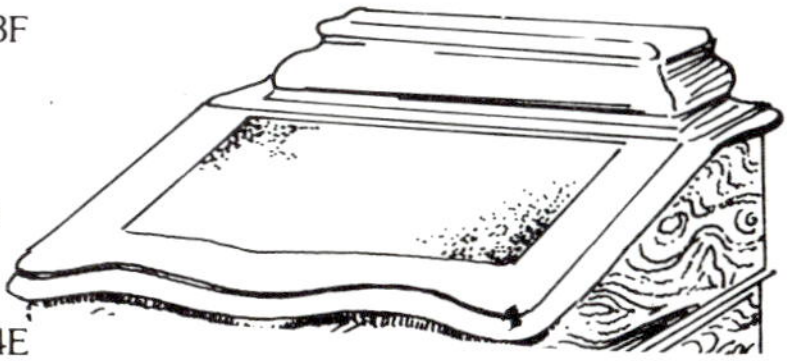

Hotspur
14 Lowndes Street, S.W.1.
Tel: 01-235 1918
Frequented by wealthy collectors and museums, there is no better place to buy the really rare pieces of 18th Century English furniture.
Map Ref. 4F

Michael Lipitch
98 Fulham Road, S.W.3.
Tel: 01-589 7327
A marvellous selection of 18th Century English fine furniture. A written guarantee is given with each purchase.
Map Ref. 6D

GLASS

Howard Phillips
11a Henrietta Place, W.1.
Tel: 01-580 9844
Very old English glassware, before 1830 and other antique glass.
Map Ref. 2F

Delomosnes and Son Ltd
4 Campden Hill Road, W.8.
Tel: 01-937 1804
Specialising in antique English and Irish glass with a special regard to 18th and early 19th Century chandeliers, Delomosnes have a beautiful stock.
Map Ref. 4B

IVORY AND JADE

Tortoise Shell & Ivory House
24 Chiltern Street, W.1.
Tel: 01-935 8031
Lovely selection of ivory, Oriental and Indian carvings.
Map Ref. 2F

J & B Antiques
1a Kensington Church Walk, W.8.
Tel: 01-937 2335
A tiny shop specialising in ivory and miniatures of all periods. Particularly strong in Victorian mistures.
Map Ref. 4C

JEWELLERY

Asprey's
165 New Bond Street, W.1.
Tel: 01-493 6767
Good selection of unusual antique jewellery.
Map Ref. 3G

Wartski
14 Grafton Street, W.1.
Tel: 01-493 1141
All antique jewellery particularly Fabergé, also objets d'art.
Map Ref. 3G

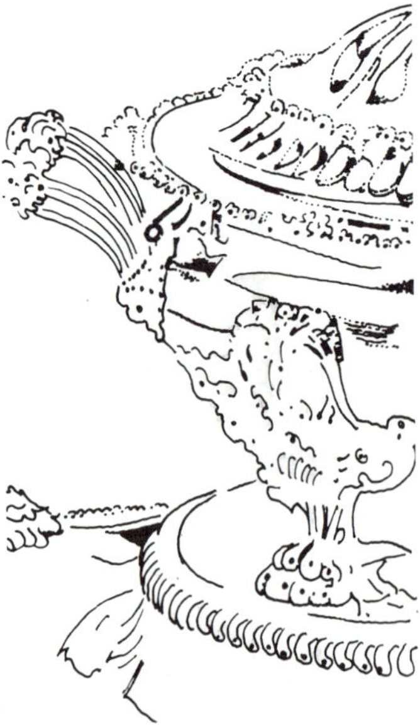

Robin Symes
3 Ormand Yard, Duke of York Street, S.W.1.
Tel: 01-938 9856
Ancient Greek, Roman, Egyptian and Mediaeval jewellery.
Map Ref. 3G

Bentley
63 New Bond Street, W.1.
Tel: 01-629 0651
Fine antique jewellery of all periods together with watches, snuff boxes and jewelled objets d'art. Modern and antique silver and Russian jewels, particularly Fabergé.
Map Ref. 3G

ORIENTAL

Bluett
48 Davies Street, W.1.
Tel: 01-629 4018
Specialises in fine quality Chinese works of art in porcelain.
Map Ref. 3F

Spink
5 King Street, S.W.1.
Tel: 01-930 7888
Marvellous selection of Chinese, Indian and Japanese antiquities.
Map Ref. 3G

Oriental Antiques
38a Kensington Church Street, W.8.
Tel: 01-937 9532
Fine quality objets d'art, Japanese and Chinese Porcelain, bronzes, jades and ivories.
Map Ref. 4E

Hugh Moss
12 Bruton Street, W.1.
Tel: 01-492 1835
Specialises in Chinese works of art including porcelain, lacquerware and enamel from the early Dynasties.
Map Ref. 3G

Nihon Token
23 Museum Street, W.1.
Tel: 01-580 6511
Specialising in Japanese antiques from before 3rd Century BC to about 1868 including armour, metalwork, lacquer, Inro and paintings.
Map Ref. 2H

Douglas J K Wright Ltd
8 Queen Street, W.1.
Tel: 01-629 9993
Chinese and Japanese works including Netsuke, lacquer, porcelain and jade.
Map Ref. 3F

PEWTER AND BRASS

Preston
1 Campden Street, W.8.
Tel: 01-727 4872
A whole range of copper and brass is found here, both antique and reproduction. Warming-pans, chestnut roasters, candlesticks are among the many objects stocked.
Map Ref. 4C

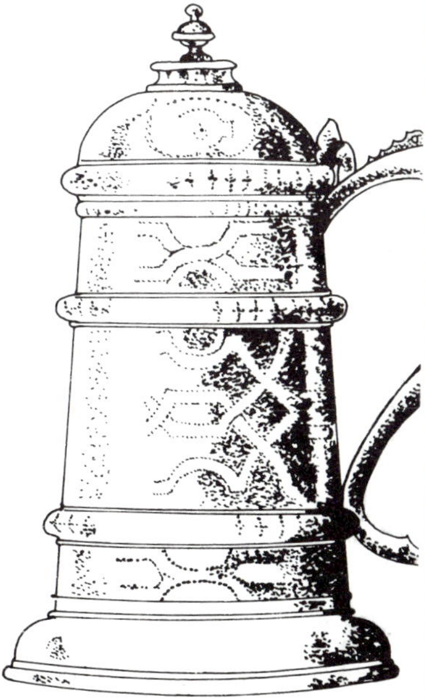

Richard Mundey
19 Chiltern Street, W.1.
Tel: 01-935 5613
Cheery owner assures us that "this is the best shop for pewter in the country". Certainly stock is wide-ranging from Roman-British times up to 19th Century and includes everything pewter. Distinguished list of customers.

Map Ref. 2F

Jack Casimir
23 Pembridge Road, W.11.
Tel: 01-727 8643
Antique brass, copper and pewter from 16th to 19th Century of good quality.

Map Ref. 3B

POTTERY AND PORCELAIN

Heirloom and Howard
1 Hay Hill, W.1.
Tel: 01-493 5868
This shop deals in anything with Armorial Bearings on it especially porcelain and china, including Chinese export china. Also glass, seals and small paintings.

Map Ref. 3F

J J May
40 Kensington Church Street, W.8.
Tel: 01-937 3575
Commemorative items in porcelain, gold and silver.

Map Ref. 5B

Richard Dennis
144 Kensington Church Street, W.8.
Tel: 01-727 2061
English Studio pottery sold here — dates 1870 to 1950.

Map Ref. 4C

Jellinek & Sampson
156 Brompton Road, S.W.3.
Tel: 01-589 5272
Specialises in 17th and 18th Century English pottery. Oak furniture and other items.

Map Ref. 4E

Oliver-Sutton
34c Kensington Church Street, W.8.
Tel: 01-937 0633
All forms and types of Staffordshire figures.

Map Ref. 4C

Vandekar
138 Brompton Road, S.W.3.
Tel: 01-589 8481
Huge selection of antique European pottery and porcelain including Sèvres, Meissen, Chelsea, Derby, Doulton and Oriental.

Map Ref. 4E

Winifred Williams
3 Bury Street, S.W.1.
Tel: 01-930 4732
18th Century English and Continental china, especially Meissen.

Map Ref. 3G

SILVER

S J Phillips
139 New Bond Street, W.1.
Tel: 01-629 6261
Large selection of early English and Continental silver.
Map Ref. 3G

T Lumley
2 Old Bond Street, W.1.
Tel: 01-629 2493
Specialises in unusual silver pieces. Noted for gilt and decorative items. Phone for appointment first.
Map Ref. 3G

How
2-3 Pickering Place, St. James Street, S.W.1.
Tel: 01-930 7140
Fine examples of early English, Irish and Scottish silver.
Map Ref. 3G

London Silver Vaults
Chancery House, 53-64 Chancery Lane, W.C.2.
Tel: 01-242 3844
One of the most famous places to see and buy all kinds of silver from antique to contemporary works.
Map Ref. 2I

N Bloom
40 Conduit Street, W.1.
Tel: 01-629 5660
Elizabethan and Victorian silver.
Map Ref. 3G

Bond Street Silver Galleries
111 New Bond Street, W.1.
Tel: 01-493 6180
Most types of silver.
Map Ref. 3G

AUCTIONEERS

If you have spare time, one of the best places to buy antiques is at one of the Auction Houses. Every auction gallery allows you to view the goods for sale prior to the auction date and there are

printed catalogues available describing each item. It is still possible to get a bargain but, if not, it is likely that you would still get the item of your choice cheaper than from the dealer as you would not be paying for his time and expense. Remember once you have successfully bid for an item you must pay for it immediately.
Details of forthcoming London auctions are published every Monday in the Daily Telegraph and every Tuesday in the Times newspapers.

Sotheby & Co.
34-35 New Bond Street, W.1.
Tel: 01-493 8080
Internationally famous as one of the oldest art auctioneers.
Map Ref. 3G

Phillips
7 Blenheim Street, W.1.
Tel: 01-409 2593 (valuations)
Good reputation for good quality antiques and unusual items.
Map Ref. 2F

Christies
8 King Street, S.W.1.
Tel: 01-839 9060
Quality antiques and fine works of art, jewellery, porcelain, etc.
Map Ref. 3G

Christies South Kensington
85 Old Brompton Road, S.W.7.
Tel: 01-589 2422
Items which are not included in the main gallery sale so it is possible to get reasonably priced bargains.
Map Ref. 5D

Bonham's Montpelier Galleries
Montpelier Street, S.W.7.
Tel: 01-584 9161
Medium price range, furniture, paintings and ceramics.
Map Ref. 4F

HYPERMARKETS

Basically, Hypermarkets consist of lots of small shops or stands under one roof, selling all kinds of antiques.

Antique Hypermarket
26 Kensington High Street, W.8.
Tel: 01-937 1572
Numerous stands in this market sell a variety of antiques. Worth a visit.
Map Ref. 4C

Antiquarius
139-141 Kings Road, S.W.3.
Tel: 01-351 5353
Excellent for costumes, books, prints, art nouveau and general antiques.
Map Ref. 5E

Chenil Galleries
181 Kings Road, S.W.3.
Tel: 01-351 5353
Mainly art deco and art nouveau, but some stalls have objets d'art and antiques.
Map Ref. 5F

Chelsea Antique Market
245 Kings Road, S.W.3.
Tel: 01-352 9695
Small items of silver, brass and some furniture. Good quality. Also old clothes.
Map Ref. 6E

Bond Street Antique Centre
124 New Bond Street, W.1.
Tel: 01-351 5353
European porcelain, watches, clocks and other collectors items.
Map Ref. 3G

STREET MARKETS

It is here that you might get a bargain, particularly if you know exactly what you are looking for. It is however very time-consuming as there are so many stalls. However, it is certainly interesting to look even if you don't want to buy.

Portobello Road, W.1.
World famous for just about everything. Friday and Saturday are best days to visit.
Map Ref. 3B

Camden Passage, N.1.
Good for reasonably priced antiques.
No Map Ref.

Bermondsey Market, S.E.1.
Open antique market with good reasonably priced antiques. Fridays only. Other areas which are good for antique shops of all kinds are:
Map Ref. 4K

Fulham Road, S.W.3. and S.W.10.
Map Ref. 5E

Kings Road, S.W.3., S.W.6. and S.W.10.
Map Ref. 4C

Church Street, W.8. Kensington.
York Street, W.1.
Map Ref. 2F

Covent Garden Piazza
Covent Garden, W.C.2.
Among the chi-chi shops in the Arcades storeholders can hire stalls for their wares. Clothes, accessories, fruit, vegetables, almost anything can be found.
Map Ref. 3H

BOOKS

Harrods
Knightsbridge, S.W.1.
Tel: 01-730 1234
A magnificent selection of books of all kinds, including one entire room for children's books.
Map Ref. 4E

Dillons
1 Malet Street, W.C.1.
Tel: 01-636 1577
Mostly scholastic and academic, a second hand department and especially scientific books.
Map Ref. 2H

The Government Bookshop
49 High Holborn, W.C.1.
Tel: 01-928 6977
All official government titles, careers, antiques and miscellaneous books on horticulture, cooking and other subjects.
Map Ref. 2H

Truslove and Hanson
205 Sloane Street, S.W.1.
Tel: 01-235 2128
Wide selection of books.
Map Ref. 4E

Foyles
119 Charing Cross Road, W.C.2.
Tel: 01-437 5660
Probably the largest bookshop in terms of numbers of books. Anything and everything that's in print can be found here, or ordered.
Map Ref. 2H

Hatchards
187 Piccadilly, W.1.
Tel: 01-437 3924
This is London's oldest book shop and has been in Piccadilly since 1767.
Map Ref. 3G

Collet's
52 and 66 Charing Cross Road, W.C.2.
Tel: 01-836 2315/6306
Comprehensive stock of Penguin paper backs in number 52, while 66 deals with a good mixture of titles, especially on politics and economics.
Map Ref. 2H

The Pan Bookshop
158 Fulham Road, S.W.10.
Tel: 01-373 4997
Everything that is in stock in the Pan paperback range besides other publications. Intelligently arranged.
Map Ref. 6D

Compendium
234 Camden High Street, N.W.1.
Tel: 01-267 1525
Nice, friendly bookshop with impressive stock. Two floors.
No Map Ref.

Besides the above shops, the various branches of W H Smith & Co (check telephone directory for address) sell a good selection of paperbacks and hardbacks.

Most department stores have good book departments too including:

Selfridges
Harrods
Harvey Nichols
Liberty's

Addresses and telephone numbers can be found in the Department Stores section.

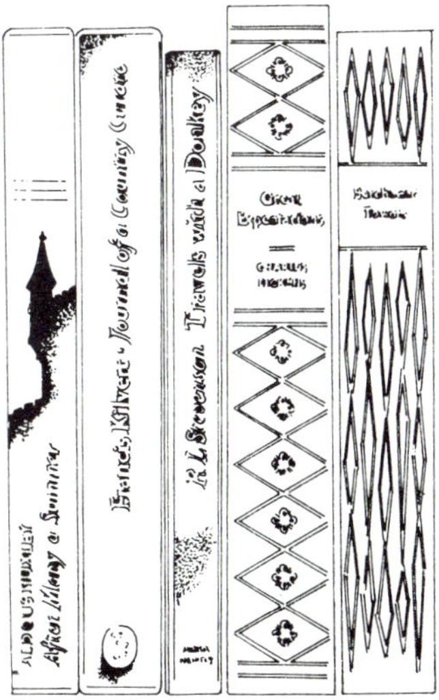

BOUTIQUES FOR WOMEN

BOND STREET

Elle
92 New Bond Street, W.1.
Tel: 01-629 4441
Chic shop specialising in the best from the continent as well as Patricia Roberts knitwear. Names to look for include Fiorucci, Rococo and Kamikaze.
Map Ref. 3G

Kurt Geiger
95 New Bond Street, W.1.
Tel: 01-499 2707
Marvellous range of shoes — lots from Magli. Very elegant styling and fine leathers. Good range of sizes.
Map Ref. 3G

Lucy's
107 New Bond Street, W.1.
Tel: 01-409 0078
Specialising in beautiful evening clothes, lots of which appear in plays on TV. Lucy's is the place to go for something glamorous.
Map Ref. 3G

Midas
72 New Bond Street, W.1.
Tel: 01-629 3633
Another lovely shoe shop — where prices are more reasonable than you would expect. Nice classic styles and colours. Clothes as well.
Map Ref. 3G

Rivoli
67 New Bond Street, W.1.
Tel: 01-629 0786
French and Italian merchandise. Beautiful evening dresses.
Map Ref. 3G

Fenwick
63 New Bond Street, W.1.
Tel: 01-629 9161
Between a boutique and a department store, this lively shop has everything you need in the way of fashion at reasonable prices. A paradise for working girls.
Map Ref. 3G

Saint-Laurent Rive Gauche
113 New Bond Street, W.1.
Tel: 01-493 1800
The Bond Street outpost of the Saint-Laurent empire where you find his ready-to-wear clothes in all their elegance. If you are a fan, this is paradise.
Map Ref. 3G

Bally
116 New Bond Street, W.1.
Tel: 01-491 7062
Another smart shoe shop in the medium to expensive range. Up-to-date styles and a good colour range.
Map Ref. 3G

Regine
43 New Bond Street, W.1.
Tel: 01-499 0788
Neat casual clothes and also some Californian sportswear feature in Regine's collection of clothes. Some star continental designers, too.
Map Ref. 3G

Fiorucci
133 New Bond Street, W.1
Tel: 01-491 3499
Highly distinctive clothes, mainly for the young. Full of casual tops and trousers. Very trendy and generally brightly coloured.
Map Ref. 3G

Celine
28 New Bond Street, W.1.
Tel: 01-493 9000
Elegance personified in this quiet, beautiful clothes, bags and leather wear shop for the woman who likes to be dressed in wool and pure silk. Also available are Fior jewellery and bags.
Map Ref. 3G

Hermes
155 New Bond Street, W.1.
Tel: 01-499 8856
Lovely headsquares, for which they are famed, plus the ultimate in leather goods are to be found in this lovely shop. Also a comprehensive range of luxurious clothes.
Map Ref. 2F

Ted Lapidus
164 New Bond Street, W.1.
Tel: 01-629 2323
Stocking Lapidus's inimitable blend of casual but smart clothes, this exciting shop has always very desirable clothes.
Map Ref. 3G

Ports
172 New Bond Street, W.1.
Tel: 01-493 9176
Beautifully made range of co-ordinate clothes inspired by Canadian Luke Tanabe. Mainly in natural fibre, classic styles, which we all need.
Map Ref. 3G

Chloe
173 New Bond Street, W.1.
Tel: 01-493 6277
Beautiful, feminine clothes that are in the upper price range — but well worth it. Gorgeous designs carried out in lovely fabrics.
Map Ref. 3G

Russell and Bromley
24 New Bond Street, W.1.
Tel: 01-629 6903
Very good and large selection of boots and shoes to be found in this popular shoe shop — most with co-ordinating bags.
Map Ref. 3G

Wardrobe
3 Grosvenor Street, W.1.
(on corner of Bond Street)
Susie Gold has assembled here a brilliant collection of designer clothes from which to choose an elegant outfit — pricey, but not so much as you would think.
Map Ref. 2F

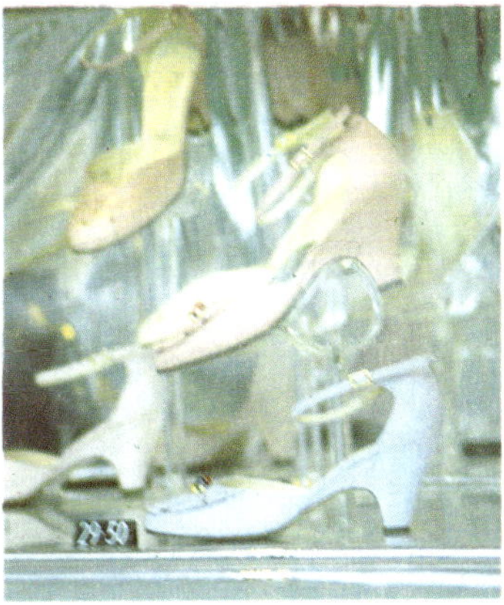

Adele Davis
10 New Bond Street, W.1.
Tel: 01-493 2795
A small collection of exclusive clothes are to be found in this little shop which would suit a woman of distinction. Fabulous evening dresses.
Map Ref. 3G

Etienne Aigner
6 New Bond Street, W.1.
Tel: 01-491 7764
Shoes, bags, leather cases for both men and women — all in exquisite leather, conservatively styled.
Map Ref. 3G

Ferragamo
24 Old Bond Street, W.1.
Tel: 01-629 5007
The famous Ferragamo tradition lives on in this smart shop with its range of enviable shoes. Still a family business.
Map Ref. 3G

Gucci
27 Old Bond Street, W.1.
Tel: 01-629 2716
Another family-owned Italian business which specialises in leather goods as well as beautiful silk scarves.
Very stylish shoes, clothes and luggage.
Map Ref. 3G

Chanel
2 Old Bond Street, W.1.
Tel: 01-493 5040
Stocking Chanel's famous little suits with her distinctive style, this newly-opened shop enables all enthusiasts to get their clothes without going to Paris.
Map Ref. 3G

Loewe
25a Old Bond Street, W.1.
Tel: 01-493 3914
Shop specialising in marvellous leather goods and pret-a-porter clothes. Also good for smaller gifts.
Map Ref. 3G

Rayne
15 Old Bond Street, W.1.
Tel: 01-439 7077
Brilliant collection of shoes, both their own make as well as from named designers — Givenchy, Jourdan and Halston. Good for evening shoes.
Map Ref. 3G

Janet Reger
12 Bond Street, W.1.
Tel: 01-493 8357
The specialist in lingerie, beautifully designed and made. Garments of which dreams are made of.
Map Ref. 3G

AROUND SLOANE STREET

Laura Ashley
9 Harriet Street, S.W.1.
183 Sloane Street, S.W.1.
Tel: 01-235 9796
One of the several Laura Ashley shops scattered about London, the Harriet Street shop has a large selection of milkmaid-type dresses plus the more sophisticated new range. The Sloane Street shop concentrates on household goods — wallpapers, fabrics and so on.
Map Ref. 4E

Elegance Maternelle
198 Sloane Street, S.W.1.
Tel: 01-235 6140
Stylish clothes for the mother-to-be, which are pretty enough to be worn by the non-pregnant! Underclothes and evening clothes as well.
Map Ref. 4E

Emilio Pucci
12a Cadogan Place, S.W.1.
Tel: 01-235 2852
Pucci is famed for his luscious print dresses. Here in his London shop you will find a good selection in a large range of sizes. Good for holiday clothes all the year round.
Map Ref. 4E

Fendi
37 Sloane Street, S.W.1.
Tel: 01-235 9966
Sportswear, Karl Lagerfeld furs, leather accessories are just some of the things that are sold in this Italian shop. Very good for bags and shoes.
Map Ref. 4E

Jorgensen
18 Sloane Street, S.W.1.
Tel: 01-235 5626
Named designer's clothes are featured in this smart shop. Very luxurious clothes in magnificent fabrics. Buy your special occasion clothes here.
Map Ref. 4E

Rodier
15 Sloane Street, S.W.1.
Tel: 01-235 3417
Paris co-ordinates which are very understated but smart. If you like your casuals with a Parisian dash this is the place for you.
Map Ref. 4E

COVENT GARDEN PIAZZA

S Fisher
12 The Market, Ground Floor.
Tel: 01-836 2576
Traditional English knitwear including Fair Isles and Shetlands. Cashmere and lambswool classics in almost any colour you can think of. Dresses too.
Map Ref. 3H

Crocodile
Unit 17, The Piazza, Ground Floor.
Tel: 01-836 9168
One of a chain of shops selling rather high-priced clothes that are in mid-stream fashion. Some American and own-label dresses.
Map Ref. 3H

Whistles
20 The Piazza, Ground Floor.
Tel: 01-379 7401
Varied range of clothes both in styles and prices. Some classic designs and also good knitwear. Original.
Map Ref. 3H

Monsoon
Unit 23, The Piazza, Ground Floor.
Tel: 01-836 9140
Full of Eastern promise — Indian cottons, Turkish designs and soft Kashmir wools make up the beautiful Monsoon mix. Always something new and lovely.
Map Ref. 3H

OTHER AREAS

Browns
27 South Molton Street, W.1.
Tel: 01-499 7833
A whole collection of shops selling high-class, chic continental designs such as Missoni. Also a Calvin Klein shop. Very desirable clothes.
Map Ref. 2F

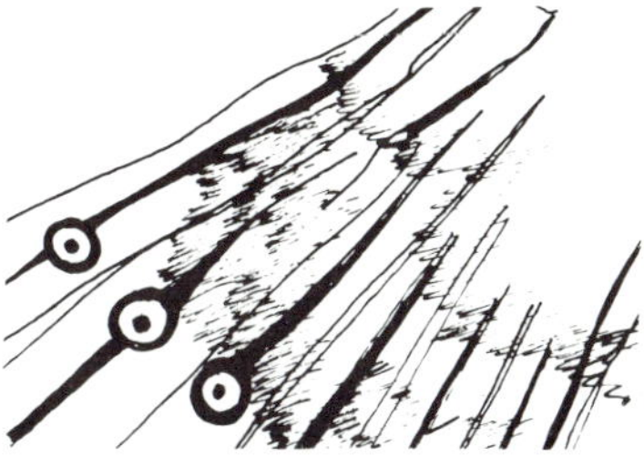

Crocodile
176 High Street, Kensington, W.8.
Tel: 01-937 6725
Also at New Bond Street and Beauchamp Place.
A chain of shops specialising in smart, expensive clothes.
Map Ref. 4E

Feathers
40 Hans Crescent, W.8.
Tel: 01-589 0350
A pretty collection of clothes is always to be found in this shop.
Map Ref. 4E

Lucienne Phillips
89 Knightsbridge, S.W.1.
Tel: 01-235 2134
All the clothes here are chosen by Lucienne Phillips, special flair for what is smart. Expensive but worth it.
Map Ref. 4C

Wakeford's
102 King's Road, S.W.3.
Tel: 01-589 2126
Also at Knightsbridge.
A good collection of established designers such as Frank Usher typifies the Wakeford's style. Very good merchandise.
Map Ref. 5E

Bellville-Sassoon
73 Pavilion Road, S.W.1.
Tel: 01-235 5801
Couture-style clothes with a very smart look. Expensive but very good.
Map Ref. 4E

Whistles
1 Theyer Street, W.1.
Tel: 01-935 7013
The best of British Designer Collections together with unique sweaters, separates and accessories.
Map Ref. 2F

Zandra Rhodes
14a Grafton Street, W.1.
Tel: 01-499 6695
Zany Zandra's beautiful dresses are an acquired taste, you either love them or hate them. Nonetheless, they are among the most beautiful around. Very expensive but only the finest materials are used. Also silk collection at under £250.
Map Ref. 2G

BOUTIQUES FOR MEN

Ebony
45 South Molton Street, W.1.
Tel: 01-408 1247
A colourful high-fashion shop with leading British and European designed clothes.
Map Ref. 2F

Browns
27 South Molton Street, W.1.
Tel: 01-491 7833
Very efficient high class boutique specialising in expensive ready-to-wear clothes.
Map Ref. 2F

Take Six
362 Oxford Street, W.1.
Tel: 01-499 9909
Also at Bond Street, W.1. & Kings Road, S.W.3.
Tel: 01-491 7141
Good range of reasonably priced fashion clothes.
Map Ref. 2F

Tommy Nutter
16 Savile Row, W.1.
Tel: 01-734 0831
Modern fashion house with a good

selection of ready-to-wear clothes and accessories. Design clothes as well.
Map Ref. 3G

Lord John
493 Oxford Street, W.1.
Tel: 01-493 9872
Well-known for casual clothes, trousers and accessories.
Map Ref. 3G

Piero de Monzi
68 Fulham Road, S.W.3.
Tel: 01-589 8765
Expensive boutique specialising in high class Italian fashion.
Map Ref. 6D

Carnaby Street, W.1.
There are many boutiques of varying standards in this street which is well worth a visit.
Map Ref. 3G

Kings Road, S.W.3.
Traditionally famous for boutiques and modern, trendy clothing shops.
Map Ref. 5E

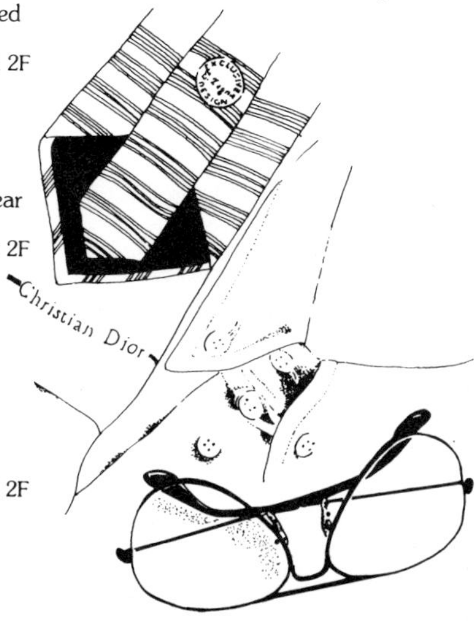

CARPETS

The following shops have a good selection of carpets which can be fitted to your own requirements in a wide range of patterns and colours. Traditional British names are Wilton, Axminster — both in high quality wool or wool and man-made mixtures. Most big department stores also have a good range of styles and colours.

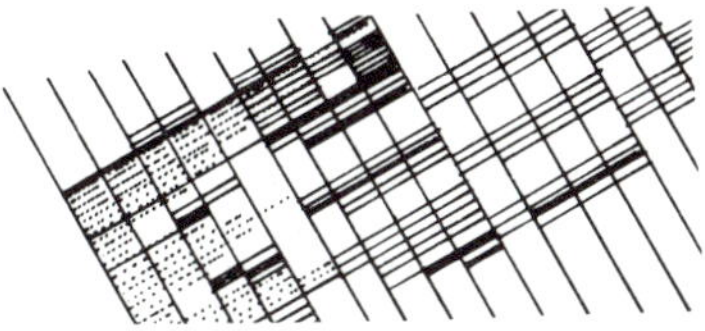

Allied Carpets
90 Edgware Road, W.2.
Also branches throughout London.
Tel: 01-402 2233
Map Ref. 2E

Chatsworth
227 Brompton Road, S.W.3.
Tel: 01-584 1386
Map Ref. 4E

Afia
60 Baker Street, W.1.
Tel: 01-935 0414
Map Ref. 2F

Resista
58a Fulham Road, S.W.6.
Tel: 01-589 3238
Map Ref. 4E

255 New King's Road, S.W.6.
Tel: 01-731 2588
Map Ref. 5D

Zarach
110 Fulham Road, S.W.3.
Tel: 01-373 1144
Also at 44 South Audley Street, W.1.
Very modern decor — furniture and accessories of the highest standard are the hallmark of the Zarach style.
Map Ref. 6D

CHINA AND GLASS

The following shops have a good selection of modern china and glass — specialist shops have a note by them. English china is particularly fine and firms such as Spode, Wedgwood and Royal Worcester produce both traditional and modern patterns so that you can be sure of finding something that will please your taste.

Chinacraft
499 Oxford Street, W.1.
Tel: 01-499 9881
Map Ref. 2F

Thomas Goode
19 South Audley Street, W.1.
Tel: 01-499 2823
High class shop with the very best china and glass.
Map Ref. 3F

Gered
173 Piccadilly, W.1.
Tel: 01-629 2614
The London showroom for Wedgwood and Spode, beautifully set out and clearly priced.
Map Ref. 3G

Lawleys
154 Regent Street, W.1.
Tel: 01-734 2621
Map Ref. 3G

House and Bargain
31 Brewer Street, W.1.
Tel: 01-734 9628
A shop with lots of interesting bits and pieces in household wares, china and cooking utensils at very good prices.
Map Ref. 3G

Royal Copenhagen
15 New Bond Street, W.1.
Tel: 01-629 3622
The London shop for the famous Danish china — small but comprehensive.
Map Ref. 3G

Wilson and Gill Studio Rosenthal
137 Regent Street, W.1.
Tel: 01-734 3076
London showroom of this elegant range of china and glass. Depends on beauty of shape rather than decoration.
Map Ref. 3G

Merchant Chandler
72 New Kings Road, S.W.6.
Tel: 01-736 6141
An amusing shop full of everything you need for your kitchen. Has great charm.
Map Ref. 5F

Central Bazaar
70 Westbourne Grove, W.2.
Tel: 01-229 3388
Specialists in Johnson's china as well as glass and luggage.
Map Ref. 2B

The Glasshouse
65 Longacre, W.C.2.
Tel: 01-836 9785
Wonderful place where you can actually see famous glassblowers at work and which also sells their wares. Very special.
Map Ref. 2H

Piddys
150 Oxford Street, W.1.
Tel: 01-637 5770
Well known names in china.
Map Ref. 2F

The following department stores also have good china and glass departments:

Harrods
Selfridges
Harvey Nichols (small but pretty)
Peter Jones

CLOCKS AND WATCHES

Camerer Cuss
32 Sloane Square, S.W.1.
Tel: 01-730 7046
First class clocks and watches that are beautiful and sometimes unusual.
Map Ref. 5F

Rolex
5 New Bond Street, W.1.
Tel: 01-491 3083
Full range of Rolex watches.
Map Ref. 3G

Watches of Switzerland
16 New Bond Street, W.1.
Tel: 01-493 5916
As one might expect there is a large selection of Swiss watches. Helpful service.
Map Ref. 3G

Cartier
175 New Bond Street, W.1.
Tel: 01-493 6962
A lovely old jewellers, famous throughout the world, which also sells very expensive watches.
Map Ref. 3G

Aspreys
165 New Bond Street, W.1.
Tel: 01-493 6767
A good selection of expensive clocks and watches.
Map Ref. 3G

Dunhills
30 Duke Street, S.W.1.
Tel: 01-499 9566
Besides being the premier tobacco and cigar store in London, Dunhills also sells a selection of unusual watches and clocks.
Map Ref. 3G

Garrards
112 Regent Street, W.1.
Tel: 01-734 7020
Famous for silverware, they also have a large selection of clocks and watches.
Map Ref. 3G

Mappin & Webb
170 Regent Street, W.1.
Tel: 01-734 0906
Fine selection of clocks and watches.
Map Ref. 3G

Harrods
Knightsbridge, S.W.1.
Tel: 01-730 1234
As might be expected of this store they have a superb collection of watches and clocks.
Map Ref. 4E

H Samuel
250 Oxford Street, W.1.
Tel: 01-493 1682
Also branches throughout London. Excellent value for lower priced clocks and watches, they also sell those in the expensive range.
Map Ref. 2F

CLOTHES AND ACCESSORIES FOR MEN

Aquascutum
100 Regent Street, W.1.
Tel: 01-734 6090
Famous for their raincoats and tweed jackets, they also have a large selection of other clothes.
Map Ref. 3G

Austin Reed
103 Regent Street, W.1.
Tel: 01-734 6789
Three floors of suits, shirts, ties and casual clothes, with the accent on quality.
Map Ref. 3G

Blades
8 Burlington Gardens, W.1.
Tel: 01-734 8911
Informal, small shop specialising in men's fashion with mainly the younger man in mind. Hand made clothes.
Map Ref. 3G

Burberry's
18 Haymarket, S.W.1.
Tel: 01-930 3343
Specialises in rainwear but also sells other clothes in traditional styles.
Map Ref. 3G

Burtons
114 Regent Street, W.1.
Tel: 01-734 1951
The main branch of this large chain selling a good selection of clothes at reasonable prices.
Map Ref. 3G

Gieves and Hawkes
1 Savile Row, W.1.
Tel: 01-734 0186
Traditional style suits and sports jackets.
Map Ref. 3G

Harrods
Knightsbridge, S.W.1.
Tel: 01-730 1234
Like everything else in this store the range and quality of their men's clothing is excellent.
Map Ref. 4E

Harry Fenton
43 Oxford Street, W.1.
Tel: 01-629 7947
Also branches throughout London. A good middle-of-the-road stockist of men's clothes.
Map Ref. 2E

C & A
Marble Arch, Oxford Street, W.1.
Tel: 01-629 7272
Also branches throughout London. A good chain store with some well priced clothes. Well worth searching through to find just what you want.
Map Ref. 2F

Dickie Dirt's
58a Westbourne Grove, W.2.
Tel: 01-229 1466
The place to get jeans at a very reasonable price.
Map Ref. 2B

Marks & Spencer
458 Oxford Street, W.1.
Tel: 01-486 6151
Also branches throughout London. The main branch of this large chain which has a world wide reputation for selling quality clothing at modest prices.
Map Ref. 2F

Moss Bros
Bedford Street, W.C.2.
Tel: 01-240 4567
Primarily a clothing hire shop, Moss Bros. have now expanded into selling excellent suits and casual wear at reasonable prices.
Map Ref. 3H

Simpsons
203 Piccadilly, W.1.
Tel: 01-734 2002
Four floors of clothing for men with the famous Daks label. Magnificent selection of accessories.
Map Ref. 3G

CLOTHES AND ACCESSORIES FOR WOMEN

The British Look — understated, classic and casual — is one that is imitated throughout the world. There are some dress firms specialising in this look and you can find it at these shops.

Map Ref. 3G

Aquascutum
100 Regent Street, W.1.
Tel: 01-734 6090
For both men and women. Beautifully tailored clothes that are also very interesting. Good quality, design and fabric are hallmarks here.

Map Ref. 3G

Burberrys
18 Haymarket, W.1.
Tel: 01-734 4060
Burberrys have given a word to the English language with the Burberry raincoat. It still exists, along with a lot of other beautiful classic clothes.

Map Ref. 3G

Jaeger
Regent Street, W.1.
Also branches throughout London.
Tel: 01-734 4050
Beautiful clothes that are classic in style but follow current fashion trends. Mix and match here to get your own special look that is still unmistakably English.

Map Ref. 3G

Scotch House
84 Regent Street, W.1.
Tel: 01-734 0203
Also branches throughout London. Here you find tartans, fine knitwear and everything that you associate with Scotland. Find your own individual tartan, wear it with a velvet jacket and jabot trimmed blouse or shirt. This is the place.

Map Ref. 3G

Peels
Burlington Arcade, W.1.
Tel: 01-493 5378
Beautiful knitwear in fine cashmere and lambswool can be found in this little shop in this pretty arcade. For the connoisseur and those wanting quality.

Map Ref. 3G

S Fisher
Burlington Arcade, W.1.
Also at Piccadilly.
Tel: 01-493 4180
Sumptuous knitwear in nearly forty colours together with dresses and other pretty things. Very good quality and finish. Luxurious but worth it.

Map Ref. 3G

Kurt Geiger
95 New Bond Street, W.1.
Tel: 01-499 2707
Marvellous range of shoes — lots from Magli. Very elegant styling and fine leathers. Good range of sizes.

Map Ref. 3G

Midas
72 New Bond Street, W.1.
Tel: 01-629 3633
Another lovely shoe shop where prices are more reasonable than you would expect. Nice classic styles and colours.

Map Ref. 3G

Fenwick
63 New Bond Street, W.1.
Tel: 01-629 9161
Between a boutique and a department store, this lively shop has everything you need in the way of fashion at reasonable prices. A paradise for working girls.

Map Ref. 3G

Bally
116 New Bond Street, W.1.
Tel: 01-629 6501
Another smart shoe shop in the medium to expensive range. Up-to-date styles and a good colour range distinguish Bally.
Map Ref. 3G

Celine
28 New Bond Street, W.1.
Tel: 01-493 9000
Beautiful clothes, bags and leather wear for the woman who likes to be nicely dressed. Also available are Fior jewellery and bags.
Map Ref. 3G

Hermes
115 Bruton Street, W.1.
(corner of Bond Street)
Tel: 01-499 8856
Lovely headsquares, for which they are famed, plus the ultimate in leather goods are to be found in this lovely shop. Also a small range of luxurious clothes.
Map Ref. 3G

Russell and Bromley
24 New Bond Street, W.1.
Tel: 01-629 6903
Very good and large selection of boots and shoes to be found in this popular shoe shop — most with co-ordinating bags.
Map Ref. 3G

Etienne Aigner
6 New Bond Street, W.1.
Tel: 01-491 7764
Shoes, bags, leather cases for both men and women — all in exquisite leather, conservatively styled.
Map Ref. 3G

Ferragamo
24 Old Bond Street, W.1.
Tel: 01-629 5007
The famous Ferragamo tradition lives on in this smart shop with its range of enviable shoes. Still a family business.
Map Ref. 3G

Loewe
25a Old Bond Street, W.1.
Tel: 01-493 3914
Another shop specialising in marvellous leather goods and clothes. Also good for smaller gifts.
Map Ref. 3G

The following department stores have excellent departments for women's clothes.

Dickins and Jones
224 Regent Street, W.1.
Tel: 01-734 7070
Map Ref. 2G

Harrods
Knightsbridge, S.W.1.
Tel: 01-730 1234
Map Ref. 4E

Marks and Spencer
458 Oxford Street, W.1.
Tel: 01-486 6151
Map Ref. 2F

C & A
Oxford Street, W.1.
Tel: 01-629 7272
Map Ref. 2F

Harvey Nichols
Knightsbridge, S.W.1.
Tel: 01-235 5000
Map Ref. 4F

Fenwicks
63 New Bond Street, W.1.
Tel: 01-629 9161
Map Ref. 3G

Selfridges
Oxford Street, W.1.
Tel: 01-629 1234
Map Ref. 2F

Simpsons
Piccadilly, W.1.
Tel: 01-734 2002
Map Ref. 3G

Bourne's
Oxford Street, W.1.
Tel: 01-636 1515
Map Ref. 2F

Debenham's
Oxford Street, W.1.
Tel: 01-580 3000
Map Ref. 3G

D. H. Evans
318 Oxford Street, W.1.
Tel: 01-629 8800
Map Ref. 2G

John Lewis
Oxford Street, W.1.
Tel: 01-629 7711
Map Ref. 2G

CLOTHES AND ACCESSORIES FOR CHILDREN

Mothercare
461 Oxford Street, W.1. and branches.
Tel: 01-629 6621
Good chain store for babies and small children — and pregnant mothers. Up to date, well priced merchandise.
Map Ref. 2F

Please Mum
69 Bond Street, W.1.
Tel: 01-486 3399
50a Wigmore Street, W.1.
Tel: 01-486 3399
Bright, modern clothes including an expensive range of leather coats. For children from 0 to 16.
Map Ref. 3G

Wonder City
22 Kensington Church Street, W.8.
Tel: 01-937 2306
Another bright shop for children with a wide range of different clothes. Very up-to-date. Toys as well.
Map Ref. 4C

Rowes
170 New Bond Street, W.1.
Tel: 01-409 1770
Very traditional clothes for top tots. Much beloved by nannies and mothers who like conventional, well-made coats and dresses.
Map Ref. 3G

La Cicogna
6a Sloane Street, S.W.1.
Tel: 01-235 3739
One of several branches of this Italian chain which specialises in baby clothes and things for the very young. Furniture, books and shoes as well.
Map Ref. 4E

Liberty's
Regent Street, W.1.
Tel: 01-732 1234
At one time every self-respecting little girl would own a Liberty print smock — and they still look marvellous. Beautiful clothes in beautiful material are the hallmark of this department.
Map Ref. 2G

Little Horrors
11a William Street, S.W.1.
Tel: 01-235 0531
16 Cheval Place, S.W.7.
Tel: 01-589 5289
Expensive silk and taffeta dresses for 10-16 year olds.
Map Ref. 4E

Little Monsoon
23 Central Avenue, Covent Garden Piazza, W.C.1.
Tel: 01-836 9140
Similar in style to the grown-up Monsoon with lots of vivid Indian cottons as well as casual clothes. Good for holiday clothes.
Map Ref. 3H

The following stores and chain stores also do children's wear.

Peter Jones
Harrods
Marks & Spencer
British Home Stores
Selfridges

CLOTHING (SPECIAL SIZES) WOMEN

Buy and Large
4 Holbein Place, Sloane Square, S.W.1.
Tel: 01-730 6534
Sizes sixteen and over, lots of the designs by named designers. Clothes in good taste with plenty of room given to armholes etc.
Map Ref. 5F

Crispin's
28 & 5 Chiltern Street, W.1.
Tel: 01-486 8924
Shoes and boots in long fittings together with long sized tights, gloves and a selection of desirable bags. Pretty designs as well as walking shoes. At No.5, narrow fittings in all sizes.
Map Ref. 2F

Dee Dawson
5 Thayer Street, W.1.
Tel: 01-935 7527
Dee Dawson designs zingy, up-to-the-minute clothes for larger sizes. Lovely colours, glamorous styles, nothing of the dowdy here.
Map Ref. 2F

Long Tall Sally
21 Chiltern Street, W.1.
Tel: 01-487 3370
Everything for the Tall Lady — particularly good for separates, though coats, raincoats and nightwear are all specially designed to fit. Large selection of trousers.
Map Ref. 2F

Nellie Frock
42 Chiltern Street, W.1.
Tel: 01-486 2712
If you are below average height then this is the shop for you. The small girl's counterpart to Long, Tall Sally! Very good merchandise.
Map Ref. 2F

Monica Flynn
137 Sloane Street, S.W.1.
Tel: 01-730 6945
(formerly Mary Durante)
For the larger lady, impeccable designs in very good fabric. Conservatively styled.
Map Ref. 5E

Tall Girls
17 Woodstock Street, W.1.
Tel: 01-499 8748
Reasonably priced clothes for the tall girl — together with a very good selection of large sized shoes of all types, including boots. Also long tights and long-fingered gloves.
Map Ref. 2F

Evans
538 Oxford Street, W.1. and branches.
Tel: 01-499 5372
Specialising in size 16 upwards with both smart and middle-of-the-road styling. Prices kept down but not at the sacrifice of quality.
Map Ref. 2F

Also:

Lilley and Skinner, Oxford Street, W.1. have, tucked away on the ground floor, a Small and Tall Shoe Department. **Jaeger** and **Aquascutum** have clothes that are longer than average.

CLOTHING (SPECIAL SIZES) MEN

High and Mighty
117 Brompton Road, S.W.1.
Tel: 01-589 7454
Everything for the large and/or tall man, including large size shoes. Helpful staff.
Map Ref. 4E

Coopers All Size
72 Edgware Road, W.2.
Tel: 01-402 8635
Coopers say that they can fit any size man. They certainly have a large selection of specialist size clothes up to 60" chest.
Map Ref. 2E

CLOTHES HIRE

Moss Bros
Bedford Street, W.C.2.
Tel: 01-240 4567
Marvellous selection of men's clothes and ladies evening dresses. Helpful and courteous staff.
Map Ref. 3H

Kritz
192 Baker Street, W.1.
Tel: 01-935 0304
Dinner and morning suits.
Map Ref. 1F

Alkit
Cambridge Circus, W.C.2.
Tel: 01-836 1814
Specialises in tropical clothing as well as dinner and morning suits.
Map Ref. 2H

CLOTHES HIRE (FANCY DRESS)

The Carnival Store
95 Hammersmith Road, W.14.
Tel: 01-603 7824
Besides making fancy dress clothes, they also hire them out.
Map Ref. 5A

C & W May
9 Garrick Street, W.C.2.
Tel: 01-836 5993
Part of Moss Bros, they specialise in English fancy dress.
Map Ref. 2H

Joker
97 Chiswick High Road, W.14.
Tel: 01-995 4118
Wonderful selection of fancy dress and costumes, many from the circus environment.
No Map Ref.

BESPOKE (CUSTOM) TAILORS FOR MEN

Hewitts
9 Savile Row, W.1.
Tel: 01-734 1505
Well-cut hand made suits with an elegant appearance. A special service is available where suits are made within a week.
Map Ref. 3G

Huntsman
11 Savile Row, W.1.
Tel: 01-734 7441
Famous for their riding clothes, they are also renowned as tailors of suits and casual wear. Very expensive but superb.
Map Ref. 3G

Anderson & Sheppard
30 Savile Row, W.1.
Tel: 01-734 1420
Old established tailors, they will make a suit quickly if necessary.
Map Ref. 3G

Douglas Hayward
95 Mount Street, W.1.
Tel: 01-499 5574
A very fashionable tailor with top quality workmanship.
Map Ref. 3F

Henry Poole
10 Cork Street, W.1.
Tel: 01-734 5985
Tailors since 1806 and suppliers of fine quality British cloth.
Map Ref. 3F

Kilgour, French & Stanbury
33a Dover Street, W.1.
Tel: 01-629 4283
A fashionable clientele, traditional styling with a good choice of cloths.
Map Ref. 3F

Cyril Grimes
48 Bishops Mansions,
Bishops Park Road, S.W.6.
Tel: 01-736 7976

Ideal for the busy man, Cyril Grimes calls at your home in the evening or at the office during lunch hours. Good quality workmanship.

Map Ref. 6A

Regent & Gordon
180 New Bond Street, W.1.
Tel: 01-629 3336
Good gentleman's tailor with a sympathetic approach to your problems, if any. Quality work.

Map Ref. 3G

Blades
8 Burlington Gardens, W.1.
Tel: 01-734 8911
Dashing styling without being too way-out, Blades is still a gentleman's tailors without being stuffy. Nice ideas about colour, too.

Map Ref. 3G

Crowe
28 Lime Street, E.C.2.
Tel: 01-627 3147
Many distinguished city men patronise Crowe's — if you're near it is worth a visit.

Map Ref. 2K

CUSTOM-MADE SHIRTS

Turnbull & Asser
71 Jermyn Street, S.W.1.
Tel: 01-930 0502
Large and unusual range of materials from these leading shirt makers. They will copy any style. Excellent ties as well.

Map Ref. 3G

Harvie & Hudson
77 Jermyn Street, S.W.1.
Tel: 01-930 3949
A traditional shirt maker specialising in quality business-style shirts and ties.

Map Ref. 3G

Hawes & Curtis
2 Burlington Gardens, W.1.
Tel: 01-493 3803
Ties and shirts, continental styling and a big range of materials.

Map Ref. 6A

Deborah & Clare
29 Beauchamp Place, S.W.3.
Tel: 01-584 2875
Specialising in silks and imported cottons. Also ready-made silk shirts.

Map Ref. 5E

Hilditch & Key
Jermyn Street, S.W.1.
Tel: 01-930 5336
Good range of shirt materials and specialist ties.

Map Ref. 3G

New & Lingwood
Jermyn Street, S.W.1.
Tel: 01-493 9621
Very helpful service — quality materials and styles.

Map Ref. 3G

CUSTOM-MADE SHOES

Alan McAfee
5 Cork Street, W.1.
Tel: 01-734 7301
Beautifully made men's shoes in all styles from moccasins to boots in all fittings.

Map Ref. 3G

R. E. Tricker Ltd
67 Jermyn Street, S.W.1.
Tel: 01-930 6395
A wonderful selection of fine hand-lasted shoes made by the same method for 150 years. Also ready-made shoes available as well as velvet slippers.

Map Ref. 3G

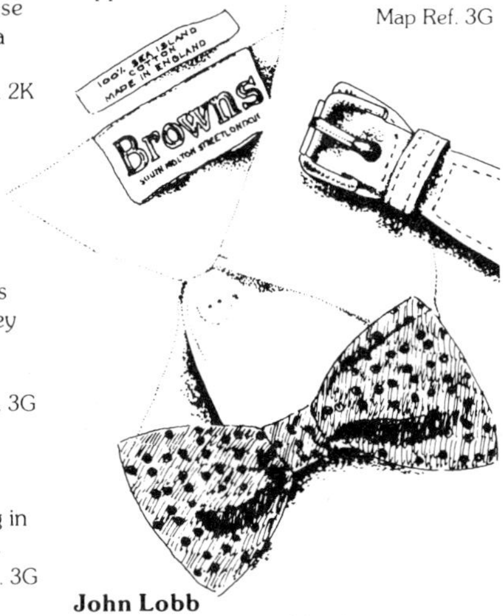

John Lobb
9 St. James Street, S.W.1.
Tel: 01-930 3664
World famous shoemaker where all shoes are entirely hand made and lasts are cut in wood.

Map Ref. 3G

Maxwell's
177 New Bond Street, W.1.
Tel: 01-493 1097
Famous for their riding boots they also hand make shoes of all kinds.

Map Ref. 3G

Anello & Davide
30 Drury Lane, W.C.2.
Tel: 01-836 1983
Specialising in theatrical shoes, they will make any type to order.

Map Ref. 2H

Chelsea Cobbler
164 Fulham Road, S.W.3.inches.
Tel: 01-373 6115
Among the beautiful boots and shoes here you are sure to find something. Otherwise you can have your own special shoes made to measure.
Map Ref. 5D

Egli
2 Windmill Street, Tottenham Court Road, W.1.
Tel: 01-636 5861
Both ladies' and men's shoes made here to a high standard and design.
Map Ref. 1G

Foster and Son
83 Jermyn Street, S.W.1.
Tel: 01-930 5385
A well-established gentlemen's boot and shoe maker. Long waiting list so it's not for those in a hurry, but worth the wait. Hunting boots a speciality.
Map Ref. 3G

Deliss
41 Beauchamp Place, S.W.1.
Tel: 01-584 3321
Pretty shoes made to your specification or own lovely styles. Boots as well.
Map Ref. 5E

THEATRICAL

Anello and Davide
96 Charing Cross Road, W.C.2.
Tel: 01-836 5019
Really for theatrical shoes but they will tackle other styles and evening shoes.
Map Ref. 2H

Frederick Freed
Cecil Court, St. Martin's Lane, W.C.2.
Tel: 01-240 0432
Also theatrical and evening shoes — very pretty. A family business where you get real attention.
Map Ref. 3H

Savva
37 Chiltern Street, W.1.
Tel: 01-935 2329
A family craftsman business which will tackle almost any style for you and take great care that you get what you want.
Map Ref. 2F

DEPARTMENT STORES

London is famous for its large Department Stores where you can buy most things if you do not have the time to visit individual shops.

Harrods
Knightsbridge, S.W.1.
Tel: 01-730 1234
It would be impossible to describe here in detail the wonder of Harrods. Suffice to say that it is possibly the best store in the world and every visitor to London should visit it.
Map Ref. 4E

Selfridges
Oxford Street, W.1.
Tel: 01-629 1234
Another London shopping institution where you can browse for hours in the vast household, furniture, fashion and toy departments.
Map Ref. 2F

Harvey Nichols
Knightsbridge, S.W.1.
Tel: 01-235 5000
A very smart store that carries all the big-name designers in fashion. furnishings and cosmetics. Has very good accessories, too, a small but good restaurant, hairdressing and beauty salon. Very feminine, though the Men's Department is good as well.
Map Ref. 4E

Fortnum & Masons
181 Piccadilly, W.1.
Tel: 01-734 8040
Yet another world-famous store which specialises in exotic foods, luxury goods and an old English atmosphere.
Map Ref. 3G

John Lewis
Oxford Street, W.1.
Tel: 01-629 7711
Modern store with the largest dress fabric department in London. Huge household displays and furnishing fabrics.
Map Ref. 2G

Liberty's
Regent Street, W.1.
Tel: 01-734 1234
A lovely store which combines 'Old-England' with modern display. Famous for printed fabrics.
Map Ref. 2G

Peter Jones
Sloane Square, S.W.3.
Tel: 01-730 3434
Largest furnishing fabric department in London but also specialises in linens, glass, china and furniture.
Map Ref. 5F

Army & Navy Stores
Victoria Street, S.W.1.
Tel: 01-834 1234
Very large store which has an excellent food hall besides a very good range of other goods.
Map Ref. 4G

Barkers
Kensington High Street, W.8.
Tel: 01-937 5432
Large store which sells a full range of goods.
Map Ref. 4C

DRY-CLEANERS

Jeeves
8 Pont Street, S.W.1.
Tel: 01-235 1101
Excellent cleaners with hand-finished articles. Collection in Central London. Laundry for shirts.
Map Ref. 4F

Liliman & Cox
34 Bruton Place, W.1.
Tel: 01-629 4555
Very high quality cleaners particularly with special articles.
Map Ref. 3F

Collins
88 Jermyn Street, S.W.1.
Tel: 01-839 5172
Same-day cleaning for some items if taken before 10.00am.
Map Ref. 3G

Lewis and Wayne
13 Elystan Street, S.W.3.
Tel: 01-589 5730
Very good cleaners for all clothes, evening wear a speciality.
Map Ref. 5E

FABRICS

Fine Dress Fabrics
87 Baker Street, W.1.
Tel: 01-935 5876
Exactly what it says — an interesting collection of dress fabrics.
Map Ref. 2F

Jasons
53 New Bond Street, W.1.
Tel: 01-629 2606
Sumptuous silks and evening dress fabrics alongside very fine wools make this a shop to linger in.
Map Ref. 3G

The Fabric Shop
6 Cale Street, S.W.3.
Tel: 01-584 8495
Paradise for furnishing fabrics — some very nice own designs found here.
Map Ref. 5E

Designer's Guild
277 King's Road, S.W.3.
Tel: 01-351 1271
Some distinctive fabrics for home furnishings can be found in this smart and modern interior design shop. Colour co-ordination a speciality.
Map Ref. 6D

Department stores having very good fabric departments are:

John Lewis
Peter Jones
Dickins and Jones
Liberty's — the home of distinguished Liberty prints.

FLOWER SHOPS AND HOUSE PLANTS

Feltons
220 Brompton Road, S.W.3.
Tel: 01-589 4433
Also Cheapside, E.C.2.
Tel: 01-236 7261
A famous shop which aims to sell cut flowers which are fresh. One of the oldest flower shops, they believe in keeping the produce properly and at the right temperature.
Map Ref. 5E

Pulbrook & Gould
181 Sloane Street, S.W.1.
Tel: 01-235 3920
Beautiful selection of fresh cut flowers and plants.
Map Ref. 5E

Moyses Stevens
Berkeley Square, W.1.
Tel: 01-493 8171
Famous for floral arrangements, dried flowers, they also make wreaths and supply flowering plants as well as fresh cut flowers.
Map Ref. 3F

Pugh & Carr
26 Gloucester Road, S.W.7.
Tel: 01-584 7181
Flower shop with fresh and dried flowers. Good Plants.
Map Ref. 5D

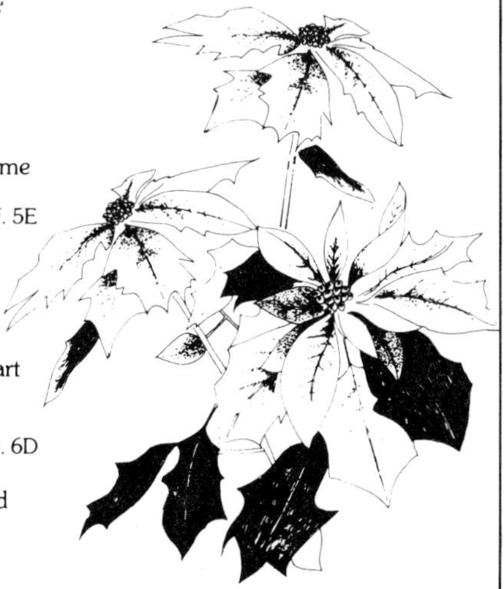

Chivers
43 Charlotte Street, W.1.
Tel: 01-580 1761
Also 68 Marchmont Street, W.C.1.
and
129 Tottenham Court Road, W.C.2.
Charlotte Street also has a vending machine outside the shop to sell flowers after hours.
Map Ref. 2G

Rassell's
80 Earls Court Road, W.8.
Tel: 01-937 0481
A total gardening service selling everything for garden and home and also landscaping.
Map Ref. 5B

Cliftons
50 Clifton Villas, Warwick Avenue, W.9.
Tel: 01-289 6851
One of the largest selection of house plants in London, and everything in the garden.
Map Ref. 1D

Flower House
315 Brompton Road, S.W.3.
Tel: 01-584 4141
Very good selection of unusual house plants, flowers and dried flowers.
Map Ref. 5E

Woolworths
See Telephone Directory for branches. Good reputation for selling inexpensive plants.
No Map Ref.

Tropical Plants Display
64 Emlyn Road, W.12.
Tel: 01-743 8777
Exotic tropical plants and palms, made into displays for offices only.
No Map Ref.

S R Milward
36 Tavistock Street, W.C.2.
Tel: 01-836 6489
Specialises in most palms and other sub-tropical plants. Contracts only.
Map Ref. 2H

FOOD SHOPS

Most food can be obtained at any small grocer, market or supermarket. This section concentrates on those shops which either specialise in particular foods or sell outstandingly good food with a personal service.

BREAD AND PATISSERIES

Maison Sagne
105 Marylebone High Street, W.1.
Tel: 01-935 6240
A delightful shop with a small café which sells mouth-watering patisseries and petit fours.
Map Ref. 2F

Patisserie Valerie
44 Old Crompton Street, W.1.
Tel: 01-437 3466
French style patisserie with delicious croissants all of which you can sample in the café section.
Map Ref. 3G

Maison Bertraux
28 Greek Street, W.1.
Tel: 01-437 6007
The oldest and one of the best French patisseries in London. Famous for French gateaux. Also has a small coffee lounge. Good croissants.
Map Ref. 3G

Dugdale & Adams
3 Gerrard Street, W.1.
Tel: 01-437 3864
Traditional underground ovens bake some of the finest French bread in London.
Map Ref. 3G

Clark's
27 Peter Street, W.1.
Tel: 01-437 6622
Home made dark rye bread is the speciality of this baker.
Map Ref. 2G

Patisserie Francaise
127 Queensway, W.2.
Tel: 01-229 0746
With nearly 30 varieties of bread and hundreds of cakes all hand baked, this is an outstanding bakery and patisserie.
Map Ref. 3C

Beatons
134 Kings Road, S.W.3
Tel: 01-589 6263
Baking on the premises, this shop is famous for its white loaves, rolls and cakes.
Map Ref. 4D

Justin de Blank
46 Walton Street, S.W.3.
Tel: 01-589 4734
Noted for traditional English crusted bread baked in brick ovens which are over a hundred years old. Also various assortments of pies, quiches and sandwiches.
Map Ref. 5E

Ceres
269 Portobello Road, W.11.
Tel: 01-229 5571
Producing exclusively wholefood and wholewheat bread. Also herbs and homeopathic remedies.
Map Ref. 3B

Rolando's
33 Tavistock Place, W.C.1.
Tel: 01-387 3876
Excellent French bread and a marvellous selection of pastries.
Map Ref. 1H

Maison Verlon
12 Bute Street, S.W.7.
Tel: 01-584 0485
Delicious cakes, tarts and pastries baked to French and Austrian recipes.
Map Ref. 5D

Le Relais Basque
28 Westbourne Grove, W.2.
Tel: 01-229 2107
Superb French patisseries, croissants and brioches.
Map Ref. 2B

Harrods
Knightsbridge, S.W.1.
Tel: 01-730 1234
In the food section of this store there is a large counter of various home made bread and cakes.
Map Ref. 4E

BUTCHERS

John Baily
116 Mount Street, W.1.
Tel: 01-499 1833
Magnificent selection of poultry and game with personal and knowledgeable service.
Map Ref. 3F

Harrods
Knightsbridge, S.W.1.
Tel: 01-730 1234
Probably the most imposing meat counter anywhere in the world. It is possible to get the very best cuts of all meat. Very wide selection of game also on show.
Map Ref. 4E

Bifulco
24 Frith Street, W.1.
Tel: 01-437 5279
Also 82 St. Johns Wood High Street, N.W.8.
Wide variety of continental cuts and specialities such as chicken kievs, kebabs, racks of lamb, home made sausages. Good, friendly service.
Map Ref. 3G

Allen
117 Mount Street, W.1.
Tel: 01-499 5831
Sell only the very best meat, Dutch veal, English lamb and Scotch beef. Established over two hundred years.
Map Ref. 3F

Druce & Craddock
24 Marylebone High Street, W.1.
Tel: 01-935 3600
Helpful service and the best meat. Also famous for their sausages.
Map Ref. 2F

J & J Dalli
78 Brewer Street, W.1.
Tel: 01-437 8870
Specialising in continental cuts, they sell only first class meat. They also cater for French, Italian and Arab cuisines.
Map Ref. 3G

W Fenn
27 Frith Street, W.1.
Tel: 01-437 4181
Excellent poultry and game and, when in season, venison.
Map Ref. 3G

Slater & Cooke
67 Brewer Street, W.1.
Tel: 01-437 2026
A lovely shop to purchase meat as each kind of meat has its own counter. Well displayed and the service is helpful.
Map Ref. 3G

Randall & Aubin
16 Brewer Street, W.1.
Tel: 01-437 3507
French cuts from top quality meat and French sausages, charcuterie.
Map Ref. 3G

C Lidgate
10 Holland Park Avenue, W.11.
Tel: 01-727 8243
Gracious and courteous, specialising in good meat and game, magnificent

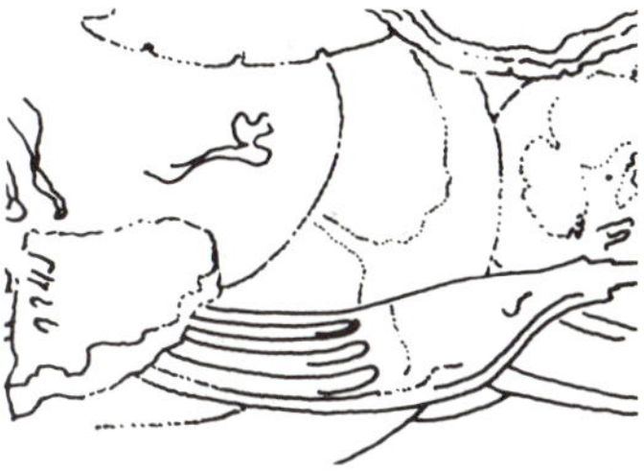

home made sausages, flans and pies. Catering service.
Map Ref. 4A

Cobb
5 Sloane Street, S.W.1.
Tel: 01-235 5377
Family-run firm with a first class reputation, they sell only the best meat.
Map Ref. 5E

Curnick
106 Draycott Avenue,
Tel: 01-589 8452
Friendly service selling continental cuts, home made sausages. English lamb and Scottish beef a speciality.
Map Ref. 5E

A A King
30 New Kings Road, S.W.6.
Tel: 01-736 4004
Good selection of meat and game.
Map Ref. 5F

CHEESE

Paxton & Whitfield
93 Jermyn Street, S.W.1.
Tel: 01-930 0259
Old fashioned but delightful shop. They let you try any cheese you may wish to purchase from the vast range. Cheddar and Stilton are specialities. Also serve cooked hams.
Map Ref. 3G

Harrods
Knightsbridge, S.W.1.
Tel: 01-730 1234
Enormous cheese department with hundreds of varieties of English and continental cheeses including some French cheeses which are difficult to obtain elsewhere.
Map Ref. 4E

Fortnum & Mason
181 Piccadilly, W.1.
Tel: 01-734 8040
A small but excellent selection of prime cheeses always in good condition, found in this luxurious store.
Map Ref. 3G

G Parmigiano Figlio
36 Old Compton Street, W.1.
Tel: 01-437 4728
If you want Italian cheese this is the shop to visit. Magnificent selection.
Map Ref. 3G

Justin de Blank
42 Elizabeth Street, W.1.
Tel: 01-730 0605
Specialises in English Cheddar and French Brie, some 2 years old. All brought straight from the farm.
Map Ref. 5F

Mr. Christians
11 Elgin Crescent, W.11.
Tel: 01-229 0501
There is an excellent range of cheeses in this deli.
Map Ref. 2B

CHOCOLATES

Prestat
40 South Molton Street, W.1.
Tel: 01-629 4838
French style handmade chocolates, they are noted for their truffles, made to a Napoleonic recipe.
Map Ref. 2F

Bendicks
55 Wigmore Street, W.1.
Tel: 01-235 4744
Also 195 Sloane Street, S.W.1.
One of the largest producers of chocolates, they specialise in Bittermints and Mint Crisps.
Map Ref. 3G

Clares
3 Park Road, Baker Street, N.W.1.
Tel: 01-262 1906
Also 163 George Street, W.1.
Superb liqueur chocolates, truffles and Easter eggs, most handmade.
Map Ref. 1F

Charbonnel et Walker
31 Old Bond Street, W.1.
Tel: 01-629 4396
Handmade chocolates with delicious centres made with fresh ingredients.
Map Ref. 3G

Fortnum & Mason
181 Piccadilly, W.1.
Tel: 01-734 8040
An excellent selection of handmade chocolates and truffles.
Map Ref. 3G

COFFEE AND TEA

Three Star Products
11 Delancey Street, N.W.1.
Tel: 01-387 4080
All types of coffee sold with friendly, helpful service.
No Map Ref.

Costa Coffee Boutique
324 Vauxhall Bridge Road, S.W.1.
Tel: 01-828 5215
An interesting shop where you can sample the coffee before making a purchase. They also sell various types of coffee making equipment.
Map Ref. 5G

Harrods
Knightsbridge, S.W.1.
Tel: 01-730 1234
An excellent selection of coffee and one of the finest ranges of tea.
Map Ref. 4E

Drury Teas & Coffee Co.
3 New Row, W.C.2.
Tel: 01-836 1960
Special blends and delicious coffee can be bought here — freshly roasted too.
Map Ref. 2H

Carwardine
70 Old Compton Street, W.1.
Tel: 01-437 4177
Fascinating shop with practically every coffee you can think of — and some more too. Also tea.
Map Ref. 3G

Fern & Co.
27 Rathbone Place, W.1.
Tel: 01-636 2237
Also at Covent Garden Piazza.
Good stock of brand name teas and coffee — very pleasant shop.
Map Ref. 2G

Fortnum & Mason
181 Piccadilly, W.1.
Tel: 01-734 8040
Very special teas and blend make an outstanding department — even the more popular names, such as Earl Grey, are blended to a particular Fortnum way. Try some of their own teas.
Map Ref. 3G

Whittards
111 Fulham Road, S.W.3.
Tel: 01-589 4261
A specialist shop that is very helpful.
Map Ref. 6D

Markus
13 Connaught Street, W.2.
Tel: 01-723 4020
Good products and special care taken in this shop. Own blends of coffee.
Map Ref. 2E

H R Higgins
42 South Molton Street, W.1.
Tel: 01-629 3913
Delicious smell of roasting coffee proclaims this small but wonderful shop full of exquisite coffee beans from all over the world.
Map Ref. 2F

FISH SHOPS

Harrods
Knightsbridge, S.W.1.
Tel: 01-730 1234
Their fish display has been photographed thousands of times. Superb selection of fresh fish of all kinds.
Map Ref. 4E

Richards
11 Brewer Street, W.1.
Tel: 01-437 1358
Unusual fish sold here as well as good lobsters and crabs.
Map Ref. 3G

Cecil & Co.
23 Romilly Street, W.1.
Tel: 01-437 4063
Small fish shop always selling an excellent selection of fresh fish.
Map Ref. 3G

John Gow
55 Connaught Street, W.2.
Tel: 01-723 1612
Popular fishmonger selling good prawns and shell fish.
Map Ref. 2E

J Mist & Sons
254 Battersea Park Road, S.W.11.
Tel: 01-228 6784
Family fishmonger established many years. Selling all types of fresh fish and their own smoked fish.
No Map Ref.

J F Blagdens
65 Paddington Street, W.1.
Tel: 01-935 8321
Specialising in crab and lobster, they also sell a marvellous selection of fresh fish and various smoked types.
Map Ref. 2F

FOREIGN FOOD SHOPS

London is full of Ethnic Food Shops which have good foods of the country of origin — generally patronised by the people of that realm who live in London. If you are nostalgic for the food of your own country do visit them, they are a home from home. If you are English buy the things you enjoyed on holiday and add variety to your eating.

ASIAN

Osaka
17 Goldhurst Terrace, N.W.6.
Tel: 01-624 4983
No Map Ref.

CHINESE

Chtong-Leen
4 Tower Street, W.1.
Tel: 01-836 5378
Map Ref. 2H

Hong Kong Supermarket Great Wall
31 Wardour Street, W.1.
Tel: 01-437 7963
Map Ref. 3G

FRENCH

Randall & Aubin
36 Brewer Street, W.1.
Tel: 01-437 3507
Map Ref. 3G

Le Cochon Rose
83 Lower Sloane Street, S.W.1.
Tel: 01-730 2898
Map Ref. 5F

Maison Bouquillon
41 Moscow Road, W.2.
Tel: 01-727 4897
Map Ref. 3C

GERMAN

The German Food Centre
44 Knightsbridge, S.W.1.
Tel: 01-235 5760
Map Ref. 4F

GREEK

Hellenic Stores
51 St. John's Wood High Street, N.W.8.
Tel: 01-586 3400
Map Ref. 2G

Athenian Grocery
16a Moscow Road, W.2.
Tel: 01-229 6280
Map Ref. 3C

INDIAN

Golden Orient
61 Berwick Street, W.1.
Tel: 01-437 1817
Map Ref. 3G

Sharuna
107 Great Russell Street, W.C.1.
Tel: 01-636 5922
Map Ref. 1H

INDONESIAN

Ganesha
6 Park Walk, S.W.10.
Tel: 01-352 8972
No Map Ref.

ITALIAN

Lina
18 Brewer Street, W.1.
Tel: 01-437 6482
Map Ref. 3G

Camisia & Son
61 Old Compton Street, W.1.
Tel: 01-437 4686
Map Ref. 3G

Fratelli Camisa
1a Berwick Street, W.1.
Tel: 01-437 7120
Map Ref. 3G

Bellusci
39 South Lambeth Road, S.W.8.
Tel: 01-582 0766
No Map Ref.

Luigi
60 New Kings Road, S.W.6.
Tel: 01-731 4994
Map Ref. 6D

JEWISH

Joelsons
28 Peter Street, W.1.
Tel: 01-437 5261
Map Ref. 2G

SCANDINAVIAN

Scandinavian Shop
170 Brompton Road, S.W.3.
Tel: 01-589 7804
Map Ref. 4E

SWISS

Swiss Centre
Leicester Square, W.C.2.
Tel: 01-734 1291
Map Ref. 3H

Bartholdi
4 Charlotte Street, W.1.
Tel: 01-636 3762
Map Ref. 2G

FRUIT AND VEGETABLES

Kirkhams
423 Kings Road, S.W.3.
Tel: 01-352 2200
An excellent greengrocer which, besides selling the more unusual vegetables, also stocks good fresh fruit.
Map Ref. 6D

Buy-Rite Fruit Store
29 Bute Street, S.W.7.
Tel: 01-581 0039
Very good value from this nice shop. Helpful service and a good range of produce.
Map Ref. 5D

Fruit Bowl
39 Marchmont Street, W.C.1.
Tel: 01-837 5531
Good selection of first class fruit and vegetables.
Map Ref. 2H

Hazell
172 Fulham Road, S.W.10.
Tel: 01-373 7943
Specialise in exotic fruits and vegetables. Very fresh and good quality.
Map Ref. 6D

Michanicou Brothers
2 Clarendon Road, W.11.
Tel: 01-727 5191
Being a family business the personal service is friendly and helpful. Excellent quality fruit and vegetables.
Map Ref. 2A

The Farm Shop
1 Neal's Yard, W.C.2.
Tel: 01-836 1066
Organically grown vegetables and fruit.
Map Ref. 3H

The following department stores also have excellent fruit and vegetable departments.

Harrods
Knightsbridge, S.W.1.
Map Ref. 4E

Selfridges
Oxford Street, W.1.
Map Ref. 2F

Fortnum & Mason
Piccadilly, W.1.
Map Ref. 3G

Barker
Kensington High Street, W.8.
Map Ref. 4C

The following streets have very good markets where you can buy an amazing amount of fruit and vegetables.

Portobello Road, W.11.
Berwick Street, W.1.
North End Road, S.W.6.

HEALTH FOOD SHOPS

The following shops specialise in Health Foods — vegetarian or otherwise. Especially good for wholemeal bread, sometimes made in specialist bakeries, together with nuts, grains, pulses and, often, cosmetics that are natural and not tested on animals.

Cranks Health Foods
8 Marshall Street, W.1.
Tel: 01-437 2915
Really a group of shops selling various aspects of vegetarian foods — also a restaurant and take-away food. Other restaurants in Heal's, Peter Robinson, Covent Garden.
Map Ref. 2G

Wholefood
112 Baker Street, W.1.
Tel: 01-935 3924
A shop selling very very good compost grown vegetables and groceries that will help you carry out the wholefood regime.
Map Ref. 2F

Ceres
269a Portobello Road, W.11.
Tel: 01-229 5571
Wholefood bakers who also sell wholegrains, beans, seeds and a good selection of health wholefoods.
Map Ref. 3B

Neal's Yard Warehouse
21 Short's Gardens, W.C.2.
Tel: 01-240 1154
A converted warehouse which sells everything in the health food line. Excellent for honey and nuts.
Map Ref. 3H

Holland and Barrett
A chain of health food shops throughout London. Addresses can be obtained through the Telephone Directory.

FURRIERS

The maxim "you get for what you pay" is particularly true when you buy a fur coat — the more you are prepared to spend, the better the skins and workmanship. And do not think that a coat you have made especially for you is going to be more expensive — it won't necessarily be, and if it is, it will give you far greater length of wear. Most furriers prefer to make for you, though many do have stocks from which you can select.
All the salons mentioned here are members of the BRITISH FUR TRADERS ASSOCIATION whose workmanship and value can be trusted. As London is the centre of the trade in furs (through the Hudson Bay Company), it is a fine place to look for a fur coat.

Berg
40/41 Conduit Street, W.1.
Tel: 01-734 5077
Beautiful and unusual skins are the hallmark of this very smart shop.
Map Ref.

Calman Links
241 Brompton Road, W.1.
Tel: 01-581 1927
All the lovely fur coats the Queen wears originated here. Calman Links will make a coat at *your* price too.
Map Ref. 4E

Fabian Furs
36 Knightsbridge, S.W.3.
Tel: 01-235 5572
A good place to find the fur you want — and great care is taken to help you.
Map Ref. 4F

Zhivago Furs
2 Portman Square, W.1.
Tel: 01-935 5092
A very smart salon which has some fantastic coats and jackets. Middle price range.
Map Ref. 2F

Furs Renée
39 Dover Street, W.1.
Tel: 01-499 4980
For really glamorous and unusual furs this is the place — besides working in one type of fur for a coat, **Furs Renée** combine often two or more furs in a design.
Map Ref. 3G

Massin Furs
50 Wigmore Street, W.1.
Tel: 01-487 4479
Very smart salon which has some unusual coats and jackets in fine mink, sable, fox and other furs.
Map Ref. 2F

Rema Furs
18 Hanover Street, W.1.
Tel: 01-629 9563
A practical company where great interest is taken that both the skins and the designs are right for you. Specialists in BLACKGLAMA Mink.
Map Ref. 3G

West Furs
21 Heddon Street, W.1.
Tel: 01-734 0777
Good designs combined with good skins just can't go wrong. Very feminine styling.
Map Ref. 3G

Witte
1 Hanover Street, W.1.
Tel: 01-734 2421/2423
Another furrier who combines good skins and good designs — and a distinctive touch.
Map Ref. 3G

Zwirn
120 Wigmore Street, W.1.
Tel: 01-486 4671
Luxurious furs and pretty designs are the thing that make Zwirn's an outstanding place to visit. Glamorous.
Map Ref. 2F

Department stores with good fur departments:
good collection of different furs at varying prices. Some very luxurious models, too.
Harvey Nichols — an exceptional fur department, including **Bradleys.**
John Lewis, Barkers, Selfridges, Dickins and Jones all have fur departments with reasonably priced furs.

GUN SHOPS

London is renowned for its fine craftsmanship when it comes to the making of guns. The following shops uphold this tradition. Expert advice and excellent workmanship are of paramount importance to these old-established places.

Holland & Holland
33 Bruton Street, W.1.
Tel: 01-499 4411
Map Ref. 3G

James Purdey & Son
57 South Audley Street, W.1.
Tel: 01-499 5292
Map Ref. 3F

Boss
13 Dover Street, W.1.
Tel: 01-493 0711
Map Ref. 3G

John Rigby
13 Pall Mall, S.W.1.
Tel: 01-734 7611
Map Ref. 3G

HAIRDRESSERS

Aldobruno
22 Motcomb Street, S.W.1.
Tel: 01-235 7275
Tube: Knightsbridge.
Stylish salon which excels in cutting and tinting. Conservative styling.
Map Ref. 4F

Andre Bernard
41 Knightsbridge, S.W.1.
Tel: 01-629 4314
Tube: Hyde Park.
Very feminine styling with emphasis on making you pretty. The London salon of a very successful chain of hairdressers.
Map Ref. 4F

Ocean Boulevard
17 Tavistock Street, Covent Garden, W.C.2.
Tel: 01-240 1450
Tube: Covent Garden.
A young, zany salon which does some very good cutting and tinting.
Map Ref. 3H

Cadogan Club
182 Sloane Street, S.W.1.
Tel: 01-235 3814
Tube: Knightsbridge.
Smart styling in this modern salon which numbers some distinguished women among its clients.
Map Ref. 4E

Crimpers
80a Baker Street, W.1.
Tel: 01-486 4522
Tube: Baker Street.
The first of the Crimpers salons — the others are at:
63 Heath Street, N.W.3.
Tel: 01-794 8625
Map Ref. 2F
231 Brompton Road, S.W.1.
Tel: 01-584 3671
Map Ref. 4E

Glemby at Fenwicks
Bond Street, W.1.
Tel: 01-629 9161
Tube: Bond Street.
One of the Glemby chain; modern do styling at reasonable prices.
prices.
Map Ref. 3G

John of Knightsbridge
31 Thurloe Place, S.W.5.
Tel: 01-589 1282
Tube: South Kensington.
Good styling and cutting is the hall-mark of this elegant salon.
Map Ref. 4E

Leonard
6 Upper Grosvenor Street, W.1.
Tel: 01-629 5757
Tube: Oxford Circus or Green Park.
Considered by many to be the best hairdresser in London. Expensive but great care is taken of your hair.
Map Ref. 3F

Michaeljohn
23a Albemarle Street, W.1.
Tel: 01-629 6969
Tube: Green Park.
Princess Anne's hairdresser — a salon where you get very pretty styling suited to you and the occasion. n.
Map Ref. 3G

Molton Brown
58 South Molton Street, W.1.
Tel: 01-629 1872
Tube: Bond Street.
Good cutting; great care taken of the health of your hair. Often herbal products are used.
Map Ref. 2F

Robert Fielding
215 Regent Street, W.1.
Tel: 01-734 3231
Tube: Piccadilly or Oxford Street, W.1.
One of a chain of good, reasonably priced hairdressers.
Map Ref. 2G

Sissors
46 King's Road, S.W.3.
Tel: 01-589 9471
Tube: Sloane Square.
Very modern salon that does superb cutting. Unisex. You don't have to have the latest style — but they are good at it!
Map Ref. 5E

Vidal Sassoon
Grosvenor House Hotel,
Park Lane, W.1.
Tel: 01-499 3740
Tube: Hyde Park.
Now the main Sassoon salon — there are several others scattered over London, including Sloane Street, S.W.1. As always you can be sure of a superb cut.
Map Ref. 3F

HAIRDRESSERS FOR MEN

Michaeljohn
6 Carlos Place, W.1.
Tel: 01-499 2125
Tube: Green Park.
Modern styling with great care taken to see that it suits you.
Map Ref. 3F

Trumpers
9 Curzon Street, W.1.
Tel: 01-499 1850
Tube: Green Park.
A traditional gentlemen's barber — used by the conservative.
Map Ref. 3F

Truefitt and Hill
23 Old Bond Street, W.1.
Tel: 01-493 2961
Tube: Green Park.
Another traditional barber which does conservative, but very good work.
Map Ref. 3G

Vidal Sassoon
56 Brook Street, W.1.
Tel: 01-409 0925
Tube: Bond Street.
The male outpost of the Sassoon Empire — very good styling and cutting.
Map Ref. 3F

Sissors
46 Kings Road, S.W.3.
Tel: 01-589 9471
Tube: Sloane Square.
Unisex salon, strictly for the young and modern. Good cutting.
Map Ref. 5E

The following shops and hotels have good hairdressing departments:

Harrods
Knightsbridge, S.W.1.
Tel: 01-730 1234
Austin Reed
Regent Street, W.1. Tel: 01-734 6789
Piccadilly Hotel
Piccadilly, W.1. Tel: 01-734 0010
Savoy Hotel
The Strand, W.C.2. Tel: 01-836 4343

HERBALISTS

Besides the Health Food Shops already listed there are many shops in London where you can find a selection of herbs both fresh and dried, among them:

Culpepper
21 Bruton Street, W.1.
Tel: 01-499 2306
A marvellous selection of dried herbs, medicines, cosmetics and pot-pourris.
Map Ref. 3F

Justin de Blank
42 Elizabeth Street, S.W.1.
Tel: 01-730 0605
Over 100 different dried and fresh herbs and a wide range of oils, vinegars and herbal teas.
Map Ref. 5E

Randall & Aubin
16 Brewer Street, W.1.
Tel: 01-437 3507
Basically a French delicatessen, they also sell fresh herbs.
Map Ref. 3G

Dandelion
256 Battersea Park Road, S.W.11.
Tel: 01-223 9211
Wide range of culinary and medicinal herbs.
No Map Ref.

HOUSEHOLD

If you are looking for household equipment of any kind the following stores have a good selection of the standard brands available:

Harrods
Knightsbridge, S.W.1.
Tel: 01-730 1234
Map Ref. 4E

Selfridges
Oxford Street, W.1.
Tel: 01-629 1234
Map Ref. 2F

John Lewis
Oxford Street, W.1.
Tel: 01-629 7711
Map Ref. 2G

Peter Jones
Sloane Square, S.W.1.
Tel: 01-730 3434
Map Ref. 5E

Barkers
Kensington High Street, W.8.
Tel: 01-937 5432
Map Ref. 4C

Heal's
Tottenham Court Road, W.1.
Tel: 01-636 1666
Map Ref. 1G

ELECTRICAL APPLIANCES

Buyers and Sellers
120 Ladbroke Grove, W.10.
Tel: 01-229 1947
Map Ref. 1A

KITCHEN FURNITURE

Wrighton Showrooms
3 Portman Square, W.1.
Tel: 01-486 4575
Map Ref. 2F

Just Kitchens
206 Upper Richmond Road, S.W.14.
Tel: 01-876 6106
No Map Ref.

Building Centre
26 Store Street, W.C.1.
Tel: 01-637 1022
Map Ref. 2G

KITCHEN EQUIPMENT

Divertimenti
68 Marylebone Lane, W.1.
Tel: 01-935 0689
A small shop with an interesting collection of batterie de cuisine — plain and good.
Map Ref. 2F

French Kitchen
86 Westbourne Grove, W.2.
Tel: 01-229 5530
Mostly French merchandise in this enterprising shop.
Map Ref. 2B

Elizabeth David
46 Bourne Street, S.W.1.
Tel: 01-730 3123
Started by the famous author-cook, though no longer run by her, this shop has everything practical that is needed in the kitchen.
Map Ref. 5F

David Mellor
4 Sloane Square, S.W.1.
Tel: 01-730 4259
Also at 26 James Street, W.C.2.
Tel: 01-374 6947
A spacious shop full of things to help you be an expert cook — modern in design and very practical.
Map Ref. 5F

Merchant Chandler
72 New King's Road, S.W.6.
Tel: 01-736 6141
A shop full of interesting items for your kitchen and house — good, original merchandise.
Map Ref. 6D

William Page
91 Shaftesbury Avenue, W.1.
Tel: 01-437 8888
Suppliers to many restaurants, Page's sell good, down-to-earth merchandise that is thoroughly professional and without decoration.
Map Ref. 3G

Richard Dare
93 Regent's Park Road, N.W.1.
Tel: 01-722 9428
A pleasant place to look for kitchen equipment in a part of London that is not well-endowed with this kind of shop. Unique French merchandise.
Map Ref. 1F

Habitat
206 King's Road, S.W.3. and branches.
Tel: 01-351 1211
With a style of its own — Habitat always has something original to please you.
Map Ref. 5E

BATHROOM FITTINGS AND FIXTURES

Bonsack
14 Mount Street, W.1.
Tel: 01-629 9981
The ultimate in bathroom fittings and fixtures — very luxurious.
Map Ref. 3F

W.1. Bathrooms
18 North Audley Street, W.1.
Tel: 01-499 1845
A pleasant place to discuss your bathroom requirements — work to a high standard.
Map Ref. 2F

Bathroom Centre
204 Great Portland Street, W.1.
Tel: 01-388 7631
A practical place which will help you to get a good bathroom.
No Map Ref.

BEDDING

London Bedding Centre
26 Sloane Street, S.W.1.
Tel: 01-235 7542
A comprehensive selection of standard beds of all shapes and sizes.
Map Ref. 4E

Bedpost Ltd
43 Wigmore Street, W.1.
Tel: 01-486 3094
An exotic selection of custom-made beds that will make any bedroom look brilliant and original.
Map Ref. 2F

Heal's
196 Tottenham Court Road, W.C.1.
Tel: 01-636 1666
Heal's will make a bed for you in almost any size, length or shape. Particularly fine beds — you can even have one side soft, the other hard if you like!
Map Ref. 1G

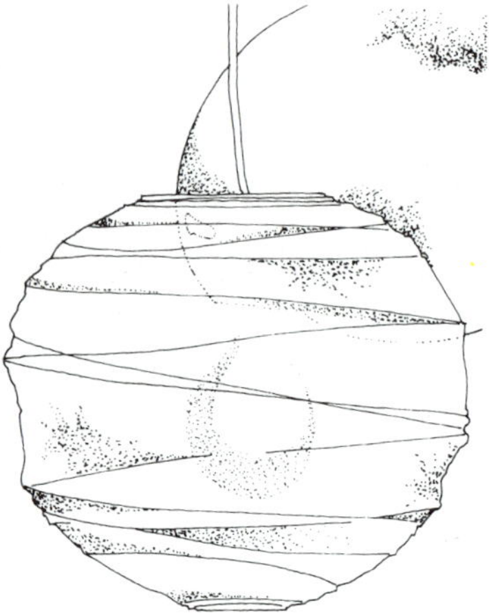

LIGHTING & LAMPS

These shops have an original and often custom-made selection of lamps and shades that are different from the standard ones found in the department stores:

Clare House
35 Elizabeth Street, S.W.1.
Tel: 01-730 8480
Map Ref. 5F

Nita Miller
42 Grosvenor Hill, W.1.
Tel: 01-629 0951
Map Ref. 3F

Arnold Montrose
47 Berners Street, W.1.
Tel: 01-580 5316
Map Ref. 2G

Christopher Wray
600 King's Road, S.W.1.
Tel: 01-736 8434
Map Ref. 6D

FURNISHING

Heal's
196 Tottenham Court Road, W.C.1.
Tel: 01-636 1666
A delightful shop that is full of the best of modern design in furniture, fabrics and carpets. A treat to wander around.
Map Ref. 1G

Maples
145 Tottenham Court Road, W.1.
Tel: 01-387 7000
One of several Maples shops which are mainly concerned with conventional furnishings.
Map Ref. 1G

Conran Shop
77 Fulham Road, S.W.18.
Tel: 01-589 7401
Full of modern ideas and original work — the standard look of today.
Map Ref. 5E

Habitat
206 King's Road, S.W.3.
Tel: 01-351 1211
One of the several shops which sell the Habitat style of furnishings and furniture. Always worth looking at.
Map Ref. 5E

Tulleys
289 Fulham Road, S.W.10.
Tel: 01-352 1078
A shop with interesting and desirable merchandise.
Map Ref. 6D

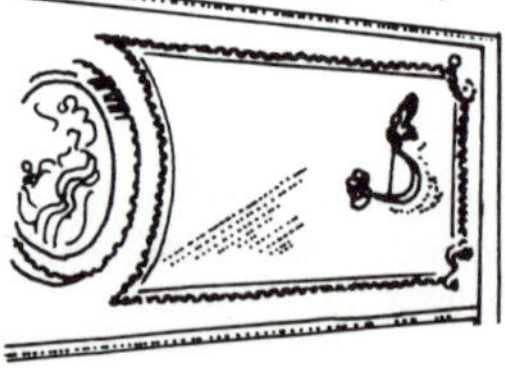

Albrizzi
1 Sloane Street, S.W.1.
Tel: 01-730 6119
A smart shop with mainly Italian styled merchandise — very modern.
Map Ref. 5F

Simmonds
180 North Gower Street, N.W.1.
Tel: 01-387 4746
Good reproduction and second hand furniture.
Map Ref. 1G

Designers Guild
277 King's Road, S.W.3.
Tel: 01-351 1271
A gentle approach to furnishings characterises the Designers Guild look.
Map Ref. 5E

Abode
779 Fulham Road, S.W.6.
Tel: 01-736 3161
Another place which has interesting ideas on interiors.
Map Ref. 6C

Aram Designs
3 Kean Street, W.C.2.
Tel: 01-240 3933
An original and interesting shop of designer's work.
Map Ref. 1H

JEWELLERS

Antrobus
11 New Bond Street, W.1.
Tel: 01-493 4557
194 Sloane Street, S.W.1.
Tel: 01-235 1154
Specialists in very pretty Victorian and antique jewellery. Charming shop with always something very special for a present.
Map Ref. 3G

Asprey's
165-169 New Bond Street, W.1.
Tel: 01-493 6767
A shop full of many beautiful things suitable for presents with a select jewellery and silver section. Everything in excellent taste.
Map Ref. 3G

Boucheron
18 New Bond Street, W.1.
Tel: 01-493 0983
Elegant designs with imagination and good stones are the hallmark of Boucheron's work. Contemporary styling.
Map Ref. 3G

Cartier
175 New Bond Street, W.1.
Tel: 01-493 6962
The bye-word for superb jewellery — always something new, designed with taste. Also look at Les Must de Cartier, a range of elegant luggage and leather accessories.
Map Ref. 3G

Charles de Temple
52 Jermyn Street, W.1.
Tel: 01-499 3639
One of the prettiest shops in London where you can find imaginative jewellery and, generally, a selection of craftsman-made works. Superb stones and a wide price range.
Map Ref. 3G

Chaumet
178 New Bond Street, W.1.
Tel: 01-493 5403
Good, charming designs with excellent craftsmanship epitomise this shop. Expensive, but as both stones and workmanship are good it is well worth it.
Map Ref. 3G

Ciro's
178 Regent Street, W.1. and branches.
Tel: 01-734 7631
The place for pearls — there is a wide range of choice. Also costume jewellery and semi-precious stones made into conventional designs.
Map Ref. 3G

Collingwood
46 Conduit Street, W.1.
Tel: 01-734 2656
Many Royal warrants. Large price range. Own workshops.
Map Ref. 3G

Garrard
112 Regent Street, W.1.
Tel: 01-734 7020
The Court jewellers — lots of choice, but the designs are generally conventional. Good for rings and other pretty things, also tiaras.
Map Ref. 3G

Graff
55 Brompton Road, S.W.3.
Tel: 01-584 8571
For glittering diamonds, principally, with the unmistakable Graff designs. Graff's work is characterised by cool elegance.
Map Ref. 4E

Grima
80 Jermyn Street, S.W.1.
Tel: 01-839 2156
Brilliant design and the unusual use of stones is the hallmark of Andrew Grima's work which is exciting and different. Look at the perspect staircase as well!
Map Ref. 3G

Hooper Bolton
17 Motcomb Street, S.W.1.
Tel: 01-235 4975
Pretty little shop that has pretty designs and very desirable pieces. You can be sure to find something delectable here.
Map Ref. 4E

John Donald
120 Cheapside, E.C.2.
Tel: 01-606 2675
Another designer that combines originality with desirability. Here you can always find the right thing for a present — reasonable or grand.
Map Ref. 2K

Kutchinsky
179 New Bond Street, W.1.
Tel: 01-629 2876
73 Brompton Road, S.W.3.
Tel: 01-584 9311
Kutchinsky's specialise in really fine stones — not the place to start worrying about the price, as these pieces are the heirlooms of the future.
Map Ref. 4E

Richard Ogden
28 Burlington Arcade, W.1.
Tel: 01-493 9136
The place for rings as here you will find a large selection of both new and secondhand ones. A great place for engagement rings and other jewellery.
Map Ref. 3G

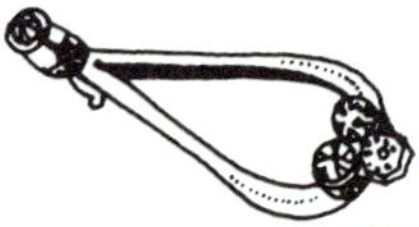

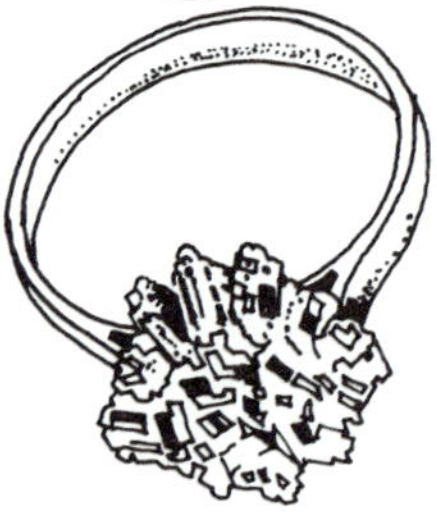

Tessiers
26 New Bond Street, W.1.
Tel: 01-629 0458
Nice place for antique and reproduction jewellery. Always some lovely brooches and small pieces for you to choose from as well as larger pieces.
Map Ref. 3G

KNITWEAR

Peels
Burlington Arcade.
Tel: 01-493 5378
Beautiful knitwear and fine cashmere can be found in this little shop in this pretty arcade. For the connoisseur and those wanting quality.
Map Ref. 3G

S Fisher
22 Burlington Arcade, W.1.
Tel: 01-493 4180
Also at 108 Piccadilly, W.1.
Tel: 01-493 6221
Superb knitwear, especially in cashmere, and traditional styling can be found in these small but lovely shops.
Map Ref. 3G

Scotch House
84 Regent Street, W.1.
Tel: 01-734 0203
Also at 2 Brompton Road, S.W.1.
Tel: 01-581 2151
Here you find tartans, fine knitwear and everything that you associate with Scotland.
Map Ref. 3G

Westaway and Westaway
29 Bloomsbury Way, W.C.1.
Tel: 01-405 2128
Marvellous shop for tartans and Scottish knitwear, especially Shetland and Fair Isle. Good large, fluffy tartan rugs are a speciality, as is cashmere at reasonable prices.
Map Ref. 2H

LINEN

Irish Linen Co.
35 Burlington Arcade, W.1.
Tel: 01-493 8949
The best in Irish Linen including beautiful double damask cloth as well as more modern designs.
Map Ref. 3G

Linen Cupboard
21 Great Castle Street, W.1.
Tel: 01-629 4062
Another shop with fine linens with a comprehensive range.
Map Ref. 2G

Vantona Linen Company
20 Brook Street, W.1.
Tel: 01-629 5000
Towels, sheets, pillowcases are some of the things to be found in this quality shop. Exclusive designs. All sorts of fabrics including percale.
Map Ref. 3G

Between the Sheets
190 Kensington Park Road, W.11.
Tel: 01-727 8768
Beautiful bed-linen made in broderie anglaise with ribbons to your choice of colour is a speciality here — other pretty linens too.
Map Ref. 2B

The Upstairs Shop
22 Pimlico Road, S.W.1.
Tel: 01-730 7502
Everything for the bedroom, including pretty sheets can be found in this original shop.
Map Ref. 5F

White House
51 New Bond Street, W.1.
Tel: 01-629 3521
Very elegant and discreet, this is the place for really beautiful linens and baby clothes as well. Expensive, but not really extravagant. Damask table cloths and napkins are a speciality here as are other elegant tableware.
Map Ref. 3G

Frette
98 New Bond Street, W.1.
Tel: 01-629 5517
Exquisite Italian table linen together with other beautiful things for your home.
Map Ref. 3G

Laura Ashley
Sloane Street and Covent Garden branches.
Tel: 01-730 1771/240 1997
Laura Ashley's inimitable period prints made up into a whole range of items for your home. Also fabric by the yard.
Map Ref. 3E

MILITARY MODEL & TRAIN COLLECTIONS

For the specialist and collector of military models these shops always have something of interest.

Hambling
29 Cecil Court, Charing Cross Road, W.C.2.
Tel: 01-836 4704
Trains only.
Map Ref. 2H

W & H Models
14 New Cavendish Street, W.1.
Tel: 01-486 3561
Trains only.
Map Ref. 2F

Tradition
5b Shepherd Street, W.1.
Tel: 01-493 7452
All items — good antique models.
Map Ref. 3F

Beatties
112 High Holborn, W.C.1.
Tel: 01-405 6285
Full range of models, also railways, cars and planes.
Map Ref. 2H

MUSIC

London Music Shop
Coldharbour Lane, S.E.5.
Tel: 01-737 2468
Mail order only.
No Map Ref.

Paxman
116 Long Acre, W.2.
Tel: 01-240 3642
Brass instruments, including French horns.
Map Ref. 2H

Bearer
7 Broadwick Street, W.1.
Tel: 01-437 1449
For violins, violas and cellos.
Map Ref. 3G

RECORD SHOPS

H.M.V.
363 Oxford Street, W.1.
Also branches throughout London.
Tel: 01-629 1240
Map Ref. 2F

Gramophone Exchange
3 Betterton Street, W.1.
Tel: 01-836 0976
Map Ref. 2G

Collectors Corner
62 New Oxford Street, W.C.1.
Tel: 01-580 6155
Map Ref. 2H

Discurio
9 Shepherd Street, W.1.
Tel: 01-493 6939
Nostalgic music of 20's, 30's and 40's.
Map Ref. 3F

Collets
180 Shaftesbury Avenue, W.C.2.
Tel: 01-240 3969
Map Ref. 3G

Virgin Records
28 Edgware Road, W.2.
Tel: 01-262 6985
Also branches throughout London.
Map Ref. 2E

Your Best Buys
9 St. Martin's Court, W.C.2.
Tel: 01-836 8514
Cassettes only.
Map Ref. 3H

SCENT

Floris
89 Jermyn Street, S.W.1.
Tel: 01-930 2885
Lovely country-fresh flower scents, talcum powders and soaps. Plus oils for burning on your lamps. Perfumes suitable for men as well as women.
Map Ref. 3G

Mary Chess
7 Shepherd Market, W.1.
Tel: 01-629 5152
Tucked away in a picturesque part of London, this little shop has an exquisite array of scents and scented gifts.
Map Ref. 3F

Penhaligon's
41 Wellington Street, W.C.2.
Tel: 01-836 4973
Old formulae are recreated by Penhaligon's into the most luscious of flowers and other scents. Plain but good looking bottles enhance the products.
Map Ref. 3H

Savory and Moore
13 Curzon Street, W.1.
Tel: 01-629 4471
In this chemist's shop you will find a dazzling number of French scents and toilet waters — and helpful staff.
Map Ref. 3G

Taylors of London
166 Sloane Street, S.W.1.
Tel: 01-235 4653
Scents, soaps and above all wonderful pot-pourri. Made to a very old recipe. Contains lots of country flowers.
Map Ref. 4E

Note: Many department stores have good perfumery and cosmetic departments, notably **Harrods, Harvey Nichols, Selfridges** and **Dickins and Jones.**
Also — **Boots** main branches (Piccadilly, Knightsbridge and Regent Street) also have a good selection of popular brands.

PETS

If you want to buy a pet there are a number of specialist shops, but if you want to take the pet out of the country, check the quarantine and health regulations. The pet shop will advise you.

Harrods
Knightsbridge, S.W.1.
Tel: 01-730 1234
There is a large department within the store and they boast that they can obtain any type of pet. Whilst this is no doubt true, they specialise in good pedigree dogs and cats.
Map Ref. 4E

Battersea Dog's Home
4 Battersea Park Road, S.W.8.
Tel: 01-622 3626
Basically a home for stray dogs and cats, nevertheless animals are sold after a period of time. There is a large selection of all breeds and prices are reasonable.
Map Ref. 6G

Animal Fair
17 Abingdon Road, W.8.
Tel: 01-937 0011
Specialising in small dogs and pedigree cats, they also have a good selection of birds, including parrots, marine fish and rodents.
Map Ref. 5C

Kensington Dog Bureau
3a Kensington Church Walk, W.8.
Tel: 01-937 4522
Will obtain any breed of dog for you and there are usually a few puppies at the Bureau and Kittens.
Map Ref. 4C

PHOTOGRAPHY

The camera enthusiast will find a good selection of photographic equipment in these shops. Listed are repair and hire shops as well.

Dixons
88 Oxford Street, W.1.
Tel: 01-636 8511
Also branches throughout London. Very large chain of camera and equipment shops, all of which sell internationally-known products.
Map Ref. 2G

Piccadilly Photo Centre
16 Piccadilly Arcade, W.1.
Tel: 01-499 4617
Little shop with a good stock of cameras and equipment and helpful advice.
Map Ref. 3G

R G Lewis
217 High Holborn, W.C.1.
Tel: 01-242 2916
Besides cameras, they also sell Kodak colour materials for those enthusiasts who want to make their own colour prints. Professional films in stock.
Map Ref. 2I

Vanguard Photo Services
156 Boston Road, W.7.
Wonderful repair shop which will mend in a day if possible. All repairs carried out on any equipment.
Map Ref.

Sendean Camera Repairs
6 D'Arblay Street, W.1.
Tel: 01-439 8418
Professional repairs carried out on any equipment. Very good service.
Map Ref. 2G

Advance Technical
24 Poland Street, W.1.
Tel: 01-734 0895
Two-day camera repairs of most makes, specialising in still and cine.
Map Ref. 2G

Pelling and Cross Rentals
104 Baker Street, W.1.
Tel: 01-487 5411
Will hire any equipment especially the more expensive and modern cameras. Good rates. Video and audio visual as well.
Map Ref. 2F

PICTURE GALLERIES

London's smaller picture galleries have an abundance of paintings both traditional and modern for sale. A browse among them quickly establishes in your mind those which will have the paintings that most appeal to you — a most individual choice. The staff are generally very knowledgeable about their stock and other paintings by the same hand.

Agnews
43 Old Bond Street, W.1.
Tel: 01-629 6176
Very well-known gallery which sells paintings both of Old Masters and 19th and 20th Century artists as well as contemporary.
Map Ref. 3G

Wildenstein
147 New Bond Street, W.1.
Tel: 01-629 6861
Has an international reputation for Old Masters and French Impressionists.
Map Ref. 3G

Lefevre
30 Bruton Street, W.1.
Tel: 01-629 2250
Specialises in good French Impressionist paintings.
Map Ref. 3F

Browse and Darby
19 Cork Street, W.1.
Tel: 01-734 7984
Good selection of 19th and 20th Century paintings. They also have some good sculptures.
Map Ref. 3G

Tryon
41 Dover Street, W.1.
Tel: 01-493 8548
Excellent examples of sporting paintings and drawings.
Map Ref. 3G

Brook Street Gallery
24 Brook Street, W.1.
Tel: 01-493 1550
Paintings, drawings and sculptures by contemporary masters.
Map Ref. 3F

Crane Kalman
178 Brompton Road, S.W.3.
Tel: 01-584 7566
Specialises in contemporary paintings by well-known English artists.
Map Ref. 4E

Marlborough Fine Art
6 Albemarle Street, W.1.
Tel: 01-629 5161
Large selection of graphics by well-known contemporary artists.
Map Ref. 3G

Redfern Gallery
Paintings, sculptures and graphics by artists such as Sutherland, Picasso and Henry Moore.
Map Ref. 3G

Waddington Galleries
34 Cork Street, W.1.
Tel: 01-439 1866
Wonderful collection of modern British and continental paintings and sculpture.
Map Ref. 3G

Hein
59 Jermyn Street, S.W.1.
Tel: 01-493 0688
Specialises in Baroque art, with a lovely collection of French and Italian sculptures.
Map Ref. 3G

Leggat
30 St. James Street, S.W.1.
Tel: 01-930 3772
Beautiful collection of Old Masters of the highest quality.
Map Ref. 3G

Maas
15 Clifford Street, W.1.
Tel: 01-734 2302
Specialises in 19th and early 20th Century paintings and watercolours.
Map Ref. 3G

PRINTS AND MAPS

Francis Edwards
83 Marylebone High Street, W.1.
Tel: 01-935 9225
Very large collection of antique maps dating back to the 15th Century.
Map Ref. 2F

Richard Green
44 Dover Street, W.1.
Tel: 01-493 7992
Good selection of 18th and 19th Century English prints.
Map Ref. 3G

Baynton-Williams
18 Lowndes Street, S.W.1.
Tel: 01-235 6595
Specialises in old maps and prints. Thousands of items in stock including charts, plans and atlases.
Map Ref. 4F

Parker Gallery
2 Albemarle Street, W.1.
Tel: 01-499 5906
Very old established dealer, specialising in military and naval prints.
Map Ref. 3G

Mapsellers
37 Southampton Street, W.C.2.
Tel: 01-836 8444
Wonderful collection of maps dating from the 15th Century.
Map Ref. 3H

Stanford
12 Longacre W.C.2.
Tel: 01-836 1321
The largest modern map shop in the world, with maps of any country to any scale.
Map Ref. 3H

RECORDS AND TAPES

Gramophone Exchange
80 Wardour Street, W.1.
Tel: 01-437 5313
One of the largest collections in London including many imports. There is a big secondhand department and they part-exchange old records.
Map Ref. 2G

Collectors Corner
62 New Oxford Street, W.C.1.
Tel: 01-580 6155
and 63 Monmouth Street, W.C.2.
Tel: 01-836 5614
Very old established record shop that specialises in English and foreign vocal, operatic and classic records. They import from many countries.
Map Ref. 2H

H.M.V.
363 Oxford Street, W.1.
Tel: 01-629 1240
Very large record shop which is run on a self-service basis. Excellent selection of L.P.'s and a whole floor devoted to tapes.
Map Ref. 2F

Discurio
9 Shepherd Street, W.1.
Tel: 01-493 6939
Mostly classical records and some foreign popular ones. Helpful staff.
Map Ref. 3F

Virgin Megastore
14-16 Oxford Street, W.1.
Tel: 01-631 1234
The largest record store in Europe which specialises in pop music of all types. Vast collection of records and tapes, also videos and photos.
Map Ref. 2G

Collet's Record Shop
180 Shaftesbury Avenue, W.C.2.
Tel: 01-240 3969
Wonderful selection of jazz and folk records both new and secondhand.
Map Ref. 3G

Dorbell's Jazz and Folk Record Shop
75 Charing Cross Road, W.C.2.
Tel: 01-437 5746
One of the largest collections in the world of folk and blues, jazz and swing records.
Map Ref. 2H

James Asman
23a New Row, W.C.2.
Tel: 01-240 1380
If you want rare jazz records then this is the shop. Magnificent selection of new and secondhand records.
Map Ref. 3H

Your Best Buys
9 St. Martin Court, W.C.2.
Tel: 01-836 8514
One of the largest collections of cassettes in Europe. Everything from classical to punk music.
Map Ref. 3H

Besides the above specialist shops there are many other general record shops in London. **Harrods** have a good department and there are branches of **Virgin Records, Harlequin,** and **Our Price** all over London.

SHOE SHOPS

Etienne Aigner
6 New Bond Street, W.1.
Tel: 01-491 7764
Shoes, bags, leather cases for both men and women — all in exquisite leather, conservatively styled.
Map Ref. 3G

Ferragamo
24 Old Bond Street, W.1.
Tel: 01-629 5007
The famous Ferragamo tradition lives on in this smart shop with its range of enviable shoes. Still a family business.
Map Ref. 3G

Rayne
15 Old Bond Street, W.1.
Tel: 01-493 9077
Brilliant collection of shoes, both their own make as well as from named designers — Givenchy, Jourdan and Halston. Good for evening shoes.
Map Ref. 3G

Midas
72 New Bond Street, W.1.
Tel: 01-629 3633
Another lovely shoe shop — where prices are more reasonable than you would expect. Nice classic styles and colours.
Map Ref. 3G

Bally
116 New Bond Street, W.1.
Tel: 01-629 6501
Another smart shoe shop in the medium to expensive range. Up-to-date styles and a good colour range distinguish Bally.
Map Ref. 3G

Kurt Geiger
95 New Bond Street, W.1.
Tel: 01-499 2707
Marvellous range of shoes — lots from Magli. Very elegant styling and fine leathers. Good range of sizes too.
Map Ref. 3G

Russell and Bromley
24 New Bond Street, W.1.
Tel: 01-629 6903
Very good and large selection of boots and shoes to be found in this popular shoe shop — most with co-ordinating bags.
Map Ref. 3G

Rayne
57 Brompton Street, S.W.3. and branches.
Tel: 01-589 5560
The Queen's shoemaker — stylish and chic.
Map Ref. 4E

Charles Jourdan
47 Brompton Road, S.W.3.
Tel: 01-584 3258
Beautiful shoes for men and women, imported from France, with some Italian men's shoes.
Map Ref. 4E

Elliots
76 New Bond Street, W.1.
Tel: 01-629 3644
Also branches throughout London. A wide range of fashionable boots and shoes. Specialists in narrow fittings. Branches throughout London.
Map Ref. 3G

Ravel
103 New Bond Street, W.1.
Tel: 01-493 6111
Also branches throughout London. Quality fashion shoes and boots from France, Italy, Spain and Brazil.
Map Ref. 3G

Other good shoe shops with branches throughout London are **Dolcis, Lilley and Skinner** and **Saxone.** Most department stores also have a good selection of shoes.

SHOE REPAIRS

Jeeves of Belgravia
10 Pont Street, S.W.1.
Tel: 01-235 1101
Excellent workmanship. 24-hour service if required.
Map Ref. 4F

Gallop's International
Good quick repair service for all types of shoes.
60 Gloucester Road, S.W.7.
Tel: 01-585 9444
16 Old Brompton Road, S.W.5.
Tel: 01-589 1734
31 Melcambe Street, N.W.1.
Tel: 01-935 4565
149 Sloane Street, S.W.1.
Tel: 01-730 7456
Map Ref. 5D, 5D, 1E, 4E.

Heel Bars can be found near all the main line stations and there are also some department stores such as **Harrods, Selfridges** and **Barkers** which have them, as do many **Woolworth** stores. They are very good for heel and sole repairs and the work is done while you wait.

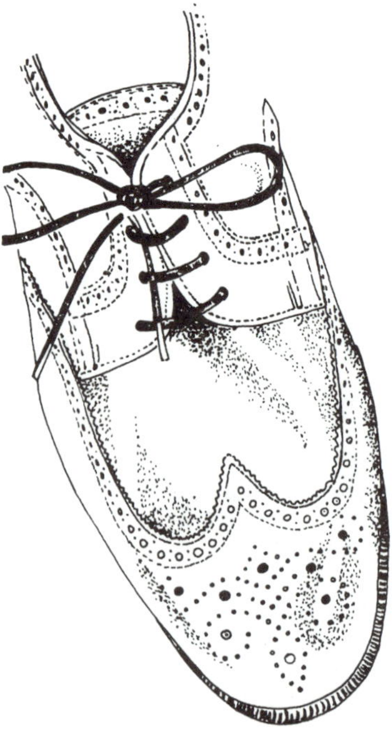

SPORTS EQUIPMENT

Lillywhites
Piccadilly Circus, S.W.1.
Tel: 01-930 3181
This is the largest general sports shop in London and every type of sports equipment including clothing can be bought here.
Map Ref. 3G

Harrods
Knightsbridge, S.W.1.
Tel: 01-730 1234
Harrods have a very good selection of sports equipment and the special department called Olympic Way usually has a display with qualified instructors.
Map Ref. 4F

Sports Day
84 Victoria Street, S.W.1.
Tel: 01-828 8377
Specialist sports shop stocking all sports footwear, clothing and equipment.
Map Ref. 4G

John Bennett
157 Old Kent Road, S.E.1.
Tel: 01-237 4411
Specialises in billiards and snooker tables. They also sell reconditioned tables as well as cues and balls.
Map Ref. 5K

Gordon Grose Sports
7 Ludgate House, Ludgate Circus, E.C.4.
Tel: 01-353 0082
Besides selling all types of general sports equipment they specialise in weight-training and lifting equipment.
Map Ref. 2J

Alpine Sports
215 Kensington High Street, W.8.
Tel: 01-938 1911
The complete ski shop with everything one would need. All top brand names at the lowest possible prices.
Map Ref. 5E

Pindisports
15 Brompton Arcade, S.W.3.
Tel: 01-584 2464
Ski shop which is the official suppliers of equipment to the Olympic ski team. Excellent selection.
Map Ref. 4E

STAMPS

Stanley Gibbons
399 The Strand, W.C.2.
Tel: 01-836 8444
The world's leading philatelists, their catalogues are taken by many to be the 'bible' for stamps.
Map Ref. 3H

E H W and Co.
12 Sicilian Avenue, W.C.1.
Tel: 01-405 5509
One of the top stamp and coin dealers in the world specialising in old British colonial and Victorian stamps.
Map Ref. 2H

Royale Stamp Co.
41 Bedford Street, W.C.2.
Tel: 01-836 6122
Specialising in British stamps from Victorian to present-day, they also deal in rare stamps from other countries.
Map Ref. 2H

J M Banin
376 The Strand, W.C.2.
Tel: 01-240 1682
Dealer in fine stamps of the British Commonwealth. Collections are a speciality.
Map Ref. 3H

W Lea
1 The Adelphi, John Adam Street, W.C.2.
Tel: 01-930 1688
Dealer in very rare postage stamps from all over the world.
Map Ref. 3H

A Constantine
124 Grand Buildings, Trafalgar Square, W.C.2.
Tel: 01-930 6933
Specialises in old stamps from Russia, China, France and Western Europe. Also present day.
Map Ref. 3H

TOBACCO, PIPES AND SNUFF

There are thousands of shops throughout London which sell cigarettes, cigars and smokers requisites, but the following are specialist shops which are well worth visiting.

Rothmans of Pall Mall
64 Pall Mall, S.W.1.
Tel: 01-930 6937
Lovely shop in St. James's which is a delight to browse through. Stockist of all Rothmans brands and many quality smokers' requisites. Very courteous and helpful staff.
Map Ref. 3G

Dunhill's
30 Duke Street, S.W.1.
Tel: 01-493 9161
A world famous shop which sells wonderful range of pipes, lighters and cigarettes. One complete floor for cigars where the selection is magnificent. Superb service.
Map Ref. 3G

James Fox
2 Burlington Gardens,
Old Bond Street, W.1.
Tel: 01-493 9009
Specialises in many types of finest Havana cigars. Very helfpul assistants in this traditional shop.
Map Ref. 3G

Astleys
109 Jermyn Street, S.W.1.
Tel: 01-930 1687
Famous for their collection of antique pipes, they also sell beautiful meerschaum and briar pipes. They also repair pipes.
Map Ref. 3G

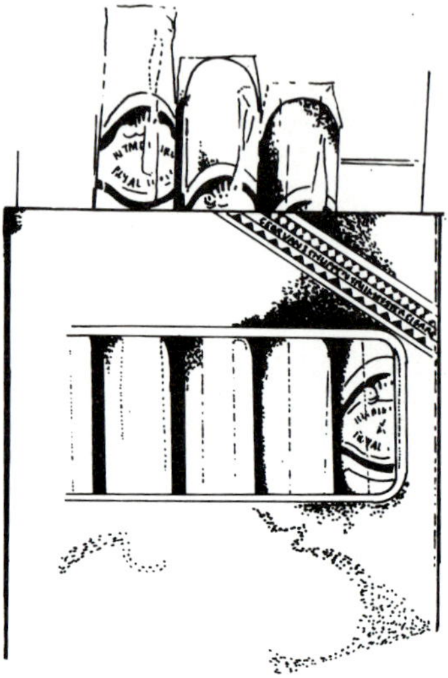

TOYS

See under 'London for Children'.

TELEVISION AND HI-FI

Lasky's
42 Tottenham Court Road, W.1.
Tel: 01-580 2573
Also branches throughout London. Very good value and a tremendous range of equipment. Full servicing facilities and good guarantees.
Map Ref. 2G

Lion House
227 Tottenham Court Road, W.1.
Tel: 01-580 7383
Large hi-fi superstore with enormous selection of equipment. There are ten separate demonstration studios.
Map Ref. 2G

Thomas Heinitz
35 Moscow Road, W.2.
Tel: 01-229 2077
Specialises in providing the best hi-fi

equipment that the customer can afford. Mr Heinitz advises on which type and also installs equipment himself. If you want the best for your pocket and don't know which range to buy, this is the place to go.
Map Ref. 3C

WINE

There are many wine shops in London and it is also possible to buy wine in supermarkets and department stores. For serious wine drinkers, however, a visit to a well-known wine merchant or wine department will be enjoyed.

Berry Bros and Rudd
3 St. James Street, S.W.1.
Tel: 01-930 1888
Very old established wine merchants. Superb list of wines and charming service.
Map Ref. 3G

Justerini & Brooks
61 St. James Street, S.W.1.
Tel: 01-493 8721
Lovely old wine shop which sells some fine wines.
Map Ref. 3G

Harrods
Knightsbridge, S.W.1.
Tel: 01-730 1234
Excellent wine department with an extensive range. Quite often there is a wine tasting. Helpful advice.
Map Ref. 4E

Fortnum & Mason
Piccadilly, W.1.
Tel: 01-734 8040
Famous for its selection of wines and incomparable service.
Map Ref. 3G

Hedges and Butler
153 Regent Street, W.1.
Tel: 01-734 4444
Very old established wine merchant with a good list and helpful service.
Map Ref. 3G

Oddbins
7 George Street, W.1.
Also branches throughout London.
Tel: 01-935 6727
Discount wine shop selling cheaper ranges. Friendly, helpful service.
Map Ref. 2F

LATE NIGHT SHOPPING

Besides the central areas of London described at the beginning of this section which have later opening hours on certain days, the following is a list of shops which stay open after hours. Chemists are in 'Helpful Information about London' section.

Great Wall
31 Wardour Street, W.1.
Tel: 01-437 7963
Open: 11.00am-2.00am, Monday to Saturday.
Chinese supermarket selling only oriental food.
Map Ref. 3H

Midnight Shop
223 Brompton Road, S.W.5.
Tel: 01-589 5030
Open: 10.00am-12.00pm, Monday to Sunday.
General provisions, meat and vegetables.
Map Ref. 5E

The Peppermill
66 Old Brompton Road, S.W.5.
Tel: 01-584 5525
Open: 9.00am-12.00pm, Monday to Sunday.
General provisions, frozen meat, fish and vegetables.
Map Ref. 5D

Partridges
132 Sloane Street, S.W.1.
Tel: 01-730 0651
Open: 9.00am-8.00pm, Monday to Saturday. 10.00am-8.00pm, Sunday.
Very good grocery and delicatessen shop.
Map Ref. 5E

Europa Foods
18 Queensway, W.2.
Tel: 01-727 3139
Open: 9.00am-11.00pm, Monday to Saturday.
Very good large supermarket.
Map Ref. 3C

24 Hour Supermarket
68 Westbourne Grove, W.2.
Tel: 01-727 4927
Open: 24 hours every day.
General provisions, both food and hardware, toiletries, fresh fruit.
Map Ref. 2B

Chivers
43 Charlotte Street, W.1.
Tel: 01-580 1761
Open: 8.45am-5.00pm, Monday to Saturday.
Map Ref. 2G

HOME ENTERTAINING

If you want food sent into your appartments or house, these people will be pleased to provide food or cook meals for you.

Hundred Acres Farm Shop
51 Hollywood Road, S.W.10.
Tel: 01-351 1053
Fresh meat for you to cook or savoury food already prepared: special delivery service for dinner parties and other entertainment.
Map Ref. 6D

Fortnum and Mason
181 Piccadilly, W.1.
Tel: 01-734 8040
Lovely cooked food department and also party department. Will show you set menus.
Map Ref. 3G

Harrods
Knightsbridge, S.W.1.
Tel: 01-730 1234
Good cooked meats and salads available for you to pick up. Also prepared meals available.
Map Ref. 4E

Justin De Blank
42 Elizabeth Street, S.W.1.
Tel: 01-730 0605
Another place where you will find delicious ready prepared pates, quiches, meats and cheeses. Will also cater for almost any function. Nice staff.
Map Ref. 5F

Hobbs and Co.
3 Garrick Street, W.C.2.
Tel: 01-240 5653
High-class provision store with many original ideas for picnics and home entertaining.
Map Ref. 3H

Lorna Wing
Tel: 01-736 3033
Lorna is a freelance cook who does Royal parties, so her cooking is impeccable. Does lovely picnic hampers as well.

Dining out in London

A
B
C
D
E
F
G
H
I
J
K
L
1
2
3
4
5
6
Kensal Green
KILBURN LANE
HARROW ROAD
FERNHEAD RD.
ELGIN AVENUE
CASTELLAIN RD.
Maida Vale
MAIDA VALE
ST. JOHN'S WOOD RD.
WELLINGTON ROAD
REGENT'S PARK
ALBANY STREET
EUSTON STATION
EUSTON ROAD
GREAT WESTERN RD
Westbourne Park
Ladbroke Grove
LADBROKE GROVE
WESTBOURNE PARK
TALBOT ROAD
CHEPSTOW RD.
CLIFTON GDNS.
Warwick Avenue
LISSON GROVE
EDGWARE ROAD
Marylebone
Baker Street
MARYLEBONE ROAD
Regent's Park
Great Portland Street
Warren Street
Goodge Street
TOTTENHAM COURT RD
GOWER STREET
SOUTHAMPTON ROW
GUILFORD ST.
GRAYS INN ROAD
KING'S CROSS ROAD
ROSEBERRY AVENUE
GOSWELL ROAD
CITY ROAD
OLD STREET
Old Street
GREAT EASTERN ST.
HACKNEY ROAD
LIVERPOOL ST. STATION
CLARENDON RD.
BLENHEIM CRES.
COLVILLE TER.
BISHOPS BRIDGE ROAD
WESTBOURNE GROVE
PADDINGTON STATION
WESTBOURNE TER
Edgware Road
SEYMOUR PLACE
PORTMAN SQUARE
BAKER STREET
MARYLEBONE HIGH ST.
PORTLAND PL.
Oxford Circus
REGENT ST.
GOODGE ST.
Tottenham Court Rd.
NEW OXFORD STREET
THEOBALDS RD.
CLERKENWELL ROAD
HOLBORN
Holborn
HOLBORN VIA
Chancery Lane
CHANCERY LANE
FARRINGDON ST.
ALDERSGATE ST.
Moorgate
MOORGATE
Bank
BISHOPSGATE
HOUNDSDITCH
Aldgate
COMMERCIAL ST.
WHITECHAPEL
ELGIN CRES.
Bayswater
QUEENSWAY
PEMBRIDGE RD.
Queensway
BAYSWATER ROAD
Lancaster Gate
Marble Arch
OXFORD STREET
GROSVENOR SQUARE
Bond Street
NEW BOND ST.
OLD BOND ST.
POLAND ST.
WARDOUR ST.
CHARING CROSS ROAD
SHAFTESBURY AV.
DRURY LANE
LONG ACRE
Covent Garden
Aldwych
STRAND
Somerset House
FLEET ST.
LUDGATE HILL
St Paul's
CHEAPSIDE
QUEEN VICTORIA ST.
Mansion House
Blackfriars
LEADENHALL ST.
FENCHURCH ST.
Monument
MINORIES
LEMAN ST.
Tower Hill
EAST SMITHFIELD
PORTLAND ROAD
Notting Hill Gate
NOTTING HILL GATE
KENSINGTON GARDENS
HYDE PARK
PARK LANE
BERKELEY SQUARE
CURZON ST.
PICCADILLY
Piccadilly Circus
Leicester Square
Temple
EMBANKMENT
RIVER THAMES
BLACKFRIARS BRIDGE
SOUTHWARK BRIDGE
LONDON BRIDGE
TOWER HILL
TOWER BRIDGE
SERPENTINE
ROTTEN ROW
Hyde Park Corner
Green Park
GREEN PARK
PALL MALL
THE MALL
ST. JAMES'S PARK
CHARING CROSS STATION
WATERLOO BRIDGE
STAMFORD ST.
SOUTHWARK STREET
TOOLEY STREET
HOLLAND PARK AVENUE
Holland Park
KENSINGTON CHURCH ST
KENSINGTON RD.
KNIGHTSBRIDGE
BIRDCAGE WALK
Westminster
VICTORIA
WESTMINSTER BRIDGE
WATERLOO ROAD
YORK ROAD
WATERLOO STATION
BLACKFRIARS RD.
SOUTH WARK BRIDGE RD.
Borough
BOROUGH HIGH ST.
ST. THOMAS
LONDON BRI. STATION
HOLLAND PARK
CAMPDEN HILL RD
KENSINGTON HIGH STREET
QUEEN'S GATE
EXHIBITION ROAD
Knightsbridge
BELGRAVE SQUARE
GROSVENOR PL.
St James's Park
WESTMINSTER BRIDGE RD.
Lambeth North
PALACE RD.
BOROUGH RD.
CAUSEWAY
LONG LANE
HOLLAND ROAD
High Street Kensington
BEAUCHAMP PLACE
SLOANE STREET
VICTORIA STREET
HORSE FERRY ROAD
LAMBETH
LAMBETH ROAD
ST GEORGE'S RD.
LONDON RD.
NEWINGTON
GREAT DOVER ST.
ABBEY STREET
South Kensington
BROMPTON ROAD
WALTON RD.
CADOGAN GDNS
KING'S ROAD
VAUXHALL BRIDGE ROAD
LAMBETH BRIDGE
Elephant and Castle
NEW KENT RD
HAMMERSMITH ROAD
WARWICK ROAD
EARLS COURT ROAD
CROMWELL ROAD
Gloucester Road
OLD BROMPTON ROAD
SYDNEY ST.
Sloane Square
BUCKINGHAM PALACE ROAD
VICTORIA STATION
MILL BANK
ALBERT EMBANKMENT
KENNINGTON ROAD
WALWORTH ROAD
OLD KENT ROAD
SHEPHERD'S BUSH RD
TALGARTH ROAD
NORTH END ROAD
WEST CROMWELL ROAD
Earls Court
FULHAM ROAD
ROYAL HOSPITAL ROAD
CHELSEA BRIDGE RD.
Pimlico
VAUXHALL BRIDGE
Vauxhall
HARLEYFORD RD.
KENNINGTON PARK ROAD
FULHAM PALACE ROAD
LILLIE ROAD
REDCLIFF GARDENS
West Brompton
ALBERT BRIDGE
CHELSEA EMBANKMENT
BATTERSEA PARK
CHELSEA BRIDGE
GROSVENOR ROAD
NINE ELMS LANE
FENTIMAN RD.
Oval
Kennington Park
ALBANY ROAD

DINING OUT IN LONDON

There is an enormous variety of national and international restaurants and eating places in London and it is possible to get food from most countries in the world, with an atmosphere to suit all moods and occasions, and prices to suit all pockets.

The range is vast from sandwich bars, small cafes, coffee houses, hamburger joints, bistros and ethnic places to the world famous restaurants.

The general purpose of this section in the Guide is to give the visitor an introduction to those restaurants offering good food, combined with a pleasant atmosphere.

Many restaurants accept informal dress but it is always wise to check this point when making your reservation because there are sometimes different policies between lunch and dinner. IT IS ESSENTIAL TO TELEPHONE THE RESTAURANT TO RESERVE A TABLE AS ALL THE PLACES WHICH WE HAVE LISTED ARE VERY POPULAR.

The prices indicated are only approximate.

AFRICAN

LONDON W.C.2.

The Calabash
38 Kings Street, W.C.2.
Tel: 01-836 1973
Approx £9
In the basement of the modern Africa Centre, Covent Garden. A variety of traditional West African cooking, with tasty interesting dishes. 2 bars and North African wine is available.
Open: 12.00 noon-11.30pm, Monday to Friday.
6.00pm-11.30pm, Saturday.
Closed Sunday.
Map Ref. 3H

AMERICAN

There are many outlets in London belonging to the well-known chains such as Macdonalds, Wimpy and Burger King, but we thought that the following were slightly different and had a much better atmosphere.

LONDON W.C.2.

Joe Allen
13 Exeter Street, W.C.2.
Tel: 01-836 0651
Approx £16
No Credit Cards.
Similar to the New York and Paris Joe Allen's, this very popular restaurant serves first rate cocktails, hamburgers, spinach salad and cheesecake.
Open: 12.00 noon-1.00am, Monday to Saturday. 12.00 noon-midnight, Sunday.
Open: 12.00 noon-2.00am, Monday to Sunday.
Map Ref. 3H

Peppermint Park
St. Martins Lane, W.C.2.
Tel: 01-836 5234
Approx £12
Major Credit Cards.
Decorated in pale pink and green with a long bar this popular restaurant serves hamburgers, American sandwiches, Caesar's and Waldorf salads and a range of splits, sundaes and shakes.
Open: 12.00 noon-2.00am, Monday to Saturday. Midnight on Sunday.
Map Ref. 3H

Le Grunts
12 Maiden Lane, W.C.2.
Tel: 01-379 772
Approx £5
No Credit Cards.
Chicago style pizza restaurant with matching decor. Excellent food and selection of cocktails available.
Open: 12.00 noon-11.30pm, Monday to Saturday.
Closed Sunday.
Map Ref. 3H

Maxwells
16 Russell Street, W.C.2.
Tel: 01-836 0303
Approx £10
Credit Cards: Barclaycard.
Los Angeles style with good American food and music. Cocktail bar and soda fountain.
Open: 12.00 noon-midnight, Monday to Sunday.
Map Ref. 3H

LONDON W.1.

Hard Rock Café
150 Old Park Lane, W.1.
Tel: 01-629 0382
Approx £15
No Credit Cards.
One of the best in London, with a large room decorated with ceiling fans, wooden tables and check table cloths, loud music and a separate bar. Hamburgers and steaks are excellent and American beer can be bought here.
Open: 12.00 noon-12.30am, Monday to Sunday.
Map Ref. 4F

Chicago Pizza Pie Factory
17 Hanover Square, W.1.
Tel: 01-629 2669
Approx £9
No Credit Cards.
Each pizza is cooked to order, all with special fillings. Lively music with Chicago radio tapes blaring. American beer and cheesecake.
Open: 11.40am-11.30pm, Monday to Saturday.
Closed Sunday.
Map Ref. 2G

Wolfe's
34 Park Lane, W.1.
Tel: 01-499 6897
Approx £12.50
Major Credit Cards.
Small and very busy with glamorous waitresses. Very good hamburgers, steaks, salads and American desserts.
Open: 11.30am-midnight, Monday to Sunday.
Map Ref. 3R

Surprise
12 Great Marlborough Street, W.1.
Tel: 01-434 2666
Approx £10
Major Credit Cards.
Excellent salad sandwiches, pancakes and starters. Fast service.
Open: 12.00 noon-3.00pm and 6.00pm-midnight, Monday to Saturday.
Closed Sunday.
Map Ref. 3G

LONDON S.W.1.

Wolfe's
25 Basil Street, S.W.1.
Tel: 01-589 8444
Approx £12
Major Credit Cards.
Plush restaurant serving very good hamburgers and other American style food.
Open: 11.30am-midnight, Monday to Sunday.
Map Ref. 4E

Drones
1 Pont Street, S.W.1.
Tel: 01-235 9638
Approx £20
Major Credit Cards.
Hamburgers, salads, steaks and grills in a beautiful setting on two floors.
Open: 12.30pm-3.00pm and 7.30pm-11.30pm, Monday to Sunday.
Map Ref. 4E

Sloanes
116 Knightsbridge, S.W.1.
Tel: 01-589 6520
Approx £9.
No Credit Cards.
A lively setting, loud music, bustling waitresses, but tasty hamburgers, steaks, toasted sandwiches and salads and baked potatoes.
Open: 12.30pm-3.00pm and 7.30pm-11.30pm, Monday to Sunday.
Map Ref. 4F

LONDON S.W.3.

Kennedy's
316 Kings Road, S.W.3.
Tel: 01-352 0025
Approx £6
No Credit Cards.
Good hamburgers, chilli and home made soups and patés. Music in the evening.
Open: 11.00am-1.00am, Monday to Sunday.
Map Ref. 5E

Adams
239 Old Brompton Road, S.W.3.
Tel: 01-373 3502
Approx £16.
No Credit Cards.
Good American style atmosphere in this restaurant which serves excellent spare ribs and brochettes.
Open: 7.00pm-11.30pm, Tuesday to Saturday and 12.00 noon-3.30pm, Sunday.
Map Ref. 5D

LONDON S.W.10.

Great American Disaster
335 Fulham Road, S.W.10.
also at
9 Beauchamp Place, S.W.3.
13 Queensway, W.2.
Approx £6.
No Credit Cards.
The Fulham Road branch was the first 'hamburger joint' in London. Good hamburgers, salads and desserts served by lively waitresses to the sound of loud music.
Open: 12.00 noon-1.00am, Monday to Saturday.
Closed Sunday.
Map Ref. 6D, 5E, 3C

Parsons
311 Fulham Road, S.W.10.
Tel: 01-352 0651
Approx £12.
No Credit Cards.
Pleasant little restaurant serving very good hamburgers as well as spaghetti and good salads.
Open: 12.30pm-1.00am, Monday to Sunday.
Map Ref. 6D

LONDON S.W.7.

Brooke's
68 Old Brompton Road, S.W.7.
Approx £12.
Major Credit Cards.
Unusual English setting for a good range of hamburgers, pies, quiches. Good value.
Open: 12.00 noon-12.30am, Monday to Sunday.
Set Price Lunch: £2.80.
Map Ref. 4E

AUSTRIAN

LONDON W.1.

Kerzenstüberl
9 St. Christopher's Place, Wigmore Street, W.1.
Tel: 01-486 3196
Approx £25.
Major Credit Cards.
Marvellous atmosphere with traditional hospitality and excellent food and wine.
Open: 12.00 noon-2.30pm and 6.00pm-11.00pm, Monday to Friday and 7.00pm-11.00pm, Saturday.
Closed Sunday and Lunch Saturday.
Map Ref. 2F

Old Vienna
94 New Bond Street W.1.
Tel: 01-629 8716
Approx £19.
Major Credit Cards.
Great fun in the cellar restaurant with the staff wearing traditional Austrian costume. Good food.
Open: 12.00 noon-2.30pm and 6.00pm-11.00pm, Monday to Thursday and 6.00pm-11.00pm, Friday.
Closed Sunday and Lunch Saturday.
Map Ref. 2F

Wunderbar
93 Dean Street, W.1.
Tel: 01-437 1261
Approx £10.
Major Credit Cards.
Good food, wine and beers with a strong Bavarian atmosphere. Music and dancing.
Open: 6.00pm-3.00am, Monday to Saturday.
Closed Sunday.
Map Ref. 2G

LONDON W.2.

Tiroler Hunt
27 Westbourne Grove, W.2.
Tel: 01-727 3981
Approx £8.
Major Credit Cards.
Accordian music, cowbells and a lively, friendly atmosphere. Good music.
Open: 6.30pm-1.00am, Monday to Saturday and 6.30pm-12.30am, Sunday.
Map Ref. 2B

BRAZILIAN

LONDON W.C.2.

Paulo's
28 Wellington Street W.C.2.
Tel: 01-240 1919
Approx £10.
Major Credit Cards.
Besides the coffee, which is superb, the decor and South American food make this a must. The whole restaurant vibrates with Brazilian enthusiasm and the crab starter and char-grilled pork are excellent.
Open: 12.30pm-3.00pm and 6.30pm-11.30pm, Monday to Saturday.
Closed Sunday.
Set Price for Lunch and Pre-Theatre — £5.95.
Map Ref. 3H

CHINESE (CANTONESE)

LONDON W.1.

Chuen Cheng Ku
17 Wardour Street, W.1.
Tel: 01-734 3509
Approx £10.
No Credit Cards.
Very popular with Chinese diners; a good selection of Cantonese dishes.
Open: 11.00am-11.30pm, Monday to Sunday.
Map Ref. 3G

Lee Ho Fook
15 Gerrard Street, W.1.
Tel: 01-734 9578
also at
Swiss Cottage
Tel: 01-722 9552
Approx £14.
Credit Cards: American Express, Visa & Access.
Very popular with Chinese customers; the cooking is excellent with generous portions. Famous for its dim sum. Nice decor.
Open: 12.00 noon-midnight, Monday to Sunday.
Map Ref. 3H

Kowloon
21 Gerrard Street W.1.
Tel: 01-437 1694
Approx £9.50.
Credit Cards: Access.
Because this is a Chinese bakery as well as a restaurant the breads are delicious. So are the noodles, duck and barbecued pork.
Open: 12.00 noon-midnight, Monday to Sunday.
Map Ref. 3H

Ho-Ho
29 Maddox Street, W.1.
Tel: 01-493 1228
Approx £11 per head.
Excellent Chinese restaurant in an area where they are scarce. Try the crispy fried lamb.
Map Ref. 2G

Loon Fung
37 Gerrard Street, W.1.
Tel: 01-437 5429
Approx £7.
Very populr with Chinese customers; Sunday lunch is quite an experience. Large choice of dim sum, chicken, duck and shellfish.
Open: 12.00 noon-11.30pm, Monday to Sunday.
Map Ref. 3H

Lok Ho Fook
4 Gerrard Street, W.1.
Tel: 01-437 8961
Approx £8.
Major Credit Cards.
Excellent variety of Cantonese dishes with generous portions. Spare ribs, dim sum and many other main courses are mouth watering.
Open: 12.00 noon-midnight, Monday to Sunday.
Set Menu: £3.50 (Lunch),
£5-£12 (Dinner).
Map Ref. 3H

Ley-On's
56 Wardour Street, W.1.
Tel: 01-437 6465
Approx £8.
Major Credit Cards.
Cantonese specialities including excellent dim sum, pork dishes and marvellous fish and shellfish.
Open: 11.30am-11.00pm, Monday to Sunday.
Map Ref. 3G

Sun Luk
2 Macclesfield Street, W.1.
Tel: 01-734 5161
Approx £15.
No Credit Cards.
Late night restaurant serving high standard Cantonese food. Specialities include wun-tun soup, duck, crab and eels.
Open: 12.00 noon-4.30am, Monday to Sunday.
Map Ref. 3H

Wong Kei
Rupert Court, Rupert Street, W.1.
Tel: 01-437 3071
Approx £7.
No Credit Cards.
Very popular restaurant which serves very good food. Sweet and sour sauces are first class; for an interesting change try braised duckweb.
Open: 12.00 noon-2.00am, Monday to Sunday.
Map Ref. 3H

LONDON W.2.

Bamboo Kitchen
442 Edgware Road, W.2.
Tel: 01-402 4841
Approx £6.
No Credit Cards.
Small restaurant serving excellent Cantonese food with interesting specialities.
Open: 12.00 noon-midnight, Monday to Saturday and 5.30pm-11.30pm, Sunday.
Map Ref. 2E

Green Jade
29 Porchester Road, W.2.
Tel: 01-229 7221
Approx £15.50.
Credit Cards: American Express & Visa.
Vast range of both Cantonese and Peking dishes. Good value.
Open: 12.00 noon-midnight, Monday to Sunday.
Map Ref. 3C

Hung Toa
54 Queensway, W.2.
Tel: 01-727 6017
Approx £7.
No Credit Cards.
A simple restaurant with an excellent reputation for many Cantonese specialities.
Open: 12.00 noon-midnight, Monday to Sunday.
Map Ref. 3C

LONDON S.W.1.

Hunan
51 Pimlico Road, S.W.1.
Tel: 01-730 5712
Approx £14 per head.
Smart ambience and delicious cooking with duck a speciality.
Map Ref. 6G

LONDON W.C.2.

Happy Garden
47 Charing Cross Road, W.C.2.
Tel: 01-437 7472
Approx £6.
No Credit Cards.
Popular restaurant particularly with Chinese customers. Good menu with interesting dishes.
Open: 12.00 noon-11.45pm, Monday to Sunday.
Map Ref. 2H

Joy King Lau
3 Leicester Street, W.C.2.
Tel: 01-437 1133
Approx £9.
Credit Cards: American Express & Diners.
Large restaurant with a huge list of Cantonese dishes. Dim sum is a speciality as well as pork and seafood; a popular and well-established restaurant.
Open: 11.00am-11.30pm, Monday to Sunday.
Map Ref. 3H

Poons & Co.
27 Lisle Street, W.C.2.
Tel: 01-437 1528
Approx £6.
Credit Cards: American Express & Diners.
Small and very popular restaurant with good Cantonese menu. Duck and pork are especially good.
Open: 12.00 noon-11.30pm, Monday to Saturday.
Closed Sunday.
Map Ref. 3H

Dynasty
10 Charing Cross Road, W.C.2.
Tel: 01-240 2796
Approx £14 per head.
Chinese restaurant with all the goodies you expect.
Map Ref. 3H

Poons of Covent Garden
41 King Street, W.C.2.
Tel: 01-240 1743
Approx £17.50.
Credit Cards: American Express & Diners.
Modern and good but also expensive. There is a marvellous range of Cantonese dishes. The staff is friendly and helpful.
Open: 12.00 noon-midnight, Monday to Saturday.
Closed Sunday.
Set Lunch: £6.00.
Map Ref. 3H

LONDON S.W.3.

Choys
172 Kings Road, S.W.3.
Tel: 01-352 9085
Approx £12.
Credit Cards: American Express, Diners & Visa.
Good menu and some interesting dishes. Friendly staff.
Open: 12.00 noon-midnight, Monday to Sunday.
Map Ref. 5E

Shangri La
233 Brompton Road, S.W.3.
Tel: 01-584 3658
Approx £16.
Major Credit Cards.
Good service and a nice choice of dishes. Very good shellfish. Quick service downstairs.
Open: 12.00 noon-2.30pm and 8.30pm-11.30pm, Monday to Sunday.
Map Ref. 4E

The Good Earth
91 King's Road, S.W.3.
Tel: 01-352 4692
Approx £13 per head.
Very good food and a lovely ambience make this an excellent restaurant to sample Chinese food.
Map Ref. 5F

CHINESE (PEKINESE)

LONDON W.1.

Gallery Rendezvous
53 Beak Street, W.1.
Tel: 01-734 0445
Approx £18.
Credit Cards: American Express & Diners.
A smart restaurant with classical North Chinese dishes. Crispy duck is especially good.
Open: 12.00 noon-2.30pm and 6.00pm-11.00pm, Monday to Sunday.
Set Price: £8.50.
Map Ref. 3G

Gragon Gate
7 Gerrard Street, W.1.
Tel: 01-734 5154
Approx £7.
Credit Cards: American Express & Diners.
An unpretentious restaurant which serves really spicy Szechuan food. Smoked duck, vegetable and port are excellent.
Open: 12.00 noon-midnight, Monday to Sunday.
Map Ref. 3H

Dumpling Inn
15a Gerrard Street, W.1.
Tel: 01-437 2567
Approx £8.
Credit Cards: Visa & Diners.
Popular and crowded. The food is delicious. Prawns in chili sauce, fried seaweed and pork dumplings are specialities.
Open: 12.00 noon-11.30pm, Monday to Saturday.
5.30pm-11.30pm, Sunday.
Map Ref. 3H

Great Shanghai
42 Dean Street, W.1.
Tel: 01-437 9455
Approx £12.
Major Credit Cards.
Elegant and sophisticated restaurant serving Pekinese and some Cantonese dishes. Good presentation and well-cooked food.
Open: 12.00 noon-11.30pm, Monday to Sunday.
Map Ref. 3G

Mr. Kai of Mayfair
65 South Audley Street, W.1.
Tel: 01-493 8933
Approx £24.
Major Credit Cards.
A plush and welcoming restaurant with immaculately laid tables. Excellent menu and waiters are efficient and helpful. Expensive but very good.
Open: 12.00 noon-2.30pm and 7.00pm-11.30pm, Monday to Sunday.
Map Ref. 3F

Soho Rendezvous
21 Romilly Street, W.1.
Tel: 01-437 1486
Approx £20.
Major Credit Cards.
Comfortable air-conditioned surroundings in which first class Pekinise dishes are served. Bean curd, stuffed dumplings, crispy duck and fried seaweed are good.
Open: 12.00 noon-2.30pm and 6.00pm-midnight, Monday to Saturday.
Closed Sunday and Bank Holidays.
Map Ref. 3G

LONDON W.8.

Fu Tong
29 Kensington High Street, W.8.
Tel: 01-937 1293
Approx £16.
Major Credit Cards.
Fine Pekinese cooking in this elegant restaurant. Service is helpful and friendly and there is also a comfortable bar.
Open: 12.30am-11.30pm, Monday to Sunday.
Set Price: £8.
Map Ref. 4C

LONDON S.W.1.

Mr. Chow
151 Knightsbridge, S.W.1.
Tel: 01-589 7347
Approx £28.
Major Credit Cards.
A top class restaurant with modern decor. Excellent food and the Peking duck, sole in wine, fried seaweed and soups are supreme. Very efficient service.
Open: 12.30pm-2.45pm and 7.00pm-11.45pm, Monday to Sunday.
Map Ref. 4F

LONDON S.W.3.

Chelsea Rendezvous
4 Sydney Street, S.W.3.
Tel: 01-352 9519
Approx £12.
Major Credit Cards.
Smart and lively, this is a very popular Pekinese restaurant. The food is excellent, particularly the Szechuan pork and the seafood in wine. Good fun and good value.
Open: 12.30pm-3.00pm and 7.00pm-midnight, Monday to Sunday.
Map Ref. 5E

LONDON S.W.10.

Golden Duck
6 Hollywood Road, S.W.10.
Tel: 01-352 3500
Approx £20.
Credit Cards: American Express, Visa & Diners.
Old established and popular restaurant with spicy Szechuan dishes. Good cooking and friendly service.
Open: 12.30pm-3.00pm and 7.00pm-midnight, Monday to Saturday and 12.30pm-3.00pm, Sunday.
Set Price Menus from £9.
Map Ref. 6C

The Red Pepper
7 Park Walk, S.W.10.
Tel: 01-352 3546
Approx £10.
Major Credit Cards.
Besides Pekinese dishes they also serve Cantonese, Singapore and Malaysian specialities. Excellent shellfish and vegetables.
Open: 12.00 noon-3.00pm and 6.00pm-midnight, Monday to Saturday.
Closed Sunday.
No Map Ref.

LONDON S.W.7.

Shu-Shan
53 Old Brompton Road, S.W.7.
Tel: 01-589 3149
Approx £20.
Major Credit Cards.
Smart restaurant with a very extensive menu. Food is well cooked and service is efficient and friendly.
Open: 12.30pm-2.30pm and 5.30pm-11.00pm, Monday to Sunday.
Map Ref. 5D

ENGLISH

LONDON W.1.

Aunties
126 Cleveland Street, W.1.
Tel: 01-387 3226
Approx £7.
No Credit Cards.
Simple home-made English cooking. Crowded at lunchtime, this is always a popular little restaurant. Try their various pies.
Open: 12.30pm-2.00pm and 7.00-9.30pm, Monday to Saturday.
Closed Sunday.
Map Ref. 2G

Baker and Oven
10 Paddington Street, W.1.
Tel: 01-935 5072
Approx £9.
Major Credit Cards.
Converted cellars of a public house, this is a very pleasant alcoved restaurant. Traditional English dishes, lovely pies and wholesome desserts.
Open: 12.00 noon-3.00pm and 6.30pm-midnight, Monday to Saturday.
Closed Sunday.
Map Ref. 2F

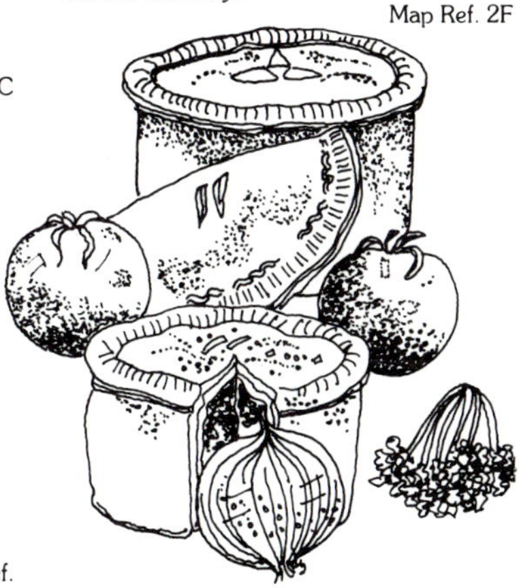

Guinea Grill
30 Bruton Place, W.1.
Tel: 01-629 5613
Approx £25.
Major Credit Cards.
Situated through the bar of the Guinea pub, this is a very popular restaurant. Excellent meat and starters and a first class wine list. Quite expensive however.
Open: 12.30pm-2.30pm and 7.00pm-11.00pm, Monday to Saturday.
Closed Sunday and Saturday Lunch.
Map Ref. 3F

Flanagans Eating House
100 Baker Street, W.1.
Tel: 01-935 1053
Approx £8.
No Credit Cards.
A good old fashioned style English eating house serving traditional English fare including soups, pies and fine fish dishes. Good, fun atmosphere.
Open: 12.00 noon-2.30pm and 6.00pm-10.45pm, Monday to Sunday.
Map Ref. 2F

Tiddy Dols
2 Hertford Street, W.1.
Tel: 01-499 2357
Approx £33.
Major Credit Cards.
An 18th Century house with quaint little rooms and twisting staircases and lots of atmosphere. Good selection of English food and some unusual specialities. Music and dancing.
Open: 6.00pm-2.00am, Monday to Sunday.
Map Ref. 3F

LONDON S.W.1.

Bens of Victoria
29 Victoria Street, S.W.1.
Tel: 01-222 0424
Approx £6.
No Credit Cards.
Elegant restaurant based on a House of Commons theme with models and cartoons of political figures. Specialities include home-made soups and pies and excellent salads.
Open: 12.00 noon-3.30pm and 5.30pm-11.30pm, Monday to Saturday.
Closed Sunday.
Map Ref. 4G

Bumbles
16 Buckingham Palace Road, S.W.1.
Tel: 01-828 2903
Approx £16.
No Credit Cards.
Popular restaurant serving plain traditional English food. Very good soups, steak and kidney pies and plain desserts.
Open: 12.00 noon-3.00pm and 6.00pm-10.30pm, Monday to Saturday.
Closed Sunday.
Map Ref. 5F

Hunting Lodge
16 Lower Regent Street, S.W.1.
Tel: 01-930 4222
Approx £20.
Major Credit Cards.
Plush restaurant with elegant decor and interesting trophies on the walls. Good food especially the game, smoked fish and roast meats.
Open: 12.30pm-3.00pm and 6.30pm-11.30pm, Monday to Saturday.
Closed Sunday.
Map Ref. 3G

Lockets
Marsham Court,
Marsham Street, S.W.1.
Tel: 01-834 9552
Approx £20.
Major Credit Cards.
Popular with members of Parliament and professional people, this elegant restaurant concentrates on traditional English food. Excellent mutton and lamb and very good desserts.
Open: 12.00 noon-3.00pm and 6.00pm-11.00pm, Monday to Saturday.
Closed Sunday.
Set Menu (Dinner) £8.50.
Map Ref. 5H

Tate Gallery
Millbank, S.W.1.
Tel: 01-834 6754
Approx £22 per head.
No Credit Cards.
After, or even before looking at the works of art, this restaurant deserves a visit. Traditional English food with some interesting variations complement one of the best wine cellars in the city.
Open: 12.00 noon-3.00pm, Monday to Saturday.
Closed Sunday.
Map Ref. 5H

English House
3 Milner Street, S.W.1.
Tel: 01-584 3002
Approx £15.
Major Credit Cards.
English restaurant in a private house with attractive decor. Interesting specialities of traditional English food. Fresh vegetables and superb desserts. Very efficient service.
Open: 12.30pm-2.30pm and 7.30pm-11.30pm, Monday to Saturday.
Closed Sunday.
Map Ref. 5E

Wiltons
27 Bury Street, S.W.1.
Tel: 01-930 8391
Approx £30-£40.
Credit Cards: American Express & Diners.
Very old established restaurant with Victorian decor serves superb food. Fish and shellfish are outstanding, game excellent, and dishes such as stews and steak and kidney pies mouth-watering.
Open: 12.30pm-2.30pm and 6.30pm-10.15pm, Monday to Friday.
Closed Friday Evening, Saturday and Sunday.
Map Ref. 3G

LONDON S.W.3.

Foxtrot
79 Royal Hospital Road, S.W.3.
Tel: 01-352 7179
Approx £10.
Major Credit Cards.
Plain, simple, very good cooking. Very popular. Under new management.
Open: 12.00 noon-2.30pm and 7.00pm-11.15pm, Monday to Saturday.
Closed Sunday.
Map Ref. 6E

Drakes
12a Pond Place, S.W.3.
Tel: 01-584 4555
Approx £24.
Major Credit Cards.
A smart split-level basement restaurant with nice decor. Well-cooked and well-presented English food with fresh vegetables. Pleasant atmosphere, and friendly staff.
Open: 12.30pm-2.15pm and 7.30pm-11.30pm, Monday to Saturday. 7.30pm-10.15pm, Sunday.
Map Ref. 6D

LONDON S.W.10.

The Click
533 Kings Road, S.W.10.
Tel: 01-352 7161
Approx £15.
Major Credit Cards.
Friendly and informal with a pleasant atmosphere. The decor is made up of changing painting exhibitions and twice-nightly cabarets are entertainment. Food is plain, wholesome and well cooked. Champagne breakfast served during second act. Over 40 cocktails available.
Open: 9.30pm-11.30pm, Monday to Sunday.
Bar opens 6.30pm.
Map Ref. 6D

Hungry Horse
196 Fulham Road, S.W.10.
Tel: 01-352 7757
Approx £22.50 per head.
Credit Cards: American Express & Diners.
Good traditional English fare served in pleasant surroundings. Try the jugged hare and boiled beef. Tasty desserts and friendly service.
Open: 12.30pm-2.30pm and 6.30pm-midnight, Monday to Sunday.
Closed Sunday Lunch.
Map Ref. 6D

LONDON W.8.

Maggie Jones
6 Old Court Place, Kensington Church Street, W.8.
Tel: 01-937 6462
Approx £25.
Credit Cards: Diners & Visa.
Small but pleasant little restaurant with a country atmosphere. Good home cooking of English food, pies and casseroles particularly tasty. Excellent patés and fresh vegetables.
Open: 12.00 noon-2.30pm and 7.00pm-11.30pm, Monday to Saturday. 6.30pm-11.30pm, Sunday.
Map Ref. 4C

LONDON W.C.2.

Rules
35 Maiden Lane, W.C.2.
Tel: 01-836 5314
Approx £18 per head.
No Credit Cards.
Very old restaurant used by Charles Dickens, Lilly Langtree and many famous personalities. Totally traditional with the very best of English food. Wonderful service.
Open: 12.15pm-2.45pm and 6.00pm-11.15pm, Monday to Saturday. Closed Sunday.
Set Menu — Pre-Theatre.
Map Ref. 3H

Simpson's-in-the-Strand
100 The Strand, W.C.2.
Approx £12.
Credit Cards: Access & Visa.
This is one of the institutions of English restaurants, and the atmosphere, particularly in the downstairs dining room, is very masculine. Classical English food served by impeccable waiters. Beef and mutton are splendid but so is the tripe and onion and the hot-pot. The rice pudding and treacle roll are worth tasting and so is the Stilton cheese.
Open: 12.00 noon-3.00pm and 6.00pm-10.00pm, Monday to Saturday.
Closed Sunday.
Map Ref. 3H

LONDON E.C.2.

Baron of Beef
Gutterlane, E.C.2.
Tel: 01-606 6961
Approx £30.
Major Credit Cards.
Panelled restaurant with elegant decor serving excellent English food. Very popular especially at lunchtime. Very efficient service.
Open: 12.00 noon-3.00pm and 6.00pm-9.30pm, Monday to Friday. Closed Saturday and Sunday.
Map Ref. 2L

FISH RESTAURANTS

LONDON W.1.

Bentley's Oyster Bar
11 Swallow Street, W.1.
Tel: 01-734 4756
Approx £15 per head.
Major Credit Cards.
Very much a 'club type' meeting place for business people. There is an upstairs restaurant and a ground floor oyster bar with a long marble counter. Oysters are excellent and so is shellfish. Service very good.
Open: 12.00 noon-2.30pm and 6.00pm-10.30pm, Monday to Saturday.
Closed Sunday.
Map Ref. 3G

Golden Carp
8a Mount Street, W.1.
Tel: 01-499 3385/01-629 5446
Approx £24.
Major Credit Cards.
Besides the speciality of carp, the sole and turbot is also excellent. There is also an oyster bar and good game.
Set Price: £8.
Open: 12.30pm-3.00pm and 6.00pm-11.30pm, Monday to Friday. 6.00pm-11.30pm, Saturday.
Closed Sunday and Lunch Saturday.
Map Ref. 3F

Grahame's Sea Fare
38 Poland Street, W.1.
Tel: 01-437 3788
Approx £12.
No Credit Cards.
A kosher restaurant with regular clientele who like the sole and plaice, the Scandinavian-style fish and the friendly service. All fresh.
Open: 12.00 noon-2.45pm and 5.30pm-8.45pm, Monday to Saturday.
Closed Sunday.
Map Ref. 2G

Scotts
20 Mount Street, W.1.
Tel: 01-629 5248
Approx £30.
Major Credit Cards.
Very plush restaurant serving excellent oysters and fresh fish. Salmon, turbot and shellfish are also excellent and it is possible to get skilfully prepared 'non-fish' dishes.
Open: 12.30pm-2.45pm and 6.30pm-11.00pm, Monday to Saturday. 7.00pm-10.00pm, Sunday.
Map Ref. 3F

Wheelers Antoines
40 Charlotte Street, W.1.
Tel: 01-636 2817
Approx £14.
Major Credit Cards.
Comfortable, intimate restaurant on three floors with cosy decor. Large selection of fish dishes and shellfish a speciality.
Open: 12.00 noon-2.30pm and 6.00pm-11.00pm, Monday to Saturday.
Closed Sunday.
Map Ref. 2G

Wheelers Braganza
56 Frith Street, W.1.
Tel: 01-437 5412
Approx £14.
Major Credit Cards.
Well-known fish restaurant with dining room upstairs and oyster bar on the ground floor. Fish dishes always well-presented.
Open: 12.00 noon-2.30pm and 6.00pm-11.00pm, Monday to Saturday.
Closed Sunday.
Map Ref. 3G

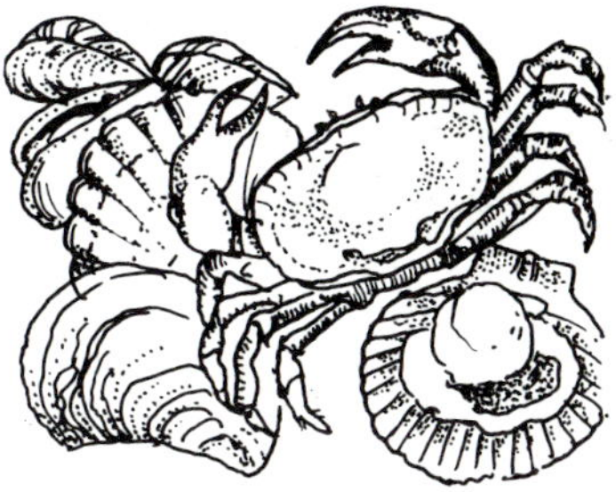

Wheelers Sovereign
17 Hertford Street, W.1.
Tel: 01-499 4679
Approx £14.
Major Credit Cards.
Elegant restaurant noted for the various presentations of Dover sole. Other fish dishes are good and the wine list is interesting.
Open: 12.30pm-2.30pm and 6.30pm-10.30pm, Monday to Saturday.
Closed Sunday.
Map Ref. 3F

Wheelers Vendôme
20 Dover Street, W.1.
Tel: 01-629 5417
Approx £14.
Major Credit Cards.
Very popular place with a downstairs oyster bar and a luxurious restaurant upstairs. Well prepared fish dishes with superb sauces. Shellfish also good. Efficient service.
Open: 12.30pm-2.30pm and 6.00pm-10.30pm, Monday to Saturday.
Closed Sunday.
Map Ref. 3G

Wheelers
19 Old Compton Street, W.1.
Tel: 01-437 2706
Approx £14.
Major Credit Cards.
A good selection of fish dishes are served in this traditional restaurant. Oysters are excellent and the service friendly.
Open: 12.30pm-2.30pm and 6.00pm-10.30pm, Monday to Saturday.
Closed Sunday.
Map Ref. 3G

LONDON S.W.1.

Overtons
5 St. James Street, S.W.1.
Tel: 01-839 3774
Approx £15 per head.
Major Credit Cards.
Club-like atmosphere in this famous fish restaurant with careful cooking and superb service. All fish and shellfish dishes are excellent.
Open: 12.00 noon-3.00pm and 6.00pm-10.00pm, Monday to Saturday.
Closed Sunday.
Map Ref. 3G

Wheelers
12a Duke of York Street, S.W.1.
Tel: 01-930 2460
Approx £12.
Major Credit Cards.
Lovely little restaurant on three floors specialising in sole dishes and lobster. Oysters are also good and the general ambience is nice.
Open: 12.00 noon-2.30pm and 6.00pm-10.45pm, Monday to Saturday.
Closed Sunday.
Map Ref. 3G

Wheelers Carafe
15 Lowndes Street, S.W.1.
Tel: 01-235 2525
Approx £12.
Major Credit Cards.
Friendly, intimate restaurant serving first class fish dishes. Shellfish are excellent, and salmon in season.
Open: 12.30pm-2.30pm and 6.30pm-10.45pm, Tuesday to Sunday.
Closed Monday.
Map Ref. 5F

LONDON S.W.3. and S.W.10.

Bill Bentley's
31 Beauchamp Place, S.W.3.
Tel: 01-589 5080
Approx £18.
Major Credit Cards.
Small dining room upstairs, a downstairs oyster bar and a happy friendly atmosphere. Fish dishes are simple, with fish pie a speciality. Good wine selection. Smoked fish.
Open: 12.00 noon-3.00pm and 5.30pm-11.00pm, Monday to Saturday.
Closed Sunday.
Map Ref. 5E

La Croisette
168 Itfield Road, S.W.10.
Tel: 01-373 3694
Approx £15.
Credit Cards: American Express.
You can really imagine you are in France in this little restaurant. Everything about it is French from the waiters to many customers. Fish is superb and the speciality is a magnificent 'fruits de mer'.
Open: 12.00pm-2.30pm and 8.00pm-11.30pm, Wednesday to Sunday.
8.00pm-11.30pm, Tuesday.
Closed Monday and Tuesday Lunch.
Set Menu £15.
Map Ref. 6C

Poissonnerie de l'avenue
82 Sloane Avenue, S.W.3.
Tel: 01-589 2457
Approx £30.
Major Credit Cards.
Cheerful French restaurant with a happy atmosphere. Well prepared fish dishes and the sauces are excellent.
Open: 12.30pm-3.00pm and 7.00pm-11.30pm, Monday to Saturday.
Closed Sunday.
Map Ref. 5E

Le Sequet
104 Draycott Avenue, S.W.3.
Tel: 01-581 1785
Approx £35.
Credit Cards: American Express.
Sister restaurant to La Croisette, this also has a marvellous atmosphere reminiscent of the South of France.

Wonderful soups and sauces accompany the fresh fish and vegetables. Fruits de mer, moules and salmon are specialities.
Open: 7.00pm-2.30am, Wednesday to Sunday and 7.30pm-11.30pm, Tuesday to Sunday.
Closed Monday and Lunch Tuesday.
Map Ref. 5E

LONDON W.8.

Geale's
2 Farmer Street, W.8.
Tel: 01-727 7969
Approx £10.
Credit Cards: American Express.
A very simple plain restaurant which has long been famous for serving excellent fresh fish and chips. Happy, friendly service. Fish delivered everyday.
Open: 12.00 noon-2.50pm and 6.00pm-12.00 midnight, Tuesday to Saturday.
Closed Sunday and Monday.
Map Ref. 3B

Wheelers Alcove
17 Kensington High Street, W.8.
Tel: 01-937 1443
Approx £12.
Major Credit Cards.
Elegant and traditional with a wide variety of well cooked fish dishes. Shellfish is also good and the wine list is extensive.
Open: 12.30pm-2.30pm and 6.30pm-10.30pm, Monday to Saturday.
Closed Sunday.
Map Ref. 4C

LONDON W.C.2.

Manzi's
1 Leicester Street, W.C.2.
Tel: 01-437 4864
Approx £18 per head.
Major Credit Cards.
Well-known fish restaurant with a smart dining room upstairs and a more simple one on the ground floor. Fish and shellfish are excellent and always very fresh.
Open: 12.00 noon-2.40pm and 5.30pm-11.40pm, Monday to Saturday and 6.00pm-11.00pm, Sunday.
Closed Lunch Sunday.
Map Ref. 3H

Sheekey's
29 St. Martin's Court, W.C.2.
Tel: 01-836 4118
Approx £24.
Major Credit Cards.
Very famous old fish restaurant which was one of the institutions of London. Now under new ownership which has smartened the decor, the quality of the cooking is still of the same high standard. Shellfish, turbot and salmon are all good and oysters superb, all packed.
Open: 12.00 noon-3.00pm and 6.00pm-11.00pm, Monday to Saturday.
Closed Sunday.
Map Ref. 3H

LONDON E.C.2.

Bill Bentley's
Swedeland Court, 202 Bishopsgate, E.C.2.
Tel: 01-283 1763
Approx £15 per head.
Major Credit Cards.
Very good luncheon place full of activity. The ground floor oyster bar is very popular and the basement dining room serves very high standard fish dishes. Friendly service.
Open: 12.00 noon-3.00pm, Monday to Friday.
Closed Saturday and Sunday.
Map Ref. 2K

Sweetings
39 Queen Victoria Street, E.C.2.
Tel: 01-248 3062
Approx £12.
No Credit Cards.
Extremely popular simple restaurant which serves excellent oysters, fish pie and salmon. Traditional puddings and cheeses are good and service is courteous.
Open: 12.00 noon-3.00pm, Monday to Friday.
Closed Saturday and Sunday.
Map Ref. 3J

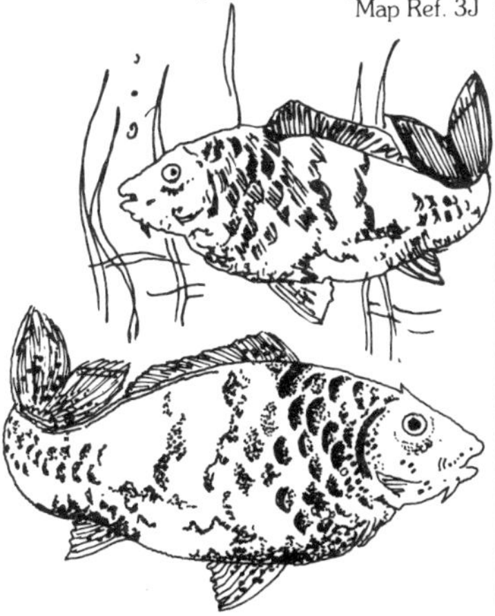

FRENCH

LONDON W.1.

Cafe Royal
Le Relais Restaurant, 68 Regent Street, W.1.
Tel: 01-437 9090
Approx £15.
Major Credit Cards.
Steeped in tradition with plush decor, this is an elegant restaurant famous throughout the world. There are two menus, one for classic French dishes and the other simpler provincial dishes. Service is outstanding.
Open: 12.00 noon-3.00pm and 7.00pm-11.30pm, Monday to Sunday.
Map Ref. 3G

Le P'tit Montmartre
15 Marylebone Lane, W.1.
Tel: 01-935 9226
Approx £30.
Major Credit Cards.
A pleasant little restaurant which has a popular lunchtime clientele. The French menu offers good choice and the service is friendly.
Open: 12.00 noon-2.30pm and 6.00pm-11.00pm, Monday to Friday. 6.00pm-11.00pm, Saturday. Closed Sunday and Lunch Saturday.
Map Ref. 2F

Connaught Hotel Restaurant
Carlos Place, W.1.
Tel: 01-499 7070
Approx £25 per head.
Credit Cards: Access.
It would be impossible in this space to write about all the virtues of this magnificent restaurant. Luxurious surroundings, marvellous service and the finest French cuisine. The specialities are too numerous to mention and are all superb, as is the wine list. Formal dress.
Open: 12.30pm-2.00pm and 6.30pm-10.30pm, Monday to Sunday.
Map Ref. 3F

L'Escargot Bienvenu
48 Greek Street, W.1.
Tel: 01-437 4460
Approx £12.
Major Credit Cards.
Long established Soho restaurant with plain decor. There is nothing simple about the food, however, which is high standard French provençal. Nice selection of cheeses.
Open: 12.00 noon-2.30pm and 5.45pm-10.30pm, Monday to Friday. 5.45pm-10.30pm, Saturday. Closed Sunday and Lunch Saturday.
Map Ref. 3G

La Gavroche
44 Upper Block Street, W.1.
Tel: 01-499 1826
Approx £25.
Major Credit Cards.
This legendary restaurant is what the very best of French cuisine is all about. It would be wrong to mention any particular creation as all are perfect, as is the superb service and the magnificent wines.
Open: 7.00pm-midnight, Monday to Saturday. Closed Sunday.
Map Ref. 5F

L'Etoile
30 Charlotte Street, W.1.
Tel: 01-636 7189
Approx £30.
Credit Cards: American Express & Diners.
A typically Parisienne restaurant with a wide choice of dishes, and a good wine list. Sauces are excellent, the hors d'oeuvre trolley a joy to behold and the service first class.
Open: 12.30pm-2.30pm and 6.30pm-10.00pm, Monday to Friday. Closed Saturday and Sunday.
Map Ref. 2G

Ici Paris
2a Duke Street, W.1.
Tel: 01-935 1864
Approx £24.
Major Credit Cards.
Pleasant little restaurant with plush decor. French cooking is simple but well prepared. Music in evenings.
Open: 12.00 noon-2.30pm and 6.30pm-11.00pm, Monday to Friday.
6.30pm-11.00pm, Saturday.
Closed Sunday and Lunch Saturday.
Map Ref. 2F

Au Jardin des Gourmets
5 Greek Street, W.1.
Tel: 01-437 1816
Approx £26.
Major Credit Cards.
Elegant, well established restaurant which serves first class French food. There are some interesting specialities and the wine list is famous as is the cheese board.
Open: 12.30pm-2.30pm and 6.30pm-11.15pm, Monday to Friday.
6.30pm-11.15pm, Saturday.
Closed Sunday and Lunch Saturday.
Map Ref. 3G

Mirabelle
56 Curzon Street, W.1.
Tel: 01-499 4636
Approx £25 per head.
Major Credit Cards.
An expensive but beautiful restaurant with flower banks and a sliding roof in the summer. The cuisine is outstanding, the choice of dishes lengthy and the service totally professional. It has held its very high reputation for 30 years.
Open: 12.30pm-2.30pm and 7.00pm-10.30pm, Monday to Saturday.
Closed Sunday.
Map Ref. 3F

LONDON S.W.1.

A l'Ecru de France
111 Jermyn Street, S.W.1.
Tel: 01-930 2837
Approx £25.
Major Credit Cards.
Very elegant and long established restaurant with a large menu of traditional French dishes. Excellent wine list.
Open: 12.30pm-3.00pm and 6.30pm-11.30pm, Monday to Friday.
6.30pm-11.30pm, Saturday.
Closed Sunday and Lunch Saturday.
Set Menu Lunch £10 50,
Dinner £14.50.
Map Ref. 3G

Chez Nico
129 Queenstown Road, S.W.1.
Tel: 01-720 6960
Approx £24 per head.
Credit Cards: American Express.
The standard of Nico's cooking has not altered since moving to these premises from South East London and the high standards which he sets himself are shown up in the superb sauces. Patés and fish dishes are specialities and the presentation of the fresh vegetables outstanding. A pretty, friendly little restaurant.
Open: 12.30pm-2.00pm and 7.00pm-10.45pm, Tuesday to Saturday.
Closed Sunday and Monday.
Map Ref. 6F

La Poule au Pot
231 Ebury Street, S.W.1.
Tel: 01-730 7763
Approx £28.
Major Credit Cards.
An informal country-kitchen type ambience with very good French regional dishes. Candle-light at night gives a soft atmosphere and the food is well prepared and simple. Helpful service.
Open: 12.30pm-2.30pm and

7.00pm-11.00pm, Monday to Saturday.
Closed Sunday.
Set Menu Lunch £8.50.
Map Ref. 5F

Mijanou
143 Ebury Street, S.W.1.
Tel: 01-730 4099
Approx £20 per head.
One of the best small restaurants in London. Nouvelle cuisine imaginately translated.
Open: 12.30pm-2.30pm and 7.30pm-10.30pm, Monday to Friday.
Map Ref. 5F

LONDON S.W.3.

Au Bon Accueil
27 Elystan Street, S.W.3.
Tel: 01-589 3718
Approx £28.
Major Credit Cards.
Popular restaurant which is always cramped and bustling. Simple cooking with fresh vegetables and imaginative presentation. Good value wine list.
Open: 12.30pm-2.30pm and 7.00pm-11.30pm, Monday to Saturday.
Closed Sunday and Saturday Lunch.
Map Ref. 5E

Bewicks
87 Walton Street, S.W.3.
Tel: 01-584 6711
Approx £35.
Major Credit Cards.
This is a cheerful intimate little restaurant with good, wholesome French cooking. Nice wine list.
Open: 12.30pm-2.15pm and 7.30pm-11.00pm, Monday to Sunday.
Map Ref. 5E

La Brasserie
272 Brompton Road, S.W.3.
Tel: 01-584 1668
Approx £25.
Major Credit Cards.
Basically an 'elegant bistro' (which was in fact its original name), the dishes are simple and well prepared and good value for money.
Open: 8.00am-midnight, Monday to Friday. 11.00am-midnight, Saturday and Sunday.
Map Ref. 5E

Capital Hotel Restaurant
22 Basil Street, S.W.3.
Tel: 01-589 5171
Approx £20 per head.
Major Credit Cards.
A modern hotel with a small restaurant which has a pleasant decor and serves a carefully chosen selection of classic

French dishes on the limited menu. Excellent desserts and a good wine list.
Open: 12.30pm-2.00pm and 6.30pm-10.00pm, Monday to Sunday.
Map Ref. 4E

Daphne's
112 Draycott Avenue, S.W.3.
Tel: 01-589 4257
Approx £30.
Major Credit Cards.
A well run restaurant which has been serving excellent French dishes over a long period of time. The specialities are written on a blackboard and all the dishes have a classic simplicity. Small and intimate surroundings.
Open: 7.30pm-12.00pm, Monday to Saturday.
Closed Sunday.
Map Ref. 5E

Le Francais
259 Fulham Road, S.W.3.
Tel: 01-352 3668
Approx £16 per head.
Credit Cards: American Express & Diners.
If you like to try regional dishes of France complemented by the wine of the area, then this restaurant does it superbly. The regions change every week. Helpful and friendly service.
Open: 12.30pm-2.30pm and 7.00pm-11.15pm, Monday to Saturday.
Closed Sunday.
Set Menu £16.
Map Ref. 5D

Mes Amis
31 Basil Street, S.W.3.
Tel: 01-584 9099
Approx £12.
Major Credit Cards.
Friendly French restaurant with nice Mediterranean decor. Simple French cooking with good ingredients and tasty sauces. Helpful service.
Open: 12.15pm-2.45pm and

7.15pm-11.00pm, Monday to Saturday.
Open Sunday.

Map Ref. 4E

La Tante Claire
68 Royal Hospital Road, S.W.3.
Tel: 01-352 6045
Approx £50.
Credit Cards: American Express.
Husband and wife team run this little restaurant with total efficiency. The French cuisine is of the very highest standard and the specialities are outstanding. Cosy dining room and excellent service. Book weeks in advance.
Open: 12.30pm-2.00pm and 7.00pm-11.00pm, Monday to Friday.
Closed Saturday and Sunday.
Set Menu Lunch, £10.50.

Map Ref. 6E

LONDON S.W.5., S.W.6., and S.W.10.

Bagatelle
5 Langton Street, S.W.10.
Tel: 01-351 4185
Approx £15 per head.
Major Credit Cards.
A charming little restaurant with simple but excellent French cooking. Sauces are very good, vegetables are fresh and there is a good cheese board.
Open: 12.00 noon-2.00pm and 7.00pm-11.00pm, Monday to Saturday.
Closed Sunday.

Map Ref. 6D

Carlos Place
855 Fulham Road, S.W.6.
Tel: 01-736 4507
Approx £24.
Major Credit Cards.
A very lively and industrial restaurant with helpful and friendly waiters. Interesting decor and the cooking is consistent, with the specialities particularly good.
Open: 12.00 noon-3.00pm and 7.00pm-11.30pm, Monday to Friday.
7.00-11.30pm, Saturday.
Closed Sunday.
Set Menu Lunch £3.95.

Map Ref. 6C

La Fringale
4 Hollywood Road, S.W.10.
Tel: 01-351 1011
Approx £22.
Credit Cards: Visa & Diners.
A pleasant Victorian styled little restaurant. Small menu but everything well prepared and excellent quality.
Open: 7.00pm-11.30pm, Monday to Saturday.
Closed Sunday.

Map Ref. 6D

LONDON W.8. and W.12.

Ark
35 Kensington High Street, W.8.
Tel: 01-937 4294
Approx £16.
Major Credit Cards.
Simple French cooking is a happy bustling atmosphere. Friendly service.
Open: 12.00 noon-3.00pm and 7.00pm-11.30pm, Monday to Saturday.
7.00pm-11.30pm, Sunday.

Map Ref. 4B

Le Detour
5 Campden Hill Road, W.8.
Tel: 01-937 9602
Approx £10.
Major Credit Cards.
Nice little restaurant with good, well cooked French dishes and some interesting specialities. Friendly service.
Open: 12.00 noon-2.30pm and 7.30pm-11.30pm, Monday to Friday.
7.30pm-11.30pm, Saturday.
Closed Sunday and Lunch Saturday.

Map Ref. 4B

Balzac Bistro
4 Wood Lane, W.12.
Tel: 01-743 6787
Approx £17.
Major Credit Cards.
Fun-type French bistro with bustling waiters and happy ambience. Blackboard menu features many provençal dishes which are well cooked and presented.
Open: 12.30pm-2.30pm and 7.00pm-11.00pm, Monday to Friday. 7.00pm-11.00pm, Saturday. Closed Sunday and Lunch Saturday. Set Menu from £6.50.
Map Ref. 4A

LONDON W.C.1. and W.C.2.

Boulestin
25 Southampton Street, W.C.2.
Tel: 01-836 7061
Approx £36.
Major Credit Cards.
Luxurious and elegant with sumptuous decor. The little bar lounge is an ideal place to study the fabulous menu of really classical French cuisine. Most dishes are superb and specialities outstanding.
Open: 12.30pm-2.30pm and 7.00pm-11.15pm, Monday to Friday. 7.00pm-11.15pm, Saturday. Closed Sunday and Lunch Saturday.
Map Ref. 3H

Brasserie du Coin
54 Lamb's Conduit Street, W.C.1.
Tel: 01-405 1717
Approx £20.
Major Credit Cards.
Very French little bistro serving traditional dishes which are well prepared. Very popular at lunchtimes.
Open: 12.00 noon-3.00pm and 6.00pm-10.30pm, Monday to Friday. Closed Saturday and Sunday.
Map Ref. 2I

Mon Plasir
21 Monmouth Street, W.C.2.
Tel: 01-836 7243
Approx £25.
A delightful little restaurant with simple provençal dishes which are well presented. Excellent cheeseboard and lovely desserts.
Open: 12.00 noon-2.00pm and 6.00pm-11.00pm, Monday to Saturday. Closed Saturday and Sunday Lunch.
Map Ref. 2H

Chez Solange
35 Cranbourn Street, W.C.2.
Tel: 01-836 0542
French restaurant with authentic French Provincial cooking. Ample portions. Piano music.
Open: 12.00 noon-4.00pm and 5.30pm-12.15am, Monday to Saturday.
Map Ref. 3H

LONDON W.11.

La Pomme d'Amour
128 Holland Park Avenue, W.11.
Approx £35 for two.
Upmarket French Restaurant with imaginative and delicious menu. Good house wine.
Open: 2.30pm-2.15pm, Monday to Friday. 7.00pm-10.00pm, Monday to Saturday.
Map Ref. 4A

L'Artiste Assoiffe
306 Westbourne Grove, W.11.
Tel: 01-727 4714
Approx £24.
Major Credit Cards.
Informal with nice candlelight atmosphere in the evening and guitarist. Authentic French cooking which is tasty and nicely presented.
Open: 6.30pm-11.30pm, Monday to Saturday. 12.30pm-2.30pm, Saturday. Closed Sunday.
Map Ref. 2B

LONDON W.9.

Didier
5 Warwick Place, W.9.
Tel: 01-286 7484
Approx £18 per head.
French Provincial atmosphere and cuisine. Not outstanding but a pleasant place to be.
Open: 2.30pm-2.30pm and 7.30pm-10.30pm, Monday to Friday.
Map Ref. 2C

LONDON E.C.1. and E.C.2.

Bubbs
329 Central Markets, E.C.1.
Tel: 01-236 2435
Approx £10.
Major Credit Cards.
Situated in Smithfield Market, this typically French bistro has lots of atmosphere. Good provincial cooking, particularly soups and fresh vegetables. Speedy efficient service.
Open: 12.15pm-2.00pm and 7.30pm-9.30pm, Monday to Friday.
Closed Saturday and Sunday.
Map Ref. 2J

Le Poulbot
45 Cheapside, E.C.2.
Tel: 01-236 4379
Approx £14.50 per head.
Major Credit Cards.
An elegant basement restaurant with high backed private booths very popular with businessmen. Limited menu but the food and sauces are of the very highest standards as in the service.
Open: 12.00 noon-3.00pm, Monday to Friday.
Closed Saturday and Sunday.
Set Menu £14.50.
Map Ref. 2K

GREEK

LONDON W.1.

Anemos
34 Charlotte Street, W.1.
Tel: 01-636 2289
Approx £20.
No Credit Cards.
Real swinging Greek restaurant where you can dance on the chairs and smash plates. Happy friendly atmosphere and typical Greek cooking. Excellent kebabs and wines.
Open: 12.00 noon-3.00pm and 6.00pm-midnight, Monday to Saturday.
Closed Sunday.
Set Menu £9.50.
Map Ref. 2G

Averof's Kebab House
86 Cleveland Street, W.1.
Tel: 01-387 2375
Approx £16.
No Credit Cards.
Lovely little Greek Restaurant run by husband and wife and serving marvellous kebabs, moussaka and other regional dishes.
Open: 12.00 noon-3.00pm and

5.00pm-midnight, Monday to Saturday.
Closed Sunday.
Map Ref. 2G

Cypriana Kebab House
11 Rathbone Street, W.1.
Tel: 01-636 1057
Approx £16.
Credit Cards: Visa & Diners.
Cypriot rather than Greek, nevertheless, the cooking is good. Specialities are talatouri salad, kleftiko and moussaka.
Open: 12.00 noon-3.00pm and 5.00pm-midnight, Monday to Friday.
5.00pm-midnight, Saturday.
Closed Sunday and Lunch Saturday.
Map Ref. 2G

Glory Kebab House
57 Goodge Street, W.1.
Tel: 01-636 9093
Approx £10.
Major Credit Cards.
Greek food is served in the restaurant. Specialities are kebabs. Friendly staff.
Open: 12.00 noon-2.00am, Monday to Saturday.
5.30pm-10.30pm, Sunday.
Map Ref. 2G

Jimmy's
23 Frith Street, W.1
Tel: 01-437 9521
Approx £12.
No Credit Cards.
Nearly 30 years old, this restaurant with its bohemian clientele and good value-for-money food is particularly an institution in London.
Open: 12.00 noon-3.00pm and 5.00pm-midnight, Monday to Friday.
12.00 noon-11.00pm, Saturday.
Closed Sunday.
Map Ref. 3G

Hellenic
30 Thayer Street, W.1.
Tel: 01-935 1257
Approx £16.

No Credit Cards.
Friendly, simple restaurant serving excellent Greek food complemented by good Greek and Cypriot wines.
Open: 12.00 noon-3.00pm and 6.30pm-10.30pm, Monday to Saturday.
Closed Saturday Lunch and Sunday.
Map Ref. 2F

Mykonas Greek Taverna
17 Frith Street, W.1.
Tel: 01-437 3603
Approx £18.
No Credit Cards.
Popular restaurant which is always full of fun with happy attentive waiters. Good food well prepared with many unusual Greek dishes.
Open: 12.00 noon-2.30pm and 5.30pm-11.00pm, Monday to Saturday.
5.30pm-11.30pm, Sunday.
Closed Saturday and Sunday Lunch.
Map Ref. 3G

White Tower
1 Percy Street, W.1.
Tel: 01-636 8141
Approx £30.
Major Credit Cards.
Consistently high standards make this old established Greek restaurant as popular as ever. The dining rooms are pleasant and so is the staff. Particularly good Greek specialities.
Open: 12.30pm-2.30pm and 6.30pm-10.30pm, Monday to Friday.
Closed Saturday and Sunday.
Map Ref. 2G

LONDON W.2.

Kalamaras
66 Inverness Mews, W.2.
Tel: 01-727 5082
Approx £14.50.
No Credit Cards.
Simple Greek Taverna which serves delicious starters and kebabs. Very friendly staff. Take own wine.
Open: 7.00pm-midnight, Monday to Saturday.
Closed Sunday.
Map Ref. 3C

Kalamaras Taverna
76 Inverness Mews, W.2.
Tel: 01-727 9122
Approx £17.
Credit Cards: American Express & Diners.
Colourfully decorated with rugs and pottery with music in the evenings. Excellent food with some interesting specialities.
Open: 7.00pm-midnight, Monday to Saturday.
Closed Sunday.
Map Ref. 4C

HUNGARIAN

LONDON W.1.

Csarda
74 Charlotte Street, W.1.
Tel: 01-580 7719
Approx £9.
Major Credit Cards.
The oldest Hungarian restaurant in London, it has a pleasant atmosphere with gipsy band and dancing until 2.00am. Good food and the deep fried mushrooms, chicken paprika and fillet steak in sour cream superb.
Open: 6.00pm-2.00am, Monday to Saturday.
Closed Sunday.
Map Ref. 2G

Gay Hussar
2 Greek Street, W.1.
Tel: 01-437 0932
Approx £28.
No Credit Cards.
Enormous menu of Hungarian specialities at this very popular restaurant. Skilful cooking which is extremely tasty, generous portions and interesting dishes.
Open: 12.30pm-2.30pm and 5.30pm-11.30pm, Monday to Saturday.
Closed Sunday.
Map Ref. 3G

LONDON W.2.

Mignon Restaurant
2 Queensway, W.2.
Tel: 01-229 0093
Approx £14.
Major Credit Cards.

Popular with Hungarian expatriates, this lively restaurant has a gipsy band, cymbalon music and good dishes such as beef goulash, a cheerful, happy place.
Open: 12.00 noon-3.00pm and 6.00pm-1.00am, Tuesday to Sunday.
Closed Monday.
Map Ref. 3C

INDIAN AND PAKISTANI

LONDON W.1.

Diwan-I-Am
161 Whitefield Street, W.1.
Tel: 01-387 0293
Approx £16.
Major Credit Cards.
Very popular little restaurant decorated to look like a cave. Specialities are tandoori chicken and prawn bhoona, but the mutton is also excellent.
Open: 12.00 noon-3.00pm and 5.30pm-midnight, Monday to Sunday.
Map Ref. 2G

Gaylord
79 Mortimer Street, W.1.
Tel: 01-580 3615
Also Albermarle Street, W.1.
Tel: 01-629 9802
Approx £9.
No Credit Cards.
Eastern style decor, this restaurant serves very good tandoori chicken, fried meat balls and pleasant curries, all appetisingly presented.
Open: 12.00 noon-3.00pm and 6.00pm-11.30pm, Monday to Sunday.
Map Ref. 3G

Geetanjli
23 Brook Street, W.1.
Tel: 01-493 1779
Approx £17.
Major Credit Cards.
If you appreciate that the best Indian food should be more aromatic than hot, then this restaurant is first-class. Specialities are the poppadoms, tandoori mixed grill from the clay oven. Ambience is exotic and service efficient.
Open: 12.00 noon-3.00pm and 6.00pm-11.00pm, Monday to Sunday.
Map Ref. 3F

Mandeer
21 Hanway Place, W.1.
Tel: 01-323 0660
Approx £13.
Major Credit Cards.
Cosy restaurant, intimate atmosphere, delicately spiced curries and well cooked vegetables make this an enjoyable place to eat.
Open: 12.00 noon-3.00pm and 6.00pm-10.30pm, Monday to Saturday.
Closed Sunday.
Map Ref. 2G

Lal Qila
117 Tottenham Court Road, W.1.
Tel: 01-387 4570
Good Tandoori Restaurant that is highly priased.
Map Ref. 2G

Tandoori of Mayfair
37a Curzon Street, W.1.
Approx £21.
Major Credit Cards.
Elegant restaurant with lovely decor and subdued lighting. Excellent specialities including chicken tikka, charcoal grilled spicy giant prawns and interesting desserts.
Open: 12.00 noon-3.00pm and 6.30pm-12.30am, Monday to Sunday.
Set Menu £9.50.
Map Ref. 3F

Veeraswamy's
99 Regent Street, W.1.
(Entrance in Swallow Street)
Tel: 01-734 1401
Approx £12.
Major Credit Cards.
Old established Indian restaurant with Victorian decor and pleasant atmosphere. Curries are mild and there are some nice tandoori dishes.
Open: 12.00 noon-3.00pm and 6.00pm-midnight, Monday to Sunday.
Map Ref. 3G

India of Mayfair
52 Hertford Street, W.1.
Tel: 01-629 1786
Approx £16.
Very good Indian cooking with Murgh-Massalam a speciality. Efficient and friendly staff.
Open: 12.00 noon-3.00pm and 6.00pm-11.30pm, Monday to Sunday.
Map Ref. 4F

LONDON W.2.

Ganges
101 Praed Street, W.2.
Tel: 01-732 4096
Approx £12.
Major Credit Cards.
Small popular restaurant which specialises in authentic Indian dishes, some not available in other restaurants. Giant fried prawns, and the chicken tikka are superb. Great care is taken in planning the menu.
Open: 12.00 noon-2.30pm and 6.00pm-11.00pm, Monday to Saturday.
Closed Sunday.
Set Menu £6.
Snack Lunch £1.25.
Map Ref. 2E

Khyber
56 Westbourne Grove, W.2.
Tel: 01-727 4385
Approx £8.
Major Credit Cards.
Pleasant little restaurant with some excellently prepared dishes, particularly the chicken and lamb curries. Nice vegetables.
Open: 12.00 noon-3.00pm and 6.00pm-midnight, Monday to Sunday.
Map Ref. 2B

LONDON W.8.

De India
14 Wrights Lane, W.8.
Tel: 01-937 8525
Approx £18.
Large restaurant on two floors with good Indian food.
Open: 12.00 noon-2.45pm and 6.00pm-11.30pm, Monday to Sunday.
Map Ref. 4C

LONDON S.W.1.

Kundan
3 Horseferry Road, S.W.1.
Tel: 01-834 3211
Approx £28.
Major Credit Cards.
Cool basement restaurant with beautiful decor maintains a very high standard of Indian and Pakistani cooking. Only the best ingredients go into the curry and tandoori dishes and the spicing is exquisite.
Open: 12.00 noon-3.00pm and 7.00pm-midnight, Monday to Saturday.
Closed Sunday.
Map Ref. 5G

LONDON S.W.3.

Tandoori
153 Fulham Road, S.W.3.
Tel: 01-589 7749
Approx £7.
Major Credit Cards.
Relaxing restaurant with pleasant decor and a little bar. Cooking is of a high standard and the lamb and chicken are beautifully spiced. Tandooris are cooked in clay ovens. Friendly service.
Open: 6.30pm-12.30am, Monday to Friday.
6.30pm-11.00pm, Saturday and Sunday.
Map Ref. 5D

LONDON S.W.5.

Naraine
10 Kenway Road, S.W.5.
Tel: 01-370 385
Approx £16.
Major Credit Cards.
Sophisticated restaurant with pleasant Indian decor. Good tandoori cooking but also some excellent hot curries. Attentive service.
Open: 12.00 noon-3.00pm and 6.00pm-midnight, Tuesday to Sunday.
Closed Monday.
Map Ref. 5C

Star of India
154 Old Brompton Road, S.W.5.
Tel: 01-373 2901

Approx £11.
Major Credit Cards.
Very high standards of Indian cooking with kebabs and prawn biryani specialities. Also very good Bangalore curries.
Open: 12.00 noon-3.00pm and 6.00pm-midnight, Monday to Saturday.
7.00pm-11.30pm, Sunday.
Map Ref. 5D

LONDON S.W.7.

Jamshid
6 Glendower Place, S.W.7.
Tel: 01-584 2309
Approx £18.
Major Credit Cards.
Old established with plush decor and one of the few places where you can get authentic Parsee cooking. Wide choice of starters. The chicken and lamb dhansak, Parsee kebabs and basmati rice are excellent. Marvellous presentation and courteous service.
Open: 12.00 noon-3.00pm and 6.00pm-11.30pm, Monday to Sunday.
Map Ref. 5C

Shezan
16 Cheval Place, S.W.7.
Tel: 01-589 7918
Approx £24.
Major Credit Cards.
Probably the best known Pakistani restaurant in London and justly lives up to its reputation. Marvellous tandooris, nans, vegetables and basmati rice. Lovely sweets, and efficient service.
Open: 12.00 noon-2.30pm and 7.00pm-11.30pm, Monday to Saturday.
Closed Sunday.
Map Ref. 5C

LONDON S.W.10.

Light of India
276 Fulham Road, S.W.10.
Tel: 01-352 5416
Approx £10.
Major Credit Cards.
There are special dishes cooked in clay ovens, which can be ordered in advance. Very helpful service. Good tandoori cooking.
Open: 12.00 noon-3.00pm and 6.00-midnight, Monday to Sunday.
Map Ref. 6C

LONDON S.W.1.

Bangla Desh
294 Upper Richmond Road, S.W.15.
Tel: 01-788 7880
Approx £12.
Superb Indian food prepared in herbs and spices, freshly ground. Cooked in traditional clay ovens.
Open: 12.00 noon-3.00pm and 6.00pm-midnight, Monday to Sunday.
Closed Bank Holiday Evenings.
Map Ref.

LONDON W.C.1.

Ganpath
372 Grays Inn Road, W.C.1.
Tel: 01-278 1938
Approx £6 per head.
Credit Cards: Access.
Good use of spices and the dals are a perfect example. Curries are hot but there are many other specialities.
Open: 12.00 noon-3.00pm and 6.00pm-10.30pm, Monday to Saturday.
Closed Sunday.
Map Ref. 1I

Tagore
8 Brunswick Centre, Bernard Street, W.C.1.
Tel: 01-837 9397
Approx £14.
Major Credit Cards.
Very good curries, prawn dishes and also well presented tandoori cooking. Interesting decor and often a cabaret in the evenings.
Open: 12.00 noon-3.00pm and 6.00pm-midnight, Monday to Sunday.
Map Ref. 1H

LONDON N.W.1.

Mumtaz
4 Park Road, N.W.1.
Tel: 01-723 0549
Approx £21.
Major Credit Cards.
Elegant and plush with exotic decor, the cooking is good with mild curries and some interesting specialities and side dishes.
Open: 12.00 noon-2.30pm and 6.00pm-11.15pm, Monday to Sunday.
Map Ref. 1E

Viceroy of India
3 Glentworth Street, N.W.1.
Tel: 01-486 3401
Approx £20.
Major Credit Cards.
Pleasant restaurant with nice decor and excellent tandoori specialities. Courteous and helpful service.
Open: 12.00 noon-3.00pm and 6.00pm-11.30pm, Monday to Sunday.
Set Menu £8.50.
Map Ref. 1E

INDONESIAN, MALAYSIAN AND SINGAPORE

LONDON W.1.

Rasa Sayang
10 Frith Street, W.1.
Tel: 01-734 8720
Approx £21.
No Credit Cards.
Authentic Singapore restaurant with a bustling atmosphere. Excellent satay, fish dishes and some spicy specialities.
Open: 12.00 noon-3.00pm and 6.00pm-11.30pm, Monday to Saturday.
Closed Sunday.
Map Ref. 3G

LONDON W.2.

Bali
101 Edgware Road, W.2.
Tel: 01-723 3303
Approx £18.
Major Credit Cards.
Split-level restaurant with nice ambience. Malaysian food on the ground floor and Indonesian in the basement. Huge portions of very good food. Try the giant king prawns and chicken satay. Charming service.
Open: 12.00 noon-2.30pm and 6.30pm-11.00pm, Monday to Sunday.
Basement Restaurant open 11.30am-midnight.
Set Price £8.50.
Map Ref. 2E

Bunga Raya
107 Westbourne Grove, W.2.
Tel: 01-229 6180
Approx £13.
No Credit Cards.
Simple restaurant with nice decor, and marvellous specialities such as hot spicy steamed crab, aram goreng and various satays.
Open: 12.00 noon-3.00pm and 6.30pm-11.30pm, Monday to Sunday.
Map Ref. 2B

LONDON W.8.

Singapore Restaurant
197a Kensington High Street, W.8.
Tel: 01-937 1551
Approx £8.
Major Credit Cards.
Large basement restaurant with many dishes and specialities of the region. Delicious satay and chicken in paper bag. Excellent sauces.
Open: 12.00 noon-3.00pm and 6.30pm-11.30pm, Monday to Sunday.
Map Ref. 4B

Singing Bamboo
35 Marloes Road, W.8.
Tel: 01-373 3410
Charming Indonesian restaurant with a wide variety of food.
Open: 6.30pm-midnight, Monday to Sunday.
Set Menus at £5.50, £7.50 and £9.50 per head.
Map Ref. 4C

INTERNATIONAL CUISINE

LONDON W.1.

Marquis
121a Mount Street, W.1.
Tel: 01-499 1256
Approx £30.
Major Credit Cards.
Very popular at lunchtime, bustling restaurant serves well prepared dishes. Prompt, friendly service.
Open: 12.00 noon-3.00pm and 6.00pm-11.00pm, Monday to Saturday.
Closed Sunday.
Map Ref. 3F

Odins
27 Devonshire Street, W.1.
Tel: 01-935 7296
Approx £50.
No Credit Cards.
Old established restaurant with a nice menu of interesting dishes. Decor is elegant and the ambience is soothing.
Open: 12.30pm-2.15pm and 7.00pm-11.15pm, Monday to Friday.
7.00pm-11.15pm, Saturday.
Closed Sunday and Lunch Saturday.
Set Menu Lunch £12.50.
Map Ref. 2F

Ritz Restaurant
Piccadilly, W.1.
Tel: 01-493 8181
Approx £15.
No Credit Cards.

Magnificent dining room reminiscent of the grand ages. Courteous and efficient service and superb cuisine and a marvellous wine list.
Open: 12.30pm-2.30pm and 7.30pm-10.30pm, Monday to Saturday.
Friday and Saturday dancing until midnight. 12.30pm-2.00pm and 7.00pm-10.30pm, Sunday.
Map Ref. 3G

LONDON S.W.1.

Le Caprice
Arlington Street, S.W.1.
Tel: 01-629 2239
Approx £24.
Major Credit Cards.
This was once the most famous restaurant in London, the Caprice. The new restaurant has recaptured the taste of the 20's and 30's with plush and elegant decor. Cuisine is also of a very high standard.
Open: 12.00 noon-3.00pm and 6.00pm-1.00am, Monday to Friday.
6.00pm-1.00am, Saturday.
Closed Sunday and Lunch Saturday.
Map Ref. 3G

Pomegranates
94 Grosvenor Road, S.W.1.
Tel: 01-828 6560
Approx £28.
Major Credit Cards.
Specialising in many varied dishes of a particularly high standard, this lovely little restaurant is a gem. Seasonal game and fish are served with fresh vegetables. Good wine list.
Open: 12.30pm-2.15pm, Monday to Friday, 7.30pm-11.15pm, Saturday.
Closed Sunday and Lunch Saturday.
Set Menu Lunch £11.00.
Map Ref. 6G

LONDON S.W.3.

Parkes
Beauchamp Place, S.W.3.
Tel: 01-589 1390
Approx £40.
Major Credit Cards.
Superb presentation, unusual and inventive cooking and a lovely, comfortable restaurant. There is no à la carte menu but the set dinner is so good there is no need for one.
Open: 12.30pm-3.00pm and 7.00pm-11.00pm, Monday to Saturday.
Closed Saturday Lunch and Sunday.
Set Menu (Dinner) £22.50.
Map Ref. 5E

Waltons
121 Waltons Street, S.W.3.
Tel: 01-584 0204
Approx £46.
Major Credit Cards.
18th Century English cooking with delicious sauces and interesting specialities. The restaurant has a soothing, glamorous atmosphere, the service is impeccable and wines outstanding.
Open: 12.30pm-2.30pm and 7.30pm-11.30pm, Monday to Sunday.
Set Price Lunch £8.50, Supper £6.
Map Ref. 5E

LONDON S.W.7., and S.W.10.

Chanterelle
119 Old Brompton Road, S.W.7.
Tel: 01-373 5522
Approx £16.
Major Credit Cards.
Intimate restaurant with alcoved tables and cooking which is good and well thought out. Nice atmosphere and the staff are friendly and efficient.
Open: 12.00 noon-2.30pm and 7.00pm-midnight, Monday to Sunday.
Set Menu Lunch £8, Supper £6.
Map Ref. 5D

Provans
306b Fulham Road, S.W.10.
Tel: 01-352 7343
Approx £25.
Major Credit Cards.
Very fashionable with a nice ambience and unusual dishes. Excellent fresh vegetables, a cosy downstairs bar and friendly waiters. Excellent English cooking.
Open: 7.00pm-midnight, Monday to Sunday.
Map Ref. 6D

LONDON S.W.8.

Alonso's
32 Queenstown Road, S.W.8.
Tel: 01-720 5986
Approx £23.
Credit Cards: American Express & Diners.
A lovely little restaurant which is quite difficult to find. Once inside however, Carmen Galvez makes you feel very much at home. Lovely presentation of really unusual dishes. Cooked to perfection.
Open: 12.30pm-2.30pm and 7.30pm-11.30pm, Monday to Friday.
7.30pm-11.30pm, Saturday.
Closed Sunday and Lunch Saturday.
Set Menu: Lunch £7.50, Dinner £11.25.
Map Ref. 6F

LONDON W.C.2.

Grange
39 King Street, W.C.2.
Tel: 01-240 2939
Approx £12.
Credit Cards: American Express.
Set menus which include adventurous dishes and marvellous crudités. Excellent service.
Open: 12.30pm-2.30pm and 7.30pm-11.30pm, Monday to Friday. 6.45-11.30pm, Saturday. Closed Sunday and Lunch Saturday. Set Menus from £10.60.
Map Ref. 3H

Inigo Jones
14 Garrick Street, W.C.2.
Tel: 01-836 6456
Approx £60.
Major Credit Cards.
Stained glass windows and luxurious decor create a pleasant atmosphere. The menu, whilst leaning towards French cooking, has other interesting specialities. French vegetables, efficient service and good wines.
Open: 12.30pm-2.30pm and 6.00pm-11.00pm, Monday to Friday. 6.00pm-11.00pm. Saturday. Closed Sunday and Lunch Saturday.
Map Ref. 3H

Neal Street Restaurant
26 Neal Street, W.C.2.
Tel: 01-836 8368
Approx £25.
Major Credit Cards.
Cool, fresh decor and a pleasant bar downstairs make this modern restaurant appealing. Mouth watering dishes and good service.
Open: 12.30pm-2.30pm and 7.00pm-11.00pm, Monday to Friday. Closed Saturday and Sunday.
Map Ref. 3H

Savoy Hotel
River Restaurant, Strand, W.C.2.
Tel: 01-836 4334
Approx £18.
Credit Cards: Access, American Express & Visa.
Recently refurbished, the dining room is luxurious. Elegant waiters give swift and attentive service, the cuisine is excellent and the presentation outstanding. Good wines.
Open: 12.30pm-2.45pm and 8.00pm-1.00am, Monday to Saturday. Closed Sunday.
Map Ref. 3H

Bates Restaurant
11 Henrietta Street, Covent Garden, W.C.2.
Tel: 01-240 7600
Sophisticated Restaurant with good meat, fowl and fish.
Open: 12.00 noon-3.00pm and 5.30pm-11.30pm, Monday to Sunday. Set Menu £8.50.
Map Ref. 3H

LONDON N.W.1.

The White House Restaurant
Albany Street, N.W.1.
Tel: 01-387 1200
Approx £20 per head.
Elegant restaurant in an area not too well-furnished with them. Good international cooking, and excellent wine list.
Open: 12.30pm-3.00pm and 6.30pm-11.30pm, Monday to Friday. Open Saturday Evenings. Closed Sunday.
Map Ref. 1F

LONDON N.W.6.

Capability Brown
351 West End Lane, N.W.6.
Tel: 01-794 3234
Approx £45.
Pretty decor and discreet service and very good food are the hallmarks of this restaurant.
Open: 12.30pm-2.30pm and 7.00pm-1.30am, Monday to Saturday. Sunday Lunchtime only.
Map Ref.

LONDON N.W.8.

Oslo Court
Prince Albert Road, N.W.8.
Tel: 01-722 8795
Approx £20 per head.
Continental cuisine and expensive but excellent wine list makes this a special place to be.
Open: 12.30pm-3.00pm and 6.30pm-11.00pm, Monday to Friday. Saturday Evening only.
Map Ref.

LONDON N.1.

Carriers
2 Camden Passage, N.1.
Tel: 01-226 5353
Approx £30 Lunch, £34 Dinner.
Credit Cards: American Express & Diners.
For many years this has been one of the best restaurants in London and the standards are as high as ever. The choice of dishes, the preparation, presentation and service could not be bettered. Set menus but with this

cuisine à la carte is irrelevant.
Open: 12.30pm-2.30pm and 7.30pm-11.30pm, Monday to Saturday.
Closed Sunday.
Set Menu, Lunch £14.74, Dinner £17.

No Map Ref.

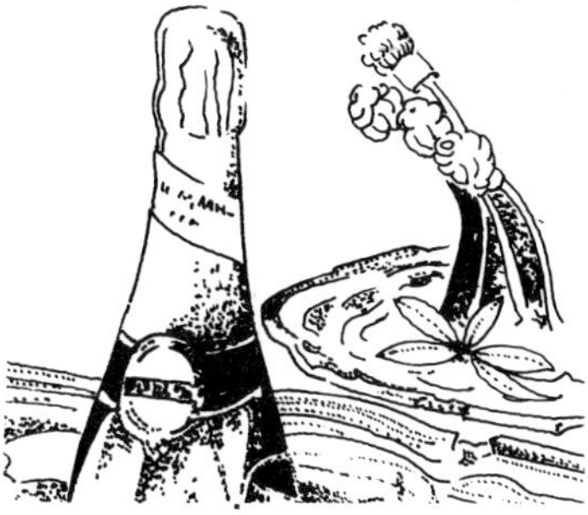

LONDON W.11.

Leith's
92 Kensington Park Road, W.11.
Tel: 01-229 4481
Approx £44.
Major Credit Cards.
Style, standards and efficient service make this restaurant an excellent place to eat. Inventive, well prepared specialities.
Open: 7.30pm-midnight, Monday to Sunday.
Set Menu £22.

Map Ref. 2B

LONDON S.W.11.

Pollyanna's
2 Battersea Road S.W.11.
Tel: 01-228 0316
Approx £40 for two.
Seductive restaurant out of the centre of London but worth the visit. Very good cooking.
Open: 7.00pm-midnight, Monday to Saturday.
Sunday Lunchtime only.

Map Ref.

LONDON E.C.2.

The City Gates Restaurant
Great Eastern Hotel,
Liverpool Street, E.C.2.
Tel: 01-283 4363
Approx £9 per head.
Splendid room redolent of former times. Buffet style service.
Open: 12.00 noon-3.00pm and 6.00pm-11.00pm, Monday to Friday. 12.00 noon-2.00pm and 7.00pm-9.30pm, Saturday and Sunday.

Map Ref.

LONDON S.E.1.

RSJ
13a Coin Street, S.E.1.
Tel: 01-928 4554
Approx £11 per head.
Informal but attractive restaurant with imaginative menu. Very popular so book.
Open: 12.00 noon-2.30pm and 7.00pm-11.00pm, Monday to Saturday.

Map Ref. 3I

ITALIAN

LONDON W.1.

Bertorelli's
19 Charlotte Street, W.1.
Tel: 01-636 4174
Also 44 Floral Street, Covent Garden, W.C.2.
Tel: 01-836 3969
Approx £20.
No Credit Cards.
One of the first Italian restaurants in London and still maintaining high standards. Friendly atmosphere and helpful staff.
Open: 12.00 noon-2.30pm and 6.00pm-10.00pm, Monday to Saturday. Covent Garden open 11.30pm. Closed Sunday.

Map Ref. 2G

Gennaro's
44 Dean Street, W.1.
Tel: 01-437 3950
Approx £20.
Major Credit Cards.
Old established restaurant with luxurious decor and efficient service. Good Italian cooking with tasty pastas, meat and lovely desserts.
Open: 12.30pm-2.30pm and 6.30pm-11.30pm, Monday to Sunday.

Map Ref. 2G

Terrazza
19 Romilly Street, W.1.
Tel: 01-734 2504
Approx £18.
Major Credit Cards.
Very busy and popular, particularly at lunchtime, the cooking is good and the specialities varied. Good selection of regional Italian wines.
Open: 12.00 noon-3.00pm and 6.00pm-midnight, Monday to Sunday.
Map Ref. 3G

Trattoria Toscana
14 Frith Street, W.1.
Tel: 01-437 6869
Approx £16.
Major Credit Cards.
Excellent Italian anti-pasta and lovely veal dishes. Friendly atmosphere and helpful staff.
Open: 12.00 noon-2.30pm and 6.00pm-11.30pm, Tuesday to Sunday.
Closed Saturday Lunch.
Map Ref. 3G

Verbanella
Blandford Street, W.1.
Tel: 01-935 2174
Approx £14.
Major Credit Cards.
A small restaurant with attentive staff and a good selection of simple Italian dishes. Anti-pasta is good as are the various fish specialities. Good wine list.
Open: 12.00 noon-3.00pm and 6.00pm-11.30pm, Monday to Saturday.
Closed Saturday and Sunday Lunch.
Map Ref. 2F

La Capannia
24 Romilly Street, W.1.
Tel: 01-437 2473
Approx £22.
Credit Cards: American Express, Diners & Visa.
A happy, bustling Italian restaurant with friendly decor and helpful staff. Excellent cooking with interesting specialities and good salads.
Open: 12.00 noon-3.00pm and 6.00pm-11.30pm, Monday to Saturday.
Closed Lunch Saturday and Sunday.
Map Ref. 3G

LONDON W.2.

Bizzarro
18 Craven Road, W.2.
Tel: 01-723 6029
Approx £20.
Major Credit Cards.
Some of the happiest Italian waiters in London and also some of the most efficient. Good atmosphere, Mediterranean decor and very good cooking. Dancing in the evening.
Open: 12.00 noon-3.00pm and 6.00pm-2.00am, Monday to Saturday.
Closed Sunday.
Map Ref. 3C

Chez Franco
3 Hereford Road, W.2.
Tel: 01-229 5079
Approx £20.
No Credit Cards.
Small restaurant with wooden chairs and benches with signed pictures of the various personalities who often eat here. Excellent selection of Italian dishes particularly the regional specialities.
Open: 12.30pm-2.30pm and 7.00pm-1.00pm, Monday to Friday.
7.00pm-11.00pm, Saturday.
Closed Sunday and Lunch Saturday.
Map Ref. 2B

LONDON S.W.1.

Como Lario
22 Holbein Place, Pimlico Road, S.W.1.
Tel: 01-730 2954
Approx £18.
No Credit Cards.
Lively and crowded, this popular trattoria is run by a hard working family who enjoy looking after their customers by providing authentic cooking and a happy atmosphere.
Open: 12.15pm-2.30pm and

6.30pm-11.30pm, Monday to Saturday.
Closed Sunday.
Map Ref. 5F

Frank's Restaurant
63 Jermyn Street, S.W.1.
Tel: 01-493 3645
Approx £18.
Major Credit Cards.
Busy, friendly restaurant which is always popular at lunchtime. Specialities include fettucine alla carbonara, veal dishes and osso bucco.
Open: 12.00 noon-3.00pm and 5.30pm-midnight.
Closed Sunday.
Map Ref. 3G

Sel e Pepe
13 Pavilion Road, S.W.1.
Tel: 01-235 0098
Approx £25.
Credit Cards: American Express, Diners & Access.
Popular and busy restaurant, especially at lunchtime. Interesting specialities with tasty liver and veal dishes. Friendly staff.
Open: 12.00 noon-3.00pm and 7.00pm-11.30pm, Monday to Saturday.
Closed Sunday.
Map Ref. 4E

Massino
42 Buckingham Palace Road, S.W.1.
Tel: 01-834 8283
Approx £20.
Credit Cards: American Express, Diners & Visa.
Busy basement restaurant always popular at lunchtime. Excellent menu with some very good specialities, fresh vegetables, fish, game and nice wines.
Open: 12.15pm-3.00pm and 6.30pm-11.30pm, Monday to Friday. 6.30pm-11.30pm, Saturday.
Closed Sunday and Lunch Saturday.
Map Ref. 4F

Mimmo d'Ischia
61 Elizabeth Street, S.W.1.
Tel: 01-730 5406
Approx £15.
Major Credit Cards.
Happy, friendly restaurant decorated with autographed pictures of famous stars. Marvellous seafood, liver and various veal dishes. Rich desserts and attentive service.
Open: 12.30pm-2.30pm and 7.00pm-11.30pm, Monday to Saturday.
Closed Sunday and Bank Holidays.
Map Ref. 5F

Mimmo and Pasquale
64 Wilton Road, S.W.1.
Tel: 01-828 6908
Approx £22.
Major Credit Cards.
Bright, Mediterranean atmosphere and some interesting Sicilian specialities. Fresh vegetables and some good fish dishes. Little terrace for eating out in the summer.
Open: 12.00 noon-3.00pm and 6.00pm-1.00am, Monday to Saturday.
Closed Sunday and Lunch Saturday.
Map Ref. 5F

LONDON S.W.3.

Don Luigi
33c Kings Road, S.W.3.
Tel: 01-730 3023
Approx £20.
Major Credit Cards.
Modern paintings, Italian tiles and a good ambience. Large menu with some unusual specialities. Nice selection of anti-pasta and desserts.
Open: 12.00 noon-3.00pm and 6.00pm-midnight, Monday to Sunday.
Map Ref. 6D

San Frediano
62 Fulham Road, S.W.3.
Tel: 01-584 8375
Approx £21.
Major Credit Cards.
Busy trattoria, very popular with a long list of devoted customers who enjoy the noisy atmosphere. Excellent food, soups and the many pasta dishes.
Open: 12.30pm-2.30pm and 7.15pm-11.15pm, Monday to Saturday.
Closed Sunday.
Map Ref. 5D

San Lorenzo
22 Beauchamp Place, S.W.3.
Tel: 01-584 1074
Approx £36.
Very well known Italian restaurant with charming decor, a nice bar and an indoor garden which opens out in the summer. Excellent pastas and some unusual specialities.
Open: 12.30pm-2.30pm and 7.00pm-11.30pm, Monday to Saturday.
Closed Sunday.
Map Ref. 5E

Meridiana
169 Fulham Road, S.W.3.
Tel: 01-589 8815
Approx £36.
Major Credit Cards.
First class restaurant with very attractive staff and a superb selection

of Italian specialities beautifully prepared and presented. Outdoor balcony for summer eating and a cosy downstairs bar.
Open: 12.30pm-3.00pm and 7.00pm-midnight, Monday to Sunday.

Map Ref. 5D

Beccofino
100 Draycott Avenue, S.W.3.
Tel: 01-584 3600
Approx £25.
Very good home-made pasta as well as other excellent Italian food. Exuberant and friendly.
Open: 12.00 noon-2.30pm and 7.30pm-11.30pm, Monday to Saturday.
Closed Sunday.

Map Ref. 5E

LONDON S.W.5.

Pontevecchio
256 Old Brompton Road, S.W.5.
Tel: 01-373 9082
Approx £16.
Credit Cards: American Express, Diners & Visa.
Modern, efficiently run restaurant which serves excellent value-for-money Italian cooking. Good selection of fish and chicken specialities, varied types of pastas and rich desserts. Outdoor seating in the summer.
Open: 12.30pm-3.00pm and 7.00pm-12.00 midnight.

Map Ref. 5C

LONDON S.W.7.

Gondoliere
3 Gloucester Road, S.W.7.
Tel: 01-584 8062
Approx £18.
Credit Cards: Access & Visa.
Pleasant restaurant. Well prepared food and a good selection of specialities.
Open: 12.00 noon-2.30pm and 6.00pm-11.30pm, Monday to Friday. 6.00pm-11.30pm, Saturday.
Closed Sunday and Lunch Saturday.

Map Ref. 5D

Montpeliano
13 Montpelier Street, S.W.7.
Tel: 01-589 0032
Approx £26.
No Credit Cards.
Charming decor with mirrors and plants give a friendly ambience to this popular restaurant. Very unusual specialities all beautifully prepared with helpful staff.
Open: 12.30pm-3.00pm and 7.00pm-midnight, Monday to Saturday.
Closed Sunday.

Map Ref. 4E

LONDON S.W.10.

La Famiglia
7 Langton Street, S.W.10.
Tel: 01-351 0761
Approx £25.
Major Credit Cards.
Popular and always busy with a happy atmosphere, the cooking is first class. The pasta is home made, the meat and fish dishes very tasty and the service is efficient.
Open: 7.30pm-11.30pm, Monday to Sunday.

Map Ref. 6D

Santa Croce
112 Cheyne Walk, S.W.10.
Tel: 01-352 7534
Approx £20.
Major Credit Cards.
Spacious, cheerful restaurant with efficient waiters bustling about. Regularly changed seasonal specialities, fresh vegetables and good cheeses and desserts.
Open: 12.30pm-2.15pm and 7.00pm-11.15pm, Monday to Saturday.
Closed Sunday.

Map Ref. 6D

LONDON W.8.

Trattoo
2 Abingdon Road, W.8.
Tel: 01-937 4448
Approx £25.
Major Credit Cards.
Hanging baskets, mirrors and lots of greenery give this attractive restaurant a pleasant ambience. There is a wide range of Italian dishes plus some very

interesting specialities. Good choice of wines.
Open: 12.00 noon-3.00pm and 7.00pm-12.00 midnight, Monday to Sunday.
Map Ref. 5B

LONDON W.C.2.

Luigi's
15 Tavistock Street, W.C.2.
Tel: 01-240 1795
Approx £25.
Credit Cards: Diners & Visa.
Good value for money, this bustling little trattoria is very popular, especially with showbusiness personalities. Authentic Italian cooking with excellent and tasty sauces.
Open: 12.00 noon-3.00pm and 5.45pm-11.30pm, Monday to Saturday.
Closed Sunday.
Map Ref. 3H

Ristorante San Martino
46 St. Martin's Lane, W.C.2.
Tel: 01-240 2336
Approx £12.50.
One of the friendliest restaurants in London with excellent Italian food. Large and popular. Good for pre or after theatre, too.
Open: 12.00 noon-2.30pm and 5.30pm-11.30pm.
Closed Saturday Lunch.
Open Sundays as weekdays.
Set Menu £6.75.
Map Ref. 3H

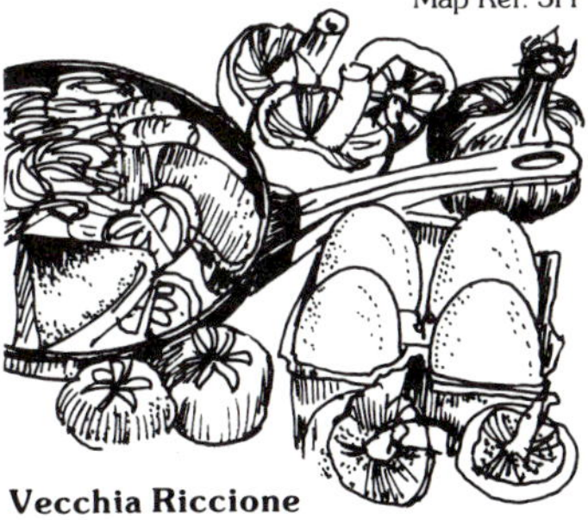

Vecchia Riccione
11 Upper St. Martins Lane, W.C.2.
Tel: 01-836 5121
Approx £24.
Major Credit Cards.
Delightful atmosphere where the waiters sing and dance, the food is well prepared and the specialities are written on a blackboard. Great fun.
Open: 12.00 noon-3.00pm and 6.00pm-11.30pm, Monday to Friday.
6.00pm-11.30pm, Saturday.
Closed Sunday and Lunch Saturday.
Map Ref. 3H

JAPANESE

LONDON W.1.

Fuji
36 Brewer Street, W.1.
Tel: 01-734 0957
Approx £16.
Major Credit Cards.
An elegant restaurant which serves easy-to-understand set menus and full mixed dishes for the knowledgeable. Many dishes are cooked at your table by pleasant waitresses.
Open: 12.30pm-2.30pm and 6.00pm-10.30pm, Monday to Friday.
6.00pm-10.30pm, Saturday.
Closed Sunday and Lunch Saturday.
Map Ref. 5G

Hokkai
59 Brewer Street, W.1.
Tel: 01-734 5826
Approx £15.
Major Credit Cards.
Good value, set menus are an excellent introduction to Japanese cooking. Interesting decor and charming service.
Open: 12.00 noon-2.30pm and 6.00pm-10.45pm, Tuesday to Saturday.
6.00pm-10.45pm, Sunday.
Closed Lunch Saturday, all day Monday.
Map Ref. 5G

Mikado
110 George Street, W.1.
Tel: 01-935 8320
Approx £40.
Major Credit Cards.
In an area where there are a number of Japanese restaurants, this lovely restaurant has a quiet air of elegance. The dishes are authentic and the preparation and presentation is superb.

Open: 12.00 noon-2.00pm and 6.00pm-10.00pm, Monday to Saturday.
Closed Sunday.
Map Ref. 2F

Saga
43 South Moltan Street, W.1.
Tel: 01-408 2236
Approx £40.
Major Credit Cards.
An atmosphere of country elegance with wooden partitions and lanterns. Lovely specialities, all of which are carefully explained by charming waitresses in national costume.
Open: 12.30pm-2.30pm and 6.30pm-10.30pm, Monday to Saturday.
Closed Sunday.
Map Ref. 3F

Sakura
9 Hanover Street, W.1.
Tel: 01-629 2961
Approx £30.
Major Credit Cards.
Traditional Japanese cooking with specialities for the western palate. Superb fish dishes and generous portions.
Open: 12.00 noon-10.30pm, Monday to Sunday.
Set Menus from £10.
Map Ref. 2G

Yamaju
16 Beak Street, W.1.
Tel: 01-437 2236
Approx £25.
Major Credit Cards.
A wonderfully decorated restaurant which consists entirely of private rooms. The food and the presentation are outstanding with a choice of four set dinners.
Open: 6.00pm-10.30pm, Monday to Saturday.
Closed Sunday.
Map Ref. 3G

LONDON S.W.1.

Suntory
72 St. James Street, S.W.1.
Tel: 01-409 0201
Approx £45.
Major Credit Cards.
Very smart restaurant owned by the Japanese whisky firm of the same name. Separate dining rooms, one for teppan cooking (meat shellfish grilled on hot plates in front of you) and the other rooms for traditional Japanese specialities. Marvellous service and a graceful ambience.
Open: 12.00 noon-2.00pm and 7.00pm-10.20pm, Monday to Saturday.
Closed Sunday.
Set Menu £19.85.
Map Ref. 3G

LONDON W.C.2.

Ajimura
51 Shelton Street, W.C.2.
Tel: 01-240 0178
Approx £26.
Major Credit Cards.
Authentic Japanese restaurant which serves beautiful varieties of fish dishes and vegetables. There are also set menus. Good value.
Open: 12.00 noon-3.00pm and 6.00pm-11.00pm, Monday to Friday.
6.00pm-11.00pm, Saturday.
Closed Sunday and Lunch Saturday.
Set Menus at various prices.
Map Ref. 2H

Azami
13 West Street, W.C.2.
Tel: 01-240 0634
Approx £18.
Major Credit Cards.
Lovely specialities explained carefully by charming waitresses. There are also excellent set menus with many interesting items. Simple and elegant with exemplary service.
Open: 12.00 noon-2.30pm and 6.00pm-10.30pm, Monday to Sunday.
Map Ref. 3H

LONDON E.C.4.

Aykoku-Kaku
9 Walbrook Street, E.C.4.
Tel: 01-236 9020
Approx £40.
Major Credit Cards.
Besides the traditional Japanese specialities there is also a range of three-course set lunches. There is a different area for teppan (grilled meat and shellfish) cooking an sushi (raw seafood). Friendly and helpful service.
Open: 12.00 noon-2.30pm and 6.00m-10.00pm, Monday to Friday.
Closed Saturday and Sunday.
Map Ref. 2I

LONDON N.W.1.

Asuka
5a Berkeley Arcade,
Baker Street, N.W.1.
Tel: 01-486 9074
Approx £32.
Major Credit Cards.
Excellent selection of seafood,

marvellous grilled meats and fresh vegetables, with easily identifiable dishes make up the menus at this little restaurant. Service is charming by waitresses in traditional costume.
Open: 12.30am-3.00pm and 6.00pm-11.00pm, Monday to Saturday.
Closed Sunday, Saturday Lunch.
Set Meal (Lunch) £6, (Dinner) £15.95.
Map Ref. 2F

JEWISH

LONDON W.1.

Grahame's Sea-Fare
38 Poland Street, W.1.
Tel: 01-437 3788
Approx £12.
No Credit Cards.
Very popular large Kosher fish restaurant. Marvellous selection either boiled, steamed or grilled, served with big portions of chips. Tasty desserts.
Open: 12.00 noon-2.45pm and 5.30pm-8.45pm, Monday to Saturday.
Closed Sunday, Monday Evening.
Map Ref. 2G

LONDON E.1.

Blooms
90 Whitechapel High Street, E.1.
Tel: 01-247 6001
Approx £7.
No Credit Cards.
The most famous of all the Jewish restaurants, this popular, bustling place serves huge portions of very appetising and well prepared food. Unlicensed.
Open: 11.30pm-9.30pm, Monday to Thursday. 11.30am-3.00pm, Friday and Saturday.
Closed Sunday and Dinner Friday and Saturday.
Map Ref. 2L

KOREAN

LONDON W.1.

Arirang
31 Poland Street, W.1.
Tel: 01-437 6633
Approx £12.
Major Credit Cards.
Traditional and authentic Korean food served by efficient and polite staff. Specialities are thinly sliced beef marinated in various sauces, barbequed spare ribs, king prawns, squid and excellent rice.
Open: 12.00 noon-3.00pm and 6.00pm-11.00pm, Monday to Saturday.
Closed Sunday.
Map Ref. 2G

Kaya
22 Dean Street, W.1.
Tel: 01-437 6630
Approx £20.
Major Credit Cards.
Although the set meals are a delight, the helpful waitresses in traditional costume will guide you through the mouth-watering à la carte menu. Many of the specialities are prepared at your table. The steamed fish is simmered in broth, and the marinated steak is delicious.
Open: 12.00 noon-3.00pm and 7.00pm-11.30pm, Monday to Saturday.
Closed Sunday, and Saturday Lunch.
Set Menu £10.
Map Ref. 3G

LONDON S.W.1.

Arirang House
3 Park Close, S.W.1.
Tel: 01-437 7608
Approx £20.
Major Credit Cards.
Elegant restaurant which serves really superb Korean dishes. Lovely, interesting specialities including barbequed spare ribs marinated in various sauces, delicious vegetables and beautifully presented fresh fruit.
Open: 12.00 noon-3.00pm and 6.00pm-11.30pm, Monday to Saturday.
Closed Sunday.
Map Ref. 4E

LEBANESE

LONDON W.2.

Al Amir
112 Edgware Road, W.2.
Tel: 01-262 6636
Approx £28.
Major Credit Cards.
A very smart restaurant with elegant decor, spacious tables and excellent service. Marvellous fresh vegetables, delicious kebabs which are flambéd at your table. The houmus, a purée of chick peas, is very tasty and the pancake desserts are also good.
Open: 12.00 noon-midnight, Monday to Sunday.

Map Ref. 2E

LONDON S.W.3.

Al Bustan
215 Brompton Road, S.W.3.
Tel: 01-584 9388
Approx £30.
Major Credit Cards.
Mediterranean decor, with a pleasant scattering of green plants, gives this restaurant a very pleasant atmosphere. Wonderful variety of charcoal grilled meats and pancakes. Entertainment at weekend. Friendly service.
Open: 12.00 noon-midnight, Monday to Sunday.

Map Ref. 4E

MEXICAN

LONDON W.1.

La Cucaracha
12 Greek Street, W.1.
Tel: 01-734 2253
Approx £10.
Major Credit Cards.
Full of atmosphere, with lots of small whitewashed rooms, bustling service and elegant Mexican style furniture. There is an extensive menu including excellent tortilla, superb meat dishes and the various salads. A happy restaurant.
Open: 12.30pm-2.30pm and 6.30pm-11.30pm, Monday to Friday. 6.30pm-11.30pm, Saturday.
Closed Sunday and Lunch Saturday.

Map Ref. 2G

MIDDLE EASTERN RESTAURANT

Salahadin
306 Earls Court Road, S.W.5.
Tel: 01-370 2445
Approx £9.
Middle-Eastern food is a speciality here though there is a European menu as well.
Open: 12.00 noon-midnight seven days a week.

Map Ref.

POLYNESIAN

LONDON W.1.

Beachcomber Restaurant
Mayfair Hotel, Berkeley Street, W.1.
Tel: 01-629 7777
Approx £26.
Major Credit Cards.
Polynesian style decor, with tropical atmosphere, live alligators and grass. Authentic food and exotic drinks. Dancing from 8.30pm.
Open: 7.00pm-2.00am, Monday to Saturday.
Closed Sunday.
Set Menu £12.95.

Map Ref. 3G

Trader Vic's
Hilton Hotel, Park Lane, W.1.
Tel: 01-493 7586
Approx £40.
Major Credit Cards.
South Sea Island setting which is both quiet and pleasant. Marvellous selection of cocktails and lovely fish and marinated lamb dishes.
Open: 12.00 noon-3.00pm and 6.30pm-midnight, Monday to Friday. 6.30pm-noon, Saturday.

Map Ref. 3F

PORTUGUESE

LONDON S.W.1.

Os Arcos
44 Hugh Street, S.W.1.
Tel: 01-828 1486
Approx £12.
Major Credit Cards.
Tiled floors, white walls with arches, mirrors and green plants, give this lovely little restaurant a cool, Mediterranean atmosphere. There is a good selection of seafood and shellfish, tasty meat dishes and excellent Portuguese wines.
Open: 12.30pm-2.30pm and 7.30pm-11.30pm, Monday to Saturday.
Closed Sunday and Saturday Lunch.
Map Ref. 5F

LONDON S.W.3.

Caravela
11 Beauchamp Place, S.W.3.
Tel: 01-581 2366
Approx £12.
Major Credit Cards.
Popular little restaurant with lots of bustle and activity. Helpful waiters and well prepared, authentic, Portuguese dishes. Delicious sardines and other fish dishes.
Open: 12.00 noon-3.00pm and 7.00pm-1.00am, Monday to Sunday.
Map Ref. 5F

O Fado
50 Beauchamp Place, S.W.3.
Tel: 01-589 3002
Approx £25.
No Credit Cards.
Friendly, intimate atmosphere with attentive service and excellent authentic Portuguese food. Interesting specialities. Singing in evening.
Open: 12.00 noon-3.00pm and 7.00pm-1.00am, Monday to Sunday.
Map Ref. 5E

RUSSIAN, CZECHOSLOVAKIAN AND POLISH

LONDON W.2.

Moravia
62 Queensway, W.2.
Tel: 01-229 4199
Approx £12.
Major Credit Cards.
Good selection of Czechoslovakian dishes such as goulash, dumplings and Moravian sausage. Log cabin atmosphere and folk songs for evening entertainment.
Open: 11.30am-midnight, Monday to Sunday.
Map Ref. 3C

LONDON S.W.3.

Borshtch 'N' Tears
46 Beauchamp Place, S.W.3.
Tel: 01-235 1892
Approx £9.
Major Credit Cards.
Popular, informal restaurant, which gets very lively in the evening, loud Russian music and a general table-thumping atmosphere. The beef stroganoff, the borscht, and other dishes are tasty and the portions are huge.
Open: 6.30pm-1.30am, Monday to Sunday.
Map Ref. 5E

Luba's Bistro
6 Yeoman's Row, S.W.3.
Tel: 01-589 2950
Approx £12.
No Credit Cards.
Busy, friendly and popular Russian restaurant, with a nice informal atmosphere good cooking. Bring your own wine.
Open: 12.00 noon-3.00pm and 6.00pm-midnight, Monday to Saturday.
Closed Sunday.
Map Ref. 5E

LONDON S.W.10.

Nikita's
65 Ifield Road, S.W.10.
Tel: 01-352 6326
Approx £18.
Major Credit Cards.
Superb Russian food such as blinis, borscht, koulebiac and other interesting dishes. Many types of flavoured vodka and a friendly, happy atmosphere.
Open: 7.30pm-11.30pm, Monday to Saturday.
Closed Sunday.
Map Ref. 6C

SCANDINAVIAN

LONDON W.2.

Hungry Viking
44 Ossington Street, W.2.
Tel: 01-727 3311
Approx £15.
Major Credit Cards.
Waitresses in national costume help you to choose among the tasty dishes on the smorgasbord in this friendly

Scandinavian type parlour restaurant.
Open: 6.30pm-11.30pm, Tuesday to Sunday.
Closed Sunday.
Map Ref. 3C

SPANISH

LONDON W.1.

Barcelona
17 Beak Street, W.1.
Tel: 01-734 6615
Approx £30.
Major Credit Cards.
Good Spanish food with some well prepared fish specialities. Nice atmosphere with guitarist in the evenings and a large choice of wines.
Open: 12.00pm-midnight, Monday to Saturday. 11.00pm, Sunday.
Map Ref. 3G

Los Espanoles
74 Charlotte Street, W.1.
Tel: 01-636 0036
Approx £12.
Major Credit Cards.
Lively restaurant, with a Spanish band and friendly staff. Good, authentic Spanish food.
Open: 12.00 noon-3.00pm and 6.00pm-2.30am, Monday to Friday.
6.00pm-2.30am, Saturday and Sunday.
Closed Lunch Saturday and Sunday.
Map Ref. 2G

Martinez
25 Swallow Street, W.1.
Tel: 01-734 5066
Approx £24.
Major Credit Cards.
Old-fashioned restaurant with authentic Spanish decor of hand painted tiles and intricate wrought iron. Excellent food particularly the calamares, gazpacho and Barzuela dishes. Courteous service. Guitar in Evening.
Open: 12.00 noon-3.00pm and 6.00pm-midnight, Monday to Sunday.
Map Ref. 3G

LONDON S.W.10.

El Bodegon
9 Park Walk, S.W.10.
Tel: 01-352 1330
Approx £20.
Major Credit Cards.
Continental atmosphere in this popular Spanish restaurant. Excellent cooking with interesting specialities, including prawns in garlic sauce, various paellas and chicken dishes.
Open: 12.00 noon-3.00pm and 7.00pm-midnight, Monday to Sunday.
Set Monday Lunch £6.
Map Ref. 6D

SWISS

LONDON W.1.

St. Moritz
161 Wardour Street, W.1.
Tel: 01-734 3324
Approx £24.
Major Credit Cards.
Very pleasant little restaurant which serves authentic Swiss dishes such as fondue bourguignonne, Kassupe and lovely pâtisseries.
Open: 12.00 noon-3.00pm and 7.00pm-11.30pm, Monday to Saturday.
6.00pm-midnight, Sunday.
Set Menu (Lunch) £6.75.
Map Ref. 3G

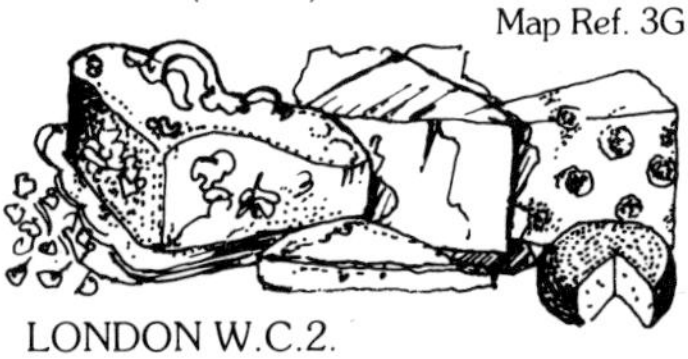

LONDON W.C.2.

Swiss Centre
2 New Coventry Street, Leicester Square, W.C.2.
Tel: 01-734 1291
Approx £10-£36.
No Credit Cards.
Four separate restaurants within one building but all within sight of each other and all offering different types of authentic Swiss dishes.

The **Imbis** coffee shop has a a self-service selection, the **Rendez-vous** has snacks and a marvellous selection of pâtisseries, the **Taverne** specialises in fondues and raclettes and the **Chesa** restaurant has an attractive decor and excellent menus.

Imbiss
Open: 8.30am-11.30pm, Monday to Sunday.
Rendez-vous
Open: 11.30am-midnight, Monday to Sunday.
Chesa
Open: 11.30am-3.00pm and 6.00pm-midnight, Monday to Sunday.
Taverne
Open: 11.30am-midnight, Monday to Sunday.
Map Ref. 3H

THAI

LONDON W.1.

Chaopraya
22 St. Christopher's Place, Oxford Street, W.1.
Tel: 01-486 0777
Approx £20.
Credit Cards: Access & Diners.
An elegant restaurant, with arches and nice decor, which serves authentic Thai cuisine. The set meals are enjoyable, but the charming waitresses are very helpful about the huge à la carte menu.
Open: 12.00 noon-3.00pm and 6.30pm-11.00pm, Monday to Saturday.
Closed Sunday.
Set Menu (Lunch) £12.80 for two.
Map Ref. 2G

Sukhothai
22 Bateman Street, W.1.
Tel: 01-434 2320
Approx £16.
Credit Cards: Access & Visa.
Smart restaurant which serves excellent food, well prepared and beautifully presented in the traditional Thai manner.
Open: 12.00 noon-3.00pm and 6.00pm-11.00pm, Monday to Saturday.
Closed Sunday.
Map Ref. 1E

LONDON W.8.

Siam
12 St. Albans Grove, W.8.
Tel: 01-937 8765
Approx £10.
No Credit Cards.
Sumptuous decor in the ground floor restaurant and elegant surroundings in the downstairs restaurant where you can recline on cushions and watch traditional Thai dancing. Lovely food served with exemplary service by charming staff.
Open: 12.30pm-2.30pm and 6.15pm-11.15pm, Tuesday to Sunday.
6.15pm-11.15pm, Monday.
Closed Lunch Sunday and Monday Lunch.
Set Menu £7.80.
Map Ref. 4C

Thai Restaurant
209 Kensington High Street, W.8.
Tel: 01-937 2260
Approx £10.
Credit Cards: American Express, Diners & Access.
Daily Thai specialities such as crispy spring greens in oyster sauce, lovely varied fish dishes and spicy meats. Pleasant little restaurant, with helpful smiling service.
Open: 12.00 noon-3.00pm and 6.00pm-10.00pm, Monday to Sunday.
Set Menu £10 for two.
Map Ref. 4C

LONDON S.W.10.

Busabong
331 Fulham Road, S.W.10.
Approx £12.
Major Credit Cards.
Either recline on cushions and watch Thai dancing while you eat in one dining room, or in the other, more formal room, sit upright and eat the same beautifully prepared cooking, with fragrant sauces, served by courteous staff.
Open: 12.30pm-3.00pm and 6.30pm-11.30pm, Monday to Saturday.
12.30pm-3.00pm and 6.30pm-10.00pm, Sunday.
Map Ref. 6D

TURKISH

LONDON W.1.

Golden Horn
134 Wardour Street, W.1.
Tel: 01-437 3027
Approx £20.
Major Credit Cards.
Pleasant restaurant which serves a large selection of Turkish specialities by friendly, helpful staff. Excellent kebabs.
Open: 12.00 noon-midnight, Monday to Saturday.
Closed Sunday.
Map Ref. 3G

Topkapi
25 Marylebone High Street, W.1.
Tel: 01-486 1872
Approx £15.
Major Credit Cards.
Very good kebabs, mezes and other Turkish specialities.
Open: 11.30am-midnight, Monday to Sunday.
Set Menu (Lunch) £4.
Map Ref. 2F

LATE NIGHT EATING

The following restaurants are a selection of where it is possible to get either a full meal or just a snack late at night.

LONDON W.1.

Far East Chinese food.
13 Gerrard Street, W.1.
Tel: 01-437 6148
Open to 5.00am.
Map Ref. 3H

Lido Chinese food.
41 Gerrard Street, W.1.
Tel: 01-437 4431
Open to 5.00am.
Map Ref. 3H

INEXPENSIVE RESTAURANTS

Eating inexpensively in London can be a hazard. There are plenty of chain restaurants, of course, like MACDONALDS, GARFUNKELS, PIZZA HUT and other various chains. Departmental stores also can sometimes have good, reasonable food — HARVEY NICHOLS, downstairs; HARRODS — the *Circle* Restaurants — PETER ROBINSON, where CRANKS have a cafe as they do in HEAL'S. And, of course, pubs and wine bars can give you good, reasonable food. But here are some more that have interesting food that is not too expensive.

LONDON W.1.

Chicago Pizza Pie Factory
17 Hanover Square, W.1.
Tel: 01-629 2669
Tube: Oxford Circus
The deepest pizzas in London and very big indeed — so two people can easily share one. Each one baked separately so don't eat here if you are in a hurry.
Map Ref. 2G

D'Artagnan
19 Blandford Street, W.1.
Tel: 01-935 1023
Approx £15.
Credit Cards: Access & Visa.
Pleasant little restaurant which serves a very tasty variety of well prepared dishes.
Open: 12.30pm-2.30pm and 7.00pm-10.30pm, Monday to Saturday.
Closed Sunday.
Set Menu £7.50.
Map Ref. 2F

L'Artiste Musclé
1 Shepherd Market, W.1.
Tel: 01-493 6150
Approx £11.
No Credit Cards.
Friendly atmosphere and well cooked steaks, salads and tasty casseroles.
Open: 12.00 noon-3.00pm and 5.30pm-11.00pm, Monday to Saturday.
5.30pm-midnight, Sunday.
Closed Lunch Sunday.
Map Ref. 3F

Creperie
56a South Molton Street, W.1.
Tel: 01-629 4794
Tube: Oxford Street or Bond Street.
Map Ref.

also at

Unit 21, Covent Garden W.C.2.
Tel: 01-836 2137
Tube: Covent Garden.
Pancakes galore with every imaginable filling you can think of — savoury, sweet, vegetarian. Pancakes are very crispy, too. In summer you can sit in the sun outside and watch the world go by. Open until midnight.
Map Ref. 6F

Granary
39 Albemarle Street, W.1.
Tel: 01-493 2978
Tube: Green Park.
Some of the best and most original food in London displayed in Large dishes for you to choose from. Delicious cakes and puddings, too. Crowded at Lunchtime so go early if you want to sit upstairs. The downstairs room tends to get rather noisy.
Map Ref. 2G

Hard Rock Cafe
150 Park Lane, W.1.
Tel: 01-629 0382
Tube: Hyde Park.
Hamburgers and American Food plus noisy music characterise this lively cafe, one of the most popular in

London. Steaks and Club sandwiches are good, too. *Open until midnight; Open Sundays.*

Map Ref. 3F

Jack Spratt
17 George Street, W.1.
Tel: 01-486 5909
Tube: Bond Street.
Every delicious dish is calorie counted for you — but Jack Spratt believes in good food not starvation and limp lettuce. Very good food and wine makes slimming a delight — and non-slimmers enjoy the fresh food, too!

Map Ref. 2E

Justin De Blank
54 Duke Street, W.1.
Tel: 01-000 0000
Tube: Marble Arch.
Part of Justin de Blank's successful series of shops purveying good food. Self-service, with very good hot and cold food. Very tempting, but remember there are also very scrumptious puddings and good cheese as well. The wine is good, too so is the coffee.

Map Ref. 2F

Heroes
11 Maddox Street, W.1.
Tel: 01-493 6596
Approx £7.
A cafe restaurant with a cocktail bar and disco dancing every evening.

Map Ref. 2G

Maison Sagne
105 Marylebone High Street, W.1.
Tel: 01-935 6240
Tube: Oxford Circus.
Closes at 5 p.m. but ideal for coffee or tea with delicious croissants and cakes. At lunchtime there are light meals of the vol-au-vent, omelette type which are also delicious.

Map Ref. 2F

Salonika Kebab Greek food.
69 Charlotte Street, W.1.
Tel: 01-636 3990
Open to 6.00am.

Map Ref. 2G

LONDON W.2.

El Greco Taverna
15 Hereford Road, W.2.
Tel: 01-229 3101
Approx £9.
Major Credit Cards.
Lovely Greek food in this small taverna which also has lots of atmosphere. Kebabs and stews are a delight.
Open: 6.00pm-1.00am, Monday to Sunday.
Meze Menu £11.

Map Ref. 2B

LONDON S.W.1.

Bendick's
195 Sloane Street, S.W.1.
Tel: 01-235 4749
Tube: Knightsbridge.
A true English tea shop with luscious cakes, scones and very good tea. At lunchtime, also offers hot dishes, soups, omelettes and so on. Small, but very English and good.

Map Ref. 4E

General Trading Company
144 Sloane Street, S.W.1.
Tel: 01-730 0411
In this famous gift shop — all the best brides have their Wedding List here — are two self-service restaurants that serve delicious, cordon bleu type food, both hot and cold. In summer you can sit outside. Pleasant staff of the Sloane Ranger variety, as is the clientele.

Map Ref. 4E

Danish Coffee House
16 Sloane Street, S.W.1.
Tube: Knightsbridge.
Downstairs, under the shop selling Danish specialities, is this clean restaurant selling Danish sandwiches, pastries and cakes. There is a wide variety catering to all tastes and the food is very fresh and appetising.

Map Ref. 4E

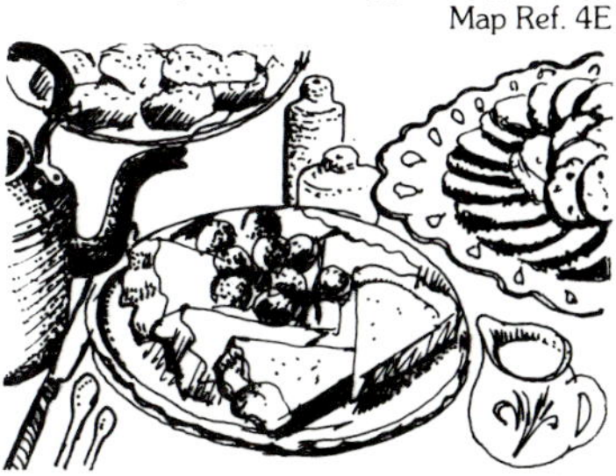

LONDON S.W.3.

Zia Teresa
6 Hans Road, S.W.3.
Tel: 01-589 7634
Approx £19.
No Credit Cards.
Italian restaurant which offers excellent pastas and generous portions of well prepared meat and fish dishes.
Open: 12.00 noon-11.00pm, Monday to Saturday.
Closed Sunday.
Map Ref. 4E

LONDON S.W.6.

Fingals
690 Fulham Road, S.W.6.
Tel: 01-736 1195
Approx £10 Lunch, £20 Dinner.
Credit Cards: Visa.
Lovely little restaurant, which serves very accomplished food and interesting specialities.
Open: 12.30pm-2.30pm and 8.00pm-11.30pm, Monday to Friday.
8.00pm-11.30pm, Saturday.
Closed Sunday and Lunch Saturday.
Map Ref. 6D

The Garden
616 Fulham Road, S.W.6.
Tel: 01-736 6056
Approx £16.
Major Credit Cards.
Soft and elegant, this little restaurant is ideal for a quiet meal. Excellent standard of food and good helpful service. Also Vegetarian Menu.
Open: 7.00pm-11.00pm, Tuesday to Sunday.
Closed Monday and Dinner Sunday.
Map Ref. 6D

LONDON S.W.7.

Bistro Vino
1 Old Brompton Road, S.W.7.
Tel: 01-584 6590
Approx £12.
No Credit Cards.
Popular haunt for those who like Anglo-French food, served in a friendly atmosphere. Good steaks.
Open: 12.00 noon-2.45pm and 6.00pm-12.00 midnight, Monday to Sunday.
Map Ref. 5D

Great British Success Hamburgers.
85 Gloucester Road, S.W.7.
Tel: 01-370 4404
Open: 24 hours.
Map Ref. 5D

LONDON W.6.

Lyric Theatre Buffet
King Street, Hammersmith, W.6.
Tel: 01-741 0824
Tube: Hammersmith.
If you should be in this area or visiting the beautiful Lyric Theatre hidden away in this office block then stop for a meal in the restaurant where you will find good home cooking and inventive, original salads. You can eat outside on the terrace on a warm day and survey the Hammersmith sky-line. Good cakes, too.
No Map Ref.

LONDON S.W.10.

Click
533 Kings Road, S.W.10.
Tel: 01-352 7161
Approx £5.
Major Credit Cards.
Smart little restaurant which offers good food, excellent hamburgers and salads and a happy atmosphere.
Open: 6.00pm-1.00am, Monday to Sunday.
Map Ref. 6D

Fox Trot Tango
14 Hollywood Road, S.W.10.
Tel: 01-352 8692
Approx £6.
Major Credit Cards.
Friendly, busy restaurant with a good menu of interesting specialities and a nice atmosphere.
Open: 12.30pm-2.30pm and 7.30pm-11.45pm, Monday to Saturday.
7.30pm-11.30pm, Sunday.
Closed Lunch Sunday.
Set Menu (Lunch) Monday-Friday £6.75.
Map Ref. 6D

Parsons
311 Fulham Road, S.W.10.
Tel: 01-352 0651
Approx £5.
No Credit Cards.
Cool in ambience, with lots of greenery, this little restaurant has long been a popular place. Tasty casseroles, excellent salads and large hamburgers.
Open: 12.30pm-1.00am, Monday to Sunday.
Map Ref. 6D

Up all Night Pancakes.
325 Fulham Road, S.W.10.
Tel: 01-352 1998
Open 24 hours.
Map Ref. 5D

LONDON W.C.1.

My Old Dutch
132 High Holborn, W.C.1.
Tel: 01-242 5200
Tube: Holborn.
Wonderful large pancakes with hundreds of different fillings are the main-stay of this attractive restaurant, though you can get cold meat and salad as well. All served on delft plates (which you can also buy) *open until midnight.*
Map Ref. 2I

LONDON W.C.2.

Farmer Brown
4 New Row, W.C.2.
Tube: Leicester Square.
Salads and sandwiches are the staple fare of this small but good cafe which will mix fillings for you. Good puddings too. Unlicensed.
Map Ref. 3H

Food for Thought
31 Neal Street, W.C.2.
Tel: 01-836 0239
Approx £5.
Simple little restaurant which serves delicious home-made food. Tasty soups, vegetable stews and a good selection of salads.
Open: 12.00 noon-8.00pm, Monday to Friday.
Closed Saturday and Sunday.
Map Ref. 2H

Cousin Jack's Cornish Shop
14 Drury Lane, W.C.2.
Tel: 01-836 7012
Tube: Holborn.
As the name suggests this does a very nice line in Cornish pasties and other Cornish delicacies such as hog's pudding. The cream is Cornish, of course. Unlicensed.
Map Ref. 2H

Porters
17 Henrietta Street, W.C.2.
Tel: 01-836 6466
Approx £12.
Credit Cards: Access & Visa.
Good, traditional English food such as fish and game pies, steak and kidney and well prepared desserts.
Open: 12.00 noon-3.00pm and 6.00pm-11.30pm, Monday to Friday.
6.00pm-11.30pm, Saturday.
Closed Sunday and Lunch Saturday.
Map Ref. 3H

Rodos Greek food.
59 St. Giles High Street, W.C.2.
Tel: 01-836 3177
Open to 5.00am.
Map Ref. 2H

LONDON E.C.4.

Oodles Country Food
31 Cathedral Place, E.C.4.
Tube: St. Pauls.
No Map Ref.

3 Fetter Lane, E.C.4.
Tube: The Temple.
Map Ref. 2I

113 High Holborn, W.C.1.
Tube: Holborn.
Map Ref. 2I

4 New Oxford Street, W.1.
Tube: Holborn.
Map Ref. 2H

A small chain of pretty shops which sell delicious wholefood type of food. Generous portions of casseroles, vegetarian dishes as well as good puddings and cheese. Excellent bread.

OPEN AIR EATING

LONDON W.2.

Le Chef
41 Connaught Street, W.2.
Tel: 01-262 5945
Approx £24.
Credit Cards: Access.
Nice little French restaurant where the tables overflow on to the pavement in fine weather. Good provincial cooking.
Open: 12.30pm-2.30pm and 7.00pm-11.30pm, Tuesday to Friday.
7.00pm-11.30pm, Saturday.
Closed Sunday/Monday and Lunch Saturday.
Map Ref. 2E

LONDON W.11.

L'Artiste Assoiffe
122 Kensington Park Road, W.11.
Tel: 01-727 5111
Approx £28.

Major Credit Cards.
French provençal cooking in an attractive restaurant with an open fire in winter. Helpful service.
Open: 12.30pm-2.30pm and 6.30pm-11.15pm, Monday to Friday. 6.30pm-11.15pm, Saturday. Closed Sunday and Lunch Saturday.
Map Ref. 3B

LONDON S.W.3.

Meridiana
169 Fulham Road, S.W.3.
Tel: 01-589 8815
Approx £22.
Major Credit Cards.
First class restaurant with an attractive staff and a super selection of Italian specialities and beautifully prepared and presented. An outdoor balcony for summer eating and a cosy downstairs bar.
Open: 12.30pm-3.00pm and 7.00pm-midnight, Monday to Saturday. Closed Sunday.
Map Ref. 5E

San Lorenzo
22 Beauchamp Place, S.W.3.
Tel: 01-584 1074
Approx £22.
Major Credit Cards.
Very well known Italian restaurant with a charming decor, a nice bar and an indoor garden which opens out in the summer. Excellent pastas and some unusual specialities.
Open: 12.30pm-2.30pm and 7.00pm-11.30m, Monday to Saturday. Closed Sunday.
Map Ref. 5E

LONDON S.W.5.

Pontevecchio
256 Old Brompton Road, S.W.5.
Tel: 01-373 9082
Approx £16.
Credit Cards: American Express, Diners & Visa.
Modern, efficiently run restaurant which serves excellent value for money Italian cooking. Good selection of fish and children specialities, varied types of pastas and rich desserts.
Open: 12.45pm-3.00pm and 6.45pm-11.45pm, Monday to Sunday.
Map Ref. 5C

LONDON S.W.7.

Chanterelle
119 Old Brompton Road, S.W.7.
Tel: 01-373 5522
Approx £22.
Major Credit Cards.
Sitting outside on a fine day is a pleasant experience, as the well prepared food and the friendly service make this a very appealing restaurant. Nice, tasty French cooking.
Open: 12.00 noon-2.30pm and 7.00pm-midnight, Monday to Sunday.
Map Ref. 5D

LONDON S.W.10.

Bagatelle
5 Langton Street, S.W.10.
Tel: 01-351 4185
Approx £30.
Major Credit Cards.
A charming restaurant with simple but excellent French cooking. Sauces are very good, vegetables fresh and there is a good cheese board.
Open: 12.00 noon-2.00pm and 7.00pm-11.30pm, Monday to Saturday. Closed Sunday.
Map Ref. 6C

Hungry Horse
196 Fulham Road, S.W.10.
Tel: 01-352 7757
Approx £22.50.
Credit Cards: American Express & Diners.
Good traditional English fare served in pleasant surroundings. Try the jugged hare and boiled beef. Tasty desserts and friendly service. Patio.
Open: 12.30pm-2.30pm and 6.30pm-midnight, Monday to Sunday.
Map Ref. 6D

RIVERSIDE EATING

LONDON W.C.2.

Hispaniola
2 Victoria Embankment, W.C.2.
Tel: 01-839 5769
Approx £28.
Credit Cards: Diners & Visa.
A converted ship which specialises in very good Spanish-type food. Prawns and other seafoods are delicious.
Open: 12.30pm-2.30pm and 7.30pm-11.30pm, Monday to Saturday. Sunday, from Easter to December. Set Menu (Lunch) £7.50.
Map Ref. 4H

LONDON S.W.1.

Villa dei Cesari
135 Grosvenor Road, S.W.1.
Tel: 01-828 7453
Approx £35.
Major Credit Cards.
Styled like an old Roman Villa, and

overlooking the Thames, it has a very romantic atmosphere. The waiters wear Roman tunics and the courses on the menu are given Roman names. Nice live bands for dancing.
Open: 7.30pm-3.00am, Tuesday to Sunday.
Map Ref. 6G

LONDON S.W.3.

Kings Head & Eight Bells
50 Cheyne Walk, S.W.3.
Tel: 01-352 1820
Approx £6.
No Credit Cards.
A lovely pub with plenty of atmosphere serving first class fare overlooking the river.
Restaurant closed Sunday.
Map Ref. 6D

LONDON E.C.4.

Samuel Pepys
Brooks Wharf, Upper Thames Street, E.C.4.
Tel: 01-248 3048
Approx £14.
Major Credit Cards.
This is a tasteful conversion of a warehouse in traditional style with two large bars and an excellent restaurant. Old lamps and prints as well as some letters by the man himself. Good English fare.
Restaurant closed Lunch Sunday.
Set Menus £6.95 and £10.95.
Map Ref. 3J

LONDON S.E.1.

Anchor
Bankside, Southwark, S.E.1.
Tel: 01-407 1577
Approx £10.
Major Credit Cards.
Excellent views of the St. Paul's Cathedral, the City of London and passing river traffic. There are three restaurants all different and serving good value wholesome food.
Open: 12.00 noon-2.00pm and 7.00pm-10.00pm, Monday to Saturday.
Restaurant closed Sunday, Saturday Lunch.
Map Ref. 3J

Royal Festival Hall Restaurants
Royal Central Hall, South Bank, S.E.1.
Tel: 01-928 2829
Approx £18.
Major Credit Cards.
Large restaurant overlooking the Thames which is ideal for a pre-concert meal.
Open: 12.30pm-2.30pm and 6.00pm-10.30pm, Monday to Saturday.
Closed Sunday and Lunch Saturday.
Set Menu £10.
Map Ref. 3I

LONDON S.E.10.

Trafalgar Tavern
Park Row, S.E.10.
Tel: 01-858 2437
Approx £10.
Major Credit Cards.
Situated near the Royal Naval College in Greenwich, this old pub has an upstairs room modelled to resemble a man o' war forecastle.
Restaurant closed Dinner Sunday.
No Map Ref.

Cutty Sark
Ballast Quay, Hassell Street, S.E.10.
Tel: 01-858 3146
Approx £18.
Major Credit Cards.
Overlooking the Thames near the famous Cutty Sark sailing ship, this old Georgian pub serves good food in a pleasant atmosphere.
Restaurant closed Sunday and Lunch Saturday, Tuesday Evening.
No Map Ref.

LONDON S.E.16.

Angel
101 Bermondsey Wall, Bermondsey, S.E.16.
Tel: 01-237 3608
Approx £20.
Major Credit Cards.
A splendid 18th century pub opposite Execution Dock. This is really a river pub and the oldest part with a delightful balcony overlooks the river. As well as having a restaurant, snacks are available in the bar.
Restaurant closed Saturday and Lunch Sunday.
Open: 12.00 noon-3.00pm and 7.00pm-10.30pm.
Map Ref. 4L

Mayflower
117 Rotherhithe Street, S.E.16.
Tel: 01-237 4088
Approx £20.
Major Credit Cards.
The Mayflower has close connections with America because it was from here in 1611 that Captain Christopher Jones and the Pilgrim Fathers first set sail for the New Land. There is a verandah overlooking the river and an excellent variety of food.
Open: 12.00 noon-2.00pm and 7.00pm-10.00pm, Monday to Saturday.
Restaurant closed Sunday.
Map Ref. 4L

LONDON E.1.

Dickens Inn
St. Katharine's Way, E.1.
Tel: 01-488 2208 (Pickwick Room)
01-488 9932 (Dickens Room)
Approx £22.
Major Credit Cards.
Two excellent restaurants: the Pickwick Room which serves traditional English food, and the Dickens Room for fish specialities. Good Atmosphere.
Open: 12.30pm-2.00pm and 7.30pm-9.30pm, Monday to Saturday.
Restaurant closed Lunch Saturday and Dinner Sunday.
Map Ref. 4L

Prospect of Whitby
57 Wapping Wall, E.1.
Tel: 01-481 1095
Approx £12.
No Credit Cards.
One of the famous pubs of London which gets very crowded, particularly on summer evenings. Samuel Pepys spent a lot of time here and there is much ancient nautical bric-a-brac. Good restaurant with balcony and varied snacks.
Restaurant closed Monday and Dinner Sunday.
No Map Ref.

Tower Hotel, Princes Room
St. Katherines Way, E.1.
Tel: 01-481 2575
Approx £18.
Major Credit Cards.
Marvellous views of the river and Tower Bridge in a very elegant restaurant setting. Excellent food with many interesting specialities.
Open: 12.30pm-3.00pm and 6.30pm-11.00pm, Monday to Sunday.
Map Ref. 4L

VEGETARIAN AND WHOLEFOOD

LONDON W.1.

Mandeer
21 Hanway Place, W.1.
Tel: 01-323 0660
Approx £12.
Major Credit Cards.
A lovely Indian vegetarian restaurant which serves strongly spiced curries. There are many specialities such as the bhajias, pakoras with dips and various dhals.
Open: 12.00 noon-3.00pm and 6.00pm-10.30pm, Monday to Saturday.
Closed Sunday.
Map Ref. 2G

Nuthouse
26 Kingly Street, W.1.
Tel: 01-437 9471
Approx £6.
No Credit Cards.
Self-service restaurant on two floors which serves a large selection of organically grown food.
Open: 10.30am-7.00pm, Monday to Friday.
11.30am-4.00pm, Saturday.
Closed Sunday and Dinner Saturday.
Map Ref. 2G

Wine bars in London

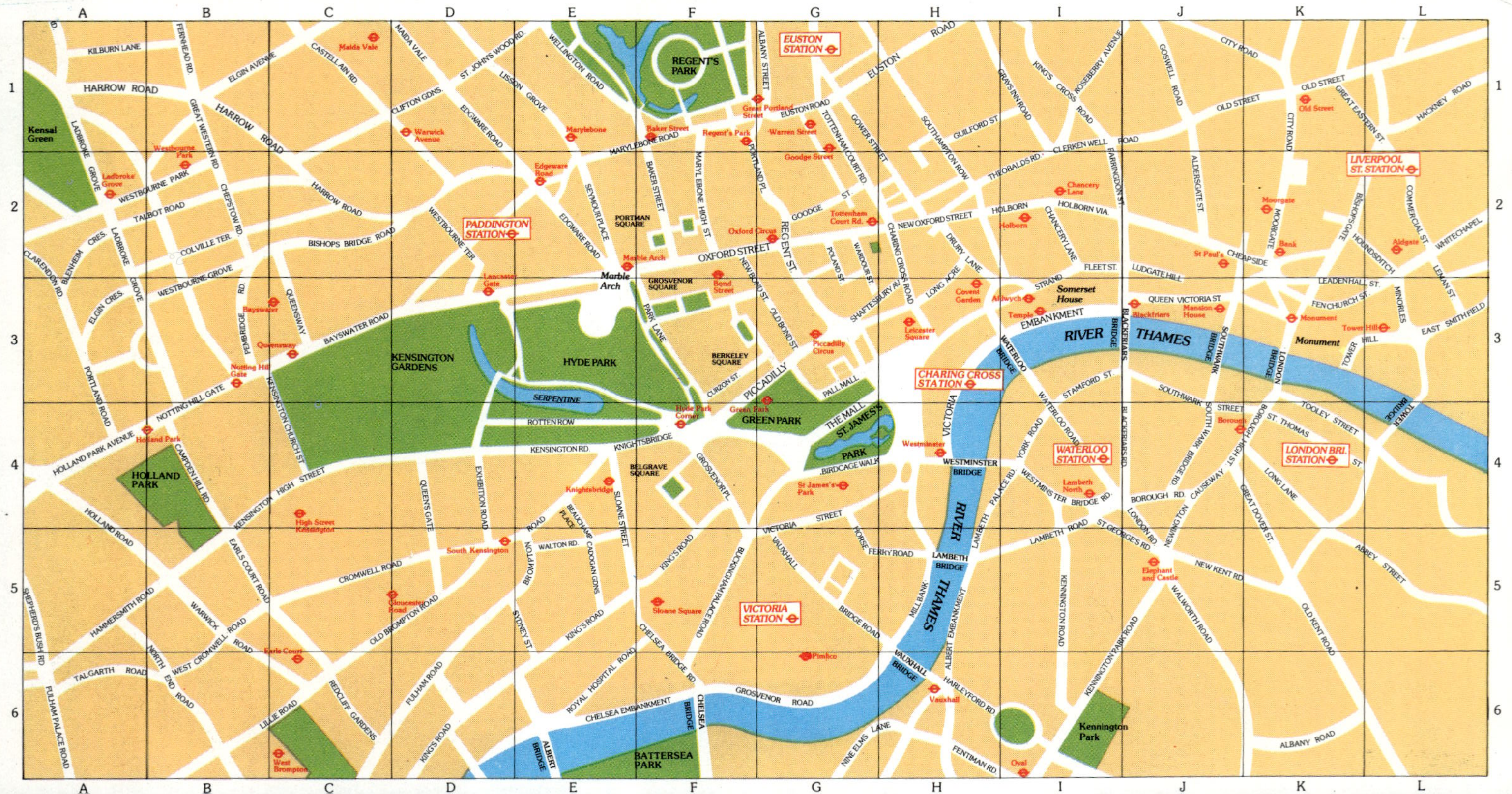
EUSTON STATION
PADDINGTON STATION
CHARING CROSS STATION
WATERLOO STATION
VICTORIA STATION
LIVERPOOL ST. STATION
LONDON BRI. STATION
REGENT'S PARK
HYDE PARK
KENSINGTON GARDENS
SERPENTINE
GREEN PARK
ST. JAMES'S PARK
HOLLAND PARK
BATTERSEA PARK
Kensington Park
Kensal Green
RIVER THAMES
PORTMAN SQUARE
GROSVENOR SQUARE
BERKELEY SQUARE
BELGRAVE SQUARE
Marble Arch
Somerset House
Monument
HARROW ROAD
OXFORD STREET
REGENT ST.
PICCADILLY
EUSTON ROAD
BAYSWATER ROAD
EDGWARE ROAD
KENSINGTON HIGH STREET
CROMWELL ROAD
KING'S ROAD
EMBANKMENT
STRAND
WATERLOO BRIDGE
WESTMINSTER BRIDGE
LAMBETH BRIDGE
VAUXHALL BRIDGE
CHELSEA BRIDGE
ALBERT BRIDGE
BLACKFRIARS BRIDGE
SOUTHWARK BRIDGE
LONDON BRIDGE
TOWER BRIDGE
Maida Vale
Warwick Avenue
Marylebone
Baker Street
Regent's Park
Great Portland Street
Warren Street
Goodge Street
Edgware Road
Ladbroke Grove
Westbourne Park
Bayswater
Queensway
Notting Hill Gate
Holland Park
Lancaster Gate
Marble Arch
Bond Street
Oxford Circus
Tottenham Court Rd.
Piccadilly Circus
Leicester Square
Covent Garden
Holborn
Chancery Lane
Aldwych
Temple
Blackfriars
Mansion House
St Paul's
Moorgate
Bank
Old Street
Aldgate
Monument
Tower Hill
Hyde Park Corner
Green Park
Knightsbridge
High Street Kensington
South Kensington
Gloucester Road
Sloane Square
Earls Court
West Brompton
St James's Park
Westminster
Lambeth North
Borough
Elephant and Castle
Pimlico
Vauxhall
Oval

WINE BARS IN LONDON

Most of the wine bars in this selection provide an interesting and informal atmosphere where you can relax and eat, drink wine and listen to music. They can offer good budget value for drinks and the food, which is often simple is usually wholesome and appetising.
Most Wine bars open around 11.00am-3.00pm and 5.30pm-11.00pm.

W.1. WINE BARS

34 Baker Street
34 Baker Street, W.1.
Tel: 01-935 1453
Excellent counter of hot and cold food in this cosy basement wine bar. Simple choice of wines. Friendly service from attractive waitresses.
Map Ref. 2G

Downs
5 Down Street, W.1.
Tel: 01-491 3810
Very smart wine bar in Mayfair that has long kept a reputation for serving delicious food and good wines bottled in country of origin.
Open 7 days a week.
Map Ref. 3F

Wolsey's
52 Wells Street, W.1.
Tel: 01-636 5121
Lots of space, this wine bar dispenses a good selection of reasonably priced wines and food.
Open: Monday-Friday.
Map Ref. 2G

Benhams
Berkeley Arcade, Baker Street, W.1.
Tel: 01-935 9429
Excellent cold buffet supplemented by hot dishes of the day. The wine list is varied and the staff are very friendly and helpful.
Map Ref. 1F

Palings
25 Hanover Square, W.1.
Tel: 01-408 0935
Basement wine bar, very popular at lunchtime. Convivial atmosphere and good selection of food.
Closed Sunday.
Map Ref. 3G

Shampers
4 Kingly Street, W.1.
Tel: 01-437 1692
Well established wine bar with a very pleasant atmosphere. Efficient service, an excellent selection of wines with

good food both hot and cold.
Open: Monday-Friday.
Map Ref. 3G

Crawfords
11 Crawford Street, W.1.
Tel: 01-486 5709
A spacious elegant cellar bar offering a large selection of wines. Hamburger and other foods are available, except Saturday.
Closed Sunday.
Map Ref. 2F

Tracks
17a Soho Square, W.1.
Tel: 01-439 2318
A new and stylish wine bar, popular with local film and office workers. In fine weather you can sit outside. Open all day for coffee.
Closed Saturday pm and Sunday.
Map Ref. 2G

Bubbles
41 North Audley Street, W.1.
Tel: 01-499 0600
A comfortable wine bar handily situated for shoppers in the Marble Arch area of Oxford Street. Good selection of wines.
Closed Saturday lunch and Sunday.
Map Ref. 3F

Fino's Wine Cellar
123 Mount Street, W.1.
Tel: 01-492 1640
Very busy, very popular wine cellar where you have to watch your elbow when drinking. Excellent wines and food.
Closed Saturday lunch and Sunday.
Map Ref. 3F

Fino's Wine Cellar
12 North Row, W.1.
Tel: 01-491 7261
Excellent food including grills and vast choice of cold buffet. Marvellous selection of wines.
Closed Saturday and Sunday.
Map Ref. 3F

Fino's Wine Cellar
37 Duke Street, W.1.
Tel: 01-935 9459

The wine bar also has a restaurant but you can choose at the bar from a vast selection of sandwiches. As with the other Fino's there is a large choice of good wines.
Closed Sunday.

Map Ref. 3F

Balls Bros.
31 Cheyne Walk, S.W.3.
Tel: 01-352 4989
Overlooking the Thames, this is one of a chain of wine bars belonging to Balls Bros. Excellent wines and selection of food. *Closed Sunday.*

Map Ref. 6E

Old Compton Wine Bar
37 Old Compton Street, W.1.
Tel: 01-437 3292
A very popular wine bar which has a different atmosphere with its glass and chrome decor. Good wines and food. Air conditioned.
Closed Sunday.

Map Ref. 3G

Casa Martinez
25 Swallow Street, W.1.
Tel: 01-734 4921
Cool and elegant, situated below a Spanish restaurant this is really a sherry bar ideally located between Regents Street and Piccadilly.
Closed Sunday.

Map Ref. 3G

S.W.7. WINE BARS

Loose Box
7 Cheval Place, S.W.7.
Tel: 01-584 9280
A large wine bar on two floors and a lively meeting place which is always crowded often with shoppers from Harrods. Modest selection of wines and good choice of food. Roof garden.

Map Ref. 4E

S.W.3. WINE BARS

Bill Bentley's Wine & Oyster Bar
31 Beauchamp Place, S.W.3.
Tel: 01-589 5080
There is a ground floor bar and small basement bar offering good seafood. Upstairs is a seafood restaurant. Good wines. *Closed Sunday.*

Map Ref. 5E

Loose Rein
221 Kings Road, S.W.3.
Tel: 01-352 9188
Basement wine bar offering a good choice of wines both by the glass and the bottle. Friendly staff and substantial well produced food.
Closed Sunday.

Map Ref. 5E

Draycott's
114 Draycott Avenue, S.W.3.
Tel: 01-584 5359
Nice decor with friendly staff serving good hot dishes and a full cold buffet. A well chosen wine list.
Brunch from 10.00am.
Open 7 days a week.

Map Ref. 5E

Downstairs Wine Bar
Basil Street Hotel, 8 Basil Street, S.W.3.
Tel: 01-730 3411
Smart basement wine bar beneath the rather staid Hotel. Very varied and good food and the wines are modestly priced. Air conditioned.
Closed Saturday evening and Sunday.

Map Ref. 4E

S.W.1. WINE BARS

Slatters
3 Panton Street, W.C.2.
Tel: 01-839 4649
Small, with classical music background and first class food this is a very civilised wine bar which also has a good selection of French wines.
Closed Saturday lunch and Sunday.

Map Ref. 3H

Ebury Wine Bar
139 Ebury Street, S.W.1.
Tel: 01-730 5447
Long established and very popular with a very interesting list of wines including some uncommon French and also English. Good food. Reservations recommended.

Map Ref. 5F

Motcombs
26 Motcomb Street, S.W.1.
Tel: 01-235 6382
Small, comfortable bar on the ground floor and a restaurant downstairs in the basement. Modest selection of

wines but the food is good.
Closed Saturday and Sunday.
Map Ref. 4F

Fino's Wine Cellar
19 Swallow Street, W.1.
Tel: 01-734 2049
Lavish cellar vaults with restaurant and buffet snacks. Good wine list and also spirits.
Open 7 days a week.
Map Ref.

Sloanes Wine Bar
51 Sloane Square, S.W.1.
Tel: 01-730 4275
Large cellar bar next to the Royal Court Theatre with good home cooked food and a modest selection of wines.
Closed Sunday.
Map Ref. 5F

Tiles
36 Buckingham Palace Road, S.W.1.
Tel: 01-834 7761
Lively wine bar with loud music and attracting the young and beautiful.
Closed Saturday and Sunday.
Map Ref. 4G

Bens of Westminster
29 Victoria Street, S.W.1.
Tel: 01-222 0424
A pleasant wine bar offering good food with waitress service and a full selection of wines.
Map Ref. 4G

Brasserie Marengo
29 Victoria Street, S.W.1.
Tel: 01-222 0424
Self-service restaurant on ground floor is open every day of week. Waitress service in well-stocked, downstairs wine bar.
Closed Saturday and Sunday.
Map Ref.

Laytons
12 Easterbrooke Street, S.W.1.
Tel: 01-828 5211
A cosy wine bar popular at lunchtimes and serving good food and an excellent selection of French wines.
Closed evenings.
Map Ref. 5G

N.W.1. WINE BARS

Bill Bentley's
239 Baker Street, N.W.1.
Tel: 01-935 3130
Mostly seafood, this formal panelled wine bar has a restaurant and food counter, which also dispenses good wines. *Closed Sundays.*
Map Ref. 1F

W.2. WINE BARS

Ruby's
28 Sussex Place, W.2.
Tel: 01-262 4654
Nice wines in particular Beaujolais. This is a friendly little wine bar also serving a variety of food where the menu is a large blackboard.
Open 7 days a week.
Map Ref. 2E

Russkies Wine Cellar
6 Wellington Terrace, Bayswater Road, W.2.
Tel: 01-229 9128
This cosy basement wine cellar, which is part owned by Andrew Henderson (a noted wine expert) is entered by a circular staircase. As one would imagine, there is a marvellous choice of wines and also imaginative food.
Closed Sunday lunch.
Map Ref. 3C

W.11. WINE BARS

Julie's
137 Portland Road, W.11.
Tel: 01-727 7985
Open all day — teas and coffees served out of licensing hours. Adjoining restaurant this is a smart, friendly place that is very popular. A la carte menu as well as snacks.
Open 7 days a week.
Map Ref.

W.8. WINE BARS

Stuntman
7 Kensington High Street, W.8.
Tel: 01-937 5501
There is a selection of over 50 wines, all very good. Excellent food.
Closed Sunday.
Map Ref.

Jimmie's Wine Bar
Kensington Palace Barracks, Kensington Church Street, W.8.
Tel: 01-937 9988
Part of the old Kensington Barracks, with good grills, salads and

sandwiches. Fine wine selection and live music in the evening.
Open 7 days a week.
Map Ref. 4C

Thackerey's
9 Young Street, W.8.
Tel: 01-937 9403
Busy wine bar with lots of noise and a friendly atmosphere. Good selection of wines and food.
Closed Sunday.
Map Ref. 4C

E.C.4. WINE BARS

El Vino
47 Fleet Street, E.C.4.
Tel: 01-353 6786
In wine bar terms this is a 'must'. El Vino's is an institution where women are traditionally not served at the bar but are waited on at tables and gentlemen must wear jackets and ties. It has not changed in years and is the haunt of journalists and lawyers. Wines are excellent and varied and at the bar they serve one of the best selection of sandwiches anywhere. Superb wine list and very reasonably priced champagnes.
Closed Saturday evening and Sunday.
Map Ref. 2I

Olde Wine Shades
6 Martin Lane, E.C.4.
Tel: 01-626 6876
Dating back to 1663 and surviving the Fire of London, this old timbered tavern is one of the oldest wine houses in London. Many famous people including Charles Dickens used to drink here. Good sandwiches at lunchtime and fine wines, sherries and ports as well as ten varieties of champagne. Lunchtime restaurant.
Closed Saturday and Sunday.
Map Ref. 3K

Bow Wine Vaults
10 Bow Churchyard, E.C.4.
Tel: 01-248 1121
Simple meals in the cellar at lunchtime only. Good wines and interesting bar food. *Closed Saturday and Sunday.*
Map Ref. 3J

Mother Bunch's
Old Seacoal Lane, E.C.4.
Tel: 01-236 5317
Beneath the arches by Ludgate Circus, this maze of vaults is a well appointed wine cellar. Good clarets and port from the wood. Large selection of sandwiches.
Closed Saturday and Sunday.
Map Ref. 2J

Balls Bros.
Laurence Pountney Hill, E.C.4.
Tel: 01-283 2947
Popular wine bar with large selection of wines and a variety of snacks.
Map Ref. 3K

Whittington's
21 College Hill, E.C.4.
Tel: 01-248 5855
Situated in Dick Whittington's vaulted cellars, with a comprehensive wine list and marvellous inventive food.
Map Ref. 2J

E.C.2. WINE BARS

Balls Bros.
6 Cheapside, E.C.2.
Tel: 01-248 2708
Smart wine bar with a large selection of wines and excellent food at lunchtime.
Closed Saturday and Sunday.
Map Ref. 2K

Coates
109 Old Broad Street, E.C.2.
Tel: 01-638 9308
Popular, panelled wine bar with a distinctly masculine character. Simple food and good sandwiches, with small, good wine list.
Closed Saturday and Sunday.
Map Ref. 2K

Coates
45 London Wall, E.C.2.
Tel: 01-628 5861
Like its sister bar in Old Broad Street, there is a discerning wine list in a Victorian atmosphere and good food in the basement.
Closed Saturday and Sunday.
Map Ref. 2K

Capataz Wine Store
89 Old Broad Street, E.C.2.
Tel: 01-588 1140
Unchanged for 50 years, with sawdust on the floor and chairs grouped around wine casks. Fine wines, including fortified ones and excellent champagnes. No food served here.
Open weekday lunchtimes only.
Map Ref. 2K

Mr. Garraway's
46 Gresham Street, E.C.2.
Tel: 01-606 8209

Traditional City wine bar built on the site of an old coffee house. Excellent clarets and vintage ports. Simple but good food.
Closed Saturday and Sunday.
Map Ref. 2J

City Boot
7 Moorfields High Walk, E.C.2.
Tel: 01-588 4766
Vintage clarets and ports as well as a fine selection of wines are served in this old wine bar. Good food.
Closed Saturday and Sunday.
Map Ref. 2K

E.C.3. WINE BARS

City Flogger
120 Fenchurch Street, E.C.3.
Tel: 01-623 3251
Another old traditional wine bar with good wines and an excellent selection of snacks and sandwiches.
Closed Saturday and Sunday.
Map Ref. 3K

Five Lamps Wine Bar
3 St. Katherines Row, E.C.3.
Tel: 01-488 1587
Simple, modern basement bar. Attractive food, friendly service and a nice selection of wines.
Closed Saturday and Sunday.
Map Ref. 3L

W.C.2. WINE BARS

Brahms and Liszt
19 Russell Street, W.C.2.
Tel: 01-240 3661
Extremely popular wine bar full of photographs and models and loud music. Modest wine selection and hot and cold snacks. Friendly service.
Closed Sunday lunch.
Map Ref. 3H

Cork and Bottle
44 Cranbourne Street, W.C.2.
Tel: 01-734 6592
Ideal for 'theatre goers' this attractive cellar bar is comfortable and inviting with friendly staff. Well chosen varied wines and the cold buffet and salads are excellent value.
Closed Sunday.
Map Ref. 3H

Fino's Wine Cellar
104 Charing Cross Road, W.C.2.
Tel: 01-836 1077
Another wine bar for shoppers and theatre goers, it also has a good restaurant as well as serving snacks. Selection of Italian wines.
Closed Sunday.
Map Ref. 2H

Renzo's
50 Kingsway, W.C.2.
Tel: 01-405 9749
Pleasant wine bar with a downstairs restaurant. Serving good Italian food. Nice selection of wines.
Closed Saturday lunch and Sunday.
Map Ref. 2H

Penny's Place
6 King Street, W.C.2.
Tel: 01-836 4553
A wine bar/bistro as you would find in France with good food prepared by chef and a traditional *plat du jour*.
Closed Saturday and Sunday.
Map Ref. 3H

Tuttons
11 Russell Street, W.C.2.
Tel: 01-836 1167
Starts with breakfast at 8.30am and is open all day serving good wines in licensing hours. A jolly place to go.
Open 7 days a week.
Map Ref. 3H

Gordon's
47 Villiers Street, W.C.2.
Tel: 01-930 1408
Gordon's Wine Cellar boasts the distinction of never having had an ordinary licence because in 1364 it was granted Royal Letters Patent by Edward III. There are two bars connected by a staircase, the upper being level with Villiers Street with wood-panelling and wine barrels and the lower with its own entrance having lots of nooks and corners. Good buffet and salads and nice wines make this wine bar a pleasant drinking house.
Open 7 days a week.
Map Ref. 3H

W.C.1. WINE BARS

Bung Hole
57 High Holborn, W.C.1.
Tel: 01-242 4318
With sawdust, wine barrels, gaslight and candle-light, this wine bar has a lot of atmosphere. Wines are good, including vintage clarets and champagne by the tankard. Cold buffet and salads are varied.
Closed Saturday and Sunday.
Map Ref. 2I

Vats Wine Bar
51 Lambs Conduit Street, W.C.1.
Tel: 01-242 8963
Crowded at lunchtime, serving good hot and cold food. Nice atmosphere with open fires in the winter and a simple but good selection of wines.
Closed Saturday and Sunday.
Map Ref. 2I

London pubs

LONDON PUBS

The English Public House (Pub) is part of the National heritage dating back to mediaeval times and, although there have been obvious changes within them, they are still today what they have always been — a public house licensed for the sale of alcoholic liquor'.
London has about 5000 pubs and the majority of these date from Victorian times. They were built to satisfy the thirst of a growing population caused by the Industrial Revolution. But there are also many which still survive from earlier centuries which were the original coaching hostels. These are mainly on the old coaching routes out of London, where the travellers used them, and in the City of London, where they were mainly for the use of businessmen.
Although a number of pubs also have restaurants the majority serve food only from the counter and usually at lunch time. This ranges from sandwiches and salads to 'one plate' hot dishes.
The main drink sold is beer, either bottled or from the tap (draught beer), and the beer is very different to that to which most tourists are accustomed. The taste is different and the beer is warmer. However it is possible to get cold lager beer in pubs as well. A pub is an essential place for any visitor to go to and in the following list we have selected a number which have atmosphere and a character all of their own.
The licensing hours when pubs are open are between 11.00am-3.00pm and 5.30pm-11.00pm on weekdays and 12.00am-2.00pm and 7.00pm-10.30pm on Sunday. There are some areas, particularly where there are markets, where the pubs have special dispensation for opening at hours other than those above.
You must be 18 years or over to buy a drink, but teenagers between 16 and 18 can go into a pub if accompanied by an adult, although they can't drink alcoholic beverages.

HISTORICAL PUBS

S.E.1. PUBS

The Anchor Tap
28 Horselydown Lane, S.E.1.
Tel: 01-407 2280
Close to Tower Bridge, this pub is 200 years old. Originally built for employees of the brewery which is next door. It is reputed to have a friendly ghost who is said to be responsible for unexplained happenings. A pleasant friendly atmosphere, with snacks and reasonably priced food.
Map Ref. 4L

S.E.16 PUBS

The Angel
101 Bermondsey Wall East, S.E.16.
Tel: 01-237 3608
A splendid 15th Century pub opposite Execution Dock. Whilst the front is not very imposing this is really a river pub and the oldest part overlooks the river with a delightful balcony. Bar snacks are limited but there is also a restaurant. Mentioned in Pepys Diary.
Map Ref. 4L

The Mayflower
117 Rotherhithe Street, S.E.16.
Tel: 01-237 4088
This genuine 17th Century pub with its exposed beams, open fireplaces and ancient bric-a-brac is one of the few licensed houses to possess a licence to sell postage stamps, including American ones. The Mayflower has close association with America because it was from here in 1611 that Captain Christopher Jones and the Pilgrim Fathers first set sail for the New Land. There is a verandah overlooking the river and an excellent variety of food.
Map Ref. 4L

A B C D E F G H I J K L
1 2 3 4 5 6
EUSTON STATION
PADDINGTON STATION
CHARING CROSS STATION
VICTORIA STATION
WATERLOO STATION
LONDON BRI. STATION
LIVERPOOL ST. STATION
REGENT'S PARK
HYDE PARK
KENSINGTON GARDENS
SERPENTINE
GREEN PARK
ST. JAMES'S PARK
HOLLAND PARK
BATTERSEA PARK
Kennington Park
Kensal Green
RIVER THAMES
Marble Arch
Somerset House
Monument
PORTMAN SQUARE
GROSVENOR SQUARE
BERKELEY SQUARE
BELGRAVE SQUARE
KILBURN LANE
HARROW ROAD
ELGIN AVENUE
FERNHEAD RD.
GREAT WESTERN RD
CASTELLAIN RD.
MAIDA VALE
ST. JOHN'S WOOD RD
WELLINGTON ROAD
LISSON GROVE
CLIFTON GDNS.
EDGWARE ROAD
LADBROKE GROVE
WESTBOURNE PARK
TALBOT ROAD
CHEPSTOW RD.
COLVILLE TER.
BISHOPS BRIDGE ROAD
WESTBOURNE TER
WESTBOURNE GROVE
BLENHEIM CRES.
CLARENDON RD.
ELGIN CRES.
PEMBRIDGE RD.
QUEENSWAY
BAYSWATER ROAD
NOTTING HILL GATE
PORTLAND ROAD
KENSINGTON CHURCH ST.
HOLLAND PARK AVENUE
CAMPDEN HILL RD
KENSINGTON HIGH STREET
HOLLAND ROAD
HAMMERSMITH ROAD
EARLS COURT ROAD
WARWICK ROAD
WEST CROMWELL ROAD
NORTH END ROAD
TALGARTH ROAD
SHEPHERD'S BUSH RD
FULHAM PALACE ROAD
LILLIE ROAD
REDCLIFF GARDENS
FULHAM ROAD
OLD BROMPTON ROAD
CROMWELL ROAD
QUEEN'S GATE
EXHIBITION ROAD
KENSINGTON RD.
ROTTEN ROW
KNIGHTSBRIDGE
BROMPTON ROAD
WALTON RD.
BEAUCHAMP PLACE
CADOGAN GDNS
SLOANE STREET
SYDNEY ST.
KING'S ROAD
ROYAL HOSPITAL ROAD
CHELSEA BRIDGE RD
CHELSEA EMBANKMENT
CHELSEA BRIDGE
ALBERT BRIDGE
GROSVENOR ROAD
BUCKINGHAM PALACE ROAD
GROSVENOR PL.
VAUXHALL BRIDGE ROAD
VICTORIA STREET
HORSE FERRY ROAD
MILLBANK
NINE ELMS LANE
VAUXHALL BRIDGE
LAMBETH BRIDGE
WESTMINSTER BRIDGE
WATERLOO BRIDGE
BLACKFRIARS BRIDGE
SOUTHWARK BRIDGE
LONDON BRIDGE
TOWER BRIDGE
ALBERT EMBANKMENT
HARLEYFORD RD
FENTIMAN RD
KENNINGTON PARK ROAD
KENNINGTON ROAD
LAMBETH ROAD
LAMBETH PALACE RD
WESTMINSTER BRIDGE RD
YORK ROAD
WATERLOO ROAD
STAMFORD ST.
BLACKFRIARS RD
SOUTHWARK STREET
SOUTH WARK BRIDGE RD
BOROUGH RD.
LONDON RD.
ST. GEORGE'S RD
NEWINGTON CAUSEWAY
BOROUGH HIGH ST.
GREAT DOVER ST.
LONG LANE
ST. THOMAS ST.
TOOLEY STREET
NEW KENT RD
WALWORTH ROAD
OLD KENT ROAD
ABBEY STREET
ALBANY ROAD
MARYLEBONE ROAD
BAKER STREET
MARYLEBONE HIGH ST.
SEYMOUR PLACE
OXFORD STREET
PARK LANE
NEW BOND ST.
OLD BOND ST.
CURZON ST.
PICCADILLY
REGENT ST.
PORTLAND PL.
ALBANY STREET
EUSTON ROAD
TOTTENHAM COURT RD.
GOWER STREET
GOODGE ST.
NEW OXFORD STREET
POLAND ST.
WARDOUR ST.
SHAFTESBURY AV.
CHARING CROSS ROAD
PALL MALL
THE MALL
BIRDCAGE WALK
VICTORIA EMBANKMENT
LONG ACRE
DRURY LANE
STRAND
FLEET ST.
HOLBORN
HOLBORN VIA
CHANCERY LANE
SOUTHAMPTON ROW
THEOBALDS RD.
GUILFORD ST
GRAYS INN ROAD
KING'S CROSS ROAD
ROSEBERRY AVENUE
CLERKEN WELL ROAD
FARRINGDON ST.
GOSWELL ROAD
ALDERSGATE ST.
LUDGATE HILL
QUEEN VICTORIA ST.
CHEAPSIDE
CITY ROAD
OLD STREET
MOORGATE
BISHOPSGATE
GREAT EASTERN ST.
HACKNEY ROAD
COMMERCIAL ST.
WHITECHAPEL
HOUNDSDITCH
LEADENHALL ST.
FENCHURCH ST.
MINORIES
LEMAN ST.
EAST SMITHFIELD
TOWER HILL
Maida Vale
Warwick Avenue
Westbourne Park
Ladbroke Grove
Bayswater
Queensway
Notting Hill Gate
Holland Park
High Street Kensington
Earls Court
West Brompton
Gloucester Road
South Kensington
Knightsbridge
Sloane Square
Lancaster Gate
Edgeware Road
Marylebone
Baker Street
Regent's Park
Great Portland Street
Warren Street
Goodge Street
Marble Arch
Bond Street
Oxford Circus
Tottenham Court Rd.
Hyde Park Corner
Green Park
Piccadilly Circus
Leicester Square
Covent Garden
St James's Park
Westminster
Pimlico
Vauxhall
Oval
Holborn
Chancery Lane
Aldwych
Temple
Blackfriars
Mansion House
St Paul's
Moorgate
Bank
Monument
Old Street
Aldgate
Tower Hill
Borough
Lambeth North
Elephant and Castle

E.C.4. PUBS

Ye Olde Cheshire Cheese
145 Fleet Street, E.C.4.
Tel: 01-353 6170
This famous pub has hardly changed since 1667, although there has been a tavern on this site since 1538. The Cheshire Cheese has been mentioned in many literary works and a small booklet which explains its history can be bought over the bars. Dr. Johnson frequently drank here and his original favourite chair is still in use. The bars are on two floors and the whole place is steeped in atmosphere. There is an excellent restaurant.
Map Ref. 2I

Ye Olde Watling
29 Watling Street, E.C.4.
Tel: 01-248 6235
Built in 1668 by Christopher Wren after the Fire of London, this pub was actually used as an office by him and his workmen whilst working on St. Paul's Cathedral. One oak beam takes the entire weight of the building and has been tested to show that it will take the strain for the next 1000 years.
Map Ref. 2J

Williamson's Tavern
1-3 Groveland Court, Bow Lane, E.C.4.
Tel: 01-248 6280
Reputed to be the oldest hostelry in the City, it was originally the first Lord Mayor's Mansion House. It is entered through iron gates presented by the Monarchs William and Mary. Buffet bar and games room.
Map Ref. 2J

Horn Tavern
29 Knightrider Street, E.C.4.
Tel: 01-248 7374
Situated close to St. Paul's Cathedral, this pub, built in 1665, was a favourite with Charles Dickens. Good snacks and separate restaurant.
Map Ref. 2J

The George
Fleet Street, E.C.4.
Tel: 01-353 9238
An imposing and original Tudor building standing opposite the Royal Courts of Justice, this is a popular pub for the legal profession. Good buffet food and a separate restaurant.
Map Ref. 2I

Black Friar
174 Victoria Street, E.C.4.
Tel: 01-236 5650
Named after the Dominican Monks, who were called Black Friars, and built on the site of the first priory. The interior is unique. The bars are decorated in marble with copper figures of friars. There is gas lighting and open fires. The Black Friar has an excellent buffet bar and a wide range of draught beers.
Map Ref. 3J

E.C.3. PUBS

Jamaica Wine House
St. Michael's Alley, Cornhill, E.C.3.
Tel: 01-626 9496
Originally one of the first coffee houses to be opened in England. Samuel Pepys, a frequent visitor, mentioned it in his diary in 1660. The building was destroyed by the Fire of London and rebuilt in 1668 in its present form. Selling an excellent selection of wines, it also sells spirits. Snacks and sandwiches are available. Closes at 8.00pm.
Map Ref. 2K

The Ship Tavern
27 Lime Street, E.C.3.
Tel: 01-626 2978
First built in 1447, the Ship is a real City pub which has always been closely connected with seamen. It has a wonderful atmosphere in its two bars and a wide variety of snacks are served.

Map Ref. 2K

Hoop and Grapes
47 Aldgate High Street, E.C.3.
Tel: 01-481 1375
One of the few pubs in London which is scheduled as an ancient monument, as it was originally built about 1200. It was partly rebuilt in the 16th Century. There is little brick, mostly wood and plaster. All the floors slope and the building leans east. Under the building are large cellars and a blocked-up tunnel which is said to lead to the Tower of London. Good snacks and a separate restaurant. Closed on Saturday and Sunday evenings.

Map Ref. 2L

E.C.2. PUBS

Ye Olde Dr Butler's Head
Masons Avenue, Coleman Street, E.C.2.
Tel: 01-606 3504
Full of antique charm, this once belonged to Dr. Butler who became Court Physician to King James I after presenting him with medicinal ale to cure his gout. Dr. Butler also prescribed for the sufferers of ague to be thrown in the Thames, and the letting off of pistols an inch away from the ear of epilepsy sufferers. He sold his medicines from the pub. It is a very popular pub serving excellent English food.

Map Ref. 2K

Dirty Dicks
202-4 Bishopsgate, E.C.2.
Tel: 01-283 5888
Founded in 1761 by Nathaniel Bentley, a well known Court dandy, this got the name 'Dirty Dicks' after he became a scruffy unkept eccentric after being jilted by his bride to be on their wedding day. The old wine and spirit vaults are still in existence and it is well worth descending to have a drink in the cobweb and sawdust atmosphere. On the ground floor there is a buffet bar.

Map Ref. 2L

E.C.1. PUBS

Olde Mitre Tavern
1 Ely Place, Hatton Garden, E.C.1.
Tel: 01-405 4751
Built in 1546 by a Bishop Goodrich, this became a prison in 1642 and later a hospital for soldiers during the Civil Wars. Inside the tavern is the trunk of a cherry tree around which Elizabeth I is said to have danced the maypole. Closes at 10.00pm.

Map Ref. 2I

Barley Mow
50 Long Lane, Smithfield, E.C.1.
Tel: 01-606 6591
Situated on Smithfield Market, the Barley Mow is 400 years old, with polished wood carvings and brass lamps. It is very homely.

Map Ref. 2J

Viaduct Tavern
126 Newgate Street, E.C.1.
Tel: 01-606 8476
Built over part of the original Newgate prison (in fact the cellars are part of it), this pub is an excellent example of good Victoriana. The decor has beautiful glass and woodwork and the ceiling is beaten metal. Snacks served over the bar. Closed Saturday evening and Sunday.

Map Ref. 2J

Hand and Shears
1 Middle Street, Cloth Fair, E.C.1.
Tel: 01-600 0257
Built in the 16th Century this pub still has its old wooden walls, hung with lanterns, an embossed ceiling and period prints. Snacks and cold meat salads.
Map Ref. 2J

W.C.2. PUBS

Lamb and Flag
33 Rose Street, Covent Garden, W.C.2.
Tel: 01-836 4108
Built in 1623 this is believed to be the only wooden framed building in the West End. The interior is traditional with exposed beams and it has a pleasant atmosphere. Excellent selection of snacks and salads. Large range of cheeses.
Map Ref. 3H

Edgar Wallace
40 Essex Street, W.C.2.
Tel: 01-353 3120
Built in the 17th Century. Dr. Johnson and his friends used to hold weekly meetings here. Sandwiches and snacks are available at the bars and there is a separate restaurant. Features author Edgar Wallace and his associates.
Map Ref. 3H

Seven Stars
53 Carey Street, W.C.2.
Tel: 01-242 8521
This is a tiny pub behind the Royal Courts of Justice, built in 1694, and is a great favourite with the legal profession. Good selection of food. Closed 8.30pm.
Map Ref. 2I

W.C.1. PUBS

Holborn Bars
22 High Holborn, W.C.1.
Tel: 01-242 7670
Built in 1690 this pub has an imposing facade. Inside, it has the longest bar in London and, with its high arched ceiling, old fashioned lamps, enormous vats and open fireplace this crowded popular pub has wonderful atmosphere. Good selection of hot and cold food.
Map Ref. 2H

W.1. PUBS

The French House
49 Dean Street, W.1.
Tel: 01-437 2799
One of the most famous pubs in London, this was originally built in the 16th Century. In 1914 the pub acquired a French landlord and it has remained 'French' ever since. During the war, the pub was the unofficial H.Q. of the Free French and there are signed photographs of famous Frenchmen throughout. Superb snacks and wines, formerly York Minster.
Map Ref. 3G

The Guinea
30 Bruton Place, W.1.
Tel: 01-629 5613
Built in 1423 this pub is not a particularly comfortable pub for drinking and does not have a lot of atmosphere. Where it really comes into its own is in the restaurant which, although expensive, is excellent. It is one of the few pubs to have a supper licence. Good steaks.
Map Ref. 3F

S.W.1. PUBS

Red Lion
2 Duke of York Street, S.W.1.
Tel: 01-930 2030
Though this is a small pub, its Victorian charm is unique with engraved glass and decorative mirrors giving the place a pleasing ambience. Although cramped, the atmosphere and friendly service make up for this. Hot and cold snacks served at the bar.
Map Ref. 3G

Red Lion
23 Crown Passage, S.W.1.
Tel: 01-930 8067
Set in a narrow alleyway off Pall Mall and St. James's Street, this has a 'village' pub atmosphere about it. The bars are small and hung with old prints. It is very popular and serves very good snacks.
Map Ref. 3G

Nags Head
53 Kinnerton Street, S.W.1.
Tel: 01-235 1135
This tiny Belgravia mews pub dates back to the early 19th Century. It has a lot of atmosphere and has bars on two floors. Selection of snacks. Darts and real ale.
Map Ref. 4F

Star Tavern
6 Belgrave Mews, S.W.1.
Tel: 01-235 2806
A beautiful Georgian pub much favoured by diplomatic personnel from nearby Embassies.
Map Ref. 4F

The Antelope
22 Eaton Terrace, S.W.1.
Tel: 01-730 7781
Established in 1780, this is now a smart pub with oil lamps, old prints and photographs. Hot and cold snacks are available at the bar and there is a wine bar with food.
Map Ref. 5F

The Grenadier
18 Wilton Row, S.W.1.
Tel: 01-235 3074
The Grenadier was originally the Officers Mess for the Duke of Wellington's soldiers and outside is the original stone used as his mounting block. When it became a pub about 1810 it was frequented by George IV. It is reputed to be haunted and in recent years received publicity when it was the centre of a High Court action which resulted in cars being refused direct access. It has a marvellous pewter bar believed to be the oldest of its kind. Good food and a separate restaurant.
Map Ref. 4F

W.2. PUBS

Victoria Tavern
10a Strathearn Place, Hyde Park Square, W.2.
Tel: 01-262 7474
Open fires in the winter. This is a Victorian pub with lots of atmosphere. Also good snacks and salads.
Map Ref. 2E

E.1. PUBS

Prospect of Whitby
57 Wapping Wall, E.1.
Tel: 01-481 1095
One of the famous pubs of London which unfortunately gets very crowded, particularly on summer evenings. Samuel Pepys spent a lot of time here and there is much ancient nautical bric-a-brac. Good restaurant with balcony and varied snacks.
Map Ref. 4L

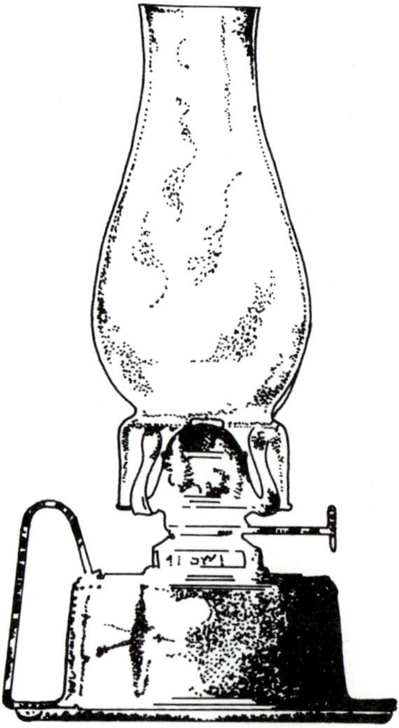

PUBS WITH GOOD RESTAURANTS

S.E.1. PUBS

The George Inn
77 Borough High Street, S.E.1.
Tel: 01-407 2056
Major Credit Cards.
Restaurant Closed Saturday Evening and Sunday.
Rebuilt after a fire in 1666, The George is the only galleried pub in London set around a courtyard where Shakespearian plays were and are today performed. There are two bars and a snack bar downstairs and two restaurants. This pub is steeped in history and well worth visiting.
Lunch and Dinner.
Map Ref. 4K

S.E.16. PUBS

The Angel
110 Bermondsey Wall East, S.E.16.
Tel: 01-237 3608
Major Credit Cards.
Restaurant Closed Saturday and Lunch Sunday.
A splendid 15th Century pub opposite Execution Dock. Whilst the front is not very imposing, this is really a river pub and the oldest part overlooks the river with a delightful balcony.
Pepys visited it.
Lunch and Dinner.
Map Ref. 4L

E.C.4. PUBS

Ye Olde Cheshire Cheese
145 Fleet Street, E.C.4.
Tel: 01-353 6170
Restaurant Closed Saturday and Sunday.
This famous pub has hardly changed since 1667, although there has been a tavern on this site since 1538. The Cheshire Cheese has been mentioned in many literary works and a small booklet which explains its history can be bought over the bars. Dr. Johnson frequently drank here and his original favourite chair is still in use. The bars are on two floors and the whole place is steeped in atmosphere. There is an excellent restaurant.
Lunch and Dinner.
Map Ref. 2I

Ye Olde Cock Tavern
22 Fleet Street, E.C.4.
Tel: 01-353 9706
Major Credit Cards.

Restaurant Closed Saturday and Sunday.
Ancient tavern with three dining rooms serving good English fare. Popular with journalists.
Lunch only.
Map Ref. 2I

Red Lion
17 Watling Street, E.C.4.
Tel: 01-248 2796
Major Credit Cards.
Restaurant Closed Saturday and Sunday.
Modern but pleasant and comfortable pub with a good restaurant and extensive menu. Also a very fine wine list.
Lunch only.
Map Ref. 2J

Brooks Wharf, Samuel Pepys
48 Upper Thames Street, E.C.4.
Tel: 01-248 3048
Major Credit Cards.
Restaurant Closed Lunch Saturday.
This is a tasteful conversion of a warehouse in traditional style with two large bars and an excellent restaurant. Old lamps and prints as well as some letters by the man himself. Good English fare.
Lunch and Dinner.
Map Ref. 3K

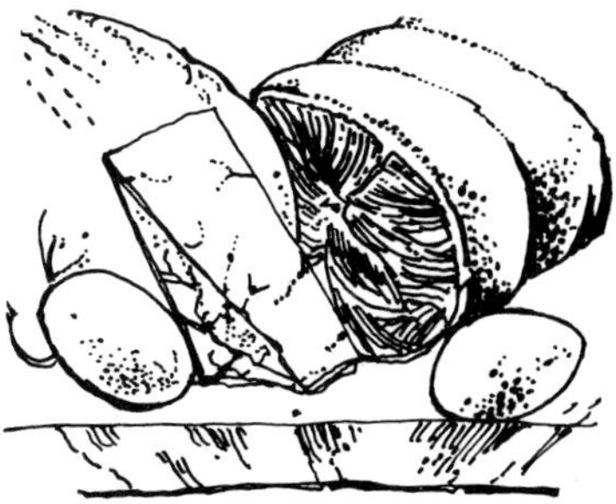

The George
Fleet Street, E.C.4.
Tel: 01-353 9238
Restaurant Closed Saturday and Sunday.
An imposing and original Tudor building standing opposite the Royal Courts of Justice, this is a popular pub for the legal profession. Good buffet food and a separate restaurant.
Lunch only.
Map Ref. 2I

E.C.3. PUBS

George and Vulture
3 Castle Court, E.C.3.
Tel: 01-626 9710
Major Credit Cards.
Restaurant Closed Saturday and Sunday.
This old Dickens Inn has a wonderful atmosphere in which to eat good, well prepared English roasts, pies and large steaks.
Lunch only.
Map Ref. 2K

W.C.2. PUBS

Gilbert and Sullivan
John Adam Street, W.C.2.
Tel: 01-839 2580
Major Credit Cards.
Restaurant Closed Sunday and Lunch Saturday.
There is a unique collection of photographs, programmes and miniature stage settings with background music from Gilbert and Sullivan. Fine English cooking.
Lunch and Dinner.
Map Ref. 3H

Sherlock Holmes
10 Northumberland Street, W.C.2.
Tel: 01-930 2644
Major Credit Cards.
Restaurant Closed Saturday Evening and Sunday.
Full of relics of the famous fictional detective and a replica of his study. Good French and English cooking.
Lunch and Dinner.
Map Ref. 3H

W.C.1. PUBS

Pindar of Wakefield
328 Grays Inn Road, W.C.1.
Tel: 01-837 1753
A fun pub with old time music hall, jazz and lots of cheerful regulars. Limited but good menu.
Dinner on music hall nights.
Map Ref. 2I

W.1. PUBS

Audley
41 Mount Street, W.1.
Tel: 01-499 1843
Restaurant Closed Sunday and Dinner Saturday.
Well-established steak restaurant on the first floor. Wine bar in basement with good food.
Lunch and Dinner.
Map Ref. 3F

The Guinea
30 Bruton Place, W.1.
Tel: 01-629 5613
Major Credit Cards.
Restaurant Closed Sunday and Lunch Saturday.
Built in 1423 this pub is not a particularly comfortable pub for drinking and does not have a lot of atmosphere. Where it really comes into its own is in the restaurant which, although expensive, is excellent. It is one of the few pubs to have a supper license. Excellent steaks.
Lunch and Dinner
Map Ref. 3F

Cock and Lion
62 Wigmore Street, W.1.
Tel: 01-935 8727
Major Credit Cards.
Restaurant Closed Sunday and Lunch Saturday.
Excellent grills and steaks where you can see what you are getting. Good helpings in a pleasant first floor restaurant.
Lunch and Dinner.
Map Ref. 2F

Baker and Oven
10 Paddington Street, W.1.
Tel: 01-935 5072
Major Credit Cards.
Restaurant Closed Sunday and Lunch Saturday.
The restaurant is in the basement and its decor is Trattoria style. It is

extremely pleasant and the food is substantial.
Lunch and Dinner.
Map Ref. 2F

Prince Regent
71 Marylebone High Street, W.1.
Tel: 01-935 2018
Major Credit Cards.
Restaurant Closed Sunday and Dinner Saturday.
Excellent food, particularly steaks and grills, but the à la carte has a varied choice. Nice atmosphere.
Lunch and Dinner.
Map Ref. 2F

Red Lion
1 Waverton Street, W.1.
Tel: 01-499 1309
Major Credit Cards.
Open 7 days a week.
Very popular, so essential to book. This pub serves traditional English food with varied starters and an excellent cheese board.
Lunch and Dinner.
Map Ref. 3F

Shepherds Tavern
50 Hertford Street, W.1.
Tel: 01-499 3017
Major Credit Cards.
Luxurious 18th Century atmosphere with prints and paintings of Mayfair. Good English food.
Lunch Monday-Friday.
Map Ref. 3F

Samuel Pepys
Clarges Street, W.1.
Tel: 01-629 5221
Major Credit Cards.
Set in the heart of Mayfair, the Samuel Pepys has a good restaurant serving traditional English food.
Lunch only, Monday-Friday.
Map Ref. 3F

S.W.1. PUBS

The Grenadier
18 Wilton Row, S.W.1.
Tel: 01-235 3074
Restaurant Open 7 Days.
The Grenadier was originally the Officers' Mess for the Duke of Wellington's soldiers and outside is the original stone used as his mounting block. When it became a pub about 1810 it was frequented by George IV. It has a marvellous pewter bar believed to be the oldest of its kind. Good food and a separate restaurant.
Lunch and Dinner.
Map Ref. 4F

St. Stephens Tavern
10 Bridge Street, S.W.1.
Tel: 01-930 2541
Major Credit Cards.
Restaurant Closed Sunday Dinner.
Because M.P.'s from the House of Commons opposite use this pub, there is a bell in the restaurant which connects the House to those Members dining to alert them for divisions. Traditional English menu with good roasts and pies.
Lunch and Dinner.
Map Ref. 4H

Tattersall's Tavern
Knightsbridge Green, S.W.1.
Tel: 01-584 7122
Major Credit Cards.
Closed Saturday and Sunday.
Last orders 9.30pm.
As its name implies, the Tavern was built on the former site of Tattersall's offices and has a long association with the horse world. The comfortable wine bar serves quality food.
Lunch only.
Map Ref. 4F

W.8. PUBS

Windsor Castle
114 Campden Hill Road, W.8.
Tel: 01-727 8491
Similar to a village-type pub, this popular tavern produces not only excellent food in its small dining room but very original bar snacks as well. Only licensed Beer Garden in London.
Lunch.
Map Ref. 3B

S.W.5. PUBS

Clarence
148 Old Brompton Road, S.W.5.
Tel: 01-373 2818
Restaurant Closed Sunday and Monday.
A first class restaurant on the first floor serving a good à la carte menu.
Lunch and Dinner.
Map Ref. 4E

RIVERSIDE PUBS

S.E.1. PUBS

The Anchor
1 Bankside, S.E.1.
Tel: 01-407 1577
Situated on the South side of the Thames. The present building, rebuilt in the 17th Century, replaced the one patronised by William Shakespeare.

The Inn has a long history; it was used by smugglers and river pirates and, because of its close proximity to the old Clink prison, was often used by escaping convicts. There are five bars with exposed beams and instruments of torture. In the summer you can sit and drink outdoors. Also an excellent restaurant. Highly recommended.
Map Ref. 4L

Crown Tavern
35 Albert Embankment, S.E.1.
Tel: 01-735 1054
A friendly modern pub with a marvellous view of the river. Snacks can be obtained at the bar.
Restaurant for lunches.
Map Ref. 5H

S.E.16. PUBS

The Angel
101 Bermondsey Wall Street, S.E.16.
Tel: 01-237 3608
A splendid 15th Century pub opposite Execution Dock. Whilst the front is not very imposing, this is really a river pub and the oldest part overlooks the river with a delightful balcony. Bar snacks are limited but there is also a restaurant. Mentioned in Pepys Diary.
Map Ref. 4L

The Mayflower
117 Rotherhithe Street, S.E.16.
Tel: 01-237 4088
This genuine 17th Century pub with its exposed beams, open fireplaces and ancient bric-a-brac is one of the few licensed houses to possess a licence to sell postage stamps including American ones. The Mayflower has close connections with America because it was from here in 1611 that Captain Christopher Jones and the Pilgrim Fathers first set sail for the New Land. There is a verandah overlooking the river and an excellent variety of food.
Map Ref. 4L

S.E.10. PUBS

Trafalgar Tavern
Park Row, S.E.10.
Tel: 01-858 2437
Situated near the Royal Naval College in Greenwich, this old pub has an upstairs room modelled to resemble a man o'war forecastle. There is a very good restaurant and a balcony overlooking the river, bars and banqueting room.
No Map Ref.

Cutty Sark
Ballast Quay, Lassell Street, S.E.10.
Tel: 01-858 3146
Overlooking the Thames near the famous Cutty Sark sailing ship, this old Georgian pub serves good food in a pleasant atmosphere.
No Map Ref.

E.1. PUBS

Prospect of Whitby
57 Wapping Wall, E.1.
Tel: 01-481 1095
One of the famous pubs of London which unfortunately gets very crowded, particularly on summer evenings. Samuel Pepys spent a lot of time here and there is much ancient nautical bric-a-brac. Good restaurant with balcony overlooking the river.
Map Ref. 4L

E.C.3. PUBS

Tiger Tavern
1 Tower Hill, E.C.3.
Tel: 01-626 5097
Situated in the new centre opposite the Tower of London one can see the panoramic view of Tower Bridge and the Tower itself. There are a number of bars and a good selection of snacks.
Map Ref. 3L

E.C.4. PUBS

Brooks Wharf, Samuel Pepys
Brooks Wharf, 48 Upper Thames Street, E.C.4.
Tel: 01-248 3048
This is a tasteful conversion of a warehouse in traditional style with two large bars and an excellent restaurant. Old lamps and prints, as well as some letters by the man himself. Good English fare.
Map Ref. 3K

S.W.3. PUBS

Kings Head and Eight Bells
50 Cheyne Walk, S.W.3.
Tel: 01-352 1820

A lovely pub with plenty of atmosphere and a dining room serving first class fare overlooking the river.
Map Ref. 6E

W.6 PUBS

Dove Inn
19 Upper Mall, Hammersmith, W.6.
This pub is 400 years old — it is where 'Rule Britannia' was written! Also mentioned in A P Herbert's 'The Water Gypsies'. It is the haunt of writers and artists and has a pretty terrace on which you can sit in the summer. Hot and cold snacks available.
No Map. Ref.

W.9. PUBS

Warwick Castle
6 Warwick Place, Little Venice, W.9.
Tel: 01-286 6868
A pleasant pub close to the canal where, on a summer evening, you can watch the canal boats plying back and forth. Good food.
Map Ref. 1C

PUBS WITH MUSIC

W.C.1. PUBS

New Merlins Cave
Margery Street, W.C.1.
Tel: 01-837 2097
Large barn-like pub with disco. Sunday lunchtime visit is a must with top names for jazz appearing.
Map Ref. 1H

W.1. PUBS

Albany
240 Great Portland Street, W.1.
Tel: 01-387 8690
A Victorian pub with regular Folk and Jazz performances.
Map Ref. 2G

Phoenix
37 Cavendish Square, W.1.
Tel: 01-629 1700
Disco every Friday. Video juke box.
Map Ref. 2G

Audley
41 Mount Street, W.1.
Tel: 01-499 1843
Stereo sound music.
Map Ref. 3F

Adam Arms
Conway Street, W.1.
Tel: 01-636 8937
This pub has been entertaining its customers for many years with Folk Singers on Wednesday evening.
Map Ref. 1G

N.W.1. PUBS

Allsop Arms
137 Gloucester Place, N.W.1.
Tel: 01-723 5864
Good piano music every night which accompanies a splendid selection of bar snacks.
Map Ref. 1F

Green Man
383 Euston Road, N.W.1.
Tel: 01-387 6977
A swinging pub with nice, friendly staff. Cocktail Bar downstairs. 'Happy Hour' from 6pm-7pm.
Map Ref. 1H

S.W.3. PUBS

Trafalgar
200 Kings Road, S.W.3.
Tel: 01-352 1076
New Lounge Bar has Victorian decor and lots of plants! Wide selection of good bar snacks.
Map Ref. 5E

Six Bells
195 Kings Road, S.W.3.
Tel: 01-352 9255
Large and famous Chelsea pub with a popular disco upstairs. Check times.
Map Ref. 5E

S.W.7. PUBS

Hoop and Toy
34 Thurloe Place, S.W.7.
Tel: 01-589 8360
Noisy and popular disco on Friday and Saturday.
Map Ref. 5D

W.2. PUBS

Shakespeare
65 Westbourne Grove, W.2.
Tel: 01-229 2233
Recorded music every night but dancing not allowed.
Map Ref. 2B

W.11. PUBS

The Elgin
96 Ladbroke Grove, W.11.
Tel: 01-727 4192
On Wednesday evening this pub has a good selection of Folk Singers.
Map Ref. 2A

W.14 PUBS

The Three Kings
North End Road, W.14
Tel: 01-603 6071
This is the place to go for real ale — there is a big selection. Full range of bar food.
Map Ref. 6B

MANNS
PR
OF

SPECT
HITBY
FREE TRADE WHARF

What to see in London

WHAT TO SEE IN LONDON

If there's a problem for a visitor to London, it's the fact that there's so much to do. Obviously, London is England's largest city and was its capital even in Roman days. Being the centre of power, government and monarchy, it remains the capital of pageantry and heritage. Being the centre of routes, it has naturally become a centre for trade and finance. Though no longer the largest city in the world, the hub of world commerce, London is still an international centre for skills and expertise. Being such a force in the nation and the world as a whole, it acts as a magnet for masterpieces of all sorts and to the men of talent who bring them about. Being the centre of so many people, London is also a city of great variety. Both Shelley and Dunbar were right when the one likened it to "hell. . . a populous and smokey city" and the other called it "the flower of cities all". Shops alone range from the sedate luxury of Knightsbridge and Harrods to the hurly-burly of the East End's Petticoat Lane. At the same time, you find the razamattazz of an area like Soho almost cheek by jowl with the decorum of Bond Street, Burlington Arcade and the Gentlemen's Clubs. All in all, London is a remarkably rich experience. There's so much that what would be a major source of interest elsewhere, even a place of pilgrimage, is a commonplace feature here. For instance, few visitors, or even Londoners, would notice or note a house in Ebury Street (behind Victoria Station) yet this is where Mozart wrote his first symphony at the age of 8.

With so much on your plate, don't expect to take it all in at once. The effect would be like trying to eat everything on a menu in one lunchtime. The result inevitably leads to exhaustion — as well as indigestion.

It's only natural to find such a feast daunting, so where to start? To help you decide, it pays to get a general grasp of what's on offer — to, in effect, read the menu. One of the best ways to do this is to take the advice that W. E. Gladstone gave to some American visitors: "The way to see London is from the top of a bus — the top of a bus, gentlemen." One of the central London tours will naturally show you the major sites but it will also highlight other areas and points of interest you could easily never hear of otherwise.

Having done this, you may well feel you must go straight for the main course, for the Tower of London, the Changing of the Guard, St. Paul's Cathedral and Westminster Abbey. You can do this effectively and efficiently in one day by taking a guided coach tour but you may prefer to wander and explore on your own. If so, I would advise avoiding the Abbey in the morning, St. Paul's Cathedral after lunch and the Tower of London in late afternoon. Why? Because you will avoid the larger crowds that way. I would also suggest arming yourself with a good map, taking one area at a time and exploring on foot. Whilst in the area of the Tower, remember that there is the charming St. Katherine's Dock (with its Historic Ships collection), the newly opened high walkway on Tower Bridge, H.M.S. Belfast — the second World War cruiser — and the ghoulish London Dungeon nearby. Whilst in the area of Westminster Abbey and the Changing of the Guard, remember there's St. James's Park to have a picnic in (and listen to the band in the summer), there's Trafalgar Square with the National Gallery (and the pigeons to feed), the Royal Mews with the Queen's horses and carriages, the Houses of Parliament where you may be able to listen to a debate, the South Bank arts centre, the Imperial Collection of replica crown jewels. . . and much more. . . all close at hand.

Whilst at St. Paul's Cathedral, remember the fascinating Museum of London, the Guildhall (the powerhouse of the City of London), the Stock Exchange (with its viewing gallery and free film show), the Overlord Tapestry of the allied landing in Europe in 1944 (D-Day); the largest and newest European arts centre at the Barbican and so many other churches by Sir Christopher Wren. . . all within striking distance. This way not only do you save energy and money — you also have the time to observe life around you and find the gems in the backwaters of London (like the Norman Church of St. Bartholomew the Great in Smithfield or the intimate Shepherd's Market in Mayfair) that are all the more enjoyable for being your own discovery and so unexpected. Having explored such areas, others will inevitably appeal — for instance, the Museums in South Kensington, Covent Garden and, by no means least, the River Thames — which is the reason why London exists in the first place. A short and simple boat trip between the Tower and Westminster gives an excellent introduction to the City's history from a totally new angle. Longer trips upstream in summer will take you to Henry VIII's Tudor Palace at Hampton Court or the Royal Botanic gardens at Kew. Go further downstream and you come to the Royal Naval College at Greenwich and the Maritime Museum (complete with the Cutty Sark) or to the latest of London's engineering feats — the flood barrier at Woolwich. On all such excursions in London leave extra time available as you'll always discover there's more to see than you at first thought.

As you explore this way, you'll soon find that the next area follows on naturally — almost suggests itself — and you'll build up something that eludes so many — a genuine feel for London itself. Of course, it can't all be done in a couple of hours, a couple of days or even a couple of years — I know, I often feel as if I've only scratched the surface myself. After all, remember you're in a city of just under seven million people which was rightly called " nation, not a city" by Mr. Gladstone's great rival, Benjamin Disraeli. However, it's surprising to see how many people try to "do" it in a few hours. It saddens me to see so many visitors — tired and dishevelled, shell shocked with culture and unresponsive — rushing from one internationally famous site to another and from one queue of tourists to another. The pressure of time means they never have a chance to stumble across the byways or chat to the Londoners themselves — the bobbies, buskers, cab drivers, shop keepers, et al — they make up the heart of the city. In the same few hours (which may be all you can spare) you can reach the heart — provided you kerb your appetite and give the city time to talk to you. You may not have collected as many "sights" as your voracious tourist friend, but you'll have had a far more genuine experience to look back on.

Guided Walks around London are noted on the back page of "The Times" each day in "The Times" Information Service.

William Forrester is a graduate in history from Magdalen College, Oxford and a qualified teacher. In 1981, he became a prizewinning London Registered Guide and in 1982 was presented with first place in the City Guide course by the Lord Mayor of London. He broadcasts frequently on television and radio and lectures on English heritage. Being in a wheelchair himself, he operates a specialist service for disabled visitors to the U.K. and has received the British Tourist Authority's I.Y.O.P. award for outstanding services for disabled people. However, he says he doesn't discriminate against able bodied visitors and that his disability in no way handicaps their visit!

MUSEUMS

The British Museum
Great Russell Street, W.C.1.
Tel: 01-636 1555
Tube: Russell Square.
Buses: 14, 24, 29, 73.

Originally founded in 1753 to house several private collections ranging from natural history to coins and drawings, and in 1759 it was opened to the public. The following years saw a great increase in the collections and in 1823 after George IV presented the magnificent ROYAL LIBRARY it was agreed that a new building would be needed. A state lottery raised £300,000 the old building was demolished, and the present building erected and finished in 1852. The earliest part of the present complex is now the long gallery which still houses the KING'S LIBRARY.

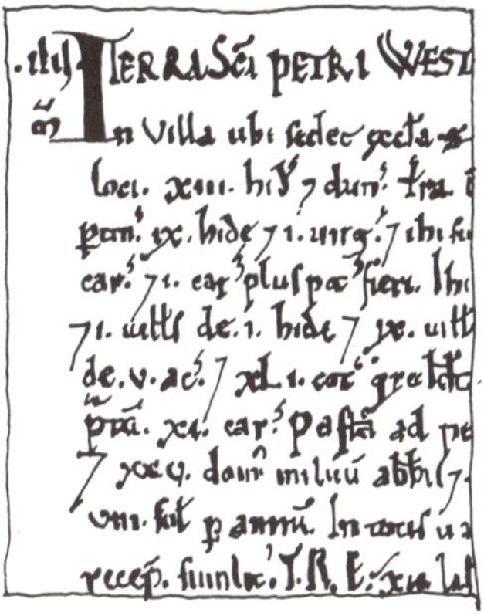
TERRA SCA PETRI WEST

The famous READING ROOM with its enormous dome was opened in 1857 and the Library, which consists of over 6 million books, is one of the most consulted in the world. By law, a copy of every publication in the United Kingdom must be deposited at the Museum, where it is kept on file.
There are so many permanent exhibits that it is difficult to decide which are the most important. One which surely rates attention is the *Elgin Marbles* situated in the Duveen Gallery. These are 5th Century BC sculptures and panels and a 500 foot long frieze of carvings by the Greek sculptor *Phidias*. The scene depicts a procession to the Acropolis and of particular interest is the way that so much depth, perspective and speed has been carved out of a shallow medium. This technique was lost until the Italian sculptor *Donatello* discovered it during the Italian Renaissance. The *Marbles* are named after the *Earl of Elgin* who, at a time when Greece was still under Turkish occupation and upon seeing them gradually being destroyed and used as building material, he decided to ship them back to England.
In ROOM 14 can be seen the marvellous *Portland Vase* which is without doubt the finest glass vase to have survived from ancient times. It is one of the earliest examples of blown glass, dating from about 2nd Century B.C. and is made up of two layers white over blue with the outer layer carved away as in a cameo.
One of the most unique collections is the range of exhibits in the ASSYRIAN

A B C D E F G H I J K L
1 2 3 4 5 6
Kensal Green
KILBURN LANE
HARROW ROAD
FERNHEAD RD.
ELGIN AVENUE
GREAT WESTERN RD
Maida Vale
CASTELLAN RD
MAIDA VALE
ST. JOHN'S WOOD RD
CLIFTON GDNS
Warwick Avenue
EDGWARE ROAD
LISSON GROVE
WELLINGTON ROAD
REGENT'S PARK
ALBANY STREET
EUSTON STATION
EUSTON ROAD
University College
GOWER STREET
TOTTENHAM COURT RD
SOUTHAMPTON ROW
GRAYS INN ROAD
KING'S CROSS ROAD
ROSEBERRY AVENUE
GOSWELL ROAD
CITY ROAD
OLD STREET
Old Street
GREAT EASTERN ST.
HACKNEY ROAD
Great Portland Street
Marylebone
Baker Street
Regent's Park
Warren Street
Goodge Street
GUILFORD ST
MARYLEBONE ROAD
CLERKEN WELL ROAD
THEOBALDS RD.
FARRINGDON ST.
Guild Hall
St. Pauls Cathedral
ALDERSGATE ST.
LIVERPOOL ST. STATION
Ladbroke Grove
Westbourne Park
WESTBOURNE PARK
TALBOT ROAD
LADBROKE GROVE
CHEPSTOW RD
Edgware Road
SEYMOUR PLACE
BAKER STREET
MARYLEBONE HIGH ST.
PORTLAND PL.
All Souls Church
GOODGE
Tottenham Court Rd.
NEW OXFORD STREET
HOLBORN
Holborn
Chancery Lane
HOLBORN VIA.
CHANCERY LANE
Moorgate
MOORGATE
BISHOPSGATE
HOUNDSDITCH
COMMERCIAL ST.
WHITECHAPEL
Aldgate
PADDINGTON STATION
WESTBOURNE TER
BISHOPS BRIDGE ROAD
COLVILLE TER.
WESTBOURNE GROVE
PORTMAN SQUARE
Oxford Circus
REGENT ST.
OXFORD STREET
CHARING CROSS ROAD
WARDOUR ST
POLAND ST
DRURY LANE
Lincolns Inn
FLEET ST.
Bank
Royal Exchange
CHEAPSIDE
St. Paul's
LUDGATE HILL
LEADENHALL ST.
CLARENDON RD
BLENHEIM CRES
ELGIN CRES.
Bayswater
QUEENSWAY
PEMBRIDGE RD
Lancaster Gate
Marble Arch
GROSVENOR SQUARE
Bond Street
NEW BOND ST.
OLD BOND ST.
Royal Academy
SHAFTESBURY AV
LONG ACRE
Covent Garden
STRAND
Somerset House
Aldwych
Temple
EMBANKMENT
QUEEN VICTORIA ST
Blackfriars
Mansion House
FENCHURCH ST.
Monument
Tower Hill
MINORIES
EAST SMITHFIELD
Queensway
BAYSWATER ROAD
KENSINGTON GARDENS
HYDE PARK
PARK LANE
BERKELEY SQUARE
Piccadilly Circus
Leicester Square
National & Portrait Galleries
St Martin's in the Fields
RIVER THAMES
BLACKFRIARS BRIDGE
SOUTHWARK BRIDGE
LONDON BRIDGE
The Tower of London
Royal Mint
Notting Hill Gate
NOTTING HILL GATE
KENSINGTON CHURCH ST
Albert Memorial
SERPENTINE
CURZON ST.
PICCADILLY
St. James's Palace
PALL MALL
Nelson's Column
CHARING CROSS STATION
WATERLOO BRIDGE
STAMFORD ST.
SOUTHWARK ST.
Southwark Cathedral
TOOLEY STREET
Tower Bridge
PORTLAND ROAD
HOLLAND PARK AVENUE
Holland Park
ROTTEN ROW
Hyde Park Corner
Green Park
GREEN PARK
THE MALL
ST. JAMES'S PARK
Houses of Parlia-ment
Westminster
VICTORIA
WATERLOO ROAD
BLACKFRIARS RD.
Borough
ST. THOMAS
LONDON BRI. STATION
HOLLAND PARK
CAMPDEN HILL RD
KENSINGTON HIGH STREET
Royal Albert Hall
KENSINGTON RD.
KNIGHTSBRIDGE
Brompton Oratory
BELGRAVE SQUARE
GROSVENOR PL.
Buckingham Palace
BIRDCAGE WALK
WESTMINSTER BRIDGE
YORK ROAD
WATERLOO STATION
SOUTHWARK BRIDGE RD
CAUSEWAY
BOROUGH RD
LONG LANE
HOLLAND ROAD
High Street Kensington
QUEENS GATE
Victoria & Albert Museum
EXHIBITION ROAD
Knightsbridge
SLOANE STREET
BEAUCHAMP PLACE
CADOGAN GDNS
St. Peter's Church
St James's Park
Westminster Abbey
RIVER
WESTMINSTER BRIDGE RD.
Lambeth North
PALACE RD
Lambeth Palace
LAMBETH ROAD
LONDON RD
ST. GEORGE'S RD
NEWINGTON
GREAT DOVER ST.
ABBEY STREET
EARLS COURT ROAD
South Kensington
BROMPTON
WALTON RD
KING'S ROAD
VICTORIA STREET
VAUXHALL
HORSE FERRY ROAD
LAMBETH BRIDGE
Tate Gallery
MILLBANK
THAMES
KENNINGTON ROAD
Imperial War Museum
Elephant and Castle
NEW KENT RD
WALWORTH ROAD
OLD KENT ROAD
SHEPHERD'S BUSH RD
HAMMERSMITH ROAD
WARWICK ROAD
CROMWELL ROAD
Gloucester Road
OLD BROMPTON ROAD
SYDNEY ST.
Sloane Square
BUCKINGHAM PALACE ROAD
Westminster Cathedral
VICTORIA STATION
BRIDGE ROAD
ALBERT EMBANKMENT
KENNINGTON PARK ROAD
TALGARTH ROAD
NORTH END ROAD
WEST CROMWELL ROAD
Earls Court
Chelsea Royal Hospital
ROYAL HOSPITAL ROAD
CHELSEA BRIDGE RD
Pimlico
VAUXHALL BRIDGE
Oval Cricket Ground
FULHAM PALACE ROAD
LILLIE ROAD
REDCLIFF GARDENS
FULHAM ROAD
CHELSEA EMBANKMENT
CHELSEA BRIDGE
GROSVENOR ROAD
Vauxhall
HARLEYFORD RD
Kennington Park
ALBANY ROAD
West Brompton
KING'S ROAD
ALBERT BRIDGE
BATTERSEA PARK
NINE ELMS LANE
FENTIMAN RD
Oval

SALOON, with carved stone slabs of battles and hunting scenes which once decorated the palace walls at Nineveh 620th Century B.C.
Even older is the EGYPTIAN COLLECTION numbering 70,000 objects. This exhibition illustrates nearly every aspect of the Ancient Egyptian civilisation and includes mummified remains and treasures from ancient burial chambers, some of which date before the 2000th Century B.C. One of the most important exhibits in this collection is the *Rosetta Stone* which provided scholars with the key to the ancient Egyptian language.
The principal medieval objects are displayed in the EARLY MEDIEVAL ROOM, which covers the years between the beginning of the 4th Century A.D. and the end of the 7th Century A.D., and the MEDIEVAL ROOM, which covers up to the 15th Century. There are *Oriental Antiquities* with treasures which date back as far back as 3500 years before Christ, and numerous clocks, coins and drinking vessels from a myriad of countries and periods.
The MANUSCRIPT ROOM houses the famous *Magna Carta* and the priceless *Codex Sinaiticus*, a 4th Century A.D. Greek Bible, as well as books, transcribed by Monks in medieval Europe.
Admission Free.
Open: 10.00am-5.00pm, Monday to Saturday.
2.30pm-6.00pm, Sunday.
Closed Christmas Eve, Christmas Day, Boxing Day, Good Friday, New Year's Day, May Bank Holiday.

Map Ref. 3H

The Victoria and Albert Museum
Cromwell Road, S.W.7.
Tel: 01-589 6371
Tube: South Kensington
Buses: 14, 30, 74.
The Victoria and Albert Museum, as its name implies, was built in commemoration of that formidable monarch and her consort. Over the Cromwell Road entrance are two portrait statues of the pair by Alfred Drury, as well as two of her son, *Edward VII*, and his Queen, *Alexandra*. The building, opened in 1909, was designed by *Sir Aston Webb*. One of the finest museums in London, devoted as it is to fine and applied arts of every country and century. Also there is a comprehensive collection of miniatures as well as water-colours, sculpture and the decorative arts, including a *Costume Court*.

THE PRIMARY COLLECTIONS arrange masterpieces of arts by style and period and need intensive study to get the best out of them. These collections start with Early Christian Art and include fine examples of Byzantine Art as well as many early representations of the Virgin and Child from the Mediterranean Countries. Contrasted with these fine works are those from Islamic and Far Eastern Countries. Then we come on to the MIDDLE AGES where work from France and Germany is distinguished, as is Spanish Gothic Art. And then on through each century, particularly impressive being the Collection of Italian masters *Luca Della Robbia*, *Donatello* and *Minelli* in the *Renaissance Collection*.
The 16th, 17th and 18th Centuries A.D. also provide masterpieces of tapestries, furniture and bibelots which represent the epitome of style and taste in the respective eras.

One of the most magnificent possessions of the Victoria and Albert Museum is the *Raphael Cartoons* which show designs for the tapestries that Pope Leo X commissioned from the great painter. They are loaned by *H.M. The Queen.*
THE DEPARTMENTAL COLLECTIONS include the *Costume Court,* a really important collection of fashion through the ages, many of the clothes being donated by famous or distinguished women. Then there are the collections of *Decorative Arts* and *English Furniture,* which includes *Queen Elizabeth's Virginals* and *The Great Bed of Ware.* Again this collection spans the ages in an interesting and informative manner. *Domestic Silver, Ceramics, Books* and *Jewellery* are other departments which mount collections.
The Victoria and Albert Museum has also a fine LIBRARY and TEXTILE STUDY ROOMS for serious students with comprehensive and scholarly lecture courses (for details ring the Information Department). It is indeed both a place for scholars and those of the general public who like to see and know about how other ages lived.
THERE ARE ALSO SPECIAL EXHIBITIONS FROM TIME TO TIME
Admission Free except for special exhibitions.

Open: 10.00am-5.50pm, Monday to Thursday and Saturday.
2.30pm-5.50pm, Sunday.
Closed Friday and Public Holidays.

Map Ref. 5D

Tower of London
Tower Hill, E.C.3.
Tel: 01-709 0765
Tube: Tower Hill.
Buses: 42, 78.
Brooding over the River there has been no image of London more powerful in people's imagination than the **Tower of London.** Bound up with British history, its Kings and Queens, its politics and wars, this abiding building has now lost the terror it once inspired and has become a peaceful and interesting museum.
It was begun by William the Conqueror within an angle in the City walls and was extensively enlarged over the centuries. *The White Tower* is Norman and contains one of the oldest chapels in England. The architecture follows the warring pattern of the Middle Ages

with an *Inner and Outer Ward,* a moat and numerous Towers.
Many famous prisoners were kept here and their rooms are still shown to visitors. Among them were Lady Jane Grey, Anne Boleyn, the Little Princes, Sir Thomas Moore and the Earl of Essex. Queen Elizabeth I, as Princess Elizabeth, was also confined here, although, unlike the others, she lived to tell the story of her imprisonment.
Also in the Tower are the *Crown Jewels* in all their magnificence. There is generally a long queue to see these, so it is advisable to go early.
The oldest crown displayed is *St. Edward's Crown* which is used in the Coronation Ceremony for the actual crowning. Nearby is the *Imperial Crown,* which was originally made for Queen Victoria and which is used for all state occasions such as the Opening of Parliament. The other insignia of Royalty, the Orb and the Sceptre, are also here. These four pieces contain some of the most

famous jewels of history, such as the Ruby worn by Henry V at Agincourt and the two *Stars of Africa* diamonds. The *Crown of Queen Elizabeth* (now the Queen Mother) is centred round the famous *Koh-i-Noor* Diamond of 108 carats.
The only survivor of the *Medieval Crown Jewels* (King John lost the others in the Wash) is the *Anointing Spoon* and the *Ampulla* which holds the oil for the Anointing. (This probably dates back to Henry IV).
The Armouries are also very interesting and worth study. Exhibits mainly consist of 18th and 19th Century pieces although there are some earlier ones.
Admission: Varies — being more expensive in the Summer.
Open: 9.30am-4.00pm, Monday to Saturday.
2.00pm-4.00pm, Sunday.
January, February, November, December.
Open: 9.30am-5.00pm, Monday to Saturday.
2.00pm-5.00pm, Sunday.
March to October.
The Tower is closed on Maundy Thursday and Good Friday and over Christmas and New Year. Check other Bank Holidays. The Jewel House is closed throughout February.
Children and O.A.P.'s half price.

Map Ref. 3L

Natural History Museum
Cromwell Road, S.W.7.
Tel: 01-589 6323
Tube: South Kensington.
Buses: 14, 30, 74.
The Natural History Museum is part of the British Museum and was formed around the collection of *Sir Hans Sloane* who died in 1753. This was added to by bequests from *Sir Joseph Banks* and the Romanesque Building

in South Kensington was designed by *Alfred Waterhouse* when it was decided to split this collection from that of the British Museum in the 1870s.
There are five departments: Zoology, Entomology, Palaeontology, Minerology and Botany and they include many fascinating objects.
One of the most popular exhibitions is that of the DINOSAURS, around which children gather in the School Holidays. There is a wide variety of MAMMALS and BIRDS on display. FOSSILS are another attraction, while people wishing to study FISH, REPTILES and WHALES find much to consider.
MINERALS, which include many collected by *Hans Sloane,* occupy another section which contains many brilliant stones, while if INSECTS are your special hobby then again there is plenty for you to gaze at.
Admission Free.
Open: 10.00am-6.00pm, Monday to Saturday.
2.30pm-6.00pm, Sunday.
Closed Public Holidays.

Map Ref. 5D

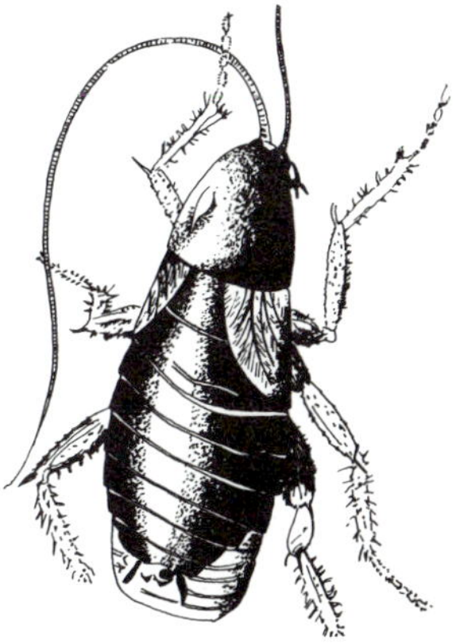

Apsley House – The Wellington Museum
149 Piccadilly, W.1.
Tel: 01-499 5676
Tube: Hyde Park Corner.
Buses: 9, 14, 19, 22, 38 and 506.
Known as No.1 Piccadilly, this beautiful house, owned by the *Duke of Wellington* and presented by the present Duke to the Nation, was built by the Adams brothers for *Lord Bathurst* and sold first to the *Wellesley* family then to the *Duke of Wellington* in 1817. The Iron Duke had extensive alterations made by the tactful hand of *Benjamin Wyatt* who added the Portico, the WELLINGTON GALLERY and faced the house in Bath Stone.
The house is dedicated to the memory of the Duke and contains many relics of him, *Napoleon* and their times. The House itself, with its spacious rooms and beautiful pieces of furniture gives a good idea of the graciousness of the Regency Period, while the contents are a lively memorial to the stirring times in which the Duke lived.
The marble statue of *Napoleon* by *Canova* dominates the Vestibule, while portraits of the Duke by *Goya* and *Lawrence*, as well as paintings by *Rubens, Murillo* and *Ribera* are well worth looking at. There is also a fine collection of *Porcelain* including some from *Meissen* and *Sèvres*. THE WATERLOO GALLERY was built so that the Duke could entertain his senior officers who were with him at the great Victory.

Admission 60p (Children half price).
Open: 10.00am-5.50pm, Tuesday to Thursday and Saturday.
Closed Monday and Friday and Public Holidays.

Map Ref. 4F

Imperial War Museum
Lambeth Road, S.E.1.
Tel: 01-735 8922
Tube: Lambeth North or *Elephant and Castle.*
Buses: 3, 59, 109, 155, 159, 172 take you to Kennington Road. 10 and 44 take you outside the Entrance.
This museum is dedicated to military might since August 1914 and houses weapons, ships, transport, aircraft models as well as actual aircraft, together with thousands of drawings, paintings, sculptures and prints by leading artists who were commissioned by the government to make pictorial records of the events of all the wars. They include such luminaries as *Sargent, Wyndham Lewis, John Piper, Epstein* and *Sir Charles Wheeler.*
Another interesting section is the DOCUMENTS ROOM which contains surrender agreements, *Hitler's Will* and the *Munich Agreement.*
The number of exhibits that the museum guards is immense and only a fraction of it can be shown at any one time, but the staff do change the exhibits so there is always something fresh to see.
There is a REFERENCE LIBRARY dealing with the World Wars in many languages as well as a FILM LIBRARY.
Admission: Free.
Open: 10.00am-5.50pm, Monday to Saturday. 2.00pm-5.50pm Sunday. Closed Over Christmas and New Year and other Bank Holidays.

Map Ref. 6I

Science and Geological Museum
Exhibition Road, S.W.7.
Tel: 01-589 3456
Tube: South Kensington.
Buses: 14, 30, 74.
One of the collection of Museums in South Kensington, the **Science and Geological Museum** is housed in buildings begun at the beginning of the century by *Sir Richard Allison* and which are continually being extended. It deals in many scientific disciplines and houses an amazing collection of industrial plant, machines, instruments and also many working models.

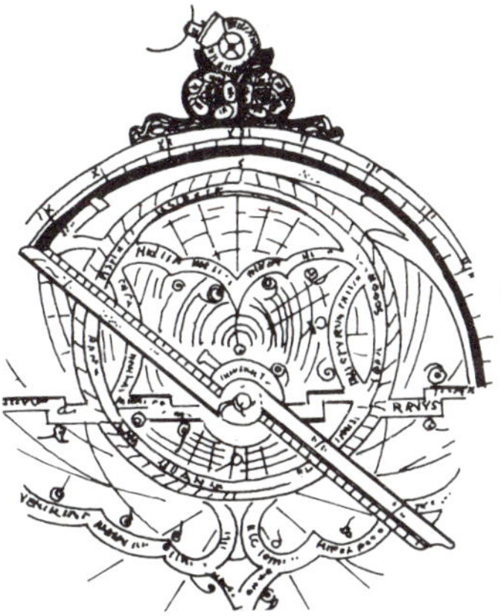

As the Museum is continually being extended, the collections also are being arranged and re-arranged, but even the non-scientific find here much to interest and amuse them. There is a CHILDREN'S GALLERY where children can put into action many exhibits and can be left safely alone. An INFORMATION OFFICE, LIBRARY and LECTURE THEATRE are other assets to this Museum, but its greatest merit is that, whatever branch of Science you are interested in, there is sure to be something of value to you. Historically minded visitors will revel in such exhibits as *Stevenson's Rocket*, and other *Old Railway Engines*, while those interested in nuclear physics will find an impressive collection devoted entirely to this subject.
AIR AND SEA NAVIGATION has its devotees as do all the various TECHNOLOGIES — Textiles, Iron and Steel, Glass and many other aspects of Science are shown both in their antique and historical forms as well as right up-to-date ones.
The adjoining **Geological Museum** is devoted to precious and ornamental stones, minerals and fossils.
Admission Free.
Open: 10.00am-5.50pm, Monday to Saturday. 2.30pm-6.00pm, Sunday. Closed Public Holidays.
Map Ref. 5D

Chelsea Royal Hospital
Chelsea Embankment, S.W.3.
Tel: 01-730 0161
Tube: Sloane Square.
Buses: 11, 137.
Many people believe that it was *Nell Gwynne* who persuaded Charles II to build this home for retired soldiers, who are often seen in London in their distinctive uniforms which date from Marlborough's day. But, in fact, it was the French *Hotel des Invalides* which was the real inspiration behind this charming and unique home.
Housing 400 pensioners, the building was designed by *Sir Christopher Wren* and there are additions by *Robert Adam* and *Sir John Sloane*. The central quadrangle contains a *Grinling Gibbons* statue of Charles II, decorated with oak leaves, to commemorate Charles's escape after the Battle of Worcester. And indeed, the Pensioners all parade on Oak Apple Day in commemoration of their Founder.
The Chapel and *The Great Hall* are fine examples of the architecture of the period with fine carvings and paintings.
The Governor's House was also designed by Wren and contains some good pictures by *Van Dyck*, *Lely* and *Kneller*.
Included in the grounds are those of *Ranelagh*, the famous place of entertainment, as well as cannon from the Battle of Waterloo.
Admission Free.
Open: 10.00am-12.00 noon and 2.00pm-4.00pm, Monday to Saturday. 2.00pm-4.00pm, Sunday.
Map Ref. 6E

Horniman Museum
London Road, Forest Hill, S.E.23.
Tel: 01-699 2339
Train: Southern to Forest Hill.
This small but fascinating Museum was built round the collection of *Frederick J. Horniman* and has been added to extensively. Its theme is *Man and his Environment* and it is mainly an ethnographical museum though it also has a fine collection of musical instruments and an aquarium. There are often temporary exhibitions, mostly on the ethnological theme, from other countries.
Other activities include concerts and lectures and there is a Children's Club on Saturday and in the School Holidays.
Admission Free.
Open: 10.00am-6.00pm, Monday to Saturday.
2.00pm-6.00pm, Sunday.
Library Closed Monday.
Museum Closed Christmas.
No Map Ref.

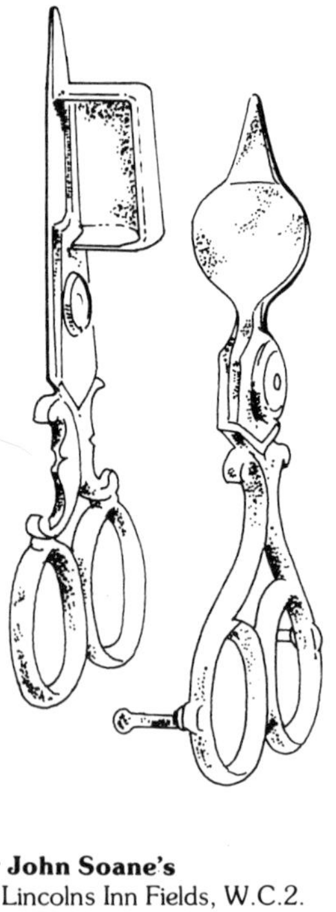

Sir John Soane's
13 Lincolns Inn Fields, W.C.2.
Tel: 01-405 2107
Tube: Holborn.
Buses: 55, 68, 77, 170, 188, 196 and 501.
This ingenious museum was built by *Sir John Soane* to house his individual and eclectic collection of paintings and sculptures. It also houses a fine collection of plans by *Sir Christopher Wren* which can be seen on request. The most amazing thing about this museum is the way the walls are in reality hinged doors which open out revealing more and more paintings, including some fine *Hogarths*. There are also works by *Canaletto* and *Watteau*. There is a crypt and the *Sarcophagus of Seti* as well as Roman funerary urns and works by *Flaxman*. The house was one of three houses in a row which was designed by Soane, himself an architect, and is a very rewarding place to visit.
Open: 10.00am-5.00pm, Tuesday to Saturday.
Closed Sunday, Monday and Public Holidays.
Admission Free.
Map Ref. 2I

Geffrye Museum
Kingsland Road, E.2.
Tel: 01-739 8368
Tube: Liverpool Street
Buses: 6, 8, 22, 35, 47 and 48.
One of the most interesting small Museums, the **Geffrye** is devoted to the domestic arts with rooms set out in the manner in which they were lived from Elizabethan times to the present day. Children are encouraged and there is a Children's Programme for them and workrooms for their use under skilled help. There is also a good library.
The Museum buildings were originally almshouses built in the early eighteenth century and donated by a former Lord Mayor, *Sir Robert Geffrye*. When new almshouses were built in 1912 this property was taken over by the then LCC. The Hall, originally the Chapel of the houses, is worth studying.
Admission Free.
Open: 10.00am-5.00pm, Tuesday to Saturday.
2.00pm-5.00pm, Sunday and Bank Holidays.
Closed Public Holidays.
Map Ref. 2K

Royal Airforce Museum
Graham Park Way, N.W.9.
Tel: 01-205 2266
Tube: Colindale.
Bus: 79.
A fantastic collection of aircraft from airships and kites to modern day bombers and missiles. Nostalgia is

created by the *Spitfires, Hurricanes* and *Lancaster Bomber* of the last war.
Admission for Battle of Britain £1.50.
Open: 10.00am-6.00pm, Monday to Saturday.
2.00pm-6.00pm, Sunday.
Closed Christmas and New Year.
No Map Ref.

Jewish Museum
Woburn House, Upper Woburn Place, W.C.1.
Tel: 01-387 3081
Tube: Euston.
Buses: 68, 77, 170, 188, 196.
There is a ten foot high Venetian *Ark* of the law, scrolls, ram's horns and *Chanukah Candlesticks* and many other beautiful ritual objects in this small museum.
Open: 12.30pm-3.00pm, Monday to Thursday.
10.30am-12.45pm, Sunday.
Closed Friday, Saturday, Jewish Holidays and Bank Holidays.
Admission Free.
Map Ref. 2H

National Maritime Museum
Romney Road, S.E.10.
Tel: 01-858 4422
Train: Southern from Charing Cross to Greenwich.
Buses: 177, 185.
The whole history of England as a maritime nation. There are superb models of ships and real boats to wander over. The *Barge House* has spectacular decorated barges which once carried VIPs in procession on the Thames.
Open: 10.00am-6.00pm, Tuesday to Saturday. 2.30pm-6.00pm. Sunday.
Closed Public Holidays, Open Bank Holidays.
No Map Ref.

National Army Museum
Royal Hospital Road, S.W.3.
Tel: 01-730 0717
Tube: Sloane Square.
Bus: 39.
New museum which features the history of the British Army from 1485 to the present day. The *Weapon Gallery* shows all the weapons used from the medieval bow to an electronic rifle range where you can test your marksmanship. There are uniforms, armour and soldiers' songs which you

can listen to on push-button machines.
Open: 10.00am-5.30pm, Monday to Saturday.
2.00pm-5.00pm, Sunday.
Closed Public Holidays.
Admission Free.
Map Ref. 6E

Museum of London
150 London Wall, E.C.2.
Tel: 01-600 3699
Tube: Moorgate/Barbican.
Buses: 141, 279, 502.
New museum which tells the story of London from the earliest times, when it was a Roman settlement, to the present giant metropolis. Beautiful displays, with rooms featured through different periods of history, shops and the various costumes worn through the years. You can also view the Lord Mayor's magnificent coach, as it is housed here between official engagements.
Open: 10.00am-6.00pm, Monday to Saturday.
2.00pm-6.00pm, Sunday.
Closed Christmas and some Public Holidays.
Map Ref. 2J

Museum of Mankind
6 Burlington Gardens, W.1.
Tel: 01-437 2224
Tube: Green Park.
Buses: 14, 19, 22, 38.
Housing ethnic cultures from Africa, South America, the Pacific Islands and some Islamic countries, this is a smaller museum than the British Museum which also features these aspects. Great favourite with children.
Open: 10.00am-5.00pm, Monday to Saturday.
2.30pm-6.00pm, Sunday.
Closed Public Holidays.
Map Ref. 3G

National Postal Museum
King Edward Street, E.C.1.
Tel: 01-432 3851
Tube: St. Pauls.
Buses: 8, 22, 25, 501.
If you are a stamp collector then this museum is definitely worth visiting. It has possibly the finest collection of stamps in the world, including the history of the *Penny Black.*
Open: 10.00am-4.30pm, Monday to Friday.
Closed Saturday and Sunday, Bank and Public Holidays.
Map Ref. 2J

Pollocks Toy Museum
1 Scala Street, W.1.
Tel: 01-636 3452
Tube: Goodge Street.
Buses: 14, 24, 29, 73, 176.
Another of London's unusual and quaint small museums, located in a tiny house. The small rooms on two floors are packed with an amazing collection of toys, both old and new, with one of the finest selections of dolls to be seen anywhere. The oldest teddy bear in England is here and there are many Victorian model theatres for which the museum is famous. There is a little shop on the ground floor which sells unusual toys and gingerbread made to an 18th Century recipe.
Open: 10.00am-5.00pm, Monday to Saturday.
Closed Sunday, Public and Bank Holidays.
Small admission charge.
Map Ref. 2G

ART GALLERIES

The National Gallery
Trafalgar Square, W.C.2.
Tel: 01-839 3321
Tube: Trafalgar Square or Charing Cross.
Buses: 3, 6, 12, 13, 15, 39, 53, 59, 88, 159, 506.
One of the last National Galleries to open in Europe, it was not until 1824, owing to two bequests by *Sir George Beaumont and John Julius Angerstein,* that the National Gallery was opened in Angerstein's old house in Pall Mall. In 1838 the Collection was moved to its present site in Trafalgar Square in a building designed by *William Wilkins,* the *Grecian Portico* being made from columns from *Sarlton House.* Extensions were made in 1876 and 1887. The *Mond Bequest* meant further extensions in 1927 and two years later came the *Duveen Room.* The Gallery is supported by Government grants and private donations and is run by a Director responsible to a Board of Trustees, appointed by the Prime Minister. Besides housing one of the finest collections of paintings in the world, the Gallery has a fine reputation for the restoration work it does, and also for the fine quality of its publications which are on sale on the ground floor. Also, it has an audio-visual room where films are shown continuously and there is also a daily lecture given in the lunch hour.

PAINTINGS
The National Gallery houses over four thousand paintings from all over the world and from all periods. It is particularly strong in Italian and Dutch paintings, and is noted for its *Rembrandts* and *Rubens.* THE BRITISH SCHOOL is only lightly

much of this is to be seen in the Tate Gallery, but the *Wilton Dyptych* is a notable example of early English painting — it depicts Richard II being presented to the Virgin and Child. *John Constable* is well represented *(The Hay Wain, Salisbury Cathedral* and others) as is *Thomas Gainsborough* and *William Hogarth. Lawrence, Reynolds* and *Turner* are English painters who also have a representative collection hung here. Among the *DUTCH SCHOOL* paintings, besides the *Rembrandts (Saskia as Flora, Two Self-Portraits* and many others) there are works by *Van Dyck,* and *Rubens.* The ITALIAN SCHOOL makes up a large portion of the collection, including, as it does, *Leonardo da Vinci (Virgin of the Rocks), Michaelangelo (The Entombment, Virgin and Child with St John and the Angels), Andrea del Sarto, Ucello* and many others. *Corregio, Mantegna, Bellini, Giorgione (Adoration of the Virgin)* and *Titian (Venus and Adonis, Bacchus and Ariadne)* and *Rintoretto (Origin of the Milky Way)* as well as *Veronese (The Family of Darius)* are other illustrious members of the ITALIAN SCHOOL who are found here with numerous works.

The SPANISH SCHOOL contains pictures by *Goya (The Duke of Wellington),* once stolen, *El Greco* — the mystical painter *(The Agony in the Garden), Murillo* and *Velasquez* whose *Rokeby Venus* was slashed by a militant suffragette in 1914. Even though it was superbly restored you can still see evidence of the attack. FRENCH PAINTING includes works by *Millet* and *Poussin* as well as *Boucher* and *Fragonard, Lancret Nattier* and *Watteau* all of whose paintings epitomise pre-Revolutionary France. The early-nineteenth century is depicted by *Corot, Courbet* and *Igres* while the Impressionists are well represented with many *Cezannes* (including *Les Grandes Baigneuses: Aix, Paysage Rocheux* and other landscapes) while there are several *Degas* and *Manets* and *Monets (La Plage de Trouville). Renoir's Les Parapluies* is only one of his masterpieces contained here, the others including a portrait of *Misia Sert* and *Danseuses.* Among Post Impressionists both *Gaugin* and *Van Gogh* have several works hung.

If you are very busy and have not a lot of time to spend, the Gallery has a leaflet which points out where the most important works are hung. In the entrance vestibule there is also a large collection of postcards, reproductions and other things to purchase which will remind you of your visit to this important Gallery.

Admission Free.
Open: 10.00am-6.00pm, Monday to Saturday.
2.00pm-6.00pm Sunday.
Closed Christmas Eve, Christmas Day, Boxing Day, Good Friday and New Year's Day.

There is a Restaurant serving simple food.

Map Ref. 4H

The Tate Gallery
Millbank, S.W.1.
Tel: 01-821 1313
Tube: Westminster and Pimlico.
Buses: 3, 59, 77, 159, 168.

The Tate Gallery is named after *Sir Harry Tate* whose generosity extended to both donating his own fine collection of paintings and commissioning the building which was designed by *Sydney R. J. Smith.* Previously, *Sir Francis Chantrey* had left money for the endowment of such a building and today many paintings are acquired under the auspices of *The Chantrey Bequest. Lord Duveen* was another art lover who donated further galleries to house his bequest of paintings and drawings particularly of *J. S. Sargent.*

The Gallery exists to show the best in the BRITISH SCHOOL of painting throughout the ages as well as modern painting from all over the world. Other painters of that time represented include *Angelica Kauffman, Joshua*

Reynolds, Romney and Stubbs. 19th Century English painting is represented by *Cotman, Landseer* and *Sir Thomas Lawrence's* portrait of *Mrs Siddons* as well as numerous *Constables (Dedham Mill, Hadleigh Church* and *The Bridges Family).*
Especially worth seeing are the works by *J. M. W. Turner* many of which were bequeathed by the artist and span his whole life-time. Another major collection is that of the *Pre-Raphaelite Brotherhood* including works by *Ford Madox Ford, Edward Burne-Jones (King Cophetua), John Millais, William Morris* (notably *La Belle Iseult)* and several major paintings by *Dante Gabriel Rossetti.*

As mentioned before, there is a special collection of works by the American artist *John Singer Sargent* including the pretty *Carnation, Lily, Lily Rose* and many distinguished portraits.
But it is for twentieth century paintings that the **Tate** is well worth a visit.

There is a whole galaxy of *Impressionist* and *Post-Impressionist* works including ones by all the major artists of that prolific period; *Cezanne* (a whole plethora of Provençal landscapes), *Degas* (horses and dancers) *Manet, Sisley* and that fantasist *Dounnier Rousseau.* Later artists include *Van Gogh (Field at Arles, The Yellow Chair)* and several marvellous works by *Utrillo (Montmartre, Porte-St-Martin).*
The great painters of the 30s and 40s are represented by *Victor Pasmore, Henry Moore, Ben Nicholson, John Piper* and some of *Graham Sutherland's* portraits. And to bring us up to date there are *Francis Bacon, David Hockney* and representatives of *Pop-Art* and *Op-Art* as well as contemporary foreign painters.
THERE ARE SOMETIMES SPECIAL EXHIBITIONS OF ONE ARTIST'S WORK
Admission Free
Open: 10.00am-6.00pm, Monday to Saturday.
2.00pm-6.00pm, Sunday.
There is a Restaurant and Snack Bar.
Map Ref. 5H

National Portrait Gallery
2 St. Martins Place, W.C.2.
Tel: 01-930 1552
Tube: Trafalgar Square: Leicester Square.
Buses: 3, 6, 12, 13, 15, 39, 53, 59, 88, 159, 506
The National Portrait Gallery is situated just behind the *National Gallery* opposite the *Edith Cavell Memorial* in St Martin's Place and opposite the celebrated church of *St Martin-in-the-Fields* (well worth a visit). It houses over four thousand drawings, paintings and sculptures of well-known British people throughout the ages. Except for members of the Royal family, a distinguished person has to have been dead for at least ten years before his or her portrait is accepted. During recent years photographs have also been included as part of this collection. Naturally, only a small part of it can be shown, but any portrait will be produced from the archives on request.
The building itself was designed by *Ewan Christian* and completed in 1896 while the extension, a gift of the art patron *Lord Duveen* was opened in 1933.
The portraits, which are not chosen for their artistic merit but from interest in the subject, make up a fascinating

collection of British physiognomy! It is also a comprehensive picture of British History, shown through the lives of illustrious men and women. Each room is arranged according to a chronological pattern and there are ample commentaries both on the walls and in leaflets. In fact, it might be said that all British History is on these walls; not only history, but expressions of British literature, arts and sciences. Whatever your particular interest, there is sure to be some important person represented here. Although the portraits are chosen for the interest of the subject, there are, however, some very good paintings here including portraits by *Lely, Kneller, Reynolds,*

Romney, Lawrence and *Millais.* Kings and Queens are well represented, as you would expect, as well as the influential men and women who surrounded them *(Thomas Cramner, Lord Burghley, Henry VIII* and *his wives: Charles II* and *his mistresses* as well as a flurry of Hanoverians and all the *Kit-Kat Club).* Literature is well to the fore including portraits of most of the poets — the *Augustans,* the *Romantics, Branwell Bronte's* portrait of his three sisters, *Rosetti, Browning,* the *Great Victorians* and many *Modern Writers.* Science brings us portraits of (among others) *Darwin* and *Huxley* while Empire builders, statesmen and soldiers are also well to the fore. And to bring us up to date there is a series of portrait busts by *Epstein* including *Yeats, Shaw* and *Somerset Maugham.* Altogether a true representation of all that was and is distinguished in British cultural life.

THERE ARE SOMETIMES SPECIAL EXHIBITIONS MOUNTED AT THIS GALLERY

Admission Free except for special exhibitions.
Open: 10.00am-5.00pm, Monday to Friday.
10.00am-6.00pm, Saturday.
Closed Most Public Holidays.

Map Ref. 4H

The Queen's Gallery
Buckingham Palace Road, S.W.1.
Tel: 01-930 4832
Tube: Green Park, St James's Park or Victoria.
Buses: 9, 14, 19, 22, 38 and 506 along Piccadilly and then walk across Park.

This is a small gallery actually contained within **Buckingham Palace** but with its own entrance (to the left as you face the Palace). It has a changing exhibition of works of Art which belong to the Queen and are generally not on public view, except when hung here.

Admission: £1.00 per adults, 50p for children, students and OAPs.
Open: 11.00am-5.00pm. Tuesday to Saturday and Bank Holiday Mondays. 2.00pm-5.00pm, Sunday. 12.00 noon-5.00pm.
Closed Christmas Day.

Map Ref. 4G

Leighton House
12 Holland Park Road, W.14.
Tel: 01-602 3316
Tube: Kensington High Street.
Buses: 9, 27, 28, 31, 33, 49 to Kensington Church Street to Holland Park Road, then walk.
Built in 1866 by *Lord Leighton* himself, a Victorian artist, this is the home for Victorian Studies. There is an astounding *Arabian Hall*, decorated with Oriental tiles (mostly medieval) with 18th century windows.
The pictures are mainly by *Lord Leighton* himself, though other Victorian artists are represented.
FROM TIME TO TIME THERE ARE SPECIAL EXHIBITIONS.
Admission Free.
Open: 11.00am-5.00pm, Monday to Saturday.
Closed Sunday and Public Holidays.
Map Ref. 5B

Kenwood House (The Iveagh Bequest)
Hampstead Lane, N.W.3.
Tel: 01-348 1286
Tube: Golders Green.
The house in which this Bequest by *Lord Iveagh* is housed was re-designed by *Robert Adam* in 1767 and the wings, by *George Saunders*, were added in 1793. The entrance is a fine example of Adam's domestic architecture while the *Library* is among his greatest work. The plaster-work by *Joseph Rose* is exquisite and there are ceiling paintings by *Zucchi*. The paintings were given by *Lord Iveagh* to the Nation in 1927 and contain some of the finest of 18th Century paintings — *Reynolds, Reyburn, Romney* and *Lawrence* among them, together with a superb collection of Dutch paintings — *Van Dyck, Franz Hals* and several good *Rembrandts*.
Spare some time for wandering around the grounds which were laid out in the 18th Century and contain many fine trees.
Admission Free.
Open: 10.00am-5.00pm, Monday to Sunday.
Closed Christmas Eve, Christmas Day and Good Friday.
No Map Ref.

Wallace Collection
Hertford House, Manchester Square, W.1.
Tel: 01-935 0687
Tube: Bond Street.
Buses: 1, 2, 6, 7, 13, 15, 16, 26 and other buses go near.
Set in one of the prettiest squares in London, Manchester Square, this collection has a romantic provenance. The collection was formed by the *Hertford* family and was given to the nation by *Lady Wallace* in 1897 together with the house.
Originally built in 1176 for the *Duke of Manchester* (hence the name of the Square) the house passed to the *Hertford* family. Most of the Collection was acquired by the fourth Marquess who lived in Paris and had access to many treasures of 18th Century France. His son, *Sir Richard Wallace* was more interested in the Renaissance period and in armoury. There are many interesting works to see in this small but unique collection. The House itself is well worth studying and the furnishings are particularly grand, including the balustrade of the marble staircase, originally made for *Louis XV*. From this monarch's reign there are also many examples of *Sevres* porcelain. *Boucher* is represented as are the two Venetian masters *Canaletto* and *Guardi*. Undoubtedly one of the finest and most popular paintings in the Collection is *Rembrandt's Portrait of Titus* and also *Franz Hals' Laughing*

Cavalier is found in the Picture Gallery. Look out also for *Romney's* portrait of the Prince Regent's first love *Perdita Robinson* as well as several *Watteaus*, a *Titian*, some *Van Dycks* and a *Pieter de Hoochs*.
In the second Picture Gallery the paintings include several by masters of early 19th Century French painting, including *Corot* and *Delacroix*, as well as more works from the romantic 18th Century pastoral school — *Watteau, Nattier, Boucher* and *Greuze*. Again here you can see some fine French furniture and further on some more *Sevres* porcelain. The *Armour*, collected by *Sir Richard Wallace* is displayed to great advantage and for students of this subject form a scholarly collection, while the rest of us can be amazed at the ingenuity men waste on killing each other!
Admission Free
Open: 10.00am-5.00pm, Monday to Saturday.
2.00pm-5.00pm, Sunday and Bank Holidays. ondays.
Closed Other Public Holidays (but check as it can vary).

Map Ref. 2F

Courtauld Institute Galleries
Woburn Square, W.C.1.
Tel: 01-580 1015
Tube: Holborn and Russell Square.
Buses: 68, 77, 188, 196.
This small gallery has a really exquisite collection of paintings bequeathed both by *Samuel Courtauld* and *Lord Lee of Fareham*. THE COURTAULD COLLECTION comprises one of the most exciting collections of IMPRESSIONIST and POST-IMPRESSIONIST paintings with examples of the works of *Degas, Monet, La Loge* by *Renoir* and the *Bar at the Folies-Bergères*, probably the best-known of *Monet's* work. *Cezanne* and *Van Gogh* are also represented. THE LEE COLLECTION is of older paintings, including some by *Bellini, Veronese, Tintoretto* and *Rubens*. There are also some impressive British Portraits of the 17th, 18th and 19th Centuries.
Other Collections are now housed in this building including the distinguished *Roger Fry Bequest* (mainly French paintings) and the *Witt and Gambier-Parry* bequests of drawings, sculptures and early Italian works.
Admission £1.00, Students and OAP's 50p.
Open: 10.00am-5.00pm, Monday to Saturday.
2.00pm-5.00pm, Sunday.
Closed Public Holidays.

Map Ref. 2H

Hayward Gallery
Belvedere Road, S.E.1.
Tel: 01-928 3144
Tube: Waterloo.
Buses: 76, 149, 168, 171, 507.
A prestigious public gallery showing contemporary British and foreign artists. It also features exhibitions of popular appeal and general interest. Arranged by the Arts Council.
Open: 10.00am-8.00pm, Monday to Thursday.
10.00am-6.00pm, Friday and Saturday.
12.00 Noon-6.00pm, Sunday.
Admission charge.

Map Ref. 4K

Royal Academy of Arts
Burlington House, Piccadilly, W.1.
Tel: 01-734 9052
Tube: Green Park.
Buses: 9, 14, 19, 22, 38.
This gallery is not supported by public funds and is a private charity. It holds a yearly summer exhibition in May, usually the work of present day artists. Opening hours and admission prices vary, so it is advisable to telephone.

Map Ref. 3G

Whitechapel Art Gallery
80 Whitechapel High Street, E.1.
Tel: 01-377 0107
Tube: Aldgate East.
Buses: 10, 25, 253.
A continuous series of contemporary British and foreign artists. ılly
Open: 11.00am-6.00pm, Sunday to Friday.
Closed Saturday and some Sundays.
Admission free except some exhibitions.

Map Ref. 2L

ROYAL BUILDINGS

Buckingham Palace
Tel: 01-930 4832
Tube: Hyde Park, Green Park, Victoria.
Buses: 9, 14, 19, 22, 38 and 506 along Piccadilly then walk across Park.
People often ask why the Queen's Residence in London (you can tell if she is in as her Standard flies when she is) is called **Buckingham Palace.** The answer is that it was originally built as the Town House of the *Duke of Buckingham* in 1703 and was then bought by *King George III* in 1767. In 1824 *George IV* (previously the Prince Regent) commissioned *John Nash* to re-design it. It came into its own when *Queen Victoria* reigned and it was she who was the first monarch to establish it as the Residence of the Monarch. An east wing was added during her reign and so now the Palace is built round a courtyard. The famous balcony, where the Royal Family appears on all State Occasions is at the front facing the *Victoria Memorial.*
This imposing monument carved in Marble, shows the redoubtable Queen surmounted by a gilt-bronze Victory, together with Courage and Constancy. Other groups represent Justice, Truth, Motherhood, Science, Art, Peace, Progress as well as Naval, Military and Industrial Power.
The Palace is never open to the public (except for the *Queen's Gallery)* although on most days there is an impressive ceremony of Changing of the Guard in the courtyard.

Map Ref. 4G

Kensington Palace
Tube: Kensington High Street.
Buses: 9, 25, 27, 28, 31, 33, 49, 73.
This Palace is probably best known in popular history as the Palace where *Queen Victoria* first heard that she was Queen and today as the residence of *HRH The Princess Margaret.* Both *Sir Christopher Wren* and *William Kent* had a hand in the design of the Palace, at various times. THE STATE APARTMENTS are open to the public.
Although the Palace was known as *Queen Victoria's* birthplace it was, in fact, the principal residence of the Sovereign since *William III* bought it and the *Hanoverian Kings* lived there until *George III* bought Buckingham Palace.
Open: Monday-Saturday 9.00am-5.00pm.
Sunday 1.00pm-5.00pm.
Admission: 40p.

Map Ref. 3D

St James's Palace
Pall Mall, S.W.1.
Tube: Green Park.
Buses: 9, 14, 19, 22, 38, 506.
This red-brick Tudor Palace, once the home of *Henry VIII,* is still a Royal residence. Ambassadors are credited to the *Court of St. James.* The Palace is not open to visitors but it is possible to wander into some of the courtyards. There is also a small Changing of the Guards between 11.15am and 11.45am.
Admission 40p.

Map Ref. 4G

Hampton Court Palace
Hampton Court, Middlesex.
Tel: 01-977 8441
How to get there.
Train: Southern to Hampton Court.
One pleasant way to visit this magnificent Palace is by river boat from Central London (see boat trips). The building of the Palace was begun by *Cardinal Wolsey,* taken over by *Henry VIII* and completed by *Sir*

Christopher Wren. Besides the interior of the Palace with its STATE APARTMENTS, the gardens are a particular delight, especially the *Sunken Garden*, the *Great Vine*, which was planted in 1769 and the famous maze where it is possible to get lost.
Open: 9.30am-6.00pm, Monday to Saturday.
11.00am-6.00pm, Sunday.
May to September.
Opening times vary between October and April therefore it is advisable for you to telephone first.
GARDENS
Open: 7.30am to one hour before dusk.
Admission charge for Palace, £1.80.
Children and OAP's half price.
No Map Ref.

Clarence House
Stable Yard Gate, S.W.1.
Tube: Green Park.
Buses: 9, 14, 19, 22, 38, 506.
It is only possible to view this Royal Residence from afar as it is the London home of *Her Majesty, Queen Elizabeth the Queen Mother.*
Map Ref. 4G

Royal Mews
Buckingham Palace Road, S.W.1.
Tel: 01-930 4832
Tube: Victoria.
Buses: 2, 16, 36.
You can see the Queen's coaches and horses, which are kept here in readiness for State Occasions, such as the *Coronation Coach* and others. The bay horses are kept on one side of the stables and the greys on the other.
Open: 2.00pm-4.00pm, Wednesday and Thursday only.
Small admission charge.
Map Ref. 4G

CATHEDRALS AND CHURCHES

St. Paul's Cathedral
Ludgate Hill, E.C.4.
Tel: 01-248 2705
Tube: St. Pauls.
Buses: 6, 8, 11, 15, 22, 25.
Built between 1675 and 1710, this cathedral is regarded as the most famous work of *Sir Christopher Wren.* It has a magnificent dome which rises some 366 feet high. Wren chose the best artists and craftsmen to work on the building, such as *Salvati* and *Stephens* who designed the mosaics, and *Tijou* who was responsible for the ironwork. The superb carvings of the choir stalls by *Grinling Gibbons,* all combine to enhance the beauty of the building. Below the Cathedral is the *Crypt* in which are the tombs of *Lord Nelson,* the *Duke of Wellington* and the grave of *Sir Christopher Wren* himself.
Of particular interest is the WHISPERING GALLERY which is reached by climbing 259 steps on route to the Dome proper. The Gallery shows an impressive view of the Concourse below and gets its name

because a whisper close to the wall is transmitted all the way around.
The staircase gets steeper and narrower for the next 130 steps leading to the STONE GALLERY which is situated at the base of the Dome where you get a marvellous view of London.
The last stage, for the really fit, is to climb to the GOLDEN GALLERY at the top of the Dome, which is 542 steps from the ground.
There are two Chapels of famous orders of Chivalry, the *Knights of St. Michael and St. George,* and the *Order of the British Empire.*
Another interesting Chapel is the AMERICAN MEMORIAL CHAPEL, dedicated to those American servicemen who lost their lives in the Second World War having left bases in the United Kingdom.
Open: Times vary — best to check first.
Crypt and Galleries Open: 10.45am-3.15pm, Monday to Saturday only.
Admission to Cathedral Free but small admission charge to CRYPT and DOME.

Map Ref. 2J

Westminster Abbey
Broad Sanctuary, S.W.1.
Tel: 01-222 5152
Tube: Westminster.
Buses: 3, 11, 12, 24, 29, 53, 88.
Because the Abbey is so large and complex it is probably better to take a guided tour in order not to miss the many interesting aspects.
The original Abbey was built by *Edward the Confessor* in 1065 and then rebuilt by *Henry III* in 1245, mostly completed in 1506, with the towers being the last part of the building finished in 1734.
The main piers of the Abbey and a lot of the flooring are solid marble and over the years many memorials and tombs have been added in the Chapels. There is beautifully-carved woodwork and stone and the wrought ironwork is considered to be some of the finest in the world.
Some of the more interesting areas are various Chapels, such as *Henry VII's* with its magnificent fan-vaulted roof, and the *Chapel and Shrine of Edward the Confessor* which has some of the oldest tombs in the Abbey. This is also where the *Coronation Chair* and the *Stone of Scone* are situated where Kings and Queens were crowned.
The Tomb of the Unknown Warrier is situated in the nave, as indeed are many other tombs of various Kings and Queens. The Abbey also has a museum with a collection of death masks and effigies.

Abbey Open: Times vary because of services — best check.
Exhibition of Abbey Treasures Open: 10.30am-4.00pm, Monday to Saturday.

Guided Tours
Telephone for times and appointment.
Free admission to Abbey

Free but small admission charge for ROYAL CHAPELS and ABBEY TREASURES.

Map Ref. 4H

Westminster Cathedral
Ashley Place, S.W.1.
Tel: 01-834 7452
Tube: Victoria.
Buses: 11, 24, 29, 39, 503, 90N, 95N, 98N.
Built in Byzantine style in red and white brick, this beautiful Roman Catholic Cathedral was started in 1895 and finished in 1910.
In recent years the surrounding area has been made into a Piazza which lends itself to the serenity of the Cathedral itself. The magnificent interior has carved marble pillars, the beautiful *High Altar*, and exquisite

mosaics. There are chapels on both sides of the wide nave and the finely carved *Stations of the Cross* is well worth a close inspection.
Among the outstanding features of the Cathedral is the BELL TOWER, the top of which is 284 feet from the ground.
There is a lift to take visitors up the tower where one is rewarded with some splendid views over London.
Open: 7.00am-8.00pm, Monday to Sunday.
Small charge for using the lift and Bell Tower.

Map Ref. 4G

Southwark Cathedral
Borough High Street, S.E.1.
Tel: 01-407 2939
Tube: London Bridge.
Buses: 35, 47, 48, 133.
Originally an Augustine Church built in 1206, it was restored in the middle of the 19th Century by *Sir Arthur Blomfield* and is considered to be one

of the lovelier small Cathedrals in Britain.
It is full of interesting tombs and epitaphs, notably those of *John Gower*, the poet and friend of *Chaucer*, and *Edmund Shakespeare* youngest brother of the great *William*.
Open: Daily.

Map Ref. 4K

St. Georges Roman Catholic Cathedral
Lambeth Road, S.E.1.
Tel: 01-928 5256
Tube: Lambeth North, Elephant and Castle.
Buses: 3, 10A, 44, 53, 59, 159.
Built by *A. W. Pugin* in 1848, the spire was never completed. Although badly damaged in the last war it has a beautifully restored interior.
Situated opposite the *Imperial War Museum*.
Open: Daily.

Map Ref. 5I

CHURCHES

All-Hallows-By-The-Tower
Byward Street, E.C.3.
Tel: 01-481 2928
Tube: Tower Hill.
Buses: 15, 25, 42, 48.
Founded in 675 A.D. this is the oldest of the City Churches, though unfortunately it suffered bomb damage during the war.
William Penn, founder of Pennsylvania, was baptised here in 1644. The Crypt is a museum with the remains of a mosaic Roman pavement and upstairs there are models of ships and ancient brassware.
Open: Daily.

Map Ref. 3L

St. Bartholomew-the-Great
West Smithfield, E.C.1.
Tel: 01-606 5171
Tube: St. Paul's, Barbican.
Buses: 5, 8, 22, 25.
Dating back to the 12th Century when a canon of *St. Paul's Cathedral* and a courtier of *Henry I* founded a priory.
The original gateway was discovered by accident when, in 1915, a Zeppelin bomb loosened some tiles.
The inside is very striking and the Church is well worth a visit.
Open: Daily.

Map Ref. 3L

St. Bride's
Fleet Street, E.C.4.
Tel: 01-353 1301
Tube: Blackfriars.
Buses: 4, 6, 11, 15, 502, 513.
Unfortunately gutted by fire in an air raid in 1940, the new building was designed from *Sir Christopher Wren's* original drawings by *Godfrey Allen.*
Named after *St. Bridget of Kildare of Ireland* who was born in the year 453 A.D., there was a church on this site at that time which existed until the middle of the 12th Century when it was again rebuilt and often used by *King John.*
Because the area became the centre of the printing trade, **St. Bride's** had a close association with many writers and *Samuel Pepys,* the diarist, was baptised here in 1633.
The church stood until the Great Fire of London in 1666 when Wren was asked to rebuild it.
Open: Daily.

Map Ref. 2I

St. Clement Danes
Strand, W.C.2.
Tel: 01-242 8282
Tube: Temple.
Buses: 4, 6, 9, 11, 15, 171.
One of the famous churches, this one is well known by every English child as the bells ring out the age-old rhyme, 'oranges and lemons, say the bells of St Clements'.
Originally built by the Danes in 886 A.D. who had a settlement in this part of London, it was replaced in 1022 until it was rebuilt by *Sir Christopher Wren.*
It was burnt down during the War and the Royal Air Force had it rebuilt to use it as their own church. Fortunately

Wren's outer walls and the steeple were intact and only the interior and the roof had to be restored.
Open: Daily.

Map Ref. 2I

St. James's
Piccadilly W.1.
Tel: 01-734 5244
Tube: Piccadilly Circus.
Buses: 9, 14, 19, 22, 25, 28.
Another *Christopher Wren* church, this one was built in 1680 and, as so often happened, this one was also damaged by fire during the War. Fortunately most of the carvings produced by the famous sculptor *Grinling Gibbons* escaped damage.
The font is especially noteworthy as it is one of Gibbons's rare sculptures in marble. It is also where *William Pitt* and the poet, *William Blake*, were baptized.
Open: Daily.

Map Ref. 3G

St. Mary-le-Bow
Cheapside, E.C.2.
Tel: 01-248 5139
Tube: Bank, St. Paul's.
Buses: 8, 22, 25.
Erected under Norman supervision during the reign of *William the Conqueror* in the 11th Century, the church has always had a close association with the City of London.
There is a legend which is still applied to this day that, to be a true cockney Londoner, you have to born within the sound of the bells of the Church. In fact, it probably originated because the *Bow Bell* was tolled during a curfew to warn people to stay within the City limits.
Rebuilt by *Sir Christopher Wren* in 1680 and partly restored after bomb damage in 1941, the tower and spire is considered by many to be one of Wren's finest works.
Open: Daily.

Map Ref. 2J

St. Martin-in-the-Fields
Trafalgar Square, W.C.2.
Tel: 01-930 1862
Tube: Trafalgar Square.
Buses: 1, 24, 29, 176.
Built between 1722 and 1724 by *James Gibbs,* it has a striking portico with its splendid *Corinthian Pillars,* and wide flight of steps. It also has an imposing square bell tower and a fine steeple.
Nell Gwynne was buried here in 1687; now in modern times the Crypt is used as a shelter for the homeless and hungry.
Open: Daily.

Map Ref. 4H

Brompton Oratory
Brompton Road, S.W.7.
Tel: 01-589 4811
Tube: South Kensington.
Buses: 14, 30, 74.
A fine example of an Italian Renaissance style church built in 1884 by *H. Gribble.* The nave is one of the widest in England and the marble interior is very beautiful. Some of the statues came from the Cathedral of Siena.

Map Ref. 4E

Temple Church
Inner Temple, E.C.4.
Tube: Temple.
Buses: 4, 6, 9, 11, 15, 109, 155, 168.
Consecrated in 1185, this is one of only five round churches in England which typifies the style of the churches built by the Knights Templars of Jerusalem. It has a close association with the legal profession.

Map Ref. 3I

Savoy Chapel
Savoy Hill, W.C.2.
Tube: Aldwych.
Buses: 1, 6, 9, 11, 13, 15, 77, 170, 176.
Known as the **Queen's Chapel of the Savoy,** it is the only building left from the huge Palace of Savoy that used to stand near the site. It is a beautiful chapel and well worth visiting.
Closed: August and September.

Map Ref. 3H

GOVERNMENT BUILDINGS

Houses of Parliament
Parliament Square, S.W.1.
Tel: 01-219 4272 (Commons)
01-219 3107 (Lords)
Tube: Westminster.
Buses: 3, 11, 12, 24, 29, 53, 88, 109, 155, 170, 184.
The correct title is the **Palace of Westminster,** as the present building is situated on the site of the old Palace. WESTMINSTER HALL, the Crypt of ST. STEPHENS HALL, and the old JEWEL TOWER are the only parts of the original building dating from the 12th Century. The first monarch to hold court in the Palace was *William the Conqueror,* and the building was used both as a Royal residence and a Parliament House up to 1512 when *Henry VIII* decided to move to a new Palace. Over the years the Palace was used by various politicians and became the central building for Government, but in 1834 it was badly damaged by fire. Between 1840 and 1860 it was rebuilt, including the famous CLOCK TOWER which houses the bell BIG BEN. When the light over BIG BEN is on, it means that Parliament is sitting at night and when the Union Jack is flown on VICTORIA TOWER, they are sitting during the day.
The WESTMINSTER HALL and the Crypt of ST. STEPHEN'S HALL can be visited by the public on guided tours and the JEWEL TOWER can be seen separately, as it is on the opposite side of the road. It is also possible to see Parliament in session by watching a debate from the public galleries in both the House of Commons and the House of Lords, but you must be sponsored by an M.P. However, it is wise to telephone first to check visiting hours.
JEWEL TOWER
Open: Daily, except Public Holidays.
DEBATES
House of Commons:
From 2.30pm, Monday to Thursday.
From 11.00am, Friday.
House of Lords:
From 2.30pm, Monday to Wednesday.
From 3.00pm, Thursday.
Map Ref. 4H

Number 10
Downing Street, S.W.1.
Tube: Westminster.
Buses: 3, 11, 12, 24, 29, 53, 77, 88.
Situated off Whitehall, Downing Street is a quiet, small street which contains the official residence of the *Prime Minister* at **Number 10,** which is also the venue for all Cabinet Meetings. Next door, *Number 11* is allocated to the *Chancellor of the Exchequer* and *Number 12* is used by the *Government Chief Whips.*
Map Ref. 4H

Whitehall, S.W.1.
Tube: Westminster, Trafalgar Square.
Buses: 3, 11, 12, 24, 29, 53, 77, 88.
This is a wide street which contains the CENOTAPH and is lined with the Government Buildings.
At the north end by Trafalgar Square there is the ADMIRALTY ARCH which was built in 1725 and going south along Whitehall you have on both sides, THE MINISTRY OF DEFENCE, THE TREASURY, THE FOREIGN OFFICE and the BANQUETING HOUSE which is open to the public between 10.00am and 5.00pm Tuesday to Saturday.
HORSE GUARDS is also situated off Whitehall. Rebuilt in 1753 as military barracks, this was the site of the old *Whitehall Palace* which used to be the residence of Kings and Queens in the 15th and 16th Centuries. It is probable that Charles I was beheaded in this area.

Map Ref. 4H

HISTORIC BUILDINGS

Albert Memorial
Kensington Gore, S.W.7.
Tube: High Street Kensington.
Buses: 9, 9A, 52, 73.
Designed by *Sir Gilbert Scott* and completed in 1876 it is a national Memorial to *Prince Albert*, the husband of *Queen Victoria*.
It is 180 feet high and is ornately decorated. The seated statue of the Prince is looking at the Catalogue of the Great Exhibition of 1851 which was his innovation and was held on a site near the Memorial.

Map Ref. 4D

Bank of England
Threadneedle Street, E.C.2.
Tel: 01-601 4444
Tube: Bank.
Buses: 6, 8, 22, 25, 43, 76, 133.
Nicknamed 'The Old Lady of Threadneedle Street', the Bank was incorporated in 1694 with the object of lending money to the Government, but not from the present site. This dates from 1734 and was later enlarged by *Sir John Soane,* who designed the present building incorporating the original.

It was renovated in the 1920s and was nationalised after the Second World War. The Vaults hold the Country's gold reserves and it is still the premier Bank in the world.

Map Ref. 3K

Burlington Arcade
Piccadilly, W.1.
Tube: Green Park.
Buses: 9, 9A, 14, 19, 22, 38, 506.
A delightful little arcade of shops, situated off Piccadilly near Bond Street. Built in 1819, it still retains an atmosphere of elegance with original shop windows and a beadle to welcome visitors.

Map Ref. 3G

Cleopatra's Needle
Victoria Embankment, S.W.1.
Tube: Embankment.
Buses: 109, 155, 168, 184, 172.
This Monument dates from 1500 B.C. and was found in Heliopolis, Egypt and presented to Britain in 1878, when it was erected by the Thames opposite the *Embankment Gardens.*

Map Ref. 4H

Carlton House Terrace, S.W.1.
Tube: Piccadilly Circus.
Buses: 9, 14, 19, 22, 38.
Situated between the Mall and Pall Mall this is a beautiful example of *Nash* architecture.
When *George IV* sold **Carlton House** in 1828, the property developers of the time pulled down his house and erected Landsane Town houses on the site. Number 1 was the home of *Lord Curzon* and is now the official residence of the *British Foreign Secretary,* Number 2 was the home of *Lord Kitchener,* the man whose face appeared on thousands of posters recruiting men for the First World War. Number 4 was the Headquarters of *General de Gaulle,* Number 6 is the home of the *Royal Society* and Number 12 the home of the *Institute of Contemporary Arts.*

Map Ref. 4G

Chelsea Royal Hospital
Chelsea Embankment, S.W.3.
Tube: Sloane Square.
Buses: 11, 39, 137.
Home of the *Chelsea Pensioners,* the Hospital was conceived by *Sir Stephen Fox,* a former Paymaster General as a home for old and disabled soldiers and in 1682 he commissioned *Sir Christopher Wren* to build it.
The *Chelsea Pensioners* still wear the frock-coat tunics of the 17th Century, Scarlet in Summer, with blue overcoats in Winter, and peaked caps or the tri-cornered hat of the era.
Open: 10.00am-12.00 noon and 2.00pm-4.00pm, Monday to Saturday. 2.00pm-4.00pm, Sunday.

Map Ref. 6E

College of Arms
Queen Victoria Street, E.C.4.
Tel: 01-248 2762
Tube: Blackfriars.
Bus: 76.
A late 17th Century building which houses the official records of English and Welsh genealogy and heraldry. Enquiries can be made to the Duty Herald between *10.00am-4.00pm, Monday to Friday.*

Map Ref. 3J

Covent Garden, W.C.2.
Tube: Covent Garden.
Buses: 1, 6, 9, 11, 13, 15, 77, 176.
Originally designed by *Inigo Jones* in 1638 as a residential Square, it was the hub of gossip and general news where Coffee and Chocolate Houses flourished and market traders brought their wares to sell. Gradually the houses were taken over, the inhabitants left and the area became famous as a fruit and vegetable market. The market has now been moved to *Nine Elms* and the area is gradually being restored to its previous grandeur, although with offices and shops rather than houses.
Within **Covent Garden** is the *Royal Opera House,* the lovely *St. Paul's Church, Bow Street* and many theatres.

Map Ref. 3H

Dickens's House
48 Doughty Street, W.C.1.
Tel: 01-405 2127
Tube: Chancery Lane.
Buses: 19, 38, 171, 172.
Charles Dickens lived here from 1837 to 1839 and the house contains original manuscripts, letters and many first editions of his works.
Admission: 70p for adults.
Open: Monday-Saturday 10.00-5.00pm.

Map Ref. 1I

The Docks
Tube: Tower Hill.
Buses: 9, 42, 78.
Stretching from the *Tower of London* to *Tilbury* on the north bank of the Thames, they are best viewed by taking a cruise down the river. There are some marvellous examples of 19th Century industrial architecture, although there are large areas which have been demolished for new development. One of the nicer areas is *St. Katharine's Dock* near *Tower Bridge* which has been redeveloped as a yacht marina, incorporating all the old buildings.

Map Ref. 4L

Drapers Company Hall
Throgmorton Avenue, E.C.2.
Tube: Bank.
Buses: 6, 8, 21, 22, 43, 76, 133.
Dating from 1667, this City livery hall has a marvellous collection of plate and a fine staircase.
To visit, you must check with the City of London Information Centre, St. Pauls Churchyard, E.C.4.
Tel: 01-606 3030.
Special visits can be arranged by appointment.

Map Ref. 3K

Goldsmiths Hall
Foster Lane, E.C.2.
Tube: St. Paul's.
Buses: 4, 6, 9, 11, 15, 18, 141.
Built in 1835 by *Hardwick,* this is a classical style palazzo and another of the famous City of London livery halls. To visit you must check with the City of London Information Centre, St. Pauls Churchyard, E.C.4.
Tel: 01-606 3030.
Visiting days obtainable from City Information Office.

Map Ref. 2J

Grays Inn
Holborn, W.C.1.
Tel: 01-242 8591
Tube: Chancery Lane.
Buses: 17, 18, 45, 46, 243, 249, 263.
One of the four remaining Inns of Court with the power to call men and women to the Bar. The Hall dates from 1556. The gardens were laid out by *Francis Bacon,* who planted the Catalpa Tree brought to England by *Sir Walter Raleigh.* The Hall is only open to the public by written application to the Under Treasurer. The Gardens are open in the Summer.

Map Ref. 2I

Greenwich
Rail: From London Bridge, Waterloo and Charing Cross.
River: From Tower Pier or Westminster Pier.
Buses: 53, 70, 185, 188.
Greenwich is a lovely area which is probably more famous for its maritime connections than the fact that it was the favourite and fashionable place for Royalty and aristocracy in the 15th, 16th and 17th Centuries.
There are many beautiful buildings to see including the ROYAL NAVAL COLLEGE which was originally a private house and then in 1447 a Royal Palace. *Henry VIII, Mary I* and *Elizabeth I* were all born here.
It was *Henry VIII's* favourite Palace.
Another lovely building is the QUEENS HOUSE, built by *Inigo Jones,* and the old ROYAL OBSERVATORY, built by *Charles II.* It is the oldest Scientific Institution in Britain and a fine example of *Christopher Wren's* work. Besides the NATIONAL MARITIME MUSEUM, there are two ships, the old tea clipper *Cutty Sark* and the Ketch *Gypsy Moth IV* in which *Sir Francis Chichester* sailed solo around the World.

No Map Ref.

Guildhall
Gresham Street, E.C.2.
Tel: 01-606 3030
Tube: Bank or Mansion House.
Buses: 6, 8, 11, 15, 22, 25, 133.
Used for Ceremonial Banquets it was built in the 15th Century with later additions. There is a good library, an art gallery, a museum of clocks and watches, and many monuments dedicated to outstanding men and women.
Open: 10.00am-5.00pm, Monday to Saturday.
2.00pm-5.00pm, Sunday.
May to September only.

Map Ref. 2J

Hammersmith Mall
Upper and Lower Mall, Hammersmith, W.6.
Tube: Hammersmith.
Buses: 9, 33, 72, 73.
Built in the late 18th Century, the Mall is a collection of houses and pubs on the banks of the Thames which are well worth visiting because of their quaintness and charm.

No Map Ref.

Law Courts
Strand, W.C.2.
Tel: 01-405 7641
Tube: Aldwych.
Buses: 4, 6, 9, 11, 15, 502, 513.
The real title is the **Royal Courts of Justice** and they are the Supreme Courts of Judicature for England and Wales. Opened in 1882 the building is most unusual.
Map Ref. 2I

Lincoln's Inn
Lincoln's Inn, W.C.2.
Tel: 01-405 1393
Tube: Aldwych.
Buses: 4, 6, 9, 11, 15, 502, 513.
Dating from the days of *Edward I,* whose legal advisor was the *Earl of Lincoln,* this is another area which is part of the legal side of London with its barristers' chambers and solicitors' offices.
The chapel, built by *Inigo Jones* in 1623 and the 15th Century Old Hall still have a Dickensian atmosphere about them. Apply to the Gate House in Chancery Lane for admission.
Map Ref. 2J

Lloyds of London
Lime Street, E.C.3.
Tube: Aldgate.
Buses: 10, 15, 25, 40, 44.
The most famous of all insurance markets handling over one billion pounds' worth of business a year, with over 10,000 members. To visit you must apply in writing to the Head of Information and Publicity and be interested professionally.
Map Ref. 2K

Mansion House
Mansion House Street, E.C.2.
(opposite the Bank of England)
Tel: 01-626 2500
Tube: Bank.
Buses: 8, 15, 22, 25, 76, 95, 149.
A beautiful Palladian building with a handsome Corinthian portico, it was built by *George Dance* in 1752.
It is the official London residence of the *Lord Mayor*. It has a number of Reception Rooms, the most famous of which is the EGYPTIAN HALL where many glittering official functions are held. THE STATE DRAWING ROOM is also a lovely room.
Open: Write to Assistant Private Secretary for permission to look around.

Map Ref. 2K

Monument
Monument Street, E.C.3.
Tube: Monument.
Buses: 35, 47, 48, 113.
Built by *Sir Christopher Wren* in 1677 to commemorate the Great Fire of London, situated near the spot where that fire started. The height of the Monument is 202 feet, which is the distance from its site to the house of the baker in Pudding Lane where the Fire was thought to have started. There is a winding staircase inside, with 311 steps, which leads to an observation platform from where one can see good views of the City.
Open: Summer 9.00am-4.00pm, Monday to Saturday. Winter 9.00am-3.40pm.
Small admission charge.

Map Ref. 3K

Nelson's Column
Trafalgar Square, S.W.1.
Tube: Trafalgar Square.
Buses: 3, 11, 12, 24, 29, 39, 53, 59, 77.
Built by *William Railton* in 1840 to commemorate *Horatio Nelson*, this is one of the land marks of London. It is situated in a square, with large bronze lions, fountains, and thousands of pigeons. The column is 145 feet high, weighs 16 tons and the statue of Nelson is by *Bailey*.

Map Ref. 3H

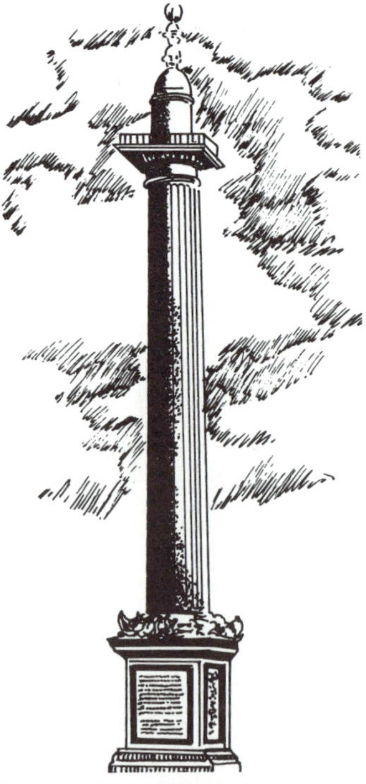

Old Bailey
Old Bailey, E.C.4.
Tel: 01-248 3277
Tube: Blackfriars or St Paul's.
Buses: 4, 6, 9, 11, 15, 18, 141.
Built on the site of the famous Newgate Prison, its real title is the **Central Criminal Court.** It was opened in 1907, the old prison finally having been demolished in 1902 after standing since the 13th Century. Its famous characteristic is the gilded figure of Justice, holding the scales on the roof. All serious crimes are tried here.
Open: 10.30am-1.00pm and 2.00pm-4.00pm, Monday to Friday. Closed Saturday and Sunday.
Minimum age 14 years.

Map Ref. 2J

Old Curiosity Shop
13 Portsmouth Street, W.C.2.
Tel: 01-405 9891
Tube: Holborn.
Buses: 55, 68, 77, 170, 172, 188, 196.
Built in 1567 and now an antique shop, this was the place that *Charles Dickens* immortalised in his book 'The Old Curiosity Shop'.
Open: 9.30am-5.30pm, Monday to Sunday. Closed Christmas Day.

Map Ref. 2I

Pall Mall, S.W.1.
Tube: Green Park or Piccadilly Circus.
Buses: 9, 14, 19, 22, 38, 506.
An elegant street leading from the south end of St. James's Street, by St. James's Palace, to the south of the Haymarket. There are a number of early 19th Century buildings including the Travellers Club, the Reform Club, the Royal Automobile Club and the Directors Club.

Map Ref. 3G

Prince Henry's Rooms
17 Fleet Street, E.C.4.
Tel: 01-353 7323
Tube: Blackfriars.
Buses: 4, 6, 9, 11, 15, 502, 513.
Named after *James I's son,* this half-timbered residence above an archway was once part of a tavern called the Prince's Arms. It is thought to have once been the Council Chamber of the Duchy of Cornwall. Dating from 1610 it is the oldest domestic building in London.
Open: 1.45pm-5.00pm, Monday to Friday.
1.45pm-4.30pm, Saturday.
Closed Sunday.
Admission: Free.

Map Ref. 2I

Royal Albert Hall
Kensington Gore, S.W.7.
Tel: 01-589 8212
Tube: High Street Kensington.
Buses: 14, 19, 22, 30, 52, 73, 74, 137.
Erected in 1867 in memory of *Prince Albert.* Opened by *Queen Victoria* in 1871.
This hall can accommodate 8000 people and is famous for the internatioanl concerts and other orchestral works held here.
Special Souvenir Shop.
Map Ref. 4D

Royal Exchange
Corner of Threadneedle Street and Cornhill, E.C.3.
Tube: Bank.
Buses: 6, 8, 22, 25, 43, 76, 133.
Originally built as a market for merchants in 1564, the original building was destroyed by the Great Fire. The present building was built in 1884 and has some fine paintings and statues.
Open: 11.30am-4.00pm, Monday to Friday.
Map Ref. 3K

Smithfield, E.C.1.
Tube: Farringdon.
Buses: 25, 50.
Present site of the famous **Smithfield Meat Market,** one of the largest in the world, this area was once where public executions, tournaments and the renowned Bartholomew Fair were held. On one side is *St. Bartholomew's Hospital,* founded in 1123, on the other the *Church of Bartholomew,* and on the Gateway is London's only statue of *King Henry VIII.*
Map Ref. 2J

St. Thomas's Old Operating Theatre
St. Thomas's Street, S.E.1.
Tel: 01-407 3662.
Tube: London Bridge.
Buses: 8, 10, 18, 43, 44, 48.
Recently discovered in the Chapel of the Old St. Thomas's Hospital, this is an early 19th Century operating theatre which has been left exactly as it was found.
Open: Monday-Wednesday and Friday afternoon.
Map Ref. 4K

Somerset House
Strand, W.C.2.
Tube: Aldwych.
Buses: 1, 4, 6, 9, 11, 13, 15, 77, 502.
A beautiful building with a massive Palladian frontage of 135 feet which dominates this part of the Strand and is also even more lovely when viewed from Waterloo Bridge. Originally *The Mansion of the Lord Protector Somerset* who ruled in the name of the boy king *Edward VI* until the Protector was executed in 1552 for treason. It then passed to the Crown and has been mainly used by various Government Departments, the most famous of which was the *Registrar of Births, Deaths and Marriages,* until their move to St. Catherine's House, Kingsway.
Map Ref. 3I

The Temple
Inner Temple
Crown Office Row, E.C.4.
Tel: 01-353 4355
Middle Temple
Middle Temple Lane, E.C.4.
Tel: 01-353 4355
Tube: Temple.
Buses: 4, 6, 9, 11, 15, 109, 155, 168.
Both are Inns of Court and on a summer's day are a delight to stroll around, with their courtyards, buildings and beautiful gardens. They are steeped in history where notables from *Shakespeare* to *Dickens* used to mix with law students.
THE INNER TEMPLE GARDENS were famous for their roses in the Middle Ages and it is here that the two leaders of the Houses of York and Lancaster are said to have each plucked a rose, one white and one red, which were to become their respective badges during their quarrel.
Map Ref. 3I

Whitefriars Crypt
30 Bouverie Street, E.C.4.
Tel: 01-353 3030
Tube: Blackfriars.
Buses: 4, 6, 9, 11, 15, 502, 513.
A beautiful 15th Century Crypt belonging to the *House of Carmelites,* it was discovered in 1895 and restored by the proprietors of the 'News of the World' newspaper, under whose offices it is buried.
Ring 01-353 3030 ext. 222 for permission to view.
Map Ref. 2I

THE RIVER

The River Thames on which the Romans first built London 2000 years ago is probably the most famous river in the world. London gradually became a major City and by 50 A.D. was considered to be the fifth largest City in the Roman Empire and has gained in importance ever since. That importance depended on the River. Besides the Romans, Saxons, Danes, Vikings, Normans and other invaders have all sailed up it stamping their character on the British race. In later years the Elizabethans set sail to conquer other territories and to the present day traders have used the Thames to carry British goods to every corner of the world. The Thames is 30 miles long between *Hampton Court* and *Greenwich* and it is possible to travel that distance by boat, during which journey you will really see the wonder of London and its different buildings. Another lovely way to watch the Thames is to stand on one of the many bridges that span it. The Thames is so important and so much a part of London that no visitor should miss the opportunity to take a boat trip. Other places to visit on the Thames:-

H.M.S. Belfast
Symons Wharf, Vine Lane,
off Tooley Street, S.E.1.
Tel: 01-407 6434
Tube: London Bridge.
Buses: 42, 47, 70, 78, 188.
Ferry: From Tower of London.
Moored between *Tower Bridge* and *London Bridge*, **H.M.S. Belfast** is a Battle Cruiser from World War II. She escorted the convoys to Russia and helped to sink the German Battleship *Scharnhorst*. She was involved with

the Normandy landings and also saw service in the Korean War.
Today she is a Naval Museum and having been carefully restored looks exactly like she did 40 years ago.
Access is available to most parts of the ship.
Open: 11.00am-5.00pm, Monday to Sunday.
April to October.
Open: 11.00am-4.00pm, Monday to Sunday.
November to March.
Admission Charge: £1.80 adults, children and OAP's half price.

Map Ref. 4K

R.R.S. Discovery
Victoria Embankment, W.C.2.
Tel: 01-836 5138
The ship in which *Captain Scott* sailed to the Antarctic in 1901.
Open: 1.00pm-4.30pm, Monday to Sunday.
Admission: £1.50, children 50p.

Map Ref. 3I

H.M.S. Crysanthemum
and
H.M.S. President
Victoria Embankment, W.C.2.
Training Ships.
Not open to public.

Map Ref. 3I

'Wellington'
Victoria Embankment, W.C.2.
Belongs to the Master Mariners.
Open: 1.00pm-4.00pm, Monday to Sunday. Not open to public.

Map Ref. 3I

STREET MARKETS

London is famous for its Street Markets and it can often be a pleasant and cheap way to buy antiques, clothes, bric-a-brac and food. They date back to the 18th and 19th Centuries and are usually open between 8.30 am and 4.30 pm Monday to Saturday. The following is a list of some of them.

Bermondsey Market
Between Tower Bridge Road and Bermondsey S.E.1.
Open: Friday only.
Mostly antique stalls aimed at dealers and collectors. Good quality.
Map Ref. 4K

Berwick Street Market
Soho, W.1.
Open: 8.00am-7.00pm, Monday to Saturday.
A good market for fruit and vegetables at reasonable prices.
Map Ref. 3G

Billingsgate
Lower Thames Street, E.C.3.
Open: From 6.00am, Daily.
Wholesale fish market for buying in bulk. The market has been here for 800 years.
Map Ref. 3K

Borough Market
Southwark Street, S.E.1.
Wholesale fruit and vegetable market for buying in bulk.
Map Ref. 4J

Brixton Market
Atlantic Road, S.W.9.
Open: 8.00am-00.00pm, Monday to Saturday.
A marvellous market specialising in West Indian food.
No Map Ref.

Cheshire Street Market
Whitechapel Road, E.C.2.
Open: Sunday 8.00am-1.00pm.
One of the labyrinth of streets in this part of the East End of London, most of which have street markets selling all kinds of merchandise and food.
Map Ref. 2L

Columbia Road Market
Hackney, W.2.
Open: Sunday 8.00am-1.00pm.
Excellent market for flowers and plants.
No Map Ref.

Covent Garden
Nine Elms, S.W.8.
Open: From 4.00am, Monday to Saturday, mornings only.
No Map Ref.

London's major wholesale market for fruit, vegetables and flowers. Bulk buying is the only way and it is also not easy to get your car in to park.
Map Ref. 6G

Farringdon Road, E.C.1.
Open: 6.00am-4.00pm, Monday to Friday.
Closed Saturday and Sunday.
Mostly old books and manuscripts.
Map Ref. 2J

Jubilee Market
Southampton Street, W.C.2.
Open: Monday to Friday.
A mixed market selling vegetables, fish, dairy produce, clothes and plants. On *Saturday* specialised craftsmen move in and sell and demonstrate their wares such as pottery, shoemaking, lacemaking, knitting and ironwork.
Map Ref. 3H

Leadenhall Market
Gracechurch Street, E.C.3.
Open: 9.00am-5.00pm, Monday to Friday.
Victorian building encloses this market which sells mainly vegetables, fruit, fish and meat and poultry.
Map Ref. 2K

Petticoat Lane
Middlesex Street, E.1.
Open: Sunday only, 9.00am-2.00pm.
London's most famous street market selling just about anything, but with a lively atmosphere.
Map Ref. 2L

Portobello Road
Notting Hill Gate, W.11.
Open: Saturday only.
Another market which has a good atmosphere. Everything from fruit and vegetables to antiques, bric-a-brac and the most amazing clothes.
Map Ref. 3B

Shepherds Bush
Goldhawk Road, W.12.
Open: Monday to Saturday.
Beside the railway arches, this is a large market which sells most things but specialises in West Indian fruit and vegetables.
No Map Ref.

Smithfield
Charterhouse Street, E.C.1.
Open: From 5.00am, Monday to Saturday.
The world's largest meat market covering 10 acres. There are shops where you can buy individual items but principally it is a wholesale market.
Map Ref. 2J

Spitalfields
Commercial Street, E.C.1.
Open: From 5.00am, Monday to Saturday.
Another wholesale market specialising in fruit, flowers and vegetables.
Map Ref. 2L

PAGEANTRY

Ceremony of the Keys
The Tower of London, E.C.3.
Tube: Tower Hill.
Buses: 15, 25, 42, 78.
You can only view this ceremony by writing for special permission to the Governor as it takes place at 9.40 pm. Every night the *Chief Warder of the Tower,* escorted by armed soldiers, locks the *West Gates,* the *Middle Tower* and the *Byward Tower* with traditional ceremony.

Map Ref. 3L

The Changing of the Queen's Guard
Buckingham Palace, S.W.1.
Tube: St. James's Park or Victoria.
Buses: 2, 11, 16, 24, 29, 36, 38, 52.
The soldiers who guard *Buckingham Palace* change every day at 11.30 am and the new Guard, following their band, march from either *Chelsea* or *Wellington* barracks in a ceremony lasting half an hour. It is not held in bad weather and only every other day in the winter.

Map Ref. 4G

The Changing of the Queen's Life Guard
Horse Guards Arch, Whitehall, S.W.1.
Tube: Trafalgar Square.
Buses: 3, 11, 12, 24, 29, 53, 77, 88.
This duty is carried out by the *Household Cavalry,* originally formed as a personal bodyguard to *Charles II* during his exile in Holland and serving every reigning Monarch since. The two regiments concerned, **The Life Guards** and the **Royal Horse Guards,** ride from *Knightsbridge Barracks* to *Horse Guards Parade* where the *Household Cavalry* first mounted guard over *Charles II* when he lived in the old Whitehall Palace.
Takes place Monday to Saturday.
10.00am Sunday.

Map Ref. 4G

The Lord Mayor's Show
City of London and Fleet Street.
Tube: St. Paul's, Blackfriars, Aldwych.
Buses: Many routes are diverted.
This takes place on the second Saturday of November when the new *Lord Mayor* drives from the *Guildhall* to the *Law Courts* to declare his loyalty and allegiance to the Queen. Although the *Lord Mayor* rides in his marvellous traditional coach, there is a type of carnival procession following with the armed forces accompanied by various assortments of floats, each one depicting a pageant-show theme.

Map Ref. 4H

Opening of the Royal Courts of Justice
Strand, W.C.2.
Tube: Westminster.
Buses: 3, 11, 12, 24, 29, 53, 88, 109, 155, 170, 184.
On the first Monday in October all Judges and Members of the Bar, dressed in State Robes, attend a service in *Westminster Abbey* and then, led by the *Lord Chancellor*, they walk in procession to the *House of Lords* and from there drive to the *Law Courts*.
The first motion taken by the *Lord Chancellor* is taken as the opening of the Courts.

Map Ref. 2I

Remembrance Sunday
Whitehall, S.W.1.
Tube: Westminster.
Buses: 3, 11, 12, 24, 29, 53, 88, 109, 155, 170, 184.
Some routes are diverted.
A very moving ceremony held on the Sunday nearest November 11th when the *Queen*, the *Prime Minister*, other Ministers and members of the Opposition party stand by the *Cenotaph* for two minutes' silence at 11.00am in respect of the armed forces killed in the two World Wars. The *Queen* then leads the laying of the wreaths.

Map Ref. 4H

Royal Tournament
Earls Court, S.W.5.
Tube: Earls Court.
Buses: 31, 74.
This is a marvellous display, held annually in mid-July for 2 weeks, by the armed forces.

Map Ref. 6C

The State Opening of Parliament
Houses of Parliament, S.W.1.
Tube: Westminster or Trafalgar Square.
Buses: 3, 11, 12, 24, 29, 53, 88, 109, 155, 170, 184.
Some routes are diverted.
Either at the end of October or early in November when Parliament reassembles after the Summer recess, or after a General Election, the *Queen*, wearing her crown and robes of state, drives from *Buckingham Palace* in her coach escorted by *Life Guards* and *Royal Horse Guards*. She goes along the Mall, down Whitehall to the *House of Lords* where she makes her speech from the throne.

Map Ref. 4H

Trooping of the Colour
Horse Guards Parade, S.W.1.
Tube: Trafalgar Square.
Buses: 3, 11, 12, 24, 29, 53, 88, 109, 155, 170, 184.
The Queen's official birthday is celebrated by **The Trooping of the Colour** which takes place on *Horse Guards Parade* on the Saturday nearest to 11th June. The ceremony dates from 1750 when troops in action had their colour paraded before them so that they would recognise their banner in battle.
The *Queen* rides from *Buckingham Palace* to the Parade where there is a march past with the colour paraded, before she returns to the Palace.

Map Ref. 4H

PARKS

Despite its size and density London has a magnificent selection of Parks, most of which are kept in perfect order throughout the year. In spring and summer they are a joy to stroll through, with a profusion of flowers, shrubs, trees, lakes and fountains. It is at times possible to think that you are in the countryside and not in the heart of a large metropolis, as the only noise you can hear is the birds.

Hyde Park, W.1.
Tel: 01-262 5484
Tube: Hyde Park Corner or Marble Arch.
Buses: 2, 12, 14, 16, 19, 22, 30, 36, 52, 73, 74, 88, 137.
Covering nearly 350 acres, **Hyde Park** became the property of the Crown in 1536 and was later opened to the public by *James I.* Stretching from Mayfair to Kensington, it is a popular place for office workers at lunch time and also for horse riding. Situated at the Marble Arch end is an area called *Speakers Corner* which is famous for its 'soap box' orators on Sundays. There is a lovely lake, the *Serpentine,* where you can hire boats for rowing and sailing, and also an area, the *Lido,* where you can swim. There are band concerts on Sundays and also two restaurants and cafes.

Map Ref. 3E

Kensington Gardens, W.2.
Tel: 01-937 4848.
Tube: Lancaster Gate or Queensway.
Buses: 12, 53, 73, 88.
Separated from *Hyde Park* by a road, **Kensington Gardens** comprises 275 acres of beautiful formal gardens. Originally they were the gardens of *Kensington Palace,* where in 1689 *William III* set up his court. *Queen Anne, George I* and *George II* gradually enlarged them until they became the size they are today. The special features are the *Sunken Gardens, Queen Anne's Orangery,* and *the Flower Walk.* For special enthusiasts the *Round Pond* is used for model boat sailing. *Queen Caroline* created the *Serpentine* by damming the Westbourne River, and also the *Long Water,* where on the west side is situated the statue of *Peter Pan.*

Map Ref. 3D

St. James's Park, S.W.1.
Tel: 01-262 5484
Tube: St. James's Park or Trafalgar Square.
Buses: 3, 11, 12, 14, 19, 22, 24, 29, 38, 53, 88.
St. James's Park is the oldest of the Royal Parks in London, having been created by *Henry VIII* and is adjacent to *Whitehall Palace.* It was, however, successive monarchs who improved the layout before *Charles II* opened it to the public.
It is also a sanctuary for wild birds with *Duck Island* a breeding and nesting ground. It is a beautiful park with lovely fountains and shrubs.

Map Ref. 4G

Green Park, S.W.1.
Tel: 01-262 5484
Tube: Green Park.
Buses: 9, 14, 19, 22, 25, 38, 506.
Although quite small and situated beside *Piccadilly* it is different in character to *St. James's Park*. It is, as its name suggests, an area of grass and shady trees. It has no flowers except daffodils and bluebells in the spring and no lakes or ponds.
Map Ref. 4G

Regents Park, N.W.1.
Tel: 01-486 7905
Tube: Regents Park, Baker Street, Great Portland Street.
Buses: 3, 27, 30, 53, 74.
Another beautiful Royal Park of 470 acres which was originally part of *Henry VIII's* hunting forest in the 16th Century. It was later granted by *Charles I* to two of his supporters as security for debts incurred by him during the Civil War. In 1811 the *Prince Regent* wanted the area connected via the newly built *Regent Street* to *Carlton House*, and asked *Nash* to design elegant houses in and around the Park. Although the scheme, which included a Palace in **Regents Park,** was never completed, *Nash* did however finish the surrounding houses. These beautiful and elegant buildings are very impressive.
The park has a fine boating lake with many species of birds, and the lovely *Queen Mary's* rose garden.
Map Ref. 1E

Battersea Park, S.W.11.
Tel: 01-228 2798
Bus: 137.
A large park on the south side of the *River Thames* between the *Albert* and *Chelsea* bridges. There is a boating lake, lovely fountains and tennis courts.
Map Ref. 6F

Crystal Palace Park, S.E.19.
Tel: 01-778 7148
British Rail: From Victoria Station to Crystal Palace.
An open park on a hill which was once the site for the *Glass Palace* brought from the Hyde Park exhibition in 1857.
No Map Ref.

Greenwich Park, S.E.10.
Tel: 01-858 2608
British Rail: From Charing Cross to Maze Hill.
Boat: River trips from Westminster Pier.
An old Royal Park which houses the *Royal Observatory* and *Flamsteed House*, with its famous red time-ball which falls exactly at 1 o'clock, Greenwich Mean Time, every day.
No Map Ref.

Hampstead Heath, N.W.3.
Tube: Hampstead Heath or Belsize Park.
Buses: 210, 268, 214.
This is a wild park where the trees and vegetation are only looked after if they are decaying, diseased or a particular danger to the public. It is an area where you can walk without seeing anyone for long periods of time and at certain places the views of London on a fine day can be stunning.

No Map Ref.

Holland Park, W.8.
Tel: 01-602 2226
Tube: Holland Park or Kensington High Street.
Buses: 9, 12, 27, 28, 33, 49, 88, 73.
A small, exquisitely landscaped park, with formal gardens, peacocks and lovely woodland walks. There is also a nice restaurant.
Map Ref. 4B

Kew Gardens, Richmond, Surrey.
Tel: 01-940 1171
Tube: Kew Gardens.
Buses: 15, 27, 65.
Covering 300 acres, these are some of the most beautiful botanical gardens in the world. They are stocked with thousands of varied flowers and trees and to appreciate their extent takes the best part of a day. There are hot-houses for orchids, ferns, palms and many other types of exotic plants. The *Palm House*, the *Temperate House* and the *Pagoda* are all interesting places to visit.
Open: 10.00am-Dusk.
Small admission charge.
No Map Ref.

Richmond Park, Richmond, Surrey.
Tel: 01-948 3209
Tube: Richmond.
Buses: 33, 37, 72, 74, 85.
Over 2000 acres in extent, this is the largest Royal Wild Park in London. There are many magnificent trees, particularly oaks, beautiful rhododendron plantations and large lakes with many species of wild fowl. The park is famous for its herds of fallow and red deer, which roam at will, and it is the best place in London for horse riding.

No Map Ref.

Syon Park, Brentford, Middlesex.
Tel: 01-560 0881
Tube: Gunnesbury.
Buses: 117, 267.
British Rail: Waterloo to Syon Lane.
Lovely landscaped gardens on the *River Thames* opposite *Kew Gardens* In the centre is the elegant *Syon House* which can also be visited.

No Map Ref.

Victoria Embankment Gardens
W.C.2.
Tube: Embankment.
Buses: 109, 155, 168, 172, 184.
Always kept in immaculate condition, these gardens are a model as to how flowers and shrubs should be grown.

Map Ref. 3I

Wimbledon Common, S.W.19.
Tel: 01-788 7655
Tube: Wimbledon then 93 bus.
Buses: 72, 74, 85, 93.
A thousand acres of wild woodland, heathland and silver birch plantations. There are a number of ponds and lakes, two golf courses and miles of horse rides. It also has a 19th Century windmill.

No Map Ref.

ZOOS

London Zoo
Regents Park, N.W.1.
Tel: 01-722 3333
Tube: Baker Street or Camden Town.
Buses: 3, 53, 74, 74b.
First opened to the public in 1847, London Zoo now has one of the most valuable and comprehensive collections of wild animals in the world. There are over 5000 animals housed here, the majority of which were actually born in the Zoo. There is a marvellous aviary, where one can observe exotic birds flying in natural surroundings, and a Moonlight Hall where day and night are reversed

and nocturnal animals which are rarely seen can be viewed. There is a large ape and monkey house, special terraces where you can see the wild cats and many more attractions. attractions including insects and reptiles.
Open: 9.00am-6.00pm, March to October.
10.00am-Dusk, November to April.
Admission: £3.50 adult, £1.55 child.

Map Ref. 1E

Chessington Zoo
Leatherhead Road, Chessington, Surrey.
Tel: Epsom 27227.
British Rail: Waterloo to Chessington.
Bus: 71.
Covering 65 acres, there is a fine selection of wild animals, including lions, giraffes, elephants and apes.
Open: Summer 10.00am-6.00pm.
Winter 10.00am-4.00pm.

No Map Ref.

THE INNS OF COURT

In England the legal profession is divided into two — Barristers, who plead cases in court, and solicitors who deal with legislation that does not require court cases and who also introduce clients to barristers when matters have to be brought to court.

The barristers, without exception, have to belong to an Inn of Court — these are the governing bodies of the profession, and regulate the conduct of barristers, train and examine candidates and, when they have passed the requisite examinations and eaten sufficient dinners in Hall admit aspirants to the Bar, as it is called. The barrister then has to find chambers — a group of practising barristers, who will allow him (or her — women were admitted to the bar in 1922) to have office space, assist, or devil, for them and eventually take on cases himself. He is then a junior and wears a stuff gown. When he is of sufficient standing a barrister may apply to the Lord Chancellor to become a Queen's Counsel or Senior Member of the Bar. If this is granted he may then take on important cases and be always attended by a junior. This is sometimes known as "taking silk" as Q.Cs wear silk gowns. Another charming custom concerns the bags in which barristers stuff their gowns and wigs. When you are first called you have a blue bag in which to carry these necessary garments. Then, after a year or two, if you have been of particular help to a silk he will give you a red bag — this is the mark of the successful junior.

There are four Inns of Court — mostly nowadays there are only offices in the quaint buildings, though some of the buildings do, still, contain private flats in which barristers can live, but these, always scarce are becoming more so, but if you get a chance to see one do so as they are very gracious and picturesque, up flights of stone stairs. Each Inn of Court has its Hall, too, in which the barristers eat their dinners and, in which, from time to time, social events are held to do with the Inns of Court and their activities. There are also chapels, the Temple Church and some pretty, private gardens — altogether the Inns of Court are charming places to wander through.

The Temple

There are two Inns of Court in the TEMPLE Inner Temple and Middle Temple. The Temple, which you find opposite the Law Courts at the end of the Strand, before it becomes Fleet Street is so called because it was originally the home of the Knights Templar, that dedicated band of religious soldiers, founded in 1119 with the express purpose of protecting the Holy Sepulchre and rescuing the Holy Land from the infidel. The order was dissolved in 1312 and the land was claimed by the Crown, who in 1324 gave it to the Knights of St. John. They, in turn, leased it to teachers of law who then set up residential schools. When Henry VII dissolved the Monasteries the land again became the property of the Crown but, during the reign of James I, the two Inns of Court were confirmed in their possession. It was, of course, at this time, that the young men went to the Inns of Court just for an education — they were a university, as indeed they are today, specialising in legal studies.

The Temple is split in two by Middle Temple Lane and this is entered by a seventeenth century gate built by Roger North — it is closed at night. Middle Temple is West of this lane and includes MIDDLE TEMPLE HALL, bombed during the war but restored to its Elizabethan Splendour. The Hammer beam roof is very magnificent and there is a beautiful carved screen (built 1671). The serving table is said to have been made from *The Golden Hind*, Drake's great ship.

The LIBRARY, also bombed with the loss of over 60,000 manuscripts has also been rebuilt and is one of the fullest legal libraries to be found.

INNER TEMPLE HALL was completely destroyed and the building is built in a Georgian Style and there is also the INNER TEMPLE LIBRARY.

THE TEMPLE CHURCH is one of the most interesting in London, being, in part, a medieval ROUND Church. It was completed in 1185 and is similar in design to the Holy Sepulchre Church in Jerusalem — there are only five existing round churches in England so this is a rarity. Added to it around 1240 is a large chancel in Early English Style. The reredos is by Sir Christopher Wren and there are several interesting tombs to be seen.

LINCOLN'S INN is the other side of Fleet Street towards Holborn — the main entrance being in CHANCERY LANE. This Inn of Court has two Halls — the OLD HALL (which is found through an archway in the Old Buildings, a group of 16th and 17th Century buildings) which was built in 1491 and extended in 1928. The oak screen may be by Inigo Jones and there is a painting by Hogarth to be seen. In Dicken's day the Hall was the place of the Court of Chancery and he describes it in BLEAK HOUSE.

THE NEW HALL AND LIBRARY is a far grander building, built in 1845 in a sort of Tudor Gothic style. The Library collection was started in 1497 and moved here when the building was completed. The Hall contains many portraits, including the controversial one of HRH Princess Margaret by Brian Organ.

The Chapel is 17th Century and built in Gothic Style — it may have been by Inigo Jones and was certainly restored by Sir Christopher Wren. The foundation stone was laid by the poet and divine, John Donne who preached the first sermon here. Cromwell's Secretary of State John Thurloe. Look out for the GATEHOUSE, a sixteenth century building built by Sir Thomas Lovell whose arms it bears.

GRAY'S INN is found in High Holborn and is entered by a gate built in the 17th Century. Although much of it was bombed it has been restored to its former glory. THE HALL, originally built in 1556-60 was restored in its original style and the glass survived and can be seen along with some modern glass donated by the American Barr Association. Gray's Inn Square is mainly late-17th century and the gardens also date from the seventh-century. It is said that Steele and Addison used to walk here and they were praised by Charles Lamb.

LITERARY LONDON

English poets and playwrights have always celebrated the city in which they have lived — this is especially true of the Londoners. Not much is left as it was originally seen by the poets, but Joy Leslie Gibson guides you through some of it that is still standing.

The first famous poem in the English language, albeit in Middle English, was written by Chaucer concerning a journey from London to Canterbury, and if the Inn from which the pilgrims started to take the ride no longer is in Talbot Yard, Southwark and to tell the tales that are still read with such delight today, at least we recognise among them types of English people who are still living. The same, too, can be said of Shakespeare's characters and although Eastcheap is very dissimilar to what it was in his day at least the name survives to remind us of Prince Hal and the rapscallion, Falstaff. But Southwark Cathedral still remains — the Church of the South Bank, near to where Shakespeare's theatres stood Philip Massinger is buried there. The Cathedral also has associations with the Founder of Harvard University, John Harvard.

Another Shakespearian building is Middle Temple Hall where it is reputed that "Twelfth Night" had its first performance and "The Comedy of Errors" was first acted in Gray's Inn Hall. Indeed, the men who thronged the Inns of Court were great patrons of the Theatre. Of all the palaces mentioned in the plays only the Tower and Hampton Court bear any resemblance to those buildings which Shakespeare could have seen, though the great names — Lancaster, York, Northumberland, Lancaster are commemorated in street names.

During Restoration times, when wit was all, the whole area around St. James's and Whitehall grew, and, indeed, Jermyn Street was built and named by one of the Restoration WITS, that coterie of men around town, by Harry Jermyn. Today it is a street of elegant shops, but look upwards and you will see the remnants of elegant facades. St. James's Church was built around this time, too, by Sir Christopher Wren and although it was damaged during the war it has been most lovingly restored and it is easy to imagine Millimant and her gallants attending Divine Service there before promenading in St. James's Park. Birdcage Walk is still with us, a reminder that there it was that you could buy little caged birds during Good King Charles's Golden Days.

Dr. Johnson spoke the most famous aphorism about London, declaring that "he who was tired of London was tired of life". The Doctor's house can still be seen in Gough Square, just off Fleet Street, and nearby is the famous Cheshire Cheese Tavern where they will show you the very chair that Dr. Johnson sat in. Sceptics say that, as Boswell never mentioned the Cheshire Cheese this is not so, but the food and wine is very good at the Cheshire Cheese so who is really worrying!

The bridge on which Wordsworth stood declaring that "Earth has nothing to show more fair" is not the same Westminster Bridge that he knew and the Houses of Parliament we now know is not that which he would have seen. The very "ships, towers, domes and theatres" have all changed but, nonetheless, the view from this and Waterloo Bridge with St. Paul's in the distance is very well worth pausing to look at. One of the nicest things about going to the Festival Hall is the view of the river it unfolds — a veritable Canaletto.

Of all poets, perhaps John Keats was the greatest Londoner, in that most of his life was passed here. The house in which he lodged in Hampstead, with the petulant Fanny Brawne next door, is still as it was when he lived there and is now the Keat's Museum, and the Mulberry tree where he is reputed to have written The Ode to the Nightingale still flourishes. But it is not so readily known that once he lodged in Westminster and his brother George's fiancee lived in Romney Street. Alas, the house is no longer there, but you can see a few early Eighteenth Century houses in this street, which the Keat's brothers must have often past.

It was in St. James's Street that Lord Byron "woke and found himself famous" on the publication of "Childe Harold", though later he moved to The Albany, that elegant set of gentleman's Chambers which is in a secluded enclave along Piccadilly. His publisher, John Murray, still inhabits the house in Albemarle Street, and it was there that Lady Byron burnt many of the poet's papers on his death.

London and Dickens are almost synonymous — the Law Courts where he spent much time as a law reporter and about which he wrote so movingly in "Bleak House", the Fleet Prison (only the site can be seen now) and the infamously named Bleeding Heart Yard (in "Little Dorrit") are all names to conjure with. A roam round the Inns of Court soon transports one back into those days, although, alas, the lamplighter no longer turns the lamps on (which he did until a few years ago). You can still eat at the George and Vulture, from which Nicholas Nickleby set out for the notorious Dotheboys Hall and walk with Kate Nickleby from her squalid lodgings to the Mantinis. Though the squalor and terrifying aspects of Dicken's London has been ameliorated by the Welfare State we can still see traces of it around and walk through streets where he once walked.

To step from his world to that of Oscar Wilde is a long step — from the East End and City to elegant Chelsea where Wilde had a substantial house in Tite Street — and nearby lived Rossetti and Thomas Carlyle. It was in Chelsea, in the Cadogan Hotel that Wilde was arrested, an event commemorated by the present day poet John Betjeman.

Among more recent work one has only to think of T. S. Eliot's magnificent invocation of London in "The Waste Land" both in the passage beginning

"Unreal City
Under the brown fog of a winter dawn,
A crowd flowed over London Bridge. . . . ."

which mentions also King William Street and Saint Mary Woolnoth and also in the third part of that poem, "The Fire Sermon", too long to quote but full of London names such as Moorgate, Greenwich, Richmond, Kew and the church

"Of Magnus Martyr hold
Inexplicable splendour of Ionian white and gold. . . . ."

John Betjeman, too, has celebrated churches, principally Holy Trinity, Sloane Street, and his long, amusing poem "Summoned by Bells" has many friendly, loving passages about London in it, particularly a lively passage about that useful, but somewhat gloomy institution, the Underground. But for the youthful Betjeman and his friend Ronald Hughes Wright it was an idyllic day when they could

". . .travel by Underground all day
Between the rush hours, so that very soon
There was no station, north of Finsbury Park,
To Barking eastwards, Clapham Common south;
No temporary platform in the west
Among the Actons and the Ealings, where
We had not once alighted. . . . ."

Yes, London has been well served by her literary men — ever since the Canterbury Pilgrims started from here and in the words of the mellifluous Spenser may the "Sweet Thames flow softly" still to inspire future poets and writers.

Southwark Cathedral
Station: London Bridge.
Buses: 25 and 35.
The first church on this site was built in 606 AD but the present building dates from the thirteenth century though traces of an earlier church are still present.
Much of the nave was re-built at the turn of the nineteenth century and is now the seat of the Bishop of Southwark. A window on the South Side contains Elizabethan glass and there is a Harvard Chapel on the East transept. There is a memorial to William Shakespeare and also to William Emerson, ancestor of the American writer Ralph Waldo Emerson. Fletcher (of Beaumont and Fletcher), Philip Massinger and "a player" Edmund Shakespeare, who may have been the poet's brother are all buried here, but the graves are unmarked.

Map Ref. 4K

Talbot Yard, Southwark
The site of the TABARD INN from where Chaucer's Pilgrims started.
Tube: Borough.
Buses: 25, 10, 35.
Near the junction of Borough High Street and Southwark Street a not very interesting place, though numbers 68 and 70 in the High Street are very old houses. In this area also was the MARSHALSEA PRISON and the KING'S BENCH both of which held some illustrious prisoners both in real life and in fiction. Among them are reputed, by Shakespeare, to be Prince Hal — though this legend has never been substantiated. In fiction Little Dorritt is the most famed inhabitant of the Marshalsea. Other prisoners in these two prisons have included (both fact and fiction) Mr. Micawber, Leigh Hunt, Edmund Bonner, Bishop of London, Tobias Smollet and John Wilkes.
In this area too was the White Hart Inn, mentioned by Shakespeare in HENRY VI.

Map Ref. 4K

Middle Temple Hall
Tube: The Temple.
Buses: 4, 6, 9, 11, 15, 502 and 513.
Situated in one of the Inns of Court this Hall was opened by Elizabeth I in 1576, and, although bombed during the war has been lovingly restored. Here, it is reputed, the first performance of TWELFTH NIGHT

took place. The whole of the Inns of Court — Inner Temple and Middle Temple are in this part of London, while Lincoln's Inn is the other side of Fleet Street: Gray's Inn being in Holborn are constantly mentioned in English Literature. The Inns of Court are the working places for barristers (also homes, though these are increasingly scarce). Among famous men of law and letters have been Sir Walter Raleigh; John Evelyn, the diarist; Henry Fielding; Edmund Burke; Sheridan; Thomas Moore; Thomas de Quincey; William Thackeray and Oliver Goldsmith, though not a lawyer, lived at 2 Brick Court.

The Temple Gardens are the Gardens in which, according to Shakespeare, the Houses of York and Lancaster chose the badges of the Red and White Roses, thus starting the Wars of the Roses.

This area is one of the oldest in London and is a quiet, fascinating place. Dickens mentions it too several times and it was here that Ruth and Tom Pinch met in MARTIN CHUZZLEWIT, and much of BLEAK HOUSE takes place in its environments.

Map Ref. 3I

Jermyn Street

Tube: Green Park.

Buses: 19, 22, 9.

Little of the original street is left as it is now all shops. But look at St. James's Church, with its Grinling Gibbons carvings. Built by Sir Christopher Wren.

Map Ref.

Romney Street, Westminster

Tube: St. James's

Buses: 507.

Some pretty eighteenth century houses which Keats must have seen, also some early Victorian houses.

Map Ref. 3G

Keats House

Tube: Chalk Farm

The poet John Keats lived here from December 1819 to September 1820 when it was known as Wentworth Place, and where he wrote many of his famous poems and fell in love with Fanny Brawne. It was built in 1815 and now houses relics of both him and Fanny. This is a pretty part of Hampstead and well worth a walk through.

Nearby in Well Walk lived the painter John Constable who lived at number 40 as did Keats in 1817.

No Map Ref.

St. James's Street

Tube: Green Park.

One of the most elegant streets in London with St. James's Palace at the end and several gentlemen's Clubs (Boodles, Brook's, Carlton) in it. The house in which the poet lived is now demolished and is replaced by Byron House.

While you are in the street have a look at Pickering Place (on the left as you face St. James's). It is a charming little court of pretty houses and one of those passed-by places which few people know of.

Map Ref. 3G

The Albany, Piccadilly

Tube: Piccadilly.

Just before you get to the Royal Academy there is a little entrance — in it you will find THE ALBANY where Byron also lived at one time. You cannot go in as it is still inhabited by the rich and famous.

Map Ref. 3G

Dickens House

24 Doughty Street, E.C.3.

Tube: Holborn.

This house, in which the writer lived from March 1837 until 1839, is now owned by the Dickens Fellowship and houses memorabilia of the novelist. It was here that he wrote PICKWICK PAPERS, OLIVER TWIST, NICHOLAS NICKLEBY and some of BARNABY RUDGE.

Map Ref. 2I

Johnson's House

Gough Square, E.C.4.

Tube: The Temple.

This 17th Century House was the home of the Doctor from 1748 to 1759 and where he worked on his Dictionary. The house is now a monument to him.

Map Ref. 3I

Literary Houses in Chelsea

Tube: Sloane Square

OSCAR WILDE lived at 34 TITE STREET; GEORGE ELIOT died at 4 Cheyne Walk; DANTE GABRIEL ROSSETTI Lived at 16 CHEYNE WALK from 1862-1882; THOMAS CARLYLE lived in CHEYNE ROW in what is now called CARLYLE HOUSE and is now in the charge of the National Trust containing many mementoes of the writer and his wife. In UPPER CHEYNE ROW, Leigh Hunt, friend of Keats, lived at Number 22, while Tobias Smollet lived round the corner in LAWRENCE STREET.

WALKING AROUND LONDON

Like most big cities one of the best ways to get to know London is to walk around it. It is, however, a very big place with all sorts of fascinating things to see, and whether your tastes are for architecture, literature, theatres, politics or anything else you can think of there are places of historic and modern interest to which you can walk about. One way to find out about walks is to look at the back page of THE TIMES, which every day lists those walks which are being held on that day, together with the subject matter *(Dickens, Shakespeare, Pubs, Ghosts etc).* Times and places are given and you just turn up, in your comfortable walking shoes, pay the fee (generally under £2) and just join in.
If you prefer to find out about a tour first, we list a number of people and organisations ready to help. Some of them specialise in one kind of interest, others will suggest several ideas.
One of the most interesting walks to do — and one of the most comprehensive is the SILVER JUBILEE WALK, initiated to commemorate the Queen's Silver Jubilee. In its entirety it is ten miles long, but if you don't feel like walking that much in a day, you can split it up. Find all about it with the London Transport's pretty and comprehensive map.
London's Canals are quaint and unusual places to walk along. They run through some very picturesque parts of London and again London Transport can provide you with the appropriate leaflet with six walks already mapped out with information as to historic places nearby, pubs where you can stop for a drink and food and other interesting data.
For a tiny, fascinating walk you may like to saunter around TOWER BRIDGE which has glass enclosed walkways giving you fantastic views over London together with exhibitions, models and a Museum.

Leaflets — all from London Transport.
Tower Bridge
Canal Walks
Silver Jubilee Walkways — 35 p

ORGANISERS OF LONDON WALKS

City Walks — Ros Tyrell, 1 Haggerston House, Clarissa Street, E.8.
London Walks — Patricia McCannan. Tel: 882 2763.
Discovering London — Alex and Peggy Cobban Brentwood (0277) 213704.
J W Travel — John Wittich, 66 St. Michael's Street, W.2.
Exciting Walks with Susan — Susan Harris. Tel: 624 9981.
Pub Walks with The Londoner — Mer Westbrook. Tel: 883 2656.
Victorian London — Victorian Society — the Secretary. Tel: 994 1019.
Karl Marx Walks — Mr. Cavell. Tel: 794 9251.
Wembley Stadium Tours — John Feenstra. Tel: 902 8833.
Regent's Canal Walk — Dr. Essex-Loprestti. Tel: 303 1289.

OUT OF LONDON

Osterley House
Nearest Underground: Osterley.
Nearest Station: Syon Lane.
Tel: 01-560 3919
Open: Tuesdays to Sundays.
Osterley Park was given to Sir Thomas Gresham by Queen Elizabeth I and on the land he built a grandiose Elizabethan House and his Queen visited it in 1577. It eventually passed into the Child Family and in 1761 Francis Child asked the famous architect Robert Adam to recreate the house. Using the Elizabethan house as a basis, Adam pulled down one side, thus making the large courtyard and colannade that we see today.
Inside the whole decoration, furniture and paintings echo his taste as no detail was too small to engage his interest — doorknobs, lamps, carpets which echo the patterns of the ceilings — all show his masterly hand. Robert Child, now head of the family, cast his eye round for a suitable bridegroom for his heiress daughter, but finally disapproved of her runaway marriage to the Earl of Westmorland that he disinherited her in favour of her daughter who eventually married Lord Villiers, the heir of the Earl of Jersey. His ancestors occupied the house until the 1950s when it was given to the nation. It is a priceless possession as it epitomises the elegant 18th century country hosue and is exquisite in all its details. The park is small but elegant and the whole place is well-worth a visit.

No Map Ref.

Syon House
Station: Syon Lane.
Tel: 01-560 0881
Open: April to September, Sundays to Thursdays.
In October, Sunday Only.
Syon House is part of the fabric of England and it is still the house of the Dukes of Northumberland though the state rooms are open to the public. It was originally a monastery with the foundation stone laid in 1415 by Henry V, though the present site was not occupied until 1431. It was dissolved by Henry VII and Queen Katherine Howard was imprisoned here. Edward VI gave the property to John Dudley, Duke of Northumberland and it was here that Lady Jane Grey heard that she was to be Queen.

Under Queen Mary it was given to some nuns, but by the time of James I the Northumberland's were again in possession. At this time Inigo Jones was asked to improve the house and Charles I's children lived here for a time after their father had been defeated. Charles II visited here as have Kings and Queens ever since.
It was in the middle of the 18th century that the house as it is seen today really came into existence. He employed Robert Adam to design the house in the so-called Roman style and it is a truly magnificent example of Adam's genius. The Great Hall and Long Gallery are superb, redolent with black and white marble and its beautiful statues.
The Drawing Rooms and dining-room are simpler in style and are warm with colour and beautiful things. Don't forget to visit the Long Gallery a feature of Adam houses. The house contains many fine paintings and furniture — many of historic interest.
THE GROUNDS OF SYON HOUSE are also magnificent and some time should be spent looking at them. In them you will also find
THE LONDON BUTTERFLY HOUSE which is a Butterfly Sanctuary which fly around in a perfect environment.
Open Daily.
Tel: 01-560 7272
There is also A GARDEN CENTRE in the grounds where you can buy plants, shrubs and flowers.
Open Daily:
Tel: 01-560 0881.
And as well the BRITISH LEYLAND HERITAGE MUSEUM for car enthusiasts.
Open Tuesdays to Sundays:
Tel: 01-560 1378

No Map Ref.

Kew Gardens
Station: Kew Gardens.
Tel: 01-940 1171
Open Daily.
Officially Kew Gardens are called the ROYAL BOTANICAL GARDENS and they are visited by experts all over the world for advice on botanical matters. But for the non-experts these gardens are a delight to roam about and enjoy as pleasure gardens. There are lakes, the famous Pagoda and the equally renowned hot-houses where you can see tropical plants growing in profusion. It is a lovely place to stroll in fine weather and a favourite with West Londoners.

No Map Ref.

Chiswick House
Burlington Lane, W.4.
Tel: 01-994 3299
Nearest Tube: Chiswick Park or Gunnersbury.
Open April to October 15 — 9.30am to 6.30pm (closed lunchtime); from October 15th, closed Mondays and Tuesdays and at 4.00pm.

Lord Burlington, on a visit to Italy, was thrilled by the beautiful Palladian Villa Rotonda at Vicenza and decided to build a similar house in Chiswick. The wings were added some thirty years later. By 18th Century standard it was a small house, but, nonetheless, it is exquisite and repays a visit. It is a minor masterpiece and stands in pleasant grounds.

No Map Ref.

CANAL WALKS
Meandering through London is the GRAND UNION CANAL much of it built in the late 18th Century and early 19th Century. THE LONDON TRANSPORT BOARD has issued an interesting booklet called CANAL WALKS which will guide you through six of these walks. The booklet details places of interest which are near the canals, pubs where you can eat and drink and other activities which take place in the vicinities of the canals. It is an unusual way of seeing various parts of London if you are a confirmed walker and like exercise.

Entertainment guide

A
B
C
D
E
F
G
H
I
J
K
L
1
2
3
4
5
6
KILBURN LANE
HARROW ROAD
Kensal Green
LADBROKE GROVE
FERNHEAD RD.
ELGIN AVENUE
GREAT WESTERN RD
HARROW ROAD
CASTELLAIN RD
Maida Vale
MAIDA VALE
ST. JOHN'S WOOD RD.
CLIFTON GDNS.
Warwick Avenue
EDGWARE ROAD
LISSON GROVE
WELLINGTON ROAD
Marylebone
REGENT'S PARK
ALBANY STREET
EUSTON STATION
EUSTON ROAD
EUSTON
ROAD
Great Portland Street
Baker Street
MARYLEBONE ROAD
Regent's Park
Warren Street
TOTTENHAM COURT RD.
GOWER STREET
GRAYS INN ROAD
KING'S CROSS ROAD
ROSEBERRY AVENUE
GOSWELL ROAD
CITY ROAD
OLD STREET
Old Street
GREAT EASTERN ST.
HACKNEY ROAD
Westbourne Park
Ladbroke Grove
WESTBOURNE PARK
TALBOT ROAD
CHEPSTOW RD.
HARROW ROAD
Edgware Road
WESTBOURNE TER
PADDINGTON STATION
SEYMOUR PLACE
EDGWARE ROAD
PORTMAN SQUARE
BAKER STREET
MARYLEBONE HIGH ST.
PORTLAND PL.
Goodge Street
GOODGE ST.
Tottenham Court Rd.
SOUTHAMPTON ROW
GUILFORD ST.
THEOBALDS RD.
CLERKEN WELL ROAD
FARRINGDON ST.
Chancery Lane
ALDERSGATE ST.
Moorgate
MOORGATE
LIVERPOOL ST. STATION
BISHOPSGATE
COMMERCIAL ST.
WHITECHAPEL
CLARENDON RD.
BLENHEIM CRES
LADBROKE GROVE
COLVILLE TER.
BISHOPS BRIDGE ROAD
WESTBOURNE GROVE
ELGIN CRES.
Oxford Circus
Marble Arch
OXFORD STREET
NEW OXFORD STREET
HOLBORN
Holborn
CHANCERY LANE
HOLBORN VIA
REGENT ST.
Lancaster Gate
Marble Arch
GROSVENOR SQUARE
Bond Street
NEW BOND ST.
POLAND ST.
WARDOUR ST.
CHARING CROSS ROAD
DRURY LANE
LONG ACRE
FLEET ST.
LUDGATE HILL
St Paul's
CHEAPSIDE
Bank
HOUNDSDITCH
Aldgate
LEMAN ST.
Bayswater
PEMBRIDGE RD
QUEENSWAY
Queensway
BAYSWATER ROAD
KENSINGTON GARDENS
HYDE PARK
PARK LANE
BERKELEY SQUARE
OLD BOND ST.
Piccadilly Circus
SHAFTESBURY AV.
Leicester Square
Covent Garden
Aldwych
STRAND
Somerset House
Temple
EMBANKMENT
Blackfriars
QUEEN VICTORIA ST.
Mansion House
LEADENHALL ST.
FENCHURCH ST.
Monument
Monument
Tower Hill
MINORIES
EAST SMITHFIELD
Notting Hill Gate
NOTTING HILL GATE
PORTLAND ROAD
KENSINGTON CHURCH ST
SERPENTINE
ROTTEN ROW
CURZON ST.
PICCADILLY
Hyde Park Corner
Green Park
GREEN PARK
PALL MALL
THE MALL
ST. JAMES'S PARK
CHARING CROSS STATION
VICTORIA
WATERLOO BRIDGE
RIVER
THAMES
BLACKFRIARS BRIDGE
SOUTHWARK BRIDGE
LONDON BRIDGE
TOWER HILL
TOWER BRIDGE
HOLLAND PARK AVENUE
Holland Park
HOLLAND PARK
CAMPDEN HILL RD
KENSINGTON HIGH STREET
KENSINGTON RD.
KNIGHTSBRIDGE
BELGRAVE SQUARE
GROSVENOR PL.
BIRDCAGE WALK
Westminster
WESTMINSTER BRIDGE
STAMFORD ST.
WATERLOO ROAD
YORK ROAD
WATERLOO STATION
BLACKFRIARS RD.
SOUTHWARK STREET
Borough
BOROUGH HIGH ST.
ST. THOMAS ST.
TOOLEY STREET
LONDON BRI. STATION
HOLLAND ROAD
High Street Kensington
QUEEN'S GATE
EXHIBITION ROAD
Knightsbridge
BEAUCHAMP PLACE
SLOANE STREET
St James's Park
VICTORIA STREET
HORSE FERRY ROAD
VAUXHALL BRIDGE ROAD
Lambeth North
WESTMINSTER BRIDGE RD
LAMBETH PALACE RD
BOROUGH RD.
SOUTHWARK BRIDGE RD
CAUSEWAY
LONG LANE
EARLS COURT ROAD
South Kensington
BROMPTON ROAD
WALTON RD.
CADOGAN GDNS
KING'S ROAD
BUCKINGHAM PALACE ROAD
LAMBETH BRIDGE
LAMBETH ROAD
ST. GEORGE'S RD.
LONDON RD.
NEWINGTON CAUSEWAY
GREAT DOVER ST.
ABBEY STREET
SHEPHERD'S BUSH RD
HAMMERSMITH ROAD
WARWICK ROAD
CROMWELL ROAD
Gloucester Road
OLD BROMPTON ROAD
SYDNEY ST.
KING'S ROAD
Sloane Square
VICTORIA STATION
MILLBANK
KENNINGTON ROAD
Elephant and Castle
NEW KENT RD
WALWORTH ROAD
OLD KENT ROAD
TALGARTH ROAD
NORTH END ROAD
WEST CROMWELL ROAD
Earls Court
CHELSEA BRIDGE RD
Pimlico
ALBERT EMBANKMENT
KENNINGTON PARK ROAD
FULHAM PALACE ROAD
LILLIE ROAD
REDCLIFF GARDENS
FULHAM ROAD
ROYAL HOSPITAL ROAD
CHELSEA EMBANKMENT
CHELSEA BRIDGE
GROSVENOR ROAD
VAUXHALL BRIDGE
Vauxhall
HARLEYFORD RD
Kennington Park
ALBANY ROAD
West Brompton
KING'S ROAD
ALBERT BRIDGE
BATTERSEA PARK
NINE ELMS LANE
FENTIMAN RD
Oval

THEATRICAL AND MUSICAL LONDON

London is prominent in the richness of its cultural life – theatres, concert halls and opera houses all present a varied entertainment of the highest standard. Joy Leslie Gibson guides you through what is available.

Dr Johnson's favourite saying about being tired of life if you are tired of London might easily be paraphrased to say that if you cannot find anything in London's cultural scene to satisfy you then you must be very jaded. Whatever your taste in theatre, music or the arts London has a variety and richness unsurpassed anywhere. Whatever your tastes you will find an opera, ballet, play or concert to suit you on every night of the week (except Sundays when the theatres are closed).

Opera and Ballet

There are three opera houses in London — the most famous being the Royal Opera House in Covent Garden. A gracious and beautiful building it is the home of the famed Royal Ballet Company who give three or four performances a week. Mostly of British and Commonwealth origins the company dance in the impeccable "Royal" style and has the best corps de ballet in the world. Its home-grown stars dazzle and there are always new, young dancers coming up to astound and delight. Added to that, the Royal has two brilliant world-renowned choreographers in Frederick Ashton and Kenneth MacMillan, besides employing the best foreign talent. What more could any balletomane ask for?

The London Festival Ballet has its headquarters in London and give regular seasons here in either the Coliseum or the Festival Hall. Mainly, however, it tours, but if they are in London go to see them. They do the classic ballets in a very straightforward manner and often revive ballets of the Diaghilev period, which one can see nowhere else.

When the Royal Ballet is not performing at the Opera House, then you may see opera at its grandest, sung in the original language with glittering stars of the calibre of Pavarootti, Domingo and Yvonne Minton. Costly to go to but well worth it for you hear the most beautiful and exciting voices in the world.

Every night of the year, excepting a short season in the summer, when it is given over to ballet, the Coliseum also resounds with opera for it is the home of the English National Opera who give an extensive repertoire of operas translated into English. The ENO also develops new talents so you can catch a new singer on the way to stardom as well as hearing a high standard of music and watching good productions.

At Sadlers Wells' you will find visiting companies, including the touring section of the Royal Ballet, who come from all over the world and the British Isles to perform operas and ballets or the national dances of their country. There is always something of interest here, as well.

Theatres

Theatres showing straight plays are either shown in the subsidised theatres (i.e. theatres with Arts Council Grants) or in the commercial theatre. The two subsidised theatres are the Royal Shakespeare Company in the Barbican, where you will find two theatres — the main one which shows mainly Shakespeare with some modern drama specially written for the company, or, sometimes, classic drama, such as Ibsen, the Russian dramatists or other classic English plays. In the Pit one will find little known plays from the wealth of English drama as well as foreign classic plays and new plays all done in an imaginative way. The RSC refer to the Pit as its experimental theatre but so inventive and brilliant is the work done in the main theatre as well that one can be sure of seeing something really amazing at the Barbican.

The National Company occupies three theatres in one building on the South Bank. But it is so much more than that. The building is open all day and you can eat and drink there, take a tour round the building, look at exhibitions and listen to chamber music in the evenings (free) or go to a poetry recital, a play reading or talk. Then there are no less than three plays given every day with a varied, eclectic repertoire of old and new plays. The National does less Shakespeare than the RSC, though they do do some, but the rest of English Drama is played along with foreign plays and new plays.

The commercial theatres, which cluster around Shaftesbury Avenue, St Martin's Lane and into the Strand show a variety of work from revivals of musicals or straight plays, farce, new plays and plays imported from abroad, particularly Broadway. And if you want something more intimate then you will find a number of small theatres, often attached to pubs, where you will find acting and productions that range from excellent to indifferent. But it is fairly cheap and always fun to watch.

Music

London has four resident orchestras — and how many other cities could boast that? — the Royal Philharmonic, the Philharmonia, the London Symphony and the London Philharmonic, but only one, the London Symphony has a permanent home in the Barbican. However, both it and the other orchestras happily play in the Festival Hall, the Albert Hall and the Fairfields Hall (just out of London). And there are plans for them to visit the Barbican as well.

The great season of BBC Proms are held during the Summer in the Albert Hall, when there is ballet in the Festival Hall and a Summer Season in the Queen Elizabeth Hall, the smaller of the Halls on the South Bank. Then there are several places for recitals and more intimate musical concerts — the Purcell Room, on the South Bank: St John's Smith Square, an old converted Church, and the Wigmore Hall where many a young soloist has made a debut.

And if you prefer jazz or pop again you will find plenty of music — notable at Ronnie Scott's in Soho and in cinemas all round London. It is up to you not to sit around your hotel feeling bored — go out to explore musical and theatrical London — you will find plenty to entertain you!

TICKET AGENTS

If you can't get to the theatre to collect tickets, or if you have difficulty in booking seats direct for a show or concert, then the easiest way is through a ticket agency. Naturally they charge commission so the price of the tickets will cost more, but it is often worth it to save time.

In Leicester Square there is a colourful booth which sells Theatre Tickets at half-price plus 50p ON THE DAY OF PERFORMANCE ONLY. Run by the Society of West End Managers this booth disposes of unsold tickets at this rate daily — on matinee days the booth is open 12 noon-2pm and for evening tickets it is open 2.30pm-6.30pm. Displayed outside is a list of the shows for which tickets are available. Of course, smash hits are not included but there is generally a selection of good plays from which you can choose. Cash only: no choice of seats but best available.

Note: Many theatres now take Credit Card Bookings — as these vary from time to time please see Daily Newspapers for details.

Abbey Box Office
27 Victoria Street, S.W.1.
Tel: 01-222 2061
This agency handles most London theatrical events and concerts but also specialises in sport.
Major credit cards accepted.

Map Ref. 4G

Keith Prowse Ltd
24 Store Street, W.C.1.
Tel: 01-836 2184
This is the biggest ticket agency in London and has branches all over town. The addresses and telephone numbers of your nearest branch can be found in the telephone directory.
Major credit cards accepted.

Map Ref. 2H

London Theatre Bookings
96 Shaftesbury Avenue, W.1.
Tel: 01-439 3371
12 Gt. Newport Street, W.1.
Tel: 01-240 0681
31 Coventry Street, W.1.
Tel: 01-839 4471
An agency specialising in rock and

musical events and difficult to obtain seats. The special tickets they have in stock are displayed on a blackboard outside the booking office.
Credit Cards: Access, Barclaycard.
Map Ref. 3G

Ibbs and Tillett
124 Wigmore Street, W.1.
Tel: 01-486 4021
Specialises in all musical events and also handles bookings for the Glyndebourne Festival.
Map Ref. 2F

Premier Box Office
188 Shaftesbury Avenue, W.C.2.
Tel: 01-240 2245 Map Ref. 3G
34 St. James Street, W.1.
Tel: 01-486 7606 Map Ref. 3G
50 Fenchurch Street, E.C.3.
Tel: 01-623 3212 Map Ref. 3K
76 Cheapside, E.C.2.
Tel: 01-248 2689 Map Ref. 2J

Very good for pop concerts but also theatre and other musical events. Instant credit card bookings for Access and Barclaycard on 836 4114. Other major credit cards accepted at branches.

Obtainables
Panton House, 25 Haymarket, S.W.1.
Tel: 01-839 5363
If you find that it is impossible to get tickets for a particular show this agency can probably help but it is very expensive.
Map Ref. 3G

WEST END THEATRES

Adelphi Theatre
Strand, W.C.2.
Tel: 01-836 7611
Tube: Embankment.
Buses: 1, 6, 9, 9a, 11, 13, 15, 77, 170.
The present theatre, the fourth on this site, was opened in 1930 and is very typical of '30s architecture. Among famous musicals presented here have been several Cochran productions and the transfer of Ivor Novello's *The Dancing Years*. Holds 1481 people.
Map Ref. 3H

Albery Theatre
St Martin's Lane, W.C.2.
Tel: 01-836 3878
Tube: Leicester Square.
Buses: 1, 24, 29, 176.
Originally known as The New Theatre, this theatre was christened in 1973 in

honour of the famous Albery Family, theatrical impressarios, who are the present managers. The war-time home of the Sadler's Wells (now the Royal Ballet) and the Old Vic Companies, this theatre was built in 1903 by Charles Wyndham. Holds 877 people and is typical of an Edwardian Theatre.
Map Ref. 3H

Aldwych Theatre
Aldwych, W.C.2.
Tel: 01-836 5332
Tube: Covent Garden.
Buses: 1, 4, 6, 9, 11, 13, 15, 55, 68, 77, 170, 171, 172, 176, 188, 239, 501.
Formerly the home of the Royal Shakespeare Company this theatre is also famous as the home of the famous Aldwych Farces which were staged here during the twenties and thirties. Built in 1905 it is a splendid example of the grandiose late Victorian style.
Map Ref. 3I

Ambassadors Theatre
West Street, Cambridge Circus, W.C.2.
Tel: 01-836 1171
Tube: Leicester Square.
Buses: 1, 14, 19, 22, 29, 38, 176.
One of London's smaller theatres, which for over twenty years housed *The Mousetrap*, London's longest running play (now next door at the St Martin's Theatre). Built just before the 1914 war it is notable for the number of revues it has presented as well as being the scene of Vivien Leigh's debut in *The Mask of Virtue*. Its capacity is 453.

Map Ref. 2H

Apollo Theatre
Shaftesbury Avenue, W.1.
Tel: 01-437 2663
Tube: Piccadilly Circus.
Buses: 14, 19, 38.
Shaftesbury Avenue was opened in 1887 and it was not long before theatres were opened along it. The Apollo was the fourth and was opened in 1901. It is in French Renaissance style and behind an unpretentious façade is very pretty. Holds 796 people.

Map Ref. 3H

Apollo Victoria
Victoria, S.W.1.
Tel: 01-828 8665
Tube: Victoria.
Buses: 2, 10, 11, 16, 24, 25, 29, 36, 38, 52, 149, 181, 185, 500, 503, 506, 507, 509.
Once a cinema, then a home for Rock concerts the Victoria Palace now houses the large, enormous musical. Very much in the style of the thirties in style and is large and comfortable.

Map Ref. 5G

Cambridge Theatre
Earlham Street, W.C.2.
Tel: 01-836 6056
Tube: Covent Garden.
Buses: 1, 14, 19, 22, 24, 29, 38, 176.
Situated in the Seven Dials district, a famous part of London, since the seventeenth century, the Cambridge was not built until 1930. It is redolent of the style of this period and refurbished in red in the 1950s it is an appealing example of a mixture of styles. There is a fine art collection on the walls and in the foyers. Capacity 1275.

Map Ref. 2H

Comedy Theatre
Panton Street, S.W.1.
Tel: 01-930 2578
Tube: Piccadilly Circus.
Buses: 1, 3, 6, 9, 12, 13, 14, 15, 19, 22, 38, 39, 53, 59, 88, 159, 505, 506.
Designed by Thomas Verity, this elegant little theatre was opened in 1881 and was re-decorated in 1954 but still retains its Victorian charm. Holding 820 people it has housed many notable productions including Alec McCowen's solo rendering of "St Mark's Gospel."

Map Ref. 3H

Criterion Theatre
Piccadilly Circus, W.1.
Tel: 01-930 3216
Tube: Piccadilly Circus.
Buses: 6, 9, 12, 14, 15, 19, 22, 25, 39, 35, 59, 88, 159.
Another Thomas Verity design, this theatre was built under the famous Criterion restaurant. To get even to the Upper Circle you have to go *down* stairs. It is charmingly decorated in beige and pink and has some unusual tile decorations. Holds 645 people.

Map Ref. 3G

Duchess Theatre
Catherine Street, W.C.2.
Tel: 01-836 8243
Tube: Covent Garden.
Buses: 1, 4, 6, 9, 11, 13, 15, 55, 68, 77, 170, 171, 172, 188, 239, 501.
Built in 1929 this theatre is notable for the fact that the circle was designed to be narrower than the stalls: it is hung from girders in the roof! Maurice Lambert designed two panels situated between the proscenium arch and the dress circle. It is a pretty theatre, holding 474 people.

Map Ref. 2H

Duke of York's Theatre
St. Martin's Lane, W.C.2.
Tel: 01-836 5122
Tube: Leicester Square.
Buses: 1, 24, 29, 176
Recently bought and sumptuously redecorated by Capital Radio, this theatre was originally opened as the Trafalgar Square Theatre in 1892. The name was changed in 1895 and it was here that Puccini saw Belasco's one act play *Madame Butterfly* that he made into an opera. It is worth looking at the outside of this theatre, too. It seats 700 people.

Map Ref. 3H

Fortune Theatre
Russell Street, W.C.2.
Tel: 01-836 2238
Tube: Covent Garden.
Buses: 1, 1A, 4, 6, 9, 11, 13, 15, 55, 77, 78, 170, 171, 176, 188, 196, 239, 501, 502, 505, 513.
Opened in 1924 this theatre was the first to be built after the 1914 war. Within the building (though with separate entrance) is the Scottish National Church. Seats 440.

Map Ref. 2H

Garrick Theatre
Charing Cross Road, W.C.2.
Tel: 01-836 4601
Tube: Leicester Square or Charing Cross.
Buses: 1, 24, 29, 176.
The originator of this theatre was W. S. Gilbert and the designer was Walter Emden. It is in a classic style and a copy of a Gainsborough portrait of Garrick hangs in the foyer. Holding 800 people, it has been the home for many stars including Beatrice Lillie, Jack Buchanan as well as, more recently, Brian Rix and William Franklyn.

Map Ref. 2H

Globe Theatre
Shaftesbury Avenue, W.1.
Tel: 01-437 1592
Tube: Piccadilly.
Buses: 14, 19, 22, 38.
Holding nearly one thousand people, this theatre was originally called the Hicks Theatre after the redoubtable Sir Seymour. It was rechristened The Globe in 1909 and has housed many successful plays by such writers as Somerset Maugham, Frederick Lonsdale and Noel Coward.

Map Ref. 3H

Haymarket Theatre (Theatre Royal Haymarket)
Haymarket W.1.
Tel: 01-930 9832
Tube: Piccadilly.
Buses: 6, 9, 12, 13, 14, 15, 19, 22, 25, 38, 39, 53, 59, 88, 159.
One of the most beautiful theatres in London. Built in 1821, the Haymarket Theatre stands on the site of the original theatre built in 1702. Although the interior has been re-constructed several times, it still retains its 18th century elegance and is mainly known for presenting good plays among them being Ibsen's *Ghost's* (in 1914), *The Heiress*, the John Gielgud Season and a number of very successful revivals. Holds an audience of 906.

Map Ref. 3G

Her Majesty's Theatre
Haymarket, S.W.1.
Tel: 01-930 6606
Tube: Piccadilly Circus.
Buses: 6, 9, 12, 13, 14, 15, 19, 22, 38, 39, 53, 59, 88, 159, 505, 506.
Under various names there has been a theatre on this site from 1705. The present building was built by Herbert Beerbohm Tree and the interior designed by Lady Tree, at Sir Herbert's request, to keep her from finding out

about his *amours!* It is in Louis XIV style and is a wide, opulent theatre. Generally has large-scale productions and musicals to delight an audience of over 1200.

Map Ref. 3G

Lyric Theatre
Shaftesbury Avenue, W.1.
Tel: 01-437 3686
Tube: Piccadilly.
Buses: 14, 19, 22, 38.
Designed by C. J. Phipps in 1888 and re-furbished in 1933 this theatre is more redolent of the thirties than of its original date. It has had a large number of successes, and recently presented the late playwright, Ben Traver's play *Bed Before Yesterday,* one of its many comedy successes including Robert Morley in *Hippo Dancing* and *The Little Hut.*

Map Ref. 3G

Mayfair Theatre
Mayfair Hotel, Berkeley Street, W.1.
Tel: 01-629 3036
Tube: Green Park.
Buses: 3, 6, 9, 12, 13, 14, 15, 19, 22, 25, 38, 39, 53, 88, 159
This tiny theatre is situated inside the Mayfair Hotel (but has also its own separate entrance). It is intimate and presents good plays and small musical entertainments. And you can dine in the hotel afterwards.

Map Ref. 3F

Mermaid Theatre
Puddle Dock, Blackfriars, E.C.4.
Tel: 01-248 7655
Tube: Blackfriars.
Buses: 89, 95, 98, 133.
Sir Bernard Miles originally started the Mermaid Theatre in his garden in Hampstead but in 1951 he moved into the City, near Shakespeare's own Theatre. Recently the land was developed and the theatre, whose fortunes are uncertain, is enclosed in an office block.

Map Ref. 3J

New London Theatre
Parker Street, Drury Lane, W.C.2.
Tel: 01-405 0072
Tube: Covent Garden or Holborn.
Buses: 1, 8, 14, 19, 22, 24, 25, 29, 38, 73, 176.
The site of this theatre has long been occupied by a theatre, notably the "Old Mo" music hall and the Winter Garden. The present theatre was opened in 1973 and is owned now by Thames Television.

Map Ref. 2H

Palace Theatre
Cambridge Circus, W.1.
Tel: 01-437 6834
Tube: Leicester Square.
Buses: 1, 14, 19, 22, 24, 29, 38, 176.
Opened in 1891 as The Royal English Opera House, this theatre is renowned for its musical productions. It is notable, architecturally for being the first theatre which eliminated the pillars that were used to support the circles.

Map Ref. 2H

Palladium Theatre
Argyll Street, W.1.
Tel: 01-437 7373
Tube: Oxford Circus.
Buses: 1, 3, 6, 7, 8, 12, 13, 15, 25, 39, 53, 59, 88, 93.
London's leading Variety and Musical Theatre, this theatre, holding nearly 2,500 people, was opened in 1908 and was designed by the celebrated Frank Matcham. The original rose and red interior is very much as it was in Matcham's day.

Map Ref. 2G

Piccadilly Theatre
Denman Street, W.1.
Tel: 01-437 4506
Tube: Piccadilly.
Buses: 3, 6, 9, 12, 13, 14, 15, 19, 22, 25, 38, 39, 53, 59, 88, 159.
First opened in 1928 on a site previously occupied by stables, this theatre was designed with opulence by Bertie Crewe. Now the West End showcase of the Royal Shakespeare Company, it is owned by the Albery family. Its capacity is 1150 and is designed to take both large-scale productions as well as smaller ones.

Map Ref. 3G

Prince Edward Theatre
Old Compton Street, W.1.
Tel: 01-437 6877
Tube: Piccadilly or Leicester Square.
Buses: 1, 14, 19, 22, 24, 29, 38.
Opened in 1930, this theatre was subsequently converted into a cabaret-restaurant called The London Casino. In 1946 it became a theatre once more but, eight years later it was converted into a cinema. Now it can be used as either a cinema or a theatre and is a very large, comfortable place.

Map Ref. 3G

Prince of Wales Theatre
Coventry Street, W.1.
Tel: 01-930 8681
Tube: Piccadilly Circus or Leicester Square.
Buses: 3, 6, 9, 12, 13, 14, 15, 19, 22, 25, 38, 39, 53, 59, 88, 159.
With a capacity of over a thousand, this theatre tends to specialise in good, sound family entertainment and jolly shows. Originally called the Prince's, the first theatre on this site was built in 1884, but in 1936 Robert Cromie redesigned the theatre on clean, simple lines. Many musicals, like *Sweet Charity, Funny Girl* and *Promises, Promises* were first presented here.
Map Ref. 3G

Queen's Theatre
Shaftesbury Avenue, W.1.
Tel: 01-734 1166
Tube: Piccadilly Circus.
Buses: 14, 19, 22, 38.
Originally built in 1907, this theatre was partially bombed during the war and in the late fifties Sir Hugh Casson was asked to design a new, exciting exterior. The actual theatre, however, still retains some of its original features. It holds around a thousand people and generally shows good, middle-of-the-road plays like *Conduct Unbecoming* and *Private Lives* though it has shown some musicals notably *Stop the World, I Want to Get Off.*
Map Ref. 3G

The Royal Court Theatre
Sloane Square, S.W.1.
Tel: 01-730 1745
Tube: Sloane Square.
Buses: 11, 19, 22, 137.
The Royal Court has always specialised in putting on new, and often controversial plays. The theatre was first known as The New Chelsea and was converted from a chapel. In 1870 the name was changed, but this theatre was demolished and the present building was opened in 1888. Bombed in 1940 it was renovated in 1952 and its name was made with John Osborne's *Look Back in Anger.*
Map Ref. 5F

Royalty Theatre
Portugal Street, W.C.2.
Tel: 01-405 8004
Tube: Holborn.
Buses: 1, 4, 6, 9, 11, 13, 15, 55, 68, 77, 170, 171, 172, 176, 188, 239, 501.
On the site of the original London Opera House which was opened in 1911, this building was opened in 1960 by Dame Edith Evans and is part of a huge office block. Holding nearly a thousand people on two levels it has excellent acoustics and sight lines. The proscenium arch is adjustable — a somewhat novel feature. It is sometimes used as a cinema.
Map Ref. 2H

St Martin's Theatre
West Street, Cambridge Circus, W.1.
Tel: 01-836 1443
Tube: Leicester Square.
Buses: 1, 14, 19, 22, 24, 29, 38.
Opened during the Great War and designed by William Sprague, this elegant theatre, holding just over five hundred people, now houses the long running play *The Mousetrap.* It has housed a number of distinguished productions and transfers, mostly light comedies.
Map Ref. 2H

Savoy Theatre
Savoy Court, W.C.2.
Tel: 01-836 8888
Tube: Covent Garden or Charing Cross.
Buses: 1, 6, 9, 11, 13, 15, 77, 170, 176.
The original theatre was opened in 1881 with Gilbert and Sullivan's *Patience* and the theatre was originally the home of the D'Oyly Carte Company. Designed by C. J. Phipps it was the first public building to have electric light and in 1929 the interior was re-designed by Basil Ionides. The theatre now houses plays, though in 1973, every one of Gilbert and Sullivan's operas was performed in the centenary celebrations for this famous duo.
Map Ref. 3H

Shaftesbury Theatre
Shaftesbury Avenue, W.C.2.
Tel: 01-836 6596
Tube: Tottenham Court Road or Holborn.
Buses: 1, 8, 14, 19, 22, 24, 25, 29, 38, 73, 176.
Opened as The Princess Theatre in 1911, this theatre has had a chequered career and has been closed more than once for repairs. It is a rich-looking theatre with seating for over a thousand people. It houses big musicals and was the London home of *Hair!*
Map Ref. 3G

Strand Theatre
Aldwych, W.C.2.
Tel: 01-836 2660
Tube: Covent Garden.
Buses: 1, 6, 9, 11, 13, 15, 77, 170, 176.
Opened in 1905 and known as The Waldorf until 1909, this is another theatre designed by William Sprague. The decor is in Louis XIV style and is very resplendent. It is noted for its long runs of comedies and farces, which delight audiences of up to 1082.
Map Ref. 3I

Theatre Royal, Drury Lane
Catherine Street, W.C.2.
Tel: 01-836 8108
Tube: Covent Garden.
Buses: 1, 4, 6, 9, 11, 13, 15, 55, 68, 77, 170, 172, 188, 239, 501.
Four theatres have been built on this site — the first in Restoration times, and always associated with the Royal Mistress, Nell Gwynne. One of the largest and most magnificent of London Theatres, the present theatre, holding well over two thousand people, was opened in 1912 with an address by Lord Byron! It houses large musicals like *My Fair Lady, Showboat, Cavalcade* and *A Chorus Line.*
Map Ref. 2H

Vaudeville Theatre
The Strand, W.C.2.
Tel: 01-836 9988
Tube: Trafalgar Square or Charing Cross.
Buses: 1, 6, 9, 11, 13, 15, 77, 170, 176.
Owned by Peter Saunders and prettily re-decorated in 1969, the original theatre was opened in 1870, the facade of the houses it replaced being kept. These were pulled down in 1891, and the whole theatre again re-constructed in 1926. Known for presenting good plays, its recent successes have been *Stevie, Move Over Mrs Markham?* and was the scene of that phenomenon *Salad Days!*
Map Ref. 3H

Victoria Palace Theatre
Victoria Street, S.W.1.
Tel: 01-834 1317
Tube: Victoria.
Buses: 2, 10, 11, 16, 24, 25, 29, 36, 38, 39, 52, 149, 181, 185, 500, 503, 506, 507, 509.
Originally The Royal Standard Music Hall, this site was bought in 1910 by Alfred Butt who got Frank Matcham to design this theatre which is typical of opulent style. It was the home of *The Crazy Gang,* and also of the *Black and White Minstrels,* during their seven-year popularity. Now it houses musicals and holds an audience of over fifteen hundred.
Map Ref. 4G

Westminster Theatre
Palace Street, Buckingham Palace Road, S.W.1.
Tel: 01-834 0283
Tube: Victoria.
Buses: 2, 10, 11, 16, 24, 25, 29, 36, 38, 39, 52, 149, 181, 185, 500, 503, 506, 507, 509.

Built as a cinema, this building was converted into a theatre in 1931 with spacious foyers and a restaurant. Originally known for avant-garde drama and verse plays it is now owned by Moral Re-Armament. Flora Robson was at one time associated with the Theatre and more recently *Joseph and the Amazing Technicolour Dreamcoat* was played here.

Map Ref. 4G

Whitehall Theatre
Whitehall, S.W.1.
Tel: 01-930 6692
Tube: Trafalgar Square.
Buses: 3, 11, 12, 24, 29, 39, 53, 59, 77, 77A, 77C, 88, 159, 169, 170.
Brian Rix popularised this 1930 theatre in the sixties with his Whitehall farces. It is a simple, uncluttered theatre where great attention was paid to concealed lighting to soften the effect. Now owned by Paul Raymond it houses his saucy, erotic productions.

Map Ref. 4H

Windmill Theatre
17 Great Windmill Street, W.1.
Tel: 01-437 6312
Tube: Piccadilly Circus.
Buses: 14, 19, 22, 38.
"We Never Close!" was the proud boast of this tiny theatre during the war when it featured its nude shows. Originally a windmill stood on this site, which gave the theatre its name! Opened in 1931, it became a cinema in the sixties. In 1974 Paul Raymond bought the lease and now runs erotic revues here.

Map Ref. 3G

Wyndham's Theatre
Charing Cross Road, W.C.2.
Tel: 01-836 3028
Tube: Leicester Square.
Buses: 1, 6, 9, 11, 13, 15, 77, 170, 176.
A small, intimate-feeling theatre, though it holds over seven hundred people, this is one of the loveliest with its pale blue, cream and gold decor. Built by Sprague for Charles Wyndham it remains as it was when it was opened in 1899. It has housed many successes including *The Prime of Miss Jean Brodie, Abelard and Heloise, Godspell* and *Once a Catholic.*

Map Ref. 3H

THE CLASSIC THEATRE

THE ROYAL SHAKESPEARE COMPANY

The Barbican, Silk Street, E.C.2.
Tel: 01-628 8795
Information: 01-628 9760/628 2295.
Tube: Barbican; Moorgate.
Buses: 4, 8, 9, 11, 21, 22, 25, 43, 76, 104, 133, 141, 214, 271.
Now the home of the Royal Shakespeare Company the Barbican Theatre is to be found on the 3rd Level (Stalls) 4th, 5th and 6th Level for Circles. The Theatre itself has a thrust stage and is very warm and intimate. No one is too far from the stage and the Stratford productions can be brought here intact. Stay to see the marvellous safety curtain. A must for all who are interested in serious theatre. Repertory is not all Shakespeare — modern plays, classics by other authors and musicals are given by the marvellous company.

Map Ref. 2K

The Pit
Tel: 01-628 8795
Tube and buses — as above.
The RSC's experimental Theatre which holds about 200 people where lesser known classics, new plays and Shakespeare is performed. The audience sits round the players who perform on the floor (no formal stage) but the work is fresh, vigorous and outstanding.

Map Ref. 2K

The Warehouse
41 Earlham Street, Covent Garden, W.C.2.
Tel: 01-836 6808
Tube: Covent Garden.
Buses: 1, 14, 19, 22, 24, 38, 176.
Situated in a Warehouse (hence its

name) this theatre was formerly occupied by the RSC, but now is under the auspices of the Albery family. The policy remains unchanged, however, and you find experimental productions of the classics featuring well-known actors and actresses, new plays and a general feeling of enthusiasm. You sit around the acting space and really feel an intimacy with the performers.

Map Ref.

THE NATIONAL THEATRE COMPANY

The National Theatre
Upper Ground, S.E.1.
Tel: 01-928 2252
Tube: Waterloo.
Buses: 1, 4, 68, 171, 176, 188, 239, 501, 502, 513.

There are three theatres in this complex, which was opened in 1976. Designed by Sir Denys Lasdun it includes bars, restaurants and terraces as well as all the backstage staff need in the way of workrooms. Each of the three auditoria has its own distinct atmosphere and tends to present different types of production. A resident repertory company is embellished with stars and the work is always interesting, sometimes controversial.

Map Ref. 31

The Olivier
Named after Lord Olivier who was the first director of the company, when it was housed in the Old Vic, this theatre has a thrust stage and immense depth. The seats rise up in tiers and slightly enfold the acting area. With lilac seats it presents a cool atmosphere, but the stage has an intimate effect, and is capable of many marvellous scenic diversities. It holds over fifteen hundred people and is especially good for Shakespearian productions.

The Lyttleton
The most conventional of the three theatres, the Lyttleton has a proscenium arch. With its concrete walls and amber coloured seats, this theatre is rather austere in appearance, but has excellent sight lines. Holding around nine hundred people, it too is capable of some effective scenic changes. It is called after the Lyttleton family who for many years campaigned rigorously for the cause of the National Theatre.

The Cottesloe
The smallest of the three theatres, the Cottesloe stages some of the most interesting work that is performed in the National, mainly new plays, or vast epics like *The Passion.* It is very adaptable with an auditorium that can be changed to make it possible to give conventional proscenium productions, theatre-in-the-round or promenade performances.

Tours
You can take a tour of the Theatres to see how they work behind the scenes — the tour lasts an hour and is at various times during the day, depending on performance times.

Exhibitions and Concerts
There are exhibitions which change regularly in the foyers. Admission is free and you do not have to be attending a performance to see them. Also every evening, around six thirty, there are free musical performances in the main foyer for anyone who cares to listen.

The Old Vic
Waterloo Road, S.E.1.
Tel: 01-928 7616
Tube: Waterloo.
Buses: 1, 4, 68, 171, 188, 239, 501, 502, 513.

At present, being re-decorated, this enchanting theatre is one of the most famous in London. It was here that the redoubtable Lilian Baylis started what has become the Royal Ballet, The English National Opera and The National Theatre. In fact, the National spent its first years here. Now the home of what was formerly the Prospect Company, the theatre carries on the policy of uncomplicated productions which also go on tour. It is markedly Victorian in character and holds over eight hundred people while still retaining a cosiness and intimacy.

Map Ref. 4I

The Young Vic
66 The Cut, S.E.1.
Tel: 01-928 6363
Tube: Waterloo.
Buses: 1, 4, 68, 171, 188, 239, 501, 513.
Once the National's experimental theatre, this vigorous theatre still carries out a policy of presenting mainly classic plays in a fresh and unconventional manner. A theatre-in-the-round with a capacity of four hundred and fifty, it appeals to mainly young audiences and is always full of life.

Map Ref. 4I

FRINGE THEATRES

Besides the West End Theatres there are also many small Fringe Theatres doing mainly new plays, though there are occasionally to be seen revivals of old plays. Often with first-rate actors and actresses, these theatres provide an exciting dimension to the London scene. Very informal and relaxed they are often worth a visit.

Action Space
16 Chenies Street, W.1.
Tel: 01-637 8270
Tube: Goodge Street.

Map Ref. 2G

Bush
Bush Hotel, Shepherd's Bush, W.12.
Tel: 01-743 3388
Tube: Shepherd's Bush.

No Map Ref.

Half Moon — Old Theatre
27 Alie Street, E.1.
Tel: 01-480 6465
Tube: Aldgate and Aldgate East.

Map Ref. 2L

Half Moon — New Theatre
213 Mile End Road, E.1.
Tel: 01-480 6455
Tube: Stepney Green.

No Map Ref.

King's Head
115 Upper Street, N.1.
Tel: 01-226 1916
Tube: Angel.

No Map Ref.

Lyric Studio
The Lyric Theatre, Hammersmith
Tel: 01-741 2311
Tube: Hammersmith.

No Map Ref.

Oval House
54 Kennington Oval, S.E.11.
Tel: 01-735 2786
Tube: Oval.

Map Ref. 6I

Orange Tree
45 Kew Road, Richmond.
Tel: 01-940 3633
Tube: Richmond.

No Map Ref.

Theatre Upstairs
Royal Court Theatre, Sloane Square, S.W.1.
Tel: 01-730 2554
Tube: Sloane Square.

Map Ref. 5F

Lyric Studio
Lyric Theatre, Hammersmith, S.W.6.
Tel: 01-741 2311
Tube: Hammersmith.
Map Ref. 6A

Shaw
100 Euston Road, N.W.1.
Tel: 01-388 1394
Tube: Euston.
A very modern theatre that has no consistent policy, but often you find an interesting production with a name there.
Map Ref. 1H

Soho Poly
16 Riding House Street, W.1.
Tel: 01-636 9050.
Tube: Oxford Circus.
Map Ref. 2G

THEATRE OUT OF TOWN

There are several theatres on the outskirts of the West End which are well worth a visit both for the standard of performances and for architectural interest. Most are served by the Tube or British Rail and have great character.

Theatre on the Green
Richmond, Surrey.
Tel: 01-940 0088
Tube: Richmond.
One of Frank Matcham's beautiful theatres, Richmond has pre-West End plays, first class tours and, at Christmas, a traditional pantomime.
No Map Ref.

Greenwich
Crooms Hill, S.E.10.
Tel: 01-858 7755
Train: British Rail Southern to Greenwich.
A modern theatre which does revivals of classics and new plays. Nearly always a star appearing in an unusual part. Rather stark architecturally, but worth a visit.
No Map Ref.

Hampstead
Swiss Cottage Centre, N.W.3.
Tel: 01-722 9301
Tube: Swiss Cottage.
A tiny theatre which puts on new plays, many of which are transferred.
No Map Ref.

Round House
Chalk Farm Road, N.W.1.
Tel: 01-267 2564
Tube: Chalk Farm.
A theatre-in-the-round built in an old railway shed, there is always something fascinating going on here. Visiting companies from abroad, from the provinces, music, dance, you name it, it happens at the Round House.
No Map Ref.

Lyric, Hammersmith
King Street, W.6.
Tel: 01-741 2311
Tube: Hammersmith.
Once a pretty Victorian theatre in Hammersmith Market, this theatre was pulled down, but the auditorium, by Matcham, was kept and restored in a modern office block. Does both classic and modern plays as well as revivals, often with star casts.
Map Ref. 6A

Riverside, Hammersmith
Crisp Road, W.6.
Tel: 01-748 3354
Tube: Hammersmith Broadway.
A studio theatre which has always something fresh and interesting to offer in the way of a classic revival or new play, or a visiting company.
No Map Ref.

For your further information
The history of the London Theatres is immensely interesting and if you want to know more about them, we recommend *The Theatres of London* by Raymond Mander and Joe Mitchenson: also handy is *The London Theatre Scene* by Frank Cook.
No Map Ref.

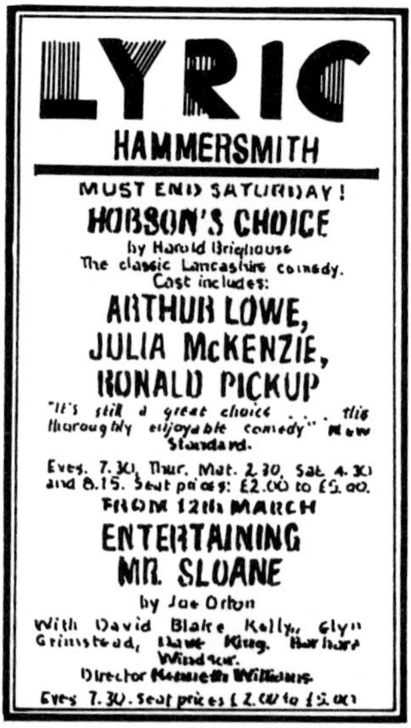

OPERA AND BALLET

London is well-endowed with opera and ballet — indeed the **Royal Ballet** is, some might say, the greatest ballet company in the world. There are no less then three houses where you can see opera and/or ballet. Except on Gala nights, when black tie and long dresses are a must, people dress nicely but not extravagantly at performances. Tickets vary greatly in price, particularly for opera, where visiting singers can put prices up to £30 in the stalls. But take heart, there are always cheaper seats available!

The Royal Opera House Covent Garden
Bow Street, W.C.2.
Tel: 01-240 1066
Tube: Covent Garden
Buses: 1, 4, 6, 9, 11, 13, 15, 68, 77, 170, 171, 172, 176, 188, 196, 239, 501, 502, 505, 513.
The first theatre on this site was built in 1732 and was one of the theatres to hold the Royal Patent. Destroyed by fire, as was the second theatre, the present building, designed by Sir Edward Barry was opened in 1858. The horseshoe shaped auditorium in red, gold and cream with cosy little boxes as well as circles is a fine example of Victorian theatre architecture and decoration. Queen Victoria's profile adorns the proscenium and there are comfortable bars and great elegance in the surroundings.

Map Ref. 3H

The Royal Opera House is the home of the **Royal Ballet** and the **Royal Opera** and the two companies alternate in repertoire. The Box Office is in Floral Street, alongside the theatre and for seat availability you can ring 01-240 1911 — a recorded information service. 55 rear amphitheatre seats are on sale every morning, together with any seats available in other parts of the house. Prices range from £1 to £13 for Ballet and from £2 to £30 for Opera. The unreserved seats sold on the day are from £2.50 to £6.50 depending on who is performing. The Opera House is generally shut during most of August and September.

The Coliseum
St. Martin's Lane, W.C.2.
Tel: 01-836 3161
Tube: Leicester Square or Trafalgar Square.
Buses: 1, 24, 29, 176.
This Theatre is now the home of the **English National Opera** which sings the operatic repertoire in English. A very grand theatre designed by the inimitable Frank Matcham it opened in 1904 and was the scene of many an illustrious ballet (including Diaghilev's), opera and musicals. It has the largest proscenium arch in London and in 1968 it became the permanent home of the then **Sadler's Wells Opera Company** which changed its name to the present one in 1974. The company is in residence for most of the year. In the summer generally, the London Festival Ballet, foreign ballet companies, and Nureyev seasons take place.
Operas are played in repertoire and enquiries can be made on 836 0111 and recorded information can be obtained on 836 7666. Seat prices are from £1.50 (£1.80 on Saturdays) to £10.30 (£11.30 on Saturdays).
The Theatre also runs a **Friends of the English National Opera Society** which holds lectures, master classes and parties. For details apply to the theatre.

Map Ref. 3H

Sadler's Wells Theatre
Rosebery Avenue, E.C.1.
Tel: 01-837 1672
Tube: Angel, Islington.
Buses: 19, 38, 172.
After the performance there is a special bus that runs to most main line stations.
There really was a well at Sadler's Wells at one time famous for their curative powers! And there has been a theatre on this site since the seventeenth century. However, the present theatre was built by the redoubtable Lilian Baylis from subscriptions she had raised. It was the North London Counterpart to the famous Old Vic and was to house the Opera and Ballet Companies she had built up. Nowadays, Sadler's Wells is host theatre to the touring section of the **Royal Ballet** and a number of foreign opera and ballet companies, as well as ethnic dancers. There is always something interesting going on here and the ticket prices are below West End prices. For repertoire, apply to the theatre.

The **London Festival Ballet** unfortunately has not a permanent theatre. It spends half its time on tour and the rest of the time in London either at the Festival Hall (in August and at Christmas time), at the Coliseum or in the Dominium Cinema. It is a very good company doing most of the classics and much of the Diaghilev repertoire. For details ring 581 1245.

CONCERT HALLS

It was once said, unfairly, that England was a land without music. Nowadays that remark is completely untrue. Every night of the week you will find really fine concerts going on in the capital. Whatever your musical taste you can find a concert in that style. Here we give you the principal places where music is being made.

CLASSICAL
Royal Albert Hall
Kensington Gore, S.W.7.
Tel: 01-589 8212
Tube: Kensington High Street.
Erected in memory of the Prince Consort this enormous hall, seating well over five thousand people is where the famous BBC/Henry Wood Promenade Concerts take place each summer. During the rest of the year you may find anything from sport to Sibelius here!
Opened in 1871 the building has many fine architectural features, notably the frieze which depicts the progress of the arts and which decorates the outside of the building. Inside is a cosy amalgam of little boxes, spacious stalls (removed during the Proms) and balconies. The Great Organ is one of the finest in the world and the whole place has a greatness and uniqueness that is rarely found in concert halls.
Map Ref. 4D

SOUTH BANK CONCERT HALLS
comprising **The Festival Hall, Queen Elizabeth Hall** and **The Purcell Room**
Belvedere Road, S.E.1.
Tel: 01-928 3191
Tube: Waterloo.
This was once one of the most controversial buildings in London, but time has mellowed both the controversy and the starkness of the

architecture! Opened for the Festival of Britain in 1951 the main hall is acoustically very fine and has an auditorium which seats nearly three thousand people. The platform can be raised to three different levels and a proscenium arch can also be fitted when ballet performances take place.

Queen Elizabeth Hall
Seating over one thousand people, the Queen Elizabeth Hall holds mainly small orchestral concerts and chamber music recitals in its elegant surroundings. The platform, a modular one, can be arranged in no fewer than thirteen different positions. It was opened in 1967.

The Purcell Room
This is a very small, intimate room, holding between three hundred and four hundred people and is devoted to recitals by solo artists and chamber music. Sometimes you will also find poetry readings here.

Wigmore Hall
36 Wigmore Street, W.1.
Tel: 01-935 2141
Tube: Oxford Circus.
Principally used for recitals and chamber music concerts, this magnificent Hall with its marble and alabaster is very lovely to look at — and its acoustics are good too! Originally built by Frederick Bechstein, opened in 1901 as the Bechstein Hall, it changed its name in 1917 and the lease is now owned by the Arts Council.
Map Ref. 2F

St John's Smith Square
Smith Square, S.W.1.
Tel: 01-222 1061
Tube: Westminster or St James's.
This concert hall was reconstructed from a bombed Church and provides an elegant centre for music. It is from here that the BBC's Monday lunchtime concerts are broadcast. These are other lunchtime concerts as well as evening ones.
Map Ref. 4H

Fairfield Hall
Croydon, Surrey.
Tel: 01-688 9291
BR Station: East Croydon.
Although a little way out of London this hall presents some very good concerts of a high standard.
No Map Ref.

JAZZ AND POP
The following places have good pop and jazz concerts — for programmes and activities ring the numbers given.

Marquee
90 Wardour Street, W.1.
Tel: 01-437 6603
Tube: Piccadilly.
Map Ref. 2G

100 Club
100 Oxford Street, W.1.
Tel: 01-636 0933
Tube: Tottenham Court Road.
Map Ref. 2G

Rainbow
232 Seven Sisters Road, N.4.
Tel: 01-263 3148
Tube: Finsbury Park.
No Map Ref.

Rock Garden
67 The Piazza, Covent Garden, W.C.2.
Tel: 01-240 3961
Tube: Covent Garden.
Map Ref. 3H

Ronnie Scott's
47 Frith Street, W.1.
Tel: 01-737 4239
Tube: Leicester Square.
Map Ref. 2G

CINEMAS

ABC Shaftesbury Avenue
Shaftesbury Avenue, W.1.
Tel: 01-836 8861.
Tube: Leicester Square.
Map Ref. 3G

Biograph
47 Wilton Road, S.W.1.
Tel: 01-834 1624
Tube: Victoria.
Map Ref. 5G

Cinecenta
Piccadilly, W.1.
Tel: 01-427 3561
Tube: Piccadilly.
Map Ref. 3G

Cinecenta
Panton Street, S.W.1.
Tel: 01-930 0631
Tube: Piccadilly.
Map Ref. 3G

Classic Cinema, Chelsea
279 King's Road, S.W.3.
Tel: 01-352 5096
Tube: Sloane Square.
Map Ref. 6D

Classic, Haymarket
Haymarket, S.W.1.
Tel: 01-839 1527
Tube: Piccadilly.
Map Ref. 3G

Classic, Leicester Square
35 Charing Cross Road, W.C.2.
Tel: 01-930 6915
Tube: Leicester Square.
Map Ref. 3H

Classic, Oxford Street
Oxford Street, W.1.
Tel: 01-636 0310
Tube: Tottenham Court Road.
Map Ref. 2G

Classic
5a Praed Street, Paddington, W.2.
Tel: 01-723 5716
Tube: Paddington.
Map Ref. 2E

Columbia
Shaftesbury Avenue, W.C.2.
Tel: 01-734 5414.
Tube: Leicester Square.
Map Ref. 3G

Dominion
Tottenham Court Road, W.C.1.
Tel: 01-580 9562
Tube: Tottenham Court Road.
Map Ref. 2H

Empire
Leicester Square, W.C.2.
Tel: 01-437 1234
Tube: Leicester Square.
Map Ref. 3H

Eros Cinema
Piccadilly Circus, W.1.
Tel: 01-437 4815
Tube: Piccadilly.
Map Ref. 3G

Filmcenta Cinema
Charing Cross Road, W.C.2.
Tel: 01-437 4815
Tube: Leicester Square.
Map Ref. 3H

Gala Royal
Marble Arch, W.2.
Tel: 01-262 2345
Tube: Edgware Road.
Arabic films only.
Map Ref. 2E

Jacey
Trafalgar Square, W.C.2.
Tel: 01-930 1143
Tube: Charing Cross.
Map Ref. 3H

Leicester Square Theatre
Leicester Square, W.C.2.
Tel: 01-930 5252
Tube: Leicester Square.
Map Ref. 3H

Liberty
Edgware Road, W.1.
Tel: 01-262 2680
Tube: Edgware Road.
Films in Hindi.
Map Ref. 2E

Londoner
Old Compton St, W.1.
Tel: 01-437 4555
Tube: Piccadilly.
Map Ref. 3G

London Pavillion
Piccadilly W.1.
Tel: 01-437 2982
Tube: Piccadilly.
Map Ref. 3G

Moulin Cinema Complex
Great Windmill Street, W.1.
Tel: 01-437 1653
Tube: Piccadilly.
Map Ref. 3G

Odeon
Haymarket, W.1.
Tel: 01-930 2738
Tube: Piccadilly.
Map Ref. 3G

Odeon
High Street, Kensington, W.8.
Tel: 01-602 6644
Tube: High Street, Kensington.
Map Ref. 5B

Odeon
Leicester Square, W.C.2.
Tel: 01-930 6111
Tube: Leicester Square.
Map Ref. 3H

Odeon
Marble Arch, W.1.
Tel: 01-262 8941
Tube: Marble Arch.
Map Ref. 2E

Odeon
St Martin's Lane, W.1.
Tel: 01-836 0691
Tube: Leicester Square.
Map Ref. 3H

Plaza
Lower Regent Street, W.1.
Tel: 01-437 1234.
Tube: Piccadilly.
Map Ref. 3G

Prince Charles
Leicester Place, W.C.2.
Tel: 01-437 7003
Tube: Piccadilly.
Map Ref. 3H

Rialto
3 Coventry Street, W.1.
Tel: 01-437 3488
Tube: Piccadilly.
Map Ref. 3H

Ritz
Leicester Square, W.C.2.
Tel: 01-437 1234
Tube: Piccadilly.
Map Ref. 3H

Scenes 1, 2, 3, 4
Swiss Centre,
Leicester Square, W.C.2.
Tel: 01-439 4446
Tube: Leicester Square.
Map Ref. 3H

Sherlock Holmes Centre
96 Baker Street, W.1.
Tel: 01-935 2772
Tube: Baker Street.
Map Ref. 2F

Soho Cinema
Brewer Street, W.1.
Tel: 01-734 4205
Tube: Piccadilly.
Map Ref. 3G

Studios 1, 2, 3, 4
225 Oxford Street, W.1.
Tel: 01-437 3300
Tube: Oxford Circus.
Map Ref. 2G

Warner West End
Leicester Square, W.1.
Tel: 01-439 0791
Tube: Leicester Square.
Map Ref. 3H

SPECIALIST, CLUBS AND SOCIETIES

Academy
Oxford Street, W.1.
Tube: Oxford Street.

Academy One
Tel: 01-437 2981

Academy Two
Tel: 01-437 5129

Academy Three
Tel: 01-437 8819
Specialises in Continental Films
Map Ref. 2G

Curzon
Curzon Street, W.1.
Tel: 01-499 3737
Tube: Green Park.
Continental or classic films.
Map Ref. 3F

Electric Cinema Club
191 Portobello Road, W.11.
Tel: 01-727 4992
Club membership 30p.
Different programme every day of old, interesting films.
Map Ref. 3B

Everyman
Holly Bush Vale, Hampstead, N.W.3.
Tel: 01-435 1525
Tube: Hampstead.
Old classic films.
No Map Ref.

Gate Mayfair
Mayfair Hotel, W.1.
Tel: 01-493 2031
Tube: Green Park.
Club membership 50p.
Map Ref. 3G

Gate Cinema
Notting Hill Gate, W.11.
Tel: 01-221 0220
Tube: Notting Hill Gate.
Foreign, classic and unusual films.
Map Ref. 3B

Gate 2
Brunswick Square, W.C.1.
Tel: 01-837 8402
Tube: Russell Square.
Map Ref. 1H

Gate 3
Parkway N.W.1.
Tel: 01-267 1201
Tube: Camden Town.
No Map Ref.

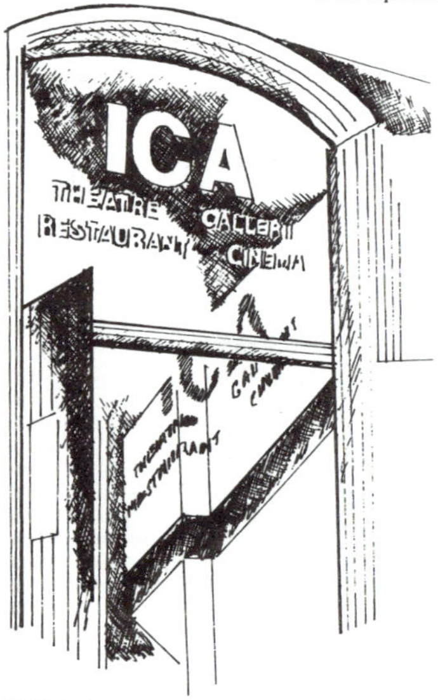

ICA Cinema
Nash House, The Mall, S.W.1.
Tel: 01-930 3647
Tube: Charing Cross.
Map Ref. 4G

Minema
Knightsbridge S.W.1.
Tel: 01-235 4225
Tube: Hyde Park or Knightsbridge.
Map Ref. 4F

National Film Theatre
South Bank, E.1. Tel: 01-928 3232
Tube: Waterloo.
Full membership £8. Temporary membership (one week) 30p.
A club with bars and restaurants which shows the best in cinema.
Map Ref. 4I

Paris Pullman
Drayton Gardens, S.W.10.
Tel: 01-373 5898
Tube: South Kensington.
Map Ref. 5D

Scala 25
Tottenham Court Road, W.1.
Tel: 01-637 9309
Tube: Goodge Street.
Membership 30p.
Map Ref. 2G

Screen on the Green
Islington, N.1. Tel: 01-226 3502
Tube: Angel.
No Map Ref.

Screen on the Hill
203 Haverstock Hill, N.W.3.
Tel: 01-435 3366
Tube: Belsize Park.
No Map Ref.

TELEVISION AND RADIO

At the present time there are three Television Stations in the London area, *BBC 1, BBC 2,* and *ITV*. The content of *BBC 1* and *ITV* is very similar in so far as they show a mixture of comedy, sport, old films, and drama programmes made for TV. The difference between them is that *ITV* is a commercial programme and consequently there are 'breaks' for advertisements. *BBC 2* is perhaps the channel with more serious content in its programmes and again there are no advertisements. They start at about mid-day (earlier at weekends) and finish approximately at midnight depending on the programme content. The main Radio Stations are *Radio 1, Radio 2, Radio 3, Radio 4, Radio London, Capital Radio, LBC* and *Radio Luxembourg*. All are commercial stations except for *Radio 1, Radio 2, Radio 3* and *Radio 4*.
Radio 3 mostly plays classical music and *Radio 4* and *LBC* are talk stations including lengthy news coverage and radio drama.
For programme times and selections for both television and radio it is best to check with a daily newspaper.

OUTDOOR SUMMER CONCERTS

There is a good variety of outdoor music in London during the summer months, from lunchtime band performances in the gardens and parks to country dancing. Many of the performances are free.
The following are some of the parks and gardens which have regular military and brass band performances in fine weather.

St. James Park, S.W.1.
Weekdays 12.30 pm and 5.30 pm.
Map Ref. 4G

Hyde Park, W.2.
Sundays 3.00 pm and 6.30 pm.
Map Ref. 3E

Regents Park, N.W.1.
Weekdays and Weekends 3.00 pm and 6.30 pm.
Map Ref. 1F

Victoria Embankment Gardens, W.C.2.
Weekdays 12.30 pm and 7.00 pm.
Weekends 3.00pm and 5.00pm.
Map Ref. 3I

Lincoln's Inn Fields, W.C.2.
Tuesdays and Thursdays 12.30 pm.
Map Ref. 3I

Paternoster Square, E.C.4.
Alternative Thursdays 12.00 pm.
Map Ref. 2J

St. Pauls Step, E.C.4.
Alternative Thursdays 12.30 pm.
Map Ref. 2J

There are other performances in other parks and squares and for details of these telephone or call at:
The Parks Department
Greater London Council,
Room 89,
County Hall, S.E.1.
Tel: 01-633 1707
Map Ref. 4H

London night life

LONDON NIGHT LIFE

NIGHT CLUBS

Apart from the fact that they are more expensive than ordinary restaurants the leading London night clubs have a very good reputation for fairness. The cost is clearly laid out on the menu and you will see what the VAT and service charge will be.
Most London night clubs employ hostesses whose job it is to boost the sale of drinks, but you do not have to have their company. If you do then you will have to pay them separately.
The following is a selection of those clubs where you can see a cabaret show and between dinner courses, dance. Prices are approximate and are for dinner for one including service and VAT, without wine. It is important to telephone and make a reservation. All clubs are closed on Sundays except where stated.

Eve Club
189 Regent Street, W.1.
Tel: 01-734 0879/0557
Major Credit Cards.
Approximate Cost £20.
Two lavish all-girl floor shows nightly at 10.45 pm and 1.45 am. French cuisine. Dancing to live music and dancing partners if required. Entrance fee is £3. Closes 3.30am.
Membership £5 but overseas visitors £1 on passport presentation.
Jacket and Tie.
Map Ref. 2G

L'Hirondelle
Swallow Street, W.1.
Tel: 01-734 6666/1511
Major Credit Cards.
Approximate Cost £20.
Small, but dazzling and sophisticated with superb menu and cabaret.
Dancing to two bands and two cabarets at 11.00 pm and 1.30 am.
International food and dancing/dining partners are available.
No Membership Fee. No Entrance Fee.
Non-diners £4.75 cover charge.
Jacket and Tie.
Map Ref. 3G

Stork
99 Regent Street, W.1.
Tel: 01-734 3686
Major Credit Cards.
Approximate Cost £20.
Intimate and relaxed, it has built up a

good reputation over 25 years.
Dancing to live bands and two cabarets at 11.45 pm and 1.45 am.
Basically English food and dancing/dining partners available. No Membership Fee. Entrance Fee £3.00.
OPEN on Sunday.
Map Ref. 3G

The Office
16 Avery Row, W.1.
Tel: 01-499 6728
Major Credit Cards.
Approximate Cost £15.
Private club admitting members only which has a restful cocktail bar and lounge. Dining room specialises in steaks and grills, dancing to live band and charming dancing partners are available. Cabaret at midnight.
Membership £10.80 per annum for U.K. residents and £5.40 for overseas residents.
Closed Saturday and Sunday.
Jacket and tie.
Map Ref. 2F

A B C D E F G H I J K L
1 2 3 4 5 6
Kensal Green
KILBURN LANE
HARROW ROAD
Maida Vale
MAIDA VALE
CASTELLAIN RD.
ELGIN AVENUE
FERNHEAD RD.
GREAT WESTERN RD.
Westbourne Park
Ladbroke Grove
LADBROKE GROVE
WESTBOURNE PARK
TALBOT ROAD
CHEPSTOW RD.
COLVILLE TER.
WESTBOURNE GROVE
BLENHEIM CRES.
CLARENDON RD.
ELGIN CRES.
BISHOPS BRIDGE ROAD
PEMBRIDGE RD.
Bayswater
QUEENSWAY
Queensway
BAYSWATER ROAD
Notting Hill Gate
NOTTING HILL GATE
PORTLAND ROAD
HOLLAND PARK AVENUE
Holland Park
HOLLAND PARK
CAMPDEN HILL RD.
KENSINGTON CHURCH ST.
KENSINGTON HIGH STREET
High Street Kensington
HOLLAND ROAD
EARLS COURT ROAD
HAMMERSMITH ROAD
WARWICK ROAD
WEST CROMWELL ROAD
Earls Court
NORTH END ROAD
TALGARTH ROAD
SHEPHERDS BUSH RD
FULHAM PALACE ROAD
LILLIE ROAD
West Brompton
REDCLIFF GARDENS
FULHAM ROAD
KING'S ROAD
CLIFTON GDNS.
Warwick Avenue
EDGWARE ROAD
ST. JOHN'S WOOD RD.
LISSON GROVE
WELLINGTON ROAD
PADDINGTON STATION
WESTBOURNE TER.
Lancaster Gate
KENSINGTON GARDENS
SERPENTINE
HYDE PARK
ROTTEN ROW
KENSINGTON RD.
QUEEN'S GATE
EXHIBITION ROAD
South Kensington
CROMWELL ROAD
Gloucester Road
OLD BROMPTON ROAD
SYDNEY ST.
Marylebone
Edgware Road
SEYMOUR PLACE
PORTMAN SQUARE
Marble Arch
Marble Arch
GROSVENOR SQUARE
PARK LANE
REGENT'S PARK
Baker Street
BAKER STREET
MARYLEBONE ROAD
MARYLEBONE HIGH ST.
Regent's Park
Great Portland Street
ALBANY STREET
EUSTON STATION
EUSTON ROAD
Warren Street
Goodge Street
PORTLAND PL.
OXFORD STREET
Oxford Circus
REGENT ST.
Bond Street
NEW BOND ST.
OLD BOND ST.
BERKELEY SQUARE
CURZON ST.
PICCADILLY
Hyde Park Corner
Green Park
GREEN PARK
KNIGHTSBRIDGE
Knightsbridge
BELGRAVE SQUARE
GROSVENOR PL.
BEAUCHAMP PLACE
CADOGAN GDNS.
WALTON RD.
BROMPTON ROAD
SLOANE STREET
Sloane Square
KING'S ROAD
BUCKINGHAM PALACE ROAD
CHELSEA BRIDGE RD.
ROYAL HOSPITAL ROAD
CHELSEA EMBANKMENT
CHELSEA BRIDGE
ALBERT BRIDGE
BATTERSEA PARK
VICTORIA STATION
Pimlico
GROSVENOR ROAD
VAUXHALL BRIDGE ROAD
VICTORIA STREET
St James's Park
BIRDCAGE WALK
ST. JAMES'S PARK
THE MALL
PALL MALL
Piccadilly Circus
SHAFTESBURY AV.
POLAND ST.
WARDOUR ST.
Tottenham Court Rd.
GOODGE ST.
TOTTENHAM COURT RD.
GOWER STREET
CHARING CROSS ROAD
NEW OXFORD STREET
Leicester Square
CHARING CROSS STATION
Covent Garden
LONG ACRE
DRURY LANE
SOUTHAMPTON ROW
GUILFORD ST.
GRAYS INN ROAD
THEOBALDS RD.
Holborn
HOLBORN
CHANCERY LANE
Chancery Lane
KING'S CROSS ROAD
ROSEBERRY AVENUE
CLERKEN WELL ROAD
FARRINGDON ST.
Aldwych
STRAND
Somerset House
Temple
EMBANKMENT
WATERLOO BRIDGE
Westminster
WESTMINSTER BRIDGE
VICTORIA
HORSEFERRY ROAD
MILL BANK
LAMBETH BRIDGE
RIVER THAMES
ALBERT EMBANKMENT
VAUXHALL BRIDGE
Vauxhall
HARLEYFORD RD.
NINE ELMS LANE
FENTIMAN RD.
Oval
Kennington Park
KENNINGTON ROAD
KENNINGTON PARK ROAD
LAMBETH PALACE RD.
LAMBETH ROAD
WESTMINSTER BRIDGE RD.
Lambeth North
WATERLOO STATION
WATERLOO ROAD
YORK ROAD
STAMFORD ST.
BLACKFRIARS BRIDGE
BLACKFRIARS RD.
Blackfriars
QUEEN VICTORIA ST.
Mansion House
LUDGATE HILL
FLEET ST.
HOLBORN VIA.
St Paul's
CHEAPSIDE
ALDERSGATE ST.
GOSWELL ROAD
CITY ROAD
OLD STREET
Old Street
Moorgate
MOORGATE
Bank
SOUTHWARK BRIDGE
SOUTHWARK STREET
SOUTHWARK BRIDGE RD.
BOROUGH RD.
LONDON RD.
ST. GEORGE'S RD.
Elephant and Castle
NEW KENT RD.
WALWORTH ROAD
NEWINGTON CAUSEWAY
Borough
BOROUGH HIGH ST.
GREAT DOVER ST.
LONG LANE
LONDON BRIDGE
Monument
Monument
LONDON BRI. STATION
ST. THOMAS ST.
TOOLEY STREET
TOWER BRIDGE
TOWER HILL
Tower Hill
FENCHURCH ST.
LEADENHALL ST.
MINORIES
Aldgate
BISHOPSGATE
HOUNDSDITCH
LIVERPOOL ST. STATION
GREAT EASTERN ST.
COMMERCIAL ST.
WHITECHAPEL
LEMAN ST.
EAST SMITHFIELD
HACKNEY ROAD
ABBEY STREET
OLD KENT ROAD
ALBANY ROAD

New Gaslight
4 Duke of York Street, S.W.1.
Tel: 01-439 7242 Daytime,
Tel: 01-930 1648 Night.
Major Credit Cards.
Approximate Cost £20.
Very elegant and plush with topless barmaids and friendly waitresses. Reasonable food and frequent cabaret spots throughout the evening. 2 bands. No Membership Fee for overseas or out of town visitors. Entrance Fee £5.75, refundable if dining before 9pm.
Jacket and Tie.
Map Ref. 3G

Bristol Suite
14 Bruton Place, W.1.
Tel: 01-402 5680
Major Credit Cards.
Approximate Cost £16.
Elegant club with nice soft atmosphere, resident pianist and gentle disco music of the '20's and '30's era. Dancing partners available and an excellent restaurant. There is a special temporary membership for overseas visitors.
Jacket and Tie.
Map Ref. 2F

The Georgian Club
4 Mill Street, W.1.
Tel: 01-629 2042
Major Credit Cards.
Approximate Cost £15.
An attractive club with a good international restaurant. Cabaret shows at 11.00pm, midnight and 12.30am. Resident band and dancing partners are available. Membership Fee £5 per year at door.
Jacket and Tie.
Map Ref. 3G

The London Room
Parker Street, W.C.2.
Tel: 01-831 8863.
Major Credit Cards.

Approximate Cost £32 approx.
Open six nights a week, there are good cabaret acts at 10.30pm, dancing and reasonable food. No Membership. No Entrance Fee.
Jacket and Tie.
Closed Sunday.
Map Ref. 2H

Boulogne
27 Gerrard Street, W.1.
Tel: 01-437 3815
Major Credit Cards.
Approximate Cost £40 inc. wine.
Established in 1852, the Edwardian decor is authentic. Good French food, dancing to live bands and cabaret at 11.30pm and 1.30am.
Dancing/dining partners available.
No Membership Fee. No Entrance Fee.
Jacket and Tie.
Closed Sunday.
Map Ref. 3G

Burlesque
14 Bruton Place, W.1.
Tel: 01-499 0938
Major Credit Cards.
Approximate Cost £50.
Dancing to live bands and continuous cabaret from 11.00pm to 2.30am. The food is French and Italian and there are dancing/dining partners available.
Membership Fee £50 per annum.
Entrance Fee £5 non members, £1 members.
Jacket and Tie.
Map Ref. 3F

Gargoyle Club
69 Dean Street, W.1.
Tel: 01-437 3278/6455
Major Credit Cards.
Approximate Cost £20.
A famous and respected strip club, with good English cooking and dancing to a live band. Strip cabaret at midnight and 1.15am.
No Membership Fee. No Entrance Fee.
Jacket and Tie.
Map Ref. 2G

Chaplins
9 Swallow Street, W.1.
Tel: 01-734 7447
Major Credit Cards.
Approximate Cost £20.
Unusual setting with the stage in the centre. Cabaret at midnight and dancing to a live band. English and French cuisine and dancing and dining partners available.
Entrance Fee £1. Gentlemen only.
Jacket and Tie.
Map Ref. 3G

Gallipolli
8 Bishopsgate Churchyard, E.C.2.
Tel: 01-588 1922
Major Credit Cards.
Approximate Cost £29.
Turkish decor, and Arabian nights atmosphere, there is dancing to live bands. Belly dance cabaret at 10.30pm. Dancing partners available and the food is Turkish and Continental.
No Membership Fee. No Entrance Fee.
Jacket and Tie.
Open for lunch Monday-Friday.
Closed Sunday.
Map Ref.

New Twilight
124 Charing Cross Road, W.C.2.
Tel: 01-836 2141
Major Credit Cards.
Approximate Cost £20.
New nightclub with a friendly, restful setting and a first class restaurant. Dancing to live music and an exotic cabaret every thirty minutes. Dancing partners available.
No Membership. Entrance Fee £5.
Jacket and Tie.
Map Ref. 2H

Empress Yildizlar
16 Berkeley Street, W.1.
Tel: 01-629 6126
Major Credit Cards.
Approximate Cost £40.
A very elegant and plush nightclub, which serves excellent cuisine. Dancing to a live band, non-stop cabaret from 12.00-6.00am.
No Membership. No Entrance Fee but cover charge of £10-£20.
Jacket and Tie.
Map Ref. 3G

DINNER DANCING

The following restaurants have been selected to give a good cross section both in price and in ambience. They differ from the Night Clubs insofar as they do not offer a floor show or cabaret, although some do have wandering players amongst the diners. Whilst not compulsory in some of the restaurants, it is advisable to wear a jacket and tie and if uncertain check when making your reservation. IT IS ESSENTIAL TO TELEPHONE TO RESERVE A TABLE.
Prices are approximate and are for dinner for one without wine.
All restaurants are closed on Sunday except where stated.

Barbarella
428 Fulham Road, S.W.6.
Tel: 01-385 9434
Major Credit Cards.
Approximate Cost £30.
Happy, Italian style restaurant serving good food in subdued surroundings. Separate area for dancing to latest disco music.
Jacket and Tie.
Map Ref. 6C

Barbarella 2
43 Thurloe Street, S.W.7.
Tel: 01-584 2000
Major Credit Cards.
Approximate Cost £30.
Like its sister restaurant this one is also full of Italian bustle. A smart restaurant with mirrored alcoves and a dance floor with disco music.
Jacket and Tie.
Closed Sunday.
Map Ref. 5D

Beachcomber
Mayfair Hotel, Berkeley Street, W.1.
Tel: 01-629 7777
Major Credit Cards.
Approximate Cost £25.
Part of the Mayfair Hotel, this long-established basement restaurant has Polynesian style decor, rock pools and alligators. International menu and dancing to two live bands.
Jacket and Tie.
Open for Lunch (except Saturday).
Closed Sunday.
Map Ref. 3G

Bizzarro
18 Craven Road, W.2.
Tel: 01-723 6029
Major Credit Cards.
Approximate Cost £25.
Italian restaurant serving appetising dishes with fresh vegetables. Dancing downstairs. Friendly service, very popular.
Closed Saturday Lunch and Sunday.
Map Ref. 3C

China Garden
66 Brewer Street, W.1.
Tel: 01-437 6500
Major Credit Cards.
Approximate Cost £15.
Very popular Chinese Restaurant which specialises in large prawns and Peking duck. Dancing in the basement.
Map Ref. 3G

Concordia Notte
29 Craven Road, W.2.
Tel: 01-402 4985
Major Credit Cards.
Approximate Cost £35.
Sumptuous decor, good dancing space, this Italian restaurant is really lively and well known celebrities are often seen here. Excellent food.
Closed Sunday.
Map Ref. 3C

The Dock
Corner of Ladbroke Grove and Kensal Road, W.10.
Tel: 01-960 5456
Approximate Cost £20.
Overlooking its own harbour, this inexpensive restaurant offers dancing both to disco and live music.
Map Ref. 1A

Dorchester Hotel
Park Lane, W.1.
Tel: 01-629 8888
Major Credit Cards.
Approximate Cost £20.
The Terrace Restaurant has long been famous for dinner dancing and it still maintains the impeccable standards of food and service with two live bands.
Jacket and Tie.
Map Ref. 3F

Hilton Hotel
Park Lane, W.1.
Tel: 01-493 8000
Major Credit Cards.
Approximate Cost £20.
The Roof Restaurant has a luxurious setting with marvellous views over London. International cuisine and dancing to two bands.
Jacket and Tie.
Map Ref. 3F

Inn on the Park
Hamilton Place, Park Lane, W.1.
Tel: 01-499 0888
Major Credit Cards.
Approximate Cost £20.

The Vintage Room restaurant has a night club atmosphere which stays open late. Superb food and dancing to a live band and to records.
Jacket and Tie.

Map Ref. 3F

Jager Hütte
42 Queensway, W.2.
Tel: 01-229 7941
Major Credit Cards.
Approximate Cost £15.
If you want to feel you are in Hungary then this is the place. Central European food and dancing to a full Gipsy band. Good fun and a place to let one's hair down.

Map Ref. 3C

La Bussola
St. Martins Lane, W.C.2.
Tel: 01-240 1148
Major Credit Cards.
Approximate Cost £50.
Deceptively large restaurant with privacy ensured by alcoved seating, white walls and a general impression of a well decorated cave. Good Italian food and dancing to two bands.

Map Ref. 3H

La Pergola
138 Cromwell Road, S.W.7.
Tel: 01-370 1363
Major Credit Cards.
Approximate Cost £15.
Nice atmosphere, good Italian food, and dancing to Latin American and Italian music.

Map Ref. 5C

Old Vienna
94 New Bond Street, W.1.
Tel: 01-629 8716
Major Credit Cards.
Approximate Cost £50.
Very enjoyable Austrian restaurant which serves excellent food and wine of the country. Service attentive, staff dressed in national costume, nice, small dance floor.
Jacket and Tie.

Map Ref. 2F

Royal Garden Hotel
Kensington Road, W.8.
Tel: 01-937 8000
Major Credit Cards.
Approximate Cost £60.
The Roof Restaurant has panoramic views across London and a particularly good one of Hyde Park and Kensington Palace Gardens. French cuisine and dancing to a live band.
Jacket and Tie.

Map Ref. 4C

Savoy Hotel
Strand, W.C.2.
Tel: 01-836 4363

Major Credit Cards.
Approximate Cost £20.
The River Restaurant of the Savoy has seen most of the famous names over the years and is one of the institutions of the London night scene. The cuisine is magnificent, the setting overlooking the river, pleasant, and the band just perfect for a memorable evening.
Jacket and Tie or Dinner Jacket.

Map Ref. 3H

Tiberio
22 Queen Street, W.1.
Tel: 01-629 3561
Major Credit Cards.
Approximate Cost £30.
Very good Italian restaurant with lovely decor and a small band to dance to after 11.00pm.
Jacket and Tie.

Map Ref. 3F

Tiddy Dols
2 Hertford Street, W.1.
Tel: 01-499 2357
Major Credit Cards.
Approximate Cost £15.
Situated in Shepherds Market, Mayfair, this is an original 18th Century house, with twisting staircases, oak beams and little rooms where one dines. Dancing to live music band and also disco music in one of the rooms, dining in any of the others. Lots of charm and atmosphere, with traditional English food. *Open on Sunday.*

Map Ref. 3F

Valencia
1 Empress Approach, Lillie Road, S.W.6.
Tel: 01-385 0039
Major Credit Cards.
Approximate Cost £30.
Spanish food, Spanish decor and even Spanish dancing, flamenco guitar, A lovely little restaurant where one dines by candlelight.
Set Price Menu £6.50.
Map Ref. 6B

Villa des Cesari
135 Grosvenor Road, S.W.1.
Tel: 01-828 7453
Major Credit Cards.
Approximate Cost £15.
Styled like and old Roman Villa and overlooking the Thames, romantic atmosphere. The waiters are in tunics and the menu has Roman names for the food. Nice live band for dancing.
Jacket and Tie.
Map Ref. 6G

DANCE HALLS

Dance halls in London are still places where you can find not only modern music to dance to, but also old fashioned ballroom dancing. They usually have different nights for each style of dancing so it is wise to telephone first to check what is happening.

Hammersmith Palais
274 Shepherds Bush Road, W.6.
Tel: 01-748 2812
Very famous and very large dance hall which is still extremely popular. No Membership Fee. Check times of opening beforehand.
Jacket and Tie.
Map Ref. 6A

Empire Ballroom
Leicester Square, W.C.2.
Tel: 01-437 1446
Disco dancing in this large dance hall. Small Membership Fee (paid at door).
Jacket and Tie, or Smart Casual.
Map Ref. 3H

Café de Paris
3 Coventry Street, W.1.
Tel: 01-437 2036
Large old-fashioned dance hall. No Membership Fee. Afternoons and Evenings.
Jacket and Tie.
Map Ref. 3H

The Lyceum
Wellington Street, Strand, W.C.2.
Tel: 01-836 3715
Friday and Saturday.
Jacket and Tie or Smart Casual.
Map Ref. 3H

DISCOTHEQUES

Discotheques have materialised within the last fifteen years in London taking over from the small groups who played in coffee bars. They cater mainly for the under 25's. Some have restaurants, some snacks only and most are licensed. Most charge an entrance fee.

Foobert's
Foubert's Place, W.1.
Tel: 01-734 3630
Modern discotheque with a restaurant and popular with overseas students.
No Membership Fee.
Open on Sunday. Admission before 9.00pm 50p £2-£3 after.
Map Ref. 2G

Café des Artistes
266 Fulham Road, S.W.10.
Tel: 01-352 6200
Large disco with a restaurant and a bar, open 8.00pm to 2.00am. No Membership Fee.
Open on Sunday.
Map Ref. 6D

Dingwalls
Camden Lock, Chalk Farm Road, N.W.1.
Tel: 01-267 4967
Live bands every night playing everything from jazz to soul, to rock and roll. Fully licensed bar serving half price drinks before 10.00pm.
Restaurant. No Membership Fee.
Open on Sunday.
Admission: £1.75-£3.50.
No Map Ref.

Reflections
Praed Street, W.2.
Tel: 01-262 7952
Fully licensed and snack meals. No Membership.
Closed on Sunday. Admission according to day, not more than £3.
Map Ref. 2E

Legends
29 Old Burlington Street, W.1.
Tel: 01-437 9933
Very popular club which has an excellent restaurant and a nice atmosphere. There's a good dance floor with loud disco music. Restaurant and bar open at lunchtimes as well as in the evenings.
Membership details given on application.
Open on Sunday.
Map Ref. 2G

Studio Valbonne
62 Kingly Street, W.1.
Tel: 01-439 7242
Elegant restaurant and discotheque. There is an excellent restaurant and a lively dance floor.
Membership £25 per annum for U.K. residents, but overseas visitors can pay £3 per visit. Entrance Fee £5.
Closed on Sunday.
Map Ref. 2G

Stringfellows
16 Upper St. Martins Lane, W.C.2.
Tel: 01-240 5534
New elegant discotheque for the over 25's, with glass dance floor, marvellous lighting effects and exotic murals. Live jazz groups upstairs and disco downstairs. Superb restaurant.
Membership Club, but non-members can pay Entrance Fee of £2, £4 and £6 depending on which day of the week they visit.
Closed on Sunday.
Map Ref. 2H

Gulliver's
11 Down Street, W.1.
Tel: 01-499 0760
Dancing to disco music and occasional live groups. Small but fun. Fully licensed.
No Membership. Entrance Fee £3.
Closed on Sunday.
Map Ref. 3F

Maximus
14 Leicester Square, W.C.2.
Tel: 01-734 4111
Popular discotheque which is crowded in the evenings. Fully licensed until closing time at 2.00am.
No Membership. Entrance Fee £3.
Open on Sunday.
Map Ref. 3H

Rock Garden
66 Piazza, Covent Garden, W.C.2.
Tel: 01-240 3961
Restaurant serving hamburgers with discotheque in the basement. No Membership Fee.
Map Ref. 3H

Samantha's
3 New Burlington Street, W.1.
Tel: 01-734 5425
A well known discotheque with live groups sometimes. Small but fun. Fully licensed. No Membership Fee.
Map Ref. 3G

Busby's
157 Charing Cross Road, W.C.2.
Tel: 01-734 6963
Vast place with a balcony overlooking the dance floor. Only open Friday and Saturday. Entrance Fee £4.
Map Ref. 2H

Thursdays
38 Kensington High Street, W.8.
Tel: 01-937 7744
A restaurant, four bars and a lively dance floor. Popular discotheque, but the wearing of jeans is banned. No Membership Fee. Closed on Sunday.
Map Ref. 5B

Tingles
Scarsdale Place, W.8.
Tel: 01-937 7211
Popular disco with a 'happy hour' between 5.30pm-7.00pm when spirits and cocktails are half price. Good restaurant. No jeans allowed, smart casual wear preferred.
No Membership.
Closed on Sunday.
Map Ref. 4C

The following discotheques are also always very popular but they are membership only. It is however sometimes possible for overseas visitors to obtain a temporary membership, so it is advisable to telephone and enquire first.

Annabel's
44 Berkeley Square, W.1.
Tel: 01-629 2350

Probably the most famous discotheque in the world, certainly the most difficult to obtain membership to. A lovely basement club serving excellent food in sumptuous surroundings. The acoustics are so good that you can barely hear the music when dining. Members only.

Map Ref. 3F

Tramps
40 Jermyn Street, S.W.1.
Tel: 01-734 3174
A younger version of Annabel's. Very loud and you will always see a selection of famous stars and personalities. Difficult to obtain admission without membership.

Map Ref. 3G

Saddle Room
1a Hamilton Mews, W.1.
Tel: 01-499 4994
Very long established and popular discotheque and restaurant. Membership £35 p.a. Temporary Membership for overseas visitors.

Map Ref. 3F

Maunkberry's
57 Jermyn Street, W.1.
Tel: 01-499 4623
Pleasant atmosphere, with loud music.
Closed Mondays.

Map Ref. 3G

Stocks
107 Kings Road, S.W.3.
Tel: 01-351 3461
Nice upstairs dining room serving good food, with a long bar. Good dance floor.
Membership £100 p.a. for Ladies, £150 p.a. for gentlemen. Special Monthly Membership for overseas visitors. Set Menu £14.

Map Ref. 4E

JAZZ CLUBS

Ronnie Scotts
47 Frith Street, W.1.
Tel: 01-439 0747
Marvellous Jazz Club usually with world famous performers. Good atmosphere, with restaurant and bar. Licensed to 3.00am. Check the weekly jazz listings in *Time Out* magazine or telephone the club to check who is playing. Admission Charge £6-£7 for non members.

Map Ref. 3G

100 Club
100 Oxford Street, W.1.
Tel: 01-636 0933
Informal and friendly club featuring mainly traditional and mainstream jazz. Admission Charge. Licensed bar.
Open on Sunday.

Map Ref. 2G

Pizza Express
10 Dean Street, W.1.
Tel: 01-439 8722
Situated beneath a pizza parlour this is a very pleasant club with big name attractions appearing frequently. Mostly mainstream. Restaurant licence means you must eat if you wish to drink alcohol. Admission Charge £3-£5.
Open on Sunday.

Map Ref. 2G

Pizza on the Park
11 Knightsbridge, S.W.1.
Tel: 01-235 5550
This little club features mainly duos, pianists and guitarists. Admission Charge. Licensed bar.
Closed on Sunday.

Map Ref. 4F

GAMING

Although all Gaming Clubs are membership clubs, most of them will give temporary membership to overseas visitors for a nominal entrance fee and production of a passport. The clubs usually open at lunchtime until 3.00am. Most have dining rooms and separate bars, but no alcohol may be served or drunk at the gaming tables. The clubs play all the known and well established gambling games. It is advisable to telephone prior to a visit to establish whether the club will accept temporary overseas visitors. It is also worth noting that there is a 48-hour wait between joining a club and being allowed to gamble, even on a temporary membership.

Aspinall's
1 Hans Street, S.W.1.
Tel: 01-235 2496
Very exclusive and small in a private house setting. Excellent restaurant.
Map Ref. 4E

Casanova
52 Grosvenor Street, W.1.
Tel: 01-629 1463
Nice atmosphere in this long established club. Good restaurant.
Map Ref. 3F

Clermont Club
44 Berkeley Street, W.1.
Tel: 01-439 5587
The more exclusive side of the Playboy Club which now owns it. Situated above Annabel's night club, it has an excellent restaurant and in the summer a terrace.
Map Ref. 3F

Knightsbridge Sporting Club
163 Knightsbridge, S.W.7.
Tel: 01-584 4252
Popular gaming club with a good restaurant.
Map Ref. 4E

Ritz Casino
Ritz Hotel, Piccadilly, W.1.
Tel: 01-491 4678
Really sumptuous surroundings in this new gaming club. Expensive but good food and wine.
Map Ref. 3G

The Sportsman
3 Tottenham Court Road, W.1.
Tel: 01-637 5464
Large gaming club with lots of tables, restaurant and bar.
Map Ref. 2G

STRIP CLUBS

Soho is the area of London where the strip clubs are situated and the unwary visitor needs to be very careful, as all the flashing neon signs and the hustlers' talk at the door doesn't necessarily mean that what you pay for you are going to see. The following list is of clubs which have been established for some time and offer good value shows.

Raymond Revuebar Theatre
Walkers Court, Brewer Street, W.1.
Tel: 01-734 1593
Major Credit Cards.
The art of strip at its best, well staged in a good theatre. Licensed bar. Shows at 7.00pm, 9.00pm and 11.00pm.
Map Ref. 3G

Pink Pussycat
10 Brewer Street, W.1.
Tel: 01-437 9439
Major Credit Cards.
Non-stop strip-cabaret, fully licensed bar and a restaurant which serves good food. Shows every thirty minutes.
Closed on Sunday.
Map Ref. 3G

Sunset Strip
30a Dean Street, W.1.
Tel: 01-437 7229
Major Credit Cards.
Good class strip shows in this fully air conditioned club.
Open 2.00pm to 11.00pm.
Closed Sunday
Entrance Fee £3.50.
Map Ref. 2G

Nell Gwynne
69 Dean Street, W.1.
Tel: 01-437 3278
Major Credit Cards.
Comfortable theatre with continuous strip shows from 6.00pm. Also a topless bar.
Map Ref. 2G

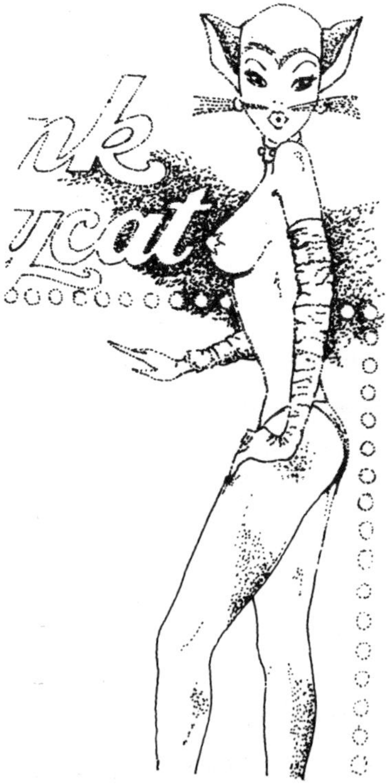

LATE NIGHT CIMEMAS

A number of cinemas show films late at night on Friday and Saturday nights starting at about 11pm and a list of these can be found in *Time Out* magazine, *Where to Go* magazine or the *New Standard*. The following cinemas show late night films every night. It is wise to telephone the cinema to check exact times.

Classic Leicester Square
Charing Cross Road, W.C.2.
Tel: 01-930 6915
All night shows.
Map Ref. 3H

Gate Cinema
Notting Hill Gate, W.11.
Tel: 01-727 5750
Late night every night.
Map Ref. 3B

Moulin Cinema Complex
Great Windmill Street, W.1.
Tel: 01-437 1653
Late night every night.
Map Ref. 3G

Eros
Piccadilly Circus, W.1.
Tel: 01-437 3839
Late night every night.
Map Ref. 3G

Gate 2
Brunswick Gardens, Nr. Russell Square, W.C.1.
Tel: 01-837 8402
Late night every night.
Map Ref. 1H

Paris Pullman
Drayton Gardens, S.W.10.
Tel: 01-373 5898
Late every night.
Map Ref. 5D

LATE NIGHT COFFEE BARS, CAFÉS AND TAKE AWAYS

Bamboo Kitchen
305 Kings Road, S.W.5.
Tel: 01-352 9281
Chinese take away.
Open to midnight weekdays and 1.00am on Friday and Saturday. Closed on Sunday.
Map Ref. 6D

Canton
11 Newport Place, W.1.
Tel: 01-437 6220
Chinese take away.
Open 24 hours every day. Open on Sunday.
Map Ref. 3G

Dunkin Donuts
2 Ludgate Circus Buildings, Farringdon Street, E.C.4.
American donuts.
Open to 1.30am weekdays.
Open to 7.00pm Sunday.
Map Ref. 2I

Elysee
13 Percy Street, W.1.
Tel: 01-636 4804
Greek food.
Open to 3.00am Monday to Saturday.
OPEN to 1.30am Sunday.
Map Ref. 2G

Far East Chinese Restaurant
13 Gerrard Street, W.1.
Tel: 01-437 6148
Chinese food and take away.
Open to 5.00am every night. OPEN on Sunday.
Map Ref. 3G

Ferrari's Restaurant
505 Central Market,
Farringdon Street, E.C.4.
Tel: 01-253 4190
Italian food.
Open 11.00pm to 4.00am Friday and Saturday only. Closed on Sunday.
Map Ref. 2J

Kentucky Fried Chicken
246 Old Brompton Road, S.W.5.
Tel: 01-370 3951
Map Ref. 4E

71 Gloucester Road, S.W.7.
Tel: 01-373 3951
Map Ref. 5D

116 Holland Park Avenue, W.11.
Tel: 01-229 6148
Map Ref. 4A

95 Westbourne Grove, W.2.
Tel: 01-229 6940
Map Ref. 2B

245 Kilburn High Road, N.W.6.
Tel: 01-328 7628
No Map Ref.

OPEN 24 hours, seven days a week.

Star Kebab House
178 Earls Court Road, S.W.5.
Indian take away
Open to 2.00am every night. OPEN on Sunday.
Map Ref. 5B

Wimpy Bars
250 Earls Court Road, S.W.5.
Tel: 01-370 2084
Map Ref. 5B

27 Euston Road, N.W.1.
Tel: 01-837 6073
Map Ref. 1G

27 London Street, W.2.
Tel: 01-723 4721
Map Ref. 2E

OPEN 24 hours, seven days a week.

Wimpy Bars
190 Shaftesbury Avenue W.C.2.
Tel: 01-836 1149
Open to 4.30am every night. OPEN on Sunday.
Map Ref. 3G

HOTEL COFFEE BARS

The following is a list of coffee bars in hotels which stay open 24 hours and are available for use by non-residents where light meals can be obtained.

Chelsea Lounge
Carlton Tower Hotel
Cadogan Place, S.W.1.
Tel: 01-235 5411
Map Ref. 5F

Ribbelsdale Restaurant
Cavendish Hotel,
Jermyn Street, S.W.1.
Tel: 01-930 2111
Map Ref. 3G

Hamburger City
Kenilworth Hotel
97 Great Russell Street, W.C.1.
Tel: 01-636 3283
Map Ref. 2H

Kensington Hilton
179 Holland Park Avenue, W.11
Tel: 01-603 3355
Map Ref. 4A

The Patio
London Hilton, Park Lane, W.1.
Tel: 01-493 8000
Map Ref. 3F

Le Café Jardin
Skyline Park Tower,
101 Knightsbridge, S.W.1.
Tel: 01-235 8050
Map Ref. 4F

MIDDLE TAR As defined by H.M. Government
DANGER: Government Health WARNING:
CIGARETTES CAN SERIOUSLY DAMAGE
YOUR HEALTH

Dunhill
LUXURY LENGTH
Distinctively longer than King Size
BY APPOINTMENT TO HER MAJESTY THE QUEEN
SUPPLIERS OF SMOKERS REQUISITES ALFRED DUNHILL LTD LONDON
dunhill
LUXURY LENGTH
FILTER DE LUXE
LONDON · PARIS · NEW YORK
LOW TO MIDDLE TAR As defined by H.M. Government
DANGER: Government Health WARNING:
CIGARETTES CAN SERIOUSLY DAMAGE
YOUR HEALTH

Health, beauty and keep fit

A B C D E F G H I J K L
1 2 3 4 5 6
Kensal Green
KILBURN LANE
HARROW ROAD
FERNHEAD RD.
ELGIN AVENUE
GREAT WESTERN RD
CASTELLAIN RD.
Maida Vale
MAIDA VALE
ST. JOHN'S WOOD RD.
WELLINGTON ROAD
REGENT'S PARK
ALBANY STREET
EUSTON STATION
EUSTON ROAD
Westbourne Park
Ladbroke Grove
WESTBOURNE PARK
TALBOT ROAD
CHEPSTOW RD.
COLVILLE TER.
BISHOPS BRIDGE ROAD
WESTBOURNE GROVE
CLIFTON GDNS.
Warwick Avenue
EDGWARE ROAD
LISSON GROVE
Marylebone
Baker Street
MARYLEBONE ROAD
Great Portland Street
Regent's Park
Warren Street
Goodge Street
TOTTENHAM COURT RD.
GOWER STREET
SOUTHAMPTON ROW
GUILFORD ST.
GRAYS INN ROAD
KING'S CROSS ROAD
ROSEBERRY AVENUE
GOSWELL ROAD
CITY ROAD
OLD STREET
Old Street
GREAT EASTERN ST.
HACKNEY ROAD
Edgeware Road
PADDINGTON STATION
WESTBOURNE TER.
SEYMOUR PLACE
PORTMAN SQUARE
BAKER STREET
MARYLEBONE HIGH ST.
PORTLAND PL.
Oxford Circus
Tottenham Court Rd.
NEW OXFORD STREET
THEOBALDS RD.
CLERKEN WELL ROAD
FARRINGDON ST.
Chancery Lane
HOLBORN
Holborn
HOLBORN VIA.
ALDERSGATE ST.
Moorgate
MOORGATE
BISHOPSGATE
LIVERPOOL ST. STATION
COMMERCIAL ST.
WHITECHAPEL
Aldgate
Bank
St Paul's
CHEAPSIDE
LUDGATE HILL
FLEET ST.
CHANCERY LANE
Marble Arch
Marble Arch
OXFORD STREET
GROSVENOR SQUARE
Bond Street
REGENT ST.
NEW BOND ST.
OLD BOND ST.
POLAND ST.
WARDOUR ST.
CHARING CROSS ROAD
DRURY LANE
LONG ACRE
Covent Garden
STRAND
Aldwych
Somerset House
Temple
EMBANKMENT
Blackfriars
QUEEN VICTORIA ST.
Mansion House
LEADENHALL ST.
FENCHURCH ST.
Monument
Monument
Tower Hill
TOWER HILL
MINORIES
LEMAN ST.
EAST SMITHFIELD
PORTLAND ROAD
Bayswater
Queensway
QUEENSWAY
PEMBRIDGE RD.
Notting Hill Gate
NOTTING HILL GATE
BAYSWATER ROAD
Lancaster Gate
KENSINGTON GARDENS
HYDE PARK
SERPENTINE
ROTTEN ROW
PARK LANE
BERKELEY SQUARE
CURZON ST.
PICCADILLY
Piccadilly Circus
SHAFTESBURY AV.
Leicester Square
PALL MALL
GREEN PARK
Green Park
Hyde Park Corner
THE MALL
ST. JAMES'S PARK
CHARING CROSS STATION
VICTORIA
WATERLOO BRIDGE
RIVER THAMES
BLACKFRIARS BRIDGE
SOUTHWARK BRIDGE
LONDON BRIDGE
TOWER BRIDGE
STAMFORD ST.
SOUTHWARK STREET
TOOLEY STREET
ST. THOMAS ST.
LONDON BRI. STATION
Borough
HOLLAND PARK AVENUE
Holland Park
HOLLAND PARK
CAMPDEN HILL RD.
KENSINGTON CHURCH ST.
KENSINGTON HIGH STREET
KENSINGTON RD.
KNIGHTSBRIDGE
BELGRAVE SQUARE
GROSVENOR PL.
BIRDCAGE WALK
Westminster
WESTMINSTER BRIDGE
WATERLOO ROAD
YORK ROAD
WATERLOO STATION
Lambeth North
WESTMINSTER BRIDGE RD.
BOROUGH RD.
SOUTH WARK BRIDGE RD.
BOROUGH HIGH ST.
LONG LANE
HOLLAND ROAD
High Street Kensington
QUEEN'S GATE
EXHIBITION ROAD
Knightsbridge
SLOANE STREET
St James's Park
VICTORIA STREET
HORSE FERRY ROAD
LAMBETH BRIDGE
LAMBETH PALACE RD.
LAMBETH ROAD
ST GEORGE'S RD.
LONDON RD.
NEWINGTON CAUSEWAY
GREAT DOVER ST.
ABBEY STREET
SHEPHERD'S BUSH RD
HAMMERSMITH ROAD
EARLS COURT ROAD
CROMWELL ROAD
South Kensington
BROMPTON ROAD
WALTON RD.
BEAUCHAMP PLACE
CADOGAN GDNS.
KING'S ROAD
BUCKINGHAM PALACE ROAD
VAUXHALL BRIDGE ROAD
VICTORIA STATION
MILLBANK
RIVER THAMES
ALBERT EMBANKMENT
KENNINGTON ROAD
Elephant and Castle
NEW KENT RD.
WALWORTH ROAD
OLD KENT ROAD
Gloucester Road
OLD BROMPTON ROAD
SYDNEY ST.
Sloane Square
Pimlico
WARWICK ROAD
WEST CROMWELL ROAD
NORTH END ROAD
TALGARTH ROAD
Earls Court
REDCLIFF GARDENS
FULHAM ROAD
ROYAL HOSPITAL ROAD
CHELSEA BRIDGE RD.
GROSVENOR ROAD
VAUXHALL BRIDGE
HARLEYFORD RD.
Vauxhall
KENNINGTON PARK ROAD
FULHAM PALACE ROAD
LILLIE ROAD
West Brompton
KINGS ROAD
ALBERT BRIDGE
CHELSEA EMBANKMENT
BATTERSEA PARK
CHELSEA BRIDGE
NINE ELMS LANE
FENTIMAN RD.
Oval
Kennington Park
ALBANY ROAD

THE HEALTH AND BEAUTY SCENE

Joy Leslie Gibson gives some advice on fitness, health and beauty while you are on holiday.

There is nothing more horrid when on holiday than to feel less than your peak in health, and less than your best in looks. And one doesn't want to go around loaded with beauty preparations, sports gear that won't be used or to have to call in doctors if at all possible. Sickness too can be caused through different food and water, so all possible steps should be taken to ensure that there are no upsets while away. Before you come to England we hope that you have consulted your own doctor who has prescribed for your usual medicines (if needed) and suggested pills for an upset stomach, but if you should need either when away you will find a list of chemists on pages 17 to 19. If you should be taken seriously ill, and we hope that you won't be, your hotel will get you a doctor. Most hotels have a liaison with one and if your country has a reciprocal agreement with us over National Insurance then, IF HE IS A NATIONAL HEALTH DOCTOR, there should be no charge. But often hotel doctors do not come under this scheme so do expect to be charged for his visit. So find out beforehand if fees will be charged. If your ailment is slight, of course, you should visit a National Health Doctor in his surgery but expect to wait some time. If you are in an accident, however slight, then you can be treated in the Emergency or Casualty Department of any large hospital. Again, unless the case is urgent, you will have to wait. Most visitors to Casualty have a letter from their doctors but explain to the nurse in charge that you are an overseas visitor and she will help you through the system. The doctors in hospital are all very competent and the British Medical Service has a high standard. If you need physio-therapy or any such ancillary services, again consult your hotel porter — they generally know of someone. As medical and dental practitioners are not allowed to advertise in the UK, porters are really the only source of information!

KEEPING FIT

If you just want to keep fit while on holiday then you will be able to find somewhere to take part in your favourite sport. Many London Councils have facilities for tennis, golf, squash and other games in Local Parks or Sports Centres. Again consult your Hotel Porter or look in the telephone directory under a specific local council — names near London to look for are CHELSEA, BATTERSEA, WESTMINSTER or (about eight miles out of London but worth visiting) RICHMOND. Also consult pages 289 to 296.

There are many exercise centres, dance centres and gyms in London and we list a lot of them on pages 284 to 285. Most of these have a membership fee, but many do do a special fee for people who have only a short time in London, or will allow you to attend on a daily basis. Ring them up, explain your needs and they will tell you of their arrangements for overseas visitors.

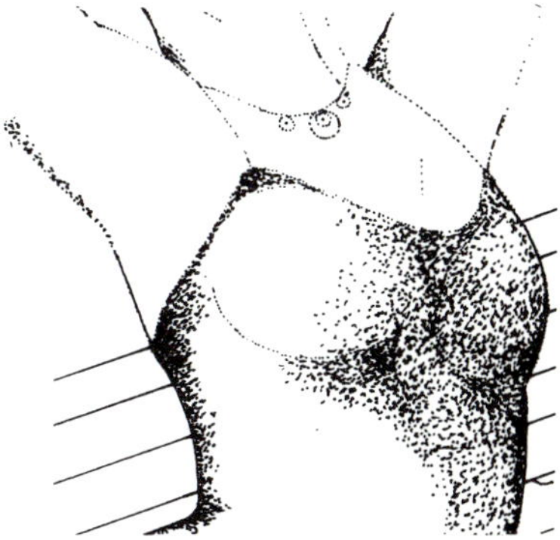

Sissors
46 King's Road, S.W.3.
Tel: 01-589 9471
Tube: Sloane Square
Very modern salon that does superb cutting. Unisex. You don't have to have the latest style — but they are good at it!
Map Ref. 5E

Vidal Sassoon
Grosvenor House Hotel,
Park Lane, W.1.
Tel: 01-499 3734
Tube: Hyde Park
Now the main Sassoon salon — there are several others scattered over London, including Sloane Street, S.W.1. You can be sure of a superb cut.
Map Ref. 3F

HAIRDRESSERS FOR MEN

Michaeljohn
6 Carlos Place, W.1.
Tel: 01-499 2125
Tube: Green Park
Modern styling with great care taken to see that it suits you.
Map Ref. 3F

Trumpers
9 Curzon Street, W.1.
Tel: 01-499 1850
Tube: Green Park
A gentleman's barber which does traditional work — used by the conservative.
Map Ref. 3F

Truefitt and Hill
23 Old Bond Street, W.1.
Tel: 01-493 2962
Tube: Green Park
Another traditional barber which does conservative, but very good, work.
Map Ref. 3G

Vidal Sassoon
56 Brook Street, W.1.
Tel: 01-409 0925
Tube: Bond Street
The male outpost of the Sassoon Empire — very good styling and cutting.
Map Ref. 2F

Sissors
46 King's Road, S.W.3.
Tel: 01-589 9471
Tube: Sloane Square
Unisex salon, strictly for the young and modern. Good cutting.
Map Ref. 5E

BEAUTY SALONS

Elizabeth Arden
20 New Bond Street, W.1.
Tel: 01-629 1200
Tube: Green Park
Everything under one roof, massage, make-up, hairdressing, manicure and a boutique, run by WARDROBE. Well-trained girls, Arden Products and an atmosphere of caring. Try the Top-to-Toe Treatment — five hours of luxury, or any other treatment.
Map Ref. 3G

Face Place
33 Cadogan Street, S.W.3.
Tel: 01-589 9062
Tube: Sloane Square
Beauty Editor Joan Price started the Face Place some years ago and gives first class treatment. You can also try products free and get expert advice of how to make-up.
Map Ref. 4E

The Sanctuary
12 Floral Street, W.C.2.
Tel: 01-836 6544
Tube: Covent Garden
A garden paradise with jacuzzi pool,

swimming pool, sauna and solarium. While you are at the Sanctuary you can take advantage of some excellent beauty treatments.

Map Ref. 3H

The Beauty Place
226 The Strand, W.C.2.
Tel: 01-353 1382
Tube: Temple
An unpretentious salon where great care is taken of you.

Map Ref. 3H

Ocean Boulevard
17 Tavistock Street, Covent Garden, W.C.2.
Tel: 01-240 1450
Tube: Covent Garden
A young, zany salon which does some very good cutting and tinting. Also available — a make-up artist and a UVA sun bed. Ocean Boulevard is open on Thursday until 11.00pm.

Map Ref. 3H

Brownies
32 Foubert's Place, W.1.
Tube: Oxford Circus
Sun tanning treatments—a day's treatment costs around £7.

Map Ref. 2G

Hawkin's Clinics
Situated in various places around and in London including 42, Beauchamp Place, S.W.1; 264 Upper Richmond Road, Putney, S.W.15.
Slimming, suntanning, beauty treatments — prices from £5 according to the treatment you have.

CYCLING

A very good way to see London is by bicycle. They can be hired by the day, week or month or bought outright. The following lists the places where you can hire bicycles. A deposit is usually required with identification.

Bicycle Revival
28 North End Parade,
North End Road, W.14.
Tel: 01-602 4499
Also at
17 Elizabeth Street, S.W.1.
Tel: 01-730 6716

Map Ref. 6B

Kensington Student Centre
Kensington Church Street, W.8.
Tel: 01-937 6089

Map Ref. 4C

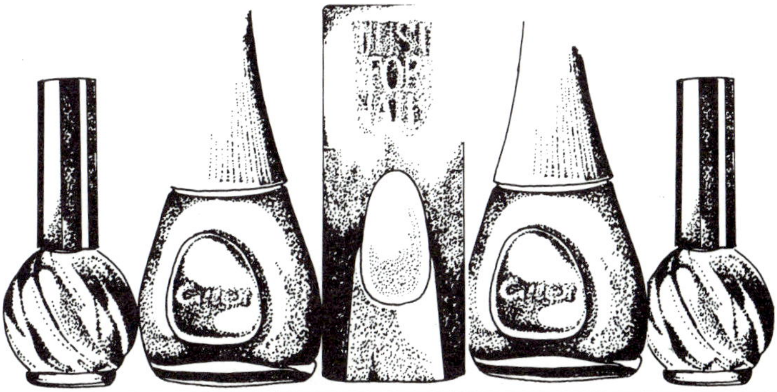

Bell Street Bikes
73 Bell Street, N.W.1.
Tel: 01-724 0456

No Map Ref.

For the enthusiasts who want further information about cycling club and professional events, contact:

British Cycle Federation
70 Brompton Road, S.W.3.
Tel: 01-584 6706

Map Ref. 4E

or

Cyclists Touring Club
69 Meadrow, Godalming, Surrey.
Tel: Godalming 7217

No Map Ref.

KEEP FIT, GYMNASIA AND DANCE CENTRES

Al Murray's City Gym
New Union Street, E.C.2.
Tel: 01-628 0786
Open to women on Tuesday and Thursday afternoons, for men on Mondays, Wednesdays and Fridays. Run by Al Murray who is consultant to Olympic teams and Champneys Health Farm. Emphasis on health and stamina. Individual programmes planned. Membership.

Map Ref. 2K

Alan Herdman
17 Homer Row, W.1.
Tel: 01-723 9953
Based on the Pilates' Technique this method uses specially designed apparatus to give you good muscle tone. Corrects posture. Approx £5 per hour.

Map Ref. 2E

Bodys
250 New King's Road, S.W.3.
Tel: 01-351 5682
Equipped with Nautilus apparatus for firming up muscles also classes for aerobics and yoga. Membership and also one-day membership (£5) with classes from £1.50.

No Map Ref.

Bodyworkshop
Lambton Squash Club, Lambton Place, Westbourne Grove, W.11.
Tel: 01-221 7989
Specially devised exercises based on Yoga, correct breathing and the relieving of tension. Gentle and effective. £3 a class.

Map Ref. 3B

Dance Centre
12 Floral Street, W.C.2.
Tel: 01-836 6544
A co-operative where many teachers of dancing and exercise hire studios and give classes in almost any type of dance or keep fit. You take your choice. Admission 25p plus the cost of your class paid direct to your teacher, generally around £2.

Map Ref. 3H

Dancercise
The Barge Durban, Isleworth, Middlesex.
Tel: 01-568 1751
Phyllis Greene Morgan's own brand of dance and exercise at various venues round and in London. Ring her for details. Energetic disco classes as well. Reasonable fees.

No Map Ref.

Danceworks
Balderton Street, W.1.
Tel: 01-629 6183
Lovely studios with a host of different classes for you to choose from. Some famous teachers use these studios — dancing, Yoga, classical ballet, Rock. Membership. Classes from £1. Saunas, showers and health-food restaurant.

Map Ref. 2F

Holmes Place Health Club
188 Fulham Road, S.W.10.
Tel: 01-352 9452
Club with large gymnasium and classes in almost every type of exercise you can think of. Showers, steam room, sauna and hairdressing. Yearly membership, but special arrangements are also made for Equity members and others.

Map Ref. 6D

Lotte Berke
29 Manchester Street, W.1.
Tel: 01-935 8905
Many beautiful women swear by Lotte Berke's system of exercise for figure

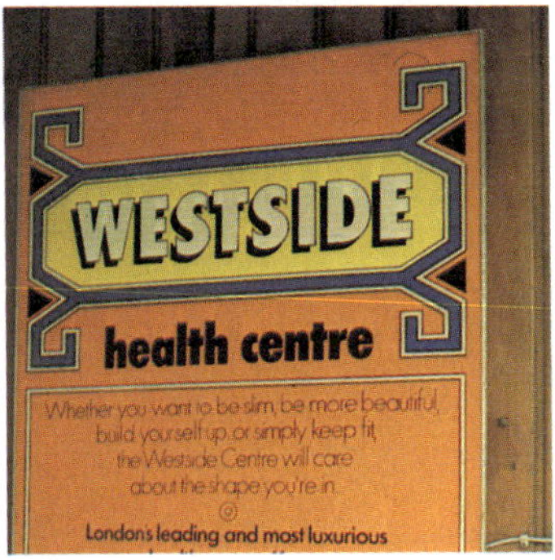

control and health. Classes, held every hour, cost from £2.50.

Map Ref. 2F

Nona's Studio
54 Glebe Place, S.W.3.
Tel: 01-352 9455
Pretty studio where you can do any number of different kinds of exercise including the Californian stretch, ballet, jazz and yoga. Showers and juice bar. Membership with classes for members at £3.75. Non-members welcome but classes then cost £6.

Map Ref. 6E

Pineapple Centre
7 Langley Place, W.C.2.
Tel: 01-836 4004

Map Ref. 3A

and

Pineapple West
60 Paddington Street, W.1.
Tel: 01-487 3444
Again a co-operative where many teachers teach different kinds of dancing and keep fit. Membership (reasonable) with classes from £1.

Map Ref. 2F

Superbody
101 Crawford Street, W.1.
Tel: 01-723 1163
Wide variety of classes in different types of dancing, yoga, aerobics are taught. Also excellent beauty salon, sauna and jacuzzi. Membership but accept non-members too. From £4 a class.

Map Ref. 2E

Sylvia Caplin
54 Stokenchurch Street, S.W.6.
Tel: 01-736 1877
Sylvia Caplin has a small studio in her home for small exercise classes — she also teaches at Pineapple. Finishes with meditation. £7 each for 2 people.

No Map Ref.

Town and Country
2 Yeoman's Row, S.W.3.
Tel: 01-584 7702
A fully equipped Health Club which concentrates on diet, exercise and beauty for women. Yoga classes as well. Membership but there are short-stay memberships as well.

Map Ref. 5E

Westside
201 Kensington High Street, W.8.
A fully equipped health club with separate days for men and women. Great care taken. Membership but short-stay memberships can be arranged.

Map Ref. 4C

SWIMMING

There are many public swimming pools around London. Here are a list of the more central ones. Telephone for opening times.

Chelsea Manor Baths
Chelsea Manor Street, S.W.3.
Tel: 01-352 6985
Map Ref. 5E

Great Smith Baths
St. Anns Street, S.W.1.
Tel: 01-352 6985
Map Ref. 4H

Dolphin Square
Grosvenor Road, S.W.1.
Tel: 01-828 1681
Map Ref. 6G

Marshall Street Baths
Marshall Street, W.1.
Tel: 01-437 7665
Map Ref. 2G

Seymour Hall
Seymour Place, W.1.
Tel: 01-723 8018
Map Ref. 2E

Oasis Pool
32 Endell Street, W.C.2.
Tel: 01-836 9555
Map Ref. 2H

Porchester Road
Queensway, W.2.
Tel: 01-229 3226
Map Ref. 3C

It is also possible to swim in the following parks. They are open from 6.00am to dusk in the summer and 7.00am to 10am in winter.

Hampstead Ponds, N.W.3.
Tel: 01-435 2366
No Map Ref.

Kennington Park, S.E.11.
Tel: 01-735 3574
Map Ref. 6I

Parliament Hill Lido, N.W.5.
Tel: 01-485 3873
No Map Ref.

Serpentine, Hyde Park, W.2.
Map Ref. 4E

Wimbledon Common, S.W.19.
No Map Ref.

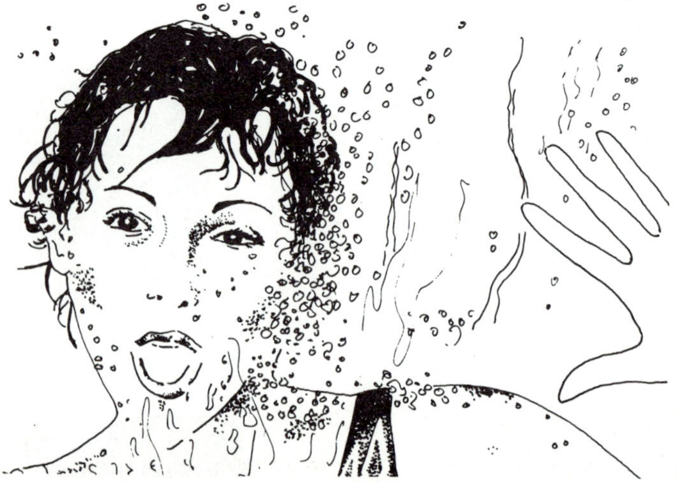

Sport in London

A B C D E F G H I J K L
1 2 3 4 5 6
EUSTON STATION
PADDINGTON STATION
LIVERPOOL ST. STATION
CHARING CROSS STATION
WATERLOO STATION
LONDON BRI. STATION
VICTORIA STATION
REGENT'S PARK
KENSINGTON GARDENS
HYDE PARK
SERPENTINE
GREEN PARK
ST. JAMES'S PARK
HOLLAND PARK
BATTERSEA PARK
Kennington Park
Kensal Green
RIVER THAMES
Marble Arch
Somerset House
Monument
PORTMAN SQUARE
GROSVENOR SQUARE
BERKELEY SQUARE
BELGRAVE SQUARE
WESTMINSTER BRIDGE
WATERLOO BRIDGE
BLACKFRIARS BRIDGE
SOUTHWARK BRIDGE
LONDON BRIDGE
TOWER BRIDGE
LAMBETH BRIDGE
VAUXHALL BRIDGE
CHELSEA BRIDGE
ALBERT BRIDGE

SPORT IN LONDON

Most sports are catered for in or around London; everything from top International Events to just playing in one of the local parks. Listed below are some of the more popular sports that can be played or watched in London but because they are very much geared to the time of year it is always best to check in *Time Out* magazine or *Where to Go* as to which sport is currently being played.

ATHLETICS

The Amateur Athletic Association
Francis House, Francis Street, S.W.1.
Tel: 01-828 9326
The Association will supply lists and fixtures of athletic events taking place in London.

Map Ref. 4E

THE MAIN SPORTS STADIUMS
Crystal Palace National Sports Centre
Crystal Palace, S.E.19.
Ledrington Road, Crystal Palace, S.E.19.
Tel: 01-778 0131
Opened in 1964, this is the largest multi-sports centre in the country. Most sports can be practised here and there are full facilities for coaching.

No Map Ref.

Empire Stadium
Wembley, Middlesex.
Tel: 01-902 1234
One of the most famous stadia in the world, it holds a great many of the International Events in a great number of sports.

No Map Ref.

White City Stadium
Wood Lane, W.12.
Tel: 01-743 7220
Box Office 01-743 7220
Completely under-cover, this stadium also stages Greyhound Racing and Speedway.

No Map Ref.

Royal Albert Hall
Kensington Gore, S.W.7.
Tel: 01-589 8212
Besides being world famous for classical music there are many indoor sporting events which take place here.

Map Ref. 4D

ARCHERY

This is an increasingly popular sport and in London alone there are over twenty archery clubs. Particulars can be obtained from the following associations.

Southern Counties Archery Society
102 Ashgrove Road, Ilford, Essex.
Tel: 01-590 4282

No Map Ref.

BILLIARDS AND SNOOKER

This is a very popular sport in the country as a whole and there are a great number of Billiards and Snooker Halls in London. The amateur side of the sport is governed by:

The Billiards and Snooker Control Council
Alexandra Chambers, 32 John William Street, Huddersfield.
Tel: 01-0484 35416

BOWLS

Another major participant sport. There are public greens in Battersea Park, Finsbury Park and many other places in London. For full details contact:

County Hall
Information Dept.,
Tel: 01-633 1705

or

The English Bowling Association
4 Lansdowne Crescent, Bournemouth.
Tel: 0202 22233

BOATING

London parks offer the best facilities for hiring small sailing dinghies and rowing boats. The two largest parks for this activity are:

The Serpentine Lake
Hyde Park.
Tel: 01-262 3751
Map Ref. 3E

and

Regents Park Lake
Regents Park.
Tel: 01-486 4759
Map Ref. 1F

It is advisable to telephone beforehand to check on weather conditions on the lakes.

CRICKET

The season for cricket is from mid-April to mid-September. The two major cricket grounds in London are:

Lords
St. Johns Wood Road, N.W.8.
Tel: 01-289 1615, Tickets.
Tel: 01-286 8011 for prospect of play.
Map Ref. 1D

and

The Oval
The Surrey Ground, Kennington Oval, Kennington, S.E.11.
Tel: 01-735 2424 or 01-735 4411 for scores etc.
Map Ref. 6I

Telephone either ground for details of matches particularly times and dates of Test Matches.

CYCLING

A very good way to see London is by bicycle. They can be hired by the day, week or month or bought outright. The following lists the places where you can hire bicycles. A deposit is usually required with identification.

Bicycle Revival
28 North End Parade, North End Road, W.14.
Tel: 01-602 4499
Map Ref. 6B

Also at
17 Elizabeth Street, S.W.1.
Tel: 01-730 6716
Map Ref. 5F

Bell Street Bikes
73 Bell Street, N.W.1.
Tel: 01-724 0456
Map Ref. 1D

For the enthusiasts who want further information about cycling club and professional events, contact:
British Cycling Federation
70 Brompton Road, S.W.3.
Tel: 01-584 6706
Map Ref. 4E

or

Cyclists Touring Club
69 Meadrow, Godalming, Surrey.
Tel: Godalming 7217.
No Map Ref.

FISHING

THAMES
To fish anywhere in the Thames, it is necessary to get a Thames Water Authority Licence. The season for fishing is between June 16th-March 14th. For details about licences contact:

London Anglers Association
183 Hoe Street, E.17.
Tel: 01-520 7477
No Map Ref.

ROYAL PARKS
To fish in the following Parks it is necessary to get a permit from:
The Royal Parks Department,
The Storeyard, Hyde Park, W.2.
Tel: 01-262 5484
Fee: £3.00 Adult, £1.50 Juveniles and OAP's.

Hampton Court
Tench, perch, pike, roach.
Hyde Park Serpentine
Roach, perch.
Richmond Park Pen Ponds
Roach, perch.
Battersea Park
Roach, tench, dace and gudgeon.
Clapham Common Eagle Pond
Carp, roach, pike, bream.
Crystal Palace
Carp, pike, roach, perch.
Finsbury Park
Gudgeon, roach.
Hampstead Heath
Roach, bream, pike, tench.
Wandsworth Common
Carp, roach, tench, pike.

FLYING

Aircraft Owners Association
50a Cambridge Street, S.W.1.
Tel: 01-834 5631
For general information and advice on anything to do with light aviation.
Map Ref. 5F

Denham Flying Club
Denham Aerodrome, Buckinghamshire.
Tel: Denham 833171
Training and hire of various types of light aircraft.

London School of Flying
The Aerodrome, Elstree, Hertfordshire.
Tel: 01-953 4343
Training and hire of various types of light aircraft.

FOOTBALL

The season is from August to April, with kick-off times at 3 p.m. on Saturdays and 7.30 p.m. for evening matches. The following are the main football clubs in the London area:

Arsenal
Highbury Stadium,
Avenell Road, N.5.
Tel: 01-359 0131

Charlton Athletic
151 Harvey Gardens, S.E.7.
Tel: 01-858 3711

Chelsea
Stamford Bridge,
Fulham Road, S.W.6.
Tel: 01-385 5545

Crystal Palace
Selhurst Park,
Whitehorse Lane, S.E.25.
Tel: 01-653 2223

Fulham
Craven Cottage,
Stevenage Road, S.W.6.
Tel: 01-736 6561

Millwall
The Den, Cold Blow Lane, S.E.14.
Tel: 01-639 3143

Orient
Leyton Stadium, Brisbane Road, E.10.
Tel: 01-539 2223

Queens Park Rangers
South Africa Road,
Shepherds Bush, W.12.
Tel: 01-743 0262

Tottenham Hotspur
748 High Road, N.17.
Tel: 01-808 3411

West Ham United
Boleyn Ground, Green Street, E.13.
Tel: 01-472 2740

GOLF

There are a great number of Golf courses in the London area and they are divided into two categories, public courses and private clubs. You can play on the public courses by payment of the green fee and it is usually possible to hire clubs as well. Entry to private clubs is more difficult and it is essential to telephone beforehand. Most clubs prefer you to be introduced by a member and all would expect you to be a member of another club and have an authorised handicap.

PUBLIC COURSES

Addington Court
Featherbed Lane, Addington,
Croydon, Surrey.
Tel: 01-657 0281

Beckenham Place Park
Beckenham, Kent.
Tel: 01-650 2292

Brent Valley
Church Road, Hanwell, W.7.
Tel: 01-567 4230

Chingford
158 Station Road, Chingford, E.4.
Tel: 01-529 5708

Coulsdon Court
Coulsdon, Surrey.
Tel: 01-660 0468

Harefield Place
The Drive, Harefield Place, Uxbridge, Middlesex.
Tel: Uxbridge 37281

Horsendon Hill
Whitton Avenue, Greenford, Middlesex.
Tel: 01-902 4555

Mitcham
Mitcham Junction, Surrey.
Tel: 01-648 1508

Perivale Park
Ruislip Road, Greenford, Middlesex.
Tel: 01-578 1693

Richmond Park
Richmond Park, S.W.15.
Tel: 01-876 3205

Royal Epping Forest
Forest Approach, Epping, E.4.
Tel: 01-529 2758

Ruislip
Ickenham Road, Ruislip, Middlesex.
Tel: Ruislip 32004

PRIVATE COURSES

The Addington
Shirley Church Road, Croydon, Surrey.
Tel: 01-777 1055

Addington Palace
Addington Park, Croydon, Surrey.
Tel: 01-654 3061

Coombe Wood
George Road, Kingston Hill, Surrey.
Tel: 01-942 3828

Croham Hurst
South Croydon, Surrey.
Tel: 01-657 1494

Finchley
Nether Court, Frith Lane, N.W.7.
Tel: 01-346 2436

Richmond
Sudbrook Park, Richmond, Surrey.
Tel: 01-940 1463

London Scottish
Windmill Enclosure, Wimbledon Common, S.W.19.
Tel: 01-788 0135

Royal Mid-Surrey
Old Deer Park, Richmond, Surrey.
Tel: 01-940 1677

Royal Wimbledon
29 Camp Road, Wimbledon Common, S.W.19.
Tel: 01-946 2125

GREYHOUND RACING

The following tracks have dog racing two or three times a week. Phone the individual stadium for details of day and times.

Catford Stadium
Catford Bridge, S.E.6.
Tel: 01-690 2261

Hackney Stadium
Waterden Road, E.15.
Tel: 01-986 3511

Harringay Stadium
Green Lanes, Harringay, N.16.
Tel: 01-800 3474

Wembley Stadium
Wembley, Middlesex.
Tel: 01-902 1234

White City
Wood Lane, Shepherds Bush, W.12.
Tel: 01-734 5544

Walthamstow Stadium
Chingford Road, E.4.
Tel: 01-527 2252

RACING

There are two very large, internationally famous race meetings. One is the Derby held in June and the other, the Royal Ascot also in June. Betting is legal both on and off the course in Britain. Flat racing is from March to November and steeplechasing from August to January. Courses within easy reach of London are:

Ascot Race Course
Ascot, Berkshire.
Home of the Royal Ascot meeting.
Tel: Ascot 22211

Epsom
Epsom Downs, Surrey.
Famous for the Derby.
Tel: Epsom 26311

Kempton Park
Sunbury-on-Thames, Middlesex.
Tel: Sunbury 82292

Sandown Park
Esher, Surrey.
Tel: Esher 63072

Jockey Club
42 Portman Square, W.1.
Tel: 01-486 4921
For information on all matters relating to Horse Racing in Britain.
Map Ref. 2F

RIDING

There are several stables around London where you can hire a horse by the hour. It is wise to telephone in advance for details and opening times.

HYDE PARK AREA

Bathurst Stables
63 Bathurst Mews, Hyde Park, W.2.
Tel: 01-723 2813
Map Ref. 2D

Lilo Blum Stables
32a Grosvenor Crescent Mews, S.W.1.
Tel: 01-235 6846
Map Ref. 4F

Ross Nye
8 Bathurst Mews, Hyde Park, W.2.
Tel: 01-262 3791
Map Ref. 2D

RICHMOND PARK AREA

Stag Lodge
Kingston Vale, S.W.15.
Tel: 01-546 9863

Roehampton Gate
Priory Lane, Richmond Park.
Tel: 01-876 7089

WIMBLEDON COMMON

Wimbledon Village Riding Stables
24b High Road, S.W.19.
Tel: 01-946 2520

LAWN TENNIS

Nearly all the London Parks have Tennis Courts and you can book in person. However it is advisable to telephone to the following parks to make a reservation as they get very crowded.

Battersea Park, S.W.8.
Tel: 01-622 2263
Map Ref. 6F

Holland Park, W.11.
Tel: 01-602 2226
Map Ref. 4B

Regents Park, N.W.1.
Tel: 01-935 8556
No reservations by telephone.
Map Ref. 1F

Lincolns Inn Fields, W.C.2.
Tel: 01-405 5194
No reservations by telephone.
Map Ref. 2I

Hurlingham Park, S.W.6.
Tel: 01-736 5186
No Map Ref.

Lawn Tennis Association
Barons Court, W.14.
Tel: 01-385 2366
The governing body of lawn tennis in Britain which will supply a list of clubs.
Map Ref. 6B

All England Lawn Tennis Club
Church Road, S.W.19.
Tel: 01-946 2244
The stage for the top event in the world, Wimbledon, held in the last week of June and first week of July.
No Map Ref.

MOTOR RACING

British Racing and Sports Car Club
Brands Hatch Circuit
Fawkham, Kent.
Tel: Ash Green 874445
Stages meetings throughout the year at various circuits and will supply a list of events.
No Map Ref.

British Automobile Racing Club
Thruxton Racing Circuit,
Nr. Andover, Hants.
Write for fixture list.

MOTOR CYCLE RACING

The Auto-Cycle Union
31 Belgrave Square, S.W.1.
Tel: 01-235 7636
Will send a handbook giving all motor cycling events.

Map Ref. 4F

MOTOR CYCLE SPEEDWAY

Racing is held at the following stadia. Telephone for times and details.

Hackney Stadium
Waterden Road, E.15.
Tel: 01-985 9822

No Map Ref.

White City
Wood Lane, W.12.
Tel: 01-743 5544

No Map Ref.

Wimbledon Stadium
Plough Lane, S.W.17.
Tel: 01-946 5361

No Map Ref.

REAL TENNIS

This is a fascinating game which dates back to the 15th Century. There are only a few courts in the London area and it is not possible to play unless you are with a member. The courts themselves can however be viewed at Hampton Court Palace and the **Queens Club,** Palliser Road, W.14. Tel: 01-385 3421, where it is also possible to have a trial game.

Map Ref. 6B

ROWING

Events take place during the summer months, the most famous being the Oxford and Cambridge boat race which is held in late March. Most of the events are held on the Thames between Putney and Mortlake bridges. The Henley Royal Regatta which is held July 5th-8th on the Thames at Henley, is also a large attraction and the town itself is also worth viewing.

The Amateur Rowing Association
6 Lower Mall, Hammersmith, W.6.
Tel: 01-748 3632
Will send details of events and lists of clubs.

No Map Ref.

RUGBY FOOTBALL

There are many rugby football grounds in the London area but the main one is Twickenham where all the important matches, including Internationals are played. Most matches are played on Saturday afternoons.

Rugby Football Union
Whitton Road, Twickenham,
Middlesex. Tel: 01-892 8161
Will send lists and venues of the more important matches taking place in the London area.

No Map Ref.

SHOW JUMPING

The two major events are the *Royal International Horse Show* at Wembley in July and the *Horse of the Year Show* at Wembley in October. There is also a Christmas event at Olympia, Kensington, W.8. in December.

The British Show Jumping Association
National Equestrian Centre,
Kenilworth, Warwickshire.
Tel: Coventry 20783
Will send fixture lists.

ICE SKATING

Queens Ice Rink
17 Queensway, W.2.
Tel: 01-229 0172
Tuition available. Ring for details and times. Café and Bar.

Map Ref. 3C

Richmond Ice Rink
Clevedon Road, Twickenham.
Tel: 01-892 3646
Café and Bar. Ring for details and times.

No Map Ref.

Silver Blades Ice Rink
386 Streatham High Road, S.W.16.
Tel: 01-769 7861

No Map Ref.

National Skating Association
117 Charterhouse Square, E.C.1.
Tel: 01-253 3824
For information about events and advice and details on other clubs.
Map Ref. 2J

SQUASH

Extremely popular, it is essential to telephone and enquire about reservations.

Squash Rackets Association
70 Brompton Road, S.W.3.
Tel: 01 584 2506
Will send a list of clubs and courts in London area.
Map Ref. 4E

Holland Park
Kensington, W.8.
Tel: 01-602 2226
Book seven days in advance.
Map Ref. 4B

Wembley Squash Centre
Empire Way, Wembley.
Tel: 01-902 9230
Book seven days in advance.
No Map Ref.

STOCK CAR RACING

Very exciting and popular spectator sport usually held on Saturday evenings in the summer. For details and times telephone the stadia.

Harringay Stadium
Green Lanes, N.4.
Tel: 01-800 3474
No Map Ref.

Wimbledon Stadium
Plough Lane, S.W.17.
Tel: 01-946 5361
No Map Ref.

SWIMMING

There are many public swimming pools around London. Here are a list of the more central ones. Telephone for opening times.

The Queen Mother Sports Centre
215 Vauxhall Bridge Road, S.W.1.
Tel: 01-834 4725
Great swimming bath and all other sports facilities in this sports centre.
Admission charges.
Open: 8.00am-7.30pm, Mondays to Fridays. (Wednesdays) 6.30pm. Saturdays to 5.30pm. Sunday 9.00am-4.30pm.
Map Ref. 5G

Chelsea Manor Baths
Chelsea Manor Street, S.W.3.
Tel: 01-352 6985
Map Ref. 6E

Great Smith Baths
St. Anns Street, S.W.1.
Tel: 01-352 6985
Map Ref. 5H

Dolphin Square
Grosvenor Road, S.W.1.
Tel: 01-834 9134
Map Ref. 6G

Marshall Street Baths
Marshall Street, W.1.
Tel: 01-437 7665
Map Ref. 2G

Seymour Hall
Seymour Place, W.1.
Tel: 01-723 8018
Map Ref. 2E

Oasis Pool
32 Endell Street, W.C.2.
Tel: 01-836 9555
Map Ref. 2H

Porchester Road
Queensway, W.2.
Tel: 01-229 3226
Map Ref. 3C

It is also possible to swim in the following parks. They are open from 6.00am to dusk in the summer and 7.00am to 10.00am winter.

Hampstead Ponds, N.W.3.
Tel: 01-435 2366
No Map Ref.

Kennington Park, S.E.11.
Tel: 01-735 3574
Map Ref. 6I

Parliament Hill Lido, N.W.5.
Tel: 01-485 3873
No Map Ref.

Serpentine, Hyde Park, W.2.
Tel: 01-262 5484
Map Ref. 3E

Wimbledon Common, S.W.19.
No Map Ref.

TEN PIN BOWLING

There used to be many more Ten Pin Bowling Clubs in Central London than now, but over the years demand has evened out and the ones listed below are very popular.

Piccadilly Bowl
30 Shaftesbury Avenue, W.1.
Tel: 01-437 1580
Map Ref. 3G

Mecca
142 Streatham Hill, S.W.2.
Tel: 01-674 5251
No Map Ref.

The businessman in London

EUSTON STATION
PADDINGTON STATION
CHARING CROSS STATION
WATERLOO STATION
VICTORIA STATION
LONDON BRI. STATION
LIVERPOOL ST. STATION
REGENT'S PARK
HYDE PARK
KENSINGTON GARDENS
SERPENTINE
GREEN PARK
ST. JAMES'S PARK
HOLLAND PARK
BATTERSEA PARK
Kennington Park
Kensal Green
Marble Arch
Somerset House
Monument
RIVER THAMES
WESTMINSTER BRIDGE
WATERLOO BRIDGE
BLACKFRIARS BRIDGE
SOUTHWARK BRIDGE
LONDON BRIDGE
TOWER BRIDGE
LAMBETH BRIDGE
VAUXHALL BRIDGE
CHELSEA BRIDGE
ALBERT BRIDGE
HARROW ROAD
KILBURN LANE
FERNHEAD RD.
ELGIN AVENUE
CASTELLAIN RD.
MAIDA VALE
ST. JOHN'S WOOD RD
WELLINGTON ROAD
LISSON GROVE
EDGWARE ROAD
CLIFTON GDNS.
MARYLEBONE ROAD
EUSTON ROAD
ALBANY STREET
TOTTENHAM COURT RD.
GOWER STREET
SOUTHAMPTON ROW
GRAYS INN ROAD
KING'S CROSS ROAD
ROSEBERRY AVENUE
GOSWELL ROAD
CITY ROAD
OLD STREET
GREAT EASTERN ST.
HACKNEY ROAD
COMMERCIAL ST.
WHITECHAPEL
LEMAN ST.
MINORIES
EAST SMITHFIELD
TOWER HILL
FENCHURCH ST.
LEADENHALL ST.
BISHOPSGATE
HOUNDSDITCH
MOORGATE
CHEAPSIDE
ALDERSGATE ST.
FARRINGDON ST.
CLERKEN WELL ROAD
THEOBALDS RD.
GUILFORD ST.
HOLBORN VIA.
CHANCERY LANE
FLEET ST.
LUDGATE HILL
QUEEN VICTORIA ST.
STRAND
EMBANKMENT
DRURY LANE
LONG ACRE
NEW OXFORD STREET
OXFORD STREET
CHARING CROSS ROAD
SHAFTESBURY AV.
WARDOUR ST.
POLAND ST.
GOODGE ST.
REGENT ST.
PORTLAND PL.
MARYLEBONE HIGH ST.
BAKER STREET
PORTMAN SQUARE
GROSVENOR SQUARE
BERKELEY SQUARE
NEW BOND ST.
OLD BOND ST.
PICCADILLY
CURZON ST.
PARK LANE
PALL MALL
THE MALL
BIRDCAGE WALK
VICTORIA STREET
VAUXHALL BRIDGE ROAD
HORSE FERRY ROAD
MILLBANK
GROSVENOR PL.
BUCKINGHAM PALACE ROAD
BELGRAVE SQUARE
KNIGHTSBRIDGE
SLOANE STREET
KING'S ROAD
BEAUCHAMP PLACE
CADOGAN GDNS.
WALTON RD.
BROMPTON ROAD
SYDNEY ST.
CHELSEA BRIDGE RD.
ROYAL HOSPITAL ROAD
CHELSEA EMBANKMENT
GROSVENOR ROAD
ROTTEN ROW
KENSINGTON RD.
EXHIBITION ROAD
QUEEN'S GATE
CROMWELL ROAD
OLD BROMPTON ROAD
FULHAM ROAD
REDCLIFF GARDENS
LILLIE ROAD
EARLS COURT ROAD
WARWICK ROAD
WEST CROMWELL ROAD
NORTH END ROAD
TALGARTH ROAD
HAMMERSMITH ROAD
FULHAM PALACE ROAD
SHEPHERD'S BUSH RD
HOLLAND ROAD
KENSINGTON HIGH STREET
KENSINGTON CHURCH ST
CAMPDEN HILL RD
HOLLAND PARK AVENUE
NOTTING HILL GATE
PORTLAND ROAD
CLARENDON RD.
BLENHEIM CRES.
ELGIN CRES.
LADBROKE GROVE
WESTBOURNE PARK
WESTBOURNE GROVE
TALBOT ROAD
COLVILLE TER.
CHEPSTOW RD.
GREAT WESTERN RD
BISHOPS BRIDGE ROAD
WESTBOURNE TER
SEYMOUR PLACE
PEMBRIDGE RD.
QUEENSWAY
BAYSWATER ROAD
STAMFORD ST.
WATERLOO ROAD
YORK ROAD
WESTMINSTER BRIDGE RD.
LAMBETH PALACE RD.
LAMBETH ROAD
ALBERT EMBANKMENT
KENNINGTON ROAD
KENNINGTON PARK ROAD
HARLEYFORD RD.
FENTIMAN RD.
NINE ELMS LANE
ST GEORGE'S RD.
LONDON RD.
BLACKFRIARS RD.
SOUTHWARK STREET
SOUTH WARK BRIDGE RD.
BOROUGH RD.
BOROUGH HIGH ST.
NEWINGTON CAUSEWAY
ST. THOMAS ST.
TOOLEY STREET
LONG LANE
GREAT DOVER ST.
NEW KENT RD.
WALWORTH ROAD
OLD KENT ROAD
ABBEY STREET
ALBANY ROAD
Maida Vale
Warwick Avenue
Marylebone
Baker Street
Regent's Park
Great Portland Street
Warren Street
Goodge Street
Tottenham Court Rd.
Oxford Circus
Bond Street
Marble Arch
Edgeware Road
Lancaster Gate
Bayswater
Queensway
Notting Hill Gate
Holland Park
Ladbroke Grove
Westbourne Park
High Street Kensington
South Kensington
Gloucester Road
Earls Court
West Brompton
Knightsbridge
Hyde Park Corner
Green Park
Piccadilly Circus
Leicester Square
Covent Garden
Holborn
Chancery Lane
Aldwych
Temple
Blackfriars
Mansion House
St Paul's
Bank
Moorgate
Old Street
Aldgate
Tower Hill
Monument
Borough
Lambeth North
Elephant and Castle
Westminster
St James's Park
Sloane Square
Pimlico
Vauxhall
Oval

THE BUSINESSMAN IN LONDON

As London is one of the major cities in the world for business and commerce, we have included in this section those aspects that a businessman, visiting either for a short trip or longer duration, would find most useful.

OFFICE HOURS

Due to the volume of people travelling to and from London to work, many companies have made separate arrangements with their staff about office hours so that they might miss the congested 'rush hours'. However, as a general basis, office hours are as follows:-

COMMERCE —
9.00am-5.00pm, Monday to Friday.
GOVERNMENT — *10.00am-1.00pm and 2.00pm-5.00pm, Monday to Friday.*

PUBLIC HOLIDAYS

England has a number of Holidays throughout the year when all offices are closed. They are:

New Year's Day (January 1st)
Good Friday
Easter Monday
May Day
Spring Bank Holiday
Summer Bank Holiday
Christmas Day (December 25th)
Boxing Day (December 26th)

BANKING

See under 'Helpful Information about London'.

OFFICE HIRE

Winter & Co. Incorporating Spacebank
36 Sackville Street, W.1.
Tel: 01-734 5043
Specialists in furnished and serviced offices in Central London.
Map Ref. 3G

World Wide Business Centre
110 Strand, W.C.2.
Tel: 01-836 8918
Provides offices on a daily, weekly or monthly basis, with full range of business services.
Map Ref. 3H

Norma Skemp Personnel Services
14 Broadway, S.W.1.
Tel: 01-222 5483
Rents desk space in offices or just an accommodation address. Also telephone answering service.
Map Ref. 3G

Management Business Services
243 Regent Street, W.1.
Tel: 01-408 1611
Has over 80 prestige offices in Mayfair available on minimum 3 month rental. Also hires board rooms and meeting rooms and give a complete range of business services.
Map Ref. 3G

SECRETARIAL SERVICES

London Secretariat
70 Queen Victoria Street, E.C.4.
Tel: 01-248 5932
For all shorthand, audio, copy typing, telex, photocopying and word-processing.
Map Ref. 3J

Rita Moore Tape Transcriptions
Room 529, High Holborn House, 52 High Holborn, W.C.1.
Tel: 01-242 5508
Conference, meetings and all office correspondence as well as legal work.
Map Ref. 2I

Red Tape
40 Great Marlborough Street, W.1.
Tel: 01-434 2821
All types of word processing services, printing and development.
Map Ref. 2G

Typing Plus
32 Rathbone Place, W.1.
Tel: 01-637 4050
Confidential secretarial services, word processing etc.
Map Ref. 2G

Tape Typing Secretarial
190 Goswell Street, E.C.1.
Tel: 01-250 3935
12 Kingly Street, W.1.
Tel: 01-734 6223
Collection and delivery of all tapes which are typed the same day, as far as possible.
Map Ref. 2K

MESSENGER SERVICES

Security Despatch
19 Russell Street, W.C.2.
Tel: 01-240 1001
Fidelity-bonded motor-cycle messengers, international couriers and nationwide delivery service.
Map Ref. 2H

Greater London Cars
251 Finchley Road, N.W.3.
Tel: 01-794 7722
Quick delivery messenger service throughout London and car passenger service.
No Map Ref.

Fleet Street Flyers
16 Bride Lane, E.C.4.
Tel: 01-353 6666
Motor-cycle messengers, worldwide courier service and express door-to-door parcel service.
Map Ref. 2I

Mercury Despatch Ltd.
17 Pindock Mews, W.9.
Tel: 01-286 8030
Quick service throughout London, and all over the World.
Map Ref. 1C

All London Radio Taxis
144 Shirland Road, W.9.
Tel: 01-286 4848
London's largest taxi network.
No Map Ref.

CAR HIRE

See under 'How to Get Around London'.

CHAUFFEUR HIRE

See under 'How to Get Around London'.

HELICOPTER RENTAL

Alan Mann Helicopters Ltd.
Fairoaks Airport, Cobham, Woking, Surrey.
Tel: Cobham (09905) 7471
For all types of helicopters.
No Map Ref.

McAlpine Helicopters Ltd.
Swallowfield Way, Hayes, Middlesex.
Tel: 01-848 3522
Long or short range helicopters. Very comprehensive service.
No Map Ref.

Bristow Helicopters
Redhill Aerodrome, Redhill, Surrey.
Tel: 01-668 6352/2353
Business and taxi charter or Nutfield Ridge.
No Map Ref.

Baff Jet Executive Travel
20 Red Lion Court, E.C.4.
Tel: 01-353 9744
Aircraft, helicopter and air ambulances.
Map Ref. 2I

C B Helicopters
Westlands Heliport, Lombard Road, S.W.11.
Tel: 01-731 5857
For all tpes of helicopter charter.
No Map Ref.

AIR TAXIS

Air London
Gatwick Airport, Sussex.
Tel: 01-0293 31653/37316
Executive jets and large aircraft for charter.
No Map Ref.

CAB Air
Elstree Aerodrome Herts.
Tel: 01-953 4411
24-hour passenger and freight service throughout Great Britain, Europe, Scandinavia and the Mediterranean.
No Map Ref.

London Executive Aviation
295 Kennington Road, S.E.11.
Tel: 01-582 2922
Aircraft brokers specialising in bookings and advice for all types of aircraft. 24 hour service.
Map Ref. 5I

Trans Care International
193 High Street, Acton, W.3.
Tel: 01-993 6151/992 5077
24-hour service with medical teams and all necessary equipment in latest planes. Doctors and qualified nurses available to attend and escort patients on scheduled airlines. Road Ambulance service also.
No Map Ref.

STOCKBROKERS

The following is a short list of international stockbrokers.

Bache Halsey Stuart Shields Inc.
5 Burlington Gardens, W.1.
Tel: 01-439 4191
Map Ref. 3G

Becker AG International
17 Lincoln's Inn Fields, W.C.2.
Tel: 01-831 6931
Map Ref. 2I

Dean Witter Reynolds Overseal Ltd.
56 Leadenhall Street, E.C.3.
Tel: 01-481 4242
Map Ref. 3K

Fox-Pitt Kelton Ltd.
2 Wilson Street, E.C.2.
Tel: 01-377 8929
Map Ref. 2K

Merrill Lynch, Pierce Fenner and Smith Ltd.
Time Life Building,
153 New Bond Street, W.1.
Tel: 01-493 7242
Map Ref. 3G

Oppenheimer and Co. Ltd.
72 Basinghall Street, E.C.2.
Tel: 01-606 3271
Map Ref. 2K

TRANSLATIONS

Berlitz Translation Service
321 Oxford Street, W.1.
Tel: 01-629 7360
Translations for all languages.
Map Ref. 2F

Bond Street Translations Ltd.
40 Old Bond Street, W.1.
Tel: 01-493 2418
All subjects, all languages, quick service on legal, financial and technical subjects.
Map Ref. 3G

Conrad Languages Ltd.
53 Theobalds Road, W.C.1.
Tel: 01-405 3609
Accurate and reliable in all languages including film and video dubbing.
Map Ref. 2I

Universal Translations
64 Queen Street, E.C.4.
Tel: 01-248 8707
Professional translators in all languages.
Map Ref. 2I

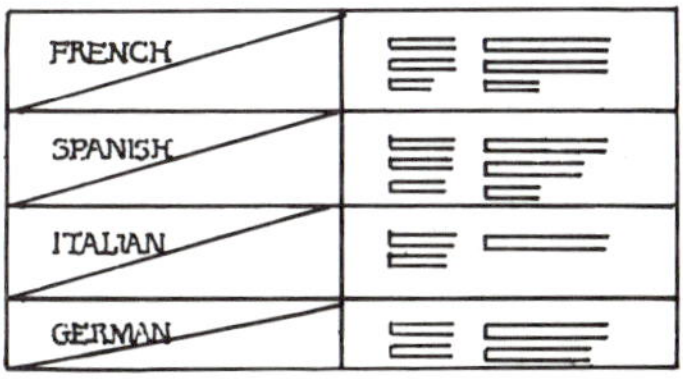

RAILWAY STATIONS

See under 'How to Get Around London'.

AIRLINES

Telephone numbers are for Passenger Reservations.

Aer Lingus
223 Regent Street, W.1.
52 Poland Street, W.1.
Tel: 01-734 1212 (Reservations)
To and from Ireland, Europe and Eastern U.S.A.
Map Ref. 2G

Aeroflot
69 Piccadilly, W.1.
Tel: 01-493 7436
To and from Russia and Eastern Europe and all the World.
Map Ref. 3G

Air Afrique
177 Piccadilly, W.1.
Tel: 01-629 6114
To West and Central Africa.
Map Ref. 3G

Air Canada
140 Regent Street, W.1.
Tel: 01-439 7941
World Wide.
Map Ref. 3G

Air France
158 New Bond Street, W.1.
Tel: 01-499 9511
World Wide.
Map Ref. 3G

Air India
17 New Bond Street, W.1.
Tel: 01-491 7979
World Wide.
Map Ref. 3G

Air Jamaica
6 Bruton Street, W.1.
Tel: 01-499 6802
To and from West Indies.
Map Ref. 3F

Air Malta
23 Pall Mall, W.1.
Tel: 01-839 5872
To and from Malta.
Map Ref. 3G

Air New Zealand
15 Charles II Street, S.W.1.
Tel: 01-930 1088
To and from New Zealand, Asia and Pacific.
Map Ref. 3G

Alia
177 Regent Street, W.1.
Tel: 01-734 2557
To and from Jordan.
Map Ref. 3G

Alitalia
251 Regent Street, W.1.
Tel: 01-734 4040
World Wide and major Italian Cities.
Map Ref. 3G

American Airlines
49 Old Bond Street, W.1.
Tel: 01-499 9701
To and from Hawaii.
Map Ref. 3G

Austrian Airlines
50 Conduit Street, W.1.
Tel: 01-439 0741
To and from Austria, Eastern Europe, Mediterranean and North Africa.
Map Ref. 3G

British Airways
75 Regent Street, W.1.
Tel: 01-370 5411
World Wide — for Sales Shops see Telephone Directory.
Map Ref. 3G

British Caledonian
Central London Air Terminal, S.W.1.
Tel: 01-834 9411
World Wide.
Map Ref. 4G

Cathay Pacific
123 Pall Mall, S.W.1.
Tel: 01-930 7878
To and from Hong Kong.
Map Ref. 3G

Delta Airlines
140 Regent Street, W.1.
Tel: 01-668 0935
To and from Atlanta.
Map Ref. 3G

Eastern Airlines
49 Old Bond Street, W.1.
Tel: 01-493 5764
To and from U.S.A., Caribbean and South America.
Map Ref. 3G

Egyptair
29 Piccadilly, W.1.
Tel: 01-734 2395
To and from Egypt.
Map Ref. 3G

El Al (Israel Airline)
185 Regent Street, W.1.
Tel: 01-437 9255
To and from Israel (Tel Aviv).
Map Ref. 3G

Gulf Air
73 Piccadilly, W.1.
Tel: 01-409 1951
To and from Middle East.
Map Ref. 3G

Iberia Airlines
169 Regent Street, W.1.
Tel: 01-437 5622
World Wide.
Map Ref. 3G

Japan Airlines
8 Hanover Street, W.1.
Tel: 01-408 1000
To and from Japan.
Map Ref. 2G

KLM Royal Dutch Airlines
Time Life Building, 153 New Bond Street, W.1.
Tel: 01-492 0336
World Wide service from the oldest airline in the world.
Map Ref. 3G

Kuwait Airways
52 Piccadilly, W.1.
Tel: 01-499 7681
To and from Middle East.
Map Ref. 3G

Lufthansa
28 Piccadilly, W.1.
Tel: 01-437 9797
World Wide.
Map Ref. 3G

Malaysian Airlines
25 St. George Street, W.1.
Tel: 01-499 6286
To and from Malaysia.
Map Ref. 3G

Middle East Airlines
80 Piccadilly, W.1.
Tel: 01-493 5681
To and from Middle East.
Map Ref. 3G

Nigeria Airways
12 Conduit Street, W.1.
Tel: 01-629 3717
To and from West Africa.
Map Ref. 3G

Olympic Airways
141 New Bond Street, W.1.
Tel: 01-499 8712
To and from Greece.
Map Ref. 3G

Pakistan International
45 Piccadilly, W.1.
Tel: 01-734 5544
To and from Far East.
Map Ref. 3G

Pan American Airways
193 Piccadilly, W.1.
Tel: 01-734 7292
World Wide.
Map Ref. 3G

T.A.P. Portuguese Airways
19 Regent Street, W.1.
Tel: 01-839 1031
To and from Portugal then World Wide.
Map Ref. 2G

Quantas Airways
182 Strand, W.C.2.
Tel: 01-240 1836
To and from Australia.
Map Ref. 3H

also at
49 Old Bond Street, W.1.

Sabena
36 Piccadilly, W.1.
Tel: 01-437 6950
World Wide — not Australia or South America.
Map Ref. 3G

Scandinavian Airlines
52 Conduit Street, W.1.
Tel: 01-734 4020
To and from Scandinavia then World Wide.
Map Ref. 3G

Singapore Airlines
143 Regent Street, W.1.
Tel: 01-439 8111
To and from Far East, Australia and New Zealand.
Map Ref. 3G

South African Airlines
251 Regent Street, W.1.
Tel: 01-734 9841
To and from South Africa.
Map Ref. 2G

Swissair
10 Wardour Street, W.1.
Tel: 01-439 4144
World Wide.
Map Ref. 3G

Trans World Airlines
200 Piccadilly, W.1.
Tel: 01-636 4090
To and from U.S.A.
Map Ref. 3G

Varig
16 Hanover Street, W.1.
Tel: 01-629 5824
To and from Brazil.
Map Ref. 2G

AIR TERMINALS

To get to Heathrow take the Piccadilly Line Train.
To get to Gatwick take the Train from Victoria.

BUSINESS SERVICES

Export Intelligence
Lirne Grove, Ruislip.
Tel: 01-866 8771
Information service for British exporters.
Map Ref. 2J

Department of Trade
Export Services
Tel: 01-215 7877
Service for foreign visitors wishing to buy British goods.

Central Office of Information
Hercules Road, S.E.1.
Tel: 01-928 2345
Map Ref. 5I

Confederation of British Industry
Centre Point, New Oxford Street, W.C.1.
Tel: 01-379 7400
Map Ref. 2H

Institute of Practitioners in Advertising
44 Belgrave Square, S.W.1.
Tel: 01-235 7020
Map Ref. 4F

CONFERENCE ADVICE

The following offer advice on planning conferences and conventions.

Conference Associates
34 Stanford Road, W.8.
Tel: 01-937 7529
Map Ref. 4C

Conference Consultants
4L Portman Mansions,
Chiltern Street, W.1.
Tel: 01-486 6582
Map Ref. 2F

London Convention Bureau
26 Grosvenor Gardens, S.W.1.
Tel: 01-730 3450
Map Ref. 4F

CHAMBER OF COMMERCE

London Chamber of Commerce
69 Cannon Street, E.C.4.
Tel: 01-248 4444
Map Ref. 3J

TELEPHONE ANSWERING

Answering Limited
16 Jacobs Wells Mews,
George Street, W.1.
Tel: 01-935 6655
Answers telephone, takes messages, radio paging etc.
Map Ref. 2F

Air Call Ltd.
176 Vauxhall Bridge Road, S.W.1.
Tel: 01-834 9000
24-hour, seven days a week answering service, radio telephones and paging.
Map Ref. 5G

Mascot Telephone Answering
331 Goswell Road, E.C.1.
Tel: 01-278 6783
Answering and Secretarial Services.
Map Ref. 1J

Basil Services
139a Sloane Street, S.W.1.
Tel: 01-730 9958
Telex service and telephone answering service. Secretarial Services.
Map Ref. 5E

ESCORT AGENCIES

There are many escort agencies in London, many with dubious backgrounds. The following is a list of agencies with presentable partners for an evening out or for sightseeing during the day.

The Portman Agency
67 Chiltern Street, W.1.
Tel: 01-935 5339
Map Ref. 2F

Chelsea Model Escorts
51 Beauchamp Place, S.W.3.
Tel: 01-584 6513
Map Ref. 5E

MONEY AFTER HOURS

See under 'Helpful Information about London'.

INTRODUCING THE CITY

by Nicholas Goodison
Chairman, The Stock Exchange

The City of London is synonymous with finance. It is a thriving market for services of many kinds — banking and finance, insurance, stocks and shares, shipbroking, commodities and many others, providing services for industry and commerce, for savers, for government, for the world.

London has been a major financial centre for centuries. Its development was founded on its position as a political and trading centre and as a port on the River Thames. Then, too, the industrial skill and knowledge, springing from the industrial revolution, were to be found in Britain, while the finance needed to develop industrial processes and new techniques was also available for use both in the UK and overseas. In these circumstances, it would have been very surprising if the financial institutions of London had failed to develop their potential.

Bank of England

A leading role among financial institutions is played by the Bank of England, the Central Bank of the United Kingdom. It was founded in 1694 as part of a scheme to raise money for King William III. At first just one bank among many in the City of London, the Bank of England was developed into the United Kingdom's central bank and the sole issuer of bank notes in England and Wales. In 1946 the Bank was nationalised.

Today the Bank of England is the government's banker, as well as being the government's adviser on monetary policy and the means of implementing that policy. For many years the Bank of England has used its influence with the commercial banks to affect their lending policies and this has generally been done on an informal basis. But with the growth in the number and range of financial institutions, this informal approach to control has been supplemented by the passing of the Banking Act in 1979, which has given a much more comprehensive legal framework for banking than the United Kingdom had before.

Commercial Banks

All five major commercial banks, Barclays, Lloyds, Midland, National Westminster and Williams and Glyn's — have their headquarters in the City, within a short walk of the Bank of England. From their head offices, their networks of over 12,000 branches spread throughout this country and the world. So "the City" is represented in every high street and beyond.

In addition, several hundred smaller banks have offices in the City. There are the British-registered overseas banks, and the "merchant banks", who provide short-term finance for their company customers as well as being a source of advice on long-term and permanent capital, corporate financial reorganisations, takeovers and mergers.

In the 19th century sterling had become the major international trading currency and Britain's financial institutions were paramount in financial world trade. Today London remains unquestionably a major financial centre on the international scene. This is largely because London's financial system has always proved flexible and adaptable. We have been prepared to change with the times and to introduce new methods and services as they are required.

London has always proved a magnet for overseas banks especially when the Eurodollar market developed in the 1950s and 1960s. There was no particular reason why it should have been based primarily in London. Frankfurt, Paris, Zurich or various other centres could have become pre-eminent. Yet London assumed this role and continues to play a leading part in the market. In 1960 there were 77 overseas banks represented in London. Today there are over 400.

The Discount Market

The so-called discount houses are a particular feature of the London money markets. There are ten of these in the City of London. In general they borrow funds from a wide range of banking institutions throughout the City, money which is repayable either on demand or at very short notice. With this money they provide the main market in treasury bills, short-term commercial bills and sterling certificates of deposit. When they are short of funds as a result of the commercial banks calling back their outstanding lending, the discount market has the right to go to the Bank of England for "lender of last resort" assistance.

The Stock Exchange

Turning now to my own institution, The Stock Exchange, readers will probably expect me to devote more space to its activities than to others. In any event, The Stock Exchange is regarded by many people as being symbolic of the City and the financial world. To its friends it epitomises all that is good in the City, but to its detractors, its four walls contain all the vices of the City, real or imaginary. When the myths have been stripped away, what is The Stock Exchange and what does it do? In its simplest terms, it is a market place where the prices of the goods traded fluctuate in accordance with the interplay of supply and demand of the users of the market. The goods in which it deals (stocks and shares) are, of course, a far cry from what one would normally expect of the local Saturday morning street market, but in essence the principles are the same. There are the stall holders (the jobbers) who quote the prices for their wares and compete with one another for the business of the brokers who act as agents for their clients, the investors. The competitive jobbing system and the strict separation of the roles of jobber and broker are what distinguish the UK Stock Exchange from other exchanges. The system ensures that the client gets the best prices at the going rate when the bargain is struck.

The Stock Exchange originated in the late 17th century when a rapidly expanding economy was demanding more funds than the early entrepreneurs could supply. As a result of this, the joint stock company came into existence and by selling shares in the ownership of new companies, funds were raised which allowed the economic expansion to continue. This also expanded the ownership of companies which hitherto had been concentrated in the hands of a powerful few. But as the spread of ownership grew, so did the need for some kind of market where shares could be traded when investors either needed their money or wished to re-invest in other companies. At first this trading was conducted in the coffee houses around Cornhill, the most notable being Jonathan's Coffee House and Garraway's. As this market grew the need for some formalised system and place of trading became more apparent and out of this need arose the London Stock Exchange, where membership was limited and rules were introduced to protect the investors.

As the industrial revolution progressed, the need for more capital stimulated the creation of many other stock exchanges around the country. Even today, although the exchanges are now united in one national institution, there are still active trading floors in four cities outside London and there are stockbrokers' offices in over 110 towns and cities throughout the UK and Ireland.

The Stock Exchange provides the trading market. Investors wanting to receive their cash back can sell the security they hold, be it a share or a gilt or some other fixed interest security. The investor receives his money from the investor to whom he sells the security and the original borrower still has use of the original funds.

This trading market falls naturally into two main sections: the market in government stocks (gilt-edged market) and that in company securities. The number of dealings in this market is much larger than in the gilt-edged market, although the total value of dealings is much smaller.

Over 7,000 securities are listed on The Stock Exchange and it has the third largest volume of any Stock Exchange in the world.

Lloyd's

Less than ten minutes walk away is the world's major insurance market, Lloyd's of London. Like The Stock Exchange, Lloyd's has its origins in the coffee houses of London in the eighteenth century. The insurance men tended to gather in Lloyd's coffee house and hence the name was born. Lloyd's has premium income in excess of £2,000m per year, around 75% of which comes from overseas. There are over 20,000 members of Lloyd's, each of whom has to demonstrate his financial ability to meet losses on an unlimited liability basis should the need arise. A UK member must show he has minimum assets of £100,000 and an overseas national, £135,000. The members are grouped into "syndicates", each of which employs professional underwriters to carry on their business.

The Baltic Exchange

The Baltic Exchange in St. Mary Axe is the world's major shipping market. Like all of the markets of the City, it has survived and prospered as a result of being flexible and quick to adapt to changing conditions. So it has become a major centre for air-chartering too, alongside its traditional business of ships and their cargoes.

Essentially, the Baltic Exchange is the meeting place of ship and air charterers and owners and their agents where ships and cargoes are matched. This is a vast and complex operation and, rather like a game of chess, the shipowners have to look two or three moves ahead all the time. Is it worth taking a cargo to North America? What cargo can be be picked up in New York and will there be another cargo ready at the next port? A central location where this sort of complex chartering can be worked out is a major contribution to the efficient transport of goods around the world. The market grew up in the City of London because in the 19th century much of the world's trade was carried in British ships, while London itself was a major port. Today neither of those remains true, but the expertise which existed on the Baltic Exchange has helped to turn it into a truly international shipping and air-freight market.

The Commodity Markets
Like the Baltic Exchange, the commodity markets grew up close to the original port of London near London Bridge. Today it is possible to deal in many commodities; sugar, tea, coffee, cocoa, tin, copper, precious metals, rubber, grains, fibres, etc., both on a "spot" and "futures" basis, that is, for delivery now or at a specified date in the future.

Despite the growth of other commodity markets around the world, London remains an important world commodities' trading centre, often dealing in deliveries of commodities which, like the ship and air charters on the Baltic, never physically come to Britain.

Financial Futures
The most recent addition to the City's market places is the London International Financial Futures Market (LIFFE). This market, opened in September 1982, enables those exposed to the risk of interest rate and currency fluctuations to offset the risk by buying or selling "futures" contracts. The market is housed in the internally reconstructed Royal Exchange building and over 250 UK and overseas financial and commodity institutions and individuals have become members.

Conclusions
"The City", as we have seen, is essentially a collection of market places. Each of them has individually a good reason for being where it is, but a major reason for London's pre-eminence as a financial and trading centre is probably the fact that so many markets are concentrated within a single square mile. The buying and selling of so many things, the means of financing their purchase, either on a short or long-term basis, insuring them from one end of the world to the other, can all be accomplished by a few short walks or a few local telephone calls.

London for children

LONDON FOR CHILDREN

Nanette Newman, wife of Brian Forbes, actress and mother suggests what to do with children in London.

ANYONE who has taken a child or children around London knows that (to quote the old song) 'It ain't what you do, it's the way that you do it' is what really counts. Having, over the years, done my fair share of London trips, I have found that there are certain things worth avoiding if you wish to find yourself reasonably sane at the end of the day, and not a contender for The Demented Parent of the Year award!

Being a Londoner myself I won't deny having some bias. I still think that — with all its faults — London remains one of the most fascinating cities in the world, but that to present it as such to a child needs some pre-planning.

First: getting to wherever you are going: try not to travel at peak hours, particularly on the return journey — queuing endlessly for a bus, or being crammed into a tube train will ensure that your day ends, not with a bang, but with a whimperer.

Second: arrange your day so that you don't have to eat at the recognised eating times. This will save you hours.

Third: always have an alternative plan at the ready. For instance, if you had been looking forward to an afternoon's boating on the Serpentine and the forecasted "perfect Summer's day" turns into our version of an Indian monsoon — before the disappointment becomes too acute, switch to Plan B. This was always known in my family as *Weather Cover,* and believe me it saved many an afternoon from turning into a minor tragedy.

Lastly: never try and cram too much into one day — the way to enjoy things is to give everybody time to stop and stare. This will prevent you tugging at small arms and saying, "Get a move on, the morning's nearly gone, and we've hardly done anything yet". That's no fun at all.

London does offer the best parks in the world — they make New York's Central Park look like a back yard. They are free and large enough never to seem over-crowded even on the hottest days. A picnic in Hyde Park, St. James's, Green Park or Regent's Park, will, weather permitting, definitely recharge the batteries. Such beauty and tranquility right in the middle of London's chaos can provide a much-needed break before you launch into the major activities of your day out.

The other important thing I have discovered over the years is that sightseeing works best when the children you are taking are not too diverse in ages. It is difficult for the teenager who is longing to get to the Science Museum not to indulge in a lot of clock-watching if made to wander around the toy department for the delight of a five-year-old. And equally, that five-year-old may not be at his best gazing at ancient monuments. So try if you can to take your children in turns or age-groups: this way everybody is happy.

Of course, as children get older, the great thrill is to be allowed to wander around London without being chaperoned by an adult. Armed with an *A to Z* and in the company of friends the same age, (not forgetting enough money to get home!) this is probably the best way the young can find out for themselves how fascinating London is. There are numerous Art Galleries, exhibitions, historic houses and places of interest, and, happily, London is still one of the safest cities during the hours of daylight.

There are some places which come under the heading of SUCCESS GUARANTEED. The Tower of London is one of these, steeped in gruesome and extraordinary history — boys and girls alike are always intrigued by the many aspects of The Tower, with its Ceremony of The Keys, and the brilliantly displayed Crown Jewels at which to wonder.

If it is purely *shopping with a difference* you are after, then the New Covent Garden complex fits the bill for all ages. There is a wide variety of shops (many of which stay open late), market stalls, plenty of reasonable places in which to have a meal or a snack, ranging from health food restaurants to Pizza Palaces, Hamburger joints and even a stall that only serves delicious jacket potatoes! In addition on many days there are entertainers performing in the Square, and close by is the famous church of St. Paul's, Covent Garden, traditionally the 'actors' church' where Ellen Terry and other notables are buried. The whole area is beautifully laid out, with ample seating under cover and exterior. If, like me, you have a *balletomane* in the family, here you are also in the heart of the ballet world. There are shops specialising in ballet gear, dance centres should any of the party wish to take in the odd class, and your day could end with a visit to the home of The Royal Ballet Company, the Royal Opera House.

As I have mentioned earlier London boasts some of the finest Museums and Public Art Galleries in the world — but, for a change, why not seek out a few of the smaller and lesser-known galleries? It is always rewarding to discover a young artist just making his name. On Sundays one can stroll along Piccadilly and the Bayswater Road and view the outdoor galleries where many unknowns get their first chance to be judged. Certainly it is well worth making the effort to find these out-of-the-way exhibitions.

It often seems to me that those of us who live in or near London take much of our capital city for granted. That is why accompanying children on a sight-seeing tour can be so rewarding. We view all the old familiars — like The Houses of Parliament, St. Paul's or the Changing of The Guard — through the eyes of a child, seeing anew things we have either forgotten or ignored simply because they have always been there on our doorstep. Children have the knack of seeing the unobvious: they gaze up at ceilings, look round corners, asking "Why?" "What For?" and "When?" And frequently we find ourselves delighting in things that our more-jaded eyes have consistently overlooked.

I suppose that during the run-up to Christmas most families will indulge in the promised trip to meet Father Christmas. Most of the larger London stores go to town with Santa. Each year his caves, grottoes or, yes, even his Space Capsules get more exotic. He will either bewitch or frighten to death most small children, and it is not an uncommon sight to see frantic mothers trying to signal to a jolly Father Christmas that he really must say "No" to the request for the large shiny dolls' pram — usually all to no avail. Santa's cheery promise of fulfilment and the mother's desperate look at the price tag: that is one trip that can be claimed a success or a failure, depending on your point of view!

Other than at Christmas or as a pre-birthday jaunt, I think that toy shops are fraught with problems. With temptation heaped on every shelf it is a rare child indeed who doesn't blatantly, or subtly indulge in a touch of the *I Wants*. So think hard before you include a toy shop in one of your London trips.

Wherever you decide to have your treat include the Regent's Park Zoo, a walk round Berwick Market (where you can buy the cheapest fruit) a look at a famous church, visit a Museum or Art Gallery, or sample what one of our many marvellous theatres has to offer, lunch in a park, or gape at the famous and infamous at Madame Tussaud's, I think you will agree with Doctor Johnson's much quoted saying that "a man who is tired of London, is tired of life".

I think that a child who is tired of London just hasn't been shown it properly — so really it is up to you.

Nanette Newman

Although best known as an actress for her award-winning performances in such films as *The Wrong Box, The Raging Moon* and *International Velvet,* Miss Newman is also the author of many childrens' books and in fact has sold well over half a million copies of her *God Bless Love* series.
More recently she starred in the television series *Let There Be Love* and played the name role in *Jessie,* a film for television written and directed by her husband, Bryan Forbes. The mother of two daughters, she has always been intensely interested in children and some years ago devised two cookery books especially aimed at the younger generation — *The Fun Food Factory* and *Fun Food Feasts.* The first of these was turned into a popular television series and was an attempt to wean children away from

junk food and teach them simple, nutritious meals. She feels very strongly that children should be encouraged to use their imaginations rather than be spoon fed with amusements that lead to dead ends. Although born in Northampton, she spent most of her early life in London and thinks it is still the most exciting city in the world to explore. "I think it offers something for everybody, young and old, and very often we praise the attractions of foreign cities and neglect the wonders of our own capital. I am grateful to the publishers of the Rothman Guide for allowing me to make this contribution and I sincerely hope that some of the ideas and advice I have put forward will point the way to hitherto undiscovered pleasures. Obviously, I have only indicated the tip of the iceberg: London is a treasure-trove of delights if only one takes the trouble to seek them out. It wasn't until this year, for instance, that Bryan and I visited the Tower of London to witness the age-old Ceremony of The Keys — and Bryan is a true Cockney! Very often we seem to ignore what is right under our noses, yet travel far afield in search of foreign places of interest."
For really up-to-date news on what is happening in London for Children during the week ring ED (STEWPOT) STEWART.
Tel: 01-246 8007
who gives a run down on all the events taking place.

KIDDING ABOUT LONDON

Tel: Chris Sparks 01-439 6288
A new Service that will entertain your children for the day. Children from seven upwards will be collected from your hotel and driven round London in a double decker bus by escorts dressed as Clowns. In the afternoon there will be a river trip, after a hamburger lunch. Balloons, hats, sweets are some of the goodies provided and there will be a prize-winning quiz.

SOME GUIDE BOOKS SPECIALISING IN CHILDREN'S LONDON

Young London — by London Transport

Family London — by London Transport

Discovering London for Children — Shire Publications

Parents' Guide to Children's London — Nicholson

all available in London Transport Information Offices at around £1.

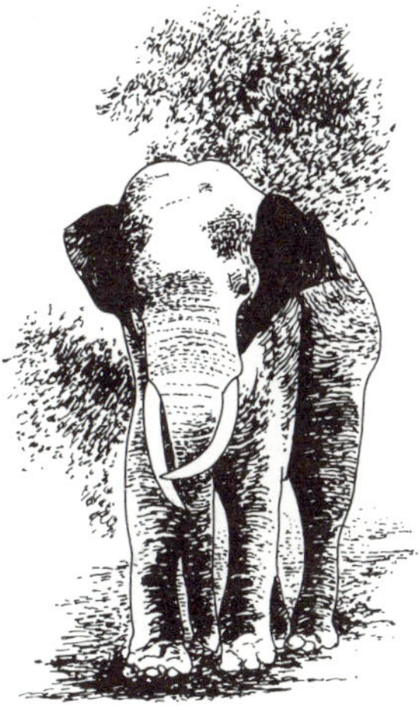

ZOOS

Chessington Zoo
Leatherhead Road, Chessington, Surrey.
Tel: Epsom 27227
Bus: Greenline Bus 714.
This has a special children's zoo, a miniature railway, boating lakes and hundreds of animals.
Open: 10.00am-6.00pm, Monday-Sunday in Summer. 10.00am-4.00pm in Winter. Special family ticket £2.
No Map Ref.

London Zoo
Regents Park, N.W.1.
Tel: 01-722 3333
Tube: Baker Street or Camden Town.
Buses: 3, 53, 74, 74b.

A
B
C
D
E
F
G
H
I
J
K
L
1
2
3
4
5
6
KILBURN LANE
HARROW ROAD
Kensal Green
LADBROKE GROVE
Ladbroke Grove
FERNHEAD RD.
ELGIN AVENUE
GREAT WESTERN RD
Westbourne Park
WESTBOURNE PARK
TALBOT ROAD
CHEPSTOW RD.
COLVILLE TER.
CLARENDON RD.
BLENHEIM CRES.
ELGIN CRES.
WESTBOURNE GROVE
PEMBRIDGE RD
Bayswater
QUEENSWAY
Queensway
Notting Hill Gate
NOTTING HILL GATE
PORTLAND ROAD
HOLLAND PARK AVENUE
Holland Park
HOLLAND PARK
CAMPDEN HILL RD
KENSINGTON CHURCH ST
KENSINGTON HIGH STREET
High Street Kensington
HOLLAND ROAD
EARLS COURT ROAD
HAMMERSMITH ROAD
WARWICK ROAD
WEST CROMWELL ROAD
NORTH END ROAD
TALGARTH ROAD
SHEPHERD'S BUSH RD
FULHAM PALACE ROAD
Earls Court
LILLIE ROAD
West Brompton
REDCLIFF GARDENS
FULHAM ROAD
KING'S ROAD
CASTELLAIN RD
Maida Vale
MAIDA VALE
CLIFTON GDNS.
Warwick Avenue
ST. JOHN'S WOOD RD
LISSON GROVE
EDGWARE ROAD
Edgeware Road
BISHOPS BRIDGE ROAD
PADDINGTON STATION
WESTBOURNE TER
Lancaster Gate
BAYSWATER ROAD
KENSINGTON GARDENS
SERPENTINE
ROTTEN ROW
KENSINGTON RD.
QUEEN'S GATE
EXHIBITION ROAD
South Kensington
CROMWELL ROAD
Gloucester Road
OLD BROMPTON ROAD
BROMPTON ROAD
SYDNEY ST.
WALTON RD.
BEAUCHAMP PLACE
CADOGAN GDNS
WELLINGTON ROAD
Marylebone
REGENT'S PARK
Baker Street
MARYLEBONE ROAD
SEYMOUR PLACE
PORTMAN SQUARE
BAKER STREET
Marble Arch
Marble Arch
HYDE PARK
GROSVENOR SQUARE
PARK LANE
MARYLEBONE HIGH ST.
Regent's Park
PORTLAND PL.
Great Portland Street
ALBANY STREET
EUSTON STATION
EUSTON ROAD
EUSTON ROAD
Warren Street
TOTTENHAM COURT RD
Goodge Street
GOODGE ST.
GOWER STREET
Oxford Circus
REGENT ST.
OXFORD STREET
Bond Street
NEW BOND ST.
OLD BOND ST.
BERKELEY SQUARE
CURZON ST.
PICCADILLY
Green Park
GREEN PARK
Hyde Park Corner
KNIGHTSBRIDGE
Knightsbridge
SLOANE STREET
BELGRAVE SQUARE
GROSVENOR PL.
KING'S ROAD
Sloane Square
BUCKINGHAM PALACE ROAD
CHELSEA BRIDGE RD
ROYAL HOSPITAL ROAD
CHELSEA EMBANKMENT
ALBERT BRIDGE
CHELSEA BRIDGE
BATTERSEA PARK
VICTORIA STATION
Pimlico
GROSVENOR ROAD
VICTORIA STREET
VAUXHALL BRIDGE ROAD
HORSE FERRY ROAD
St James's Park
BIRDCAGE WALK
THE MALL
ST. JAMES'S PARK
PALL MALL
Piccadilly Circus
POLAND ST.
WARDOUR ST.
SHAFTESBURY AV.
Tottenham Court Rd.
NEW OXFORD STREET
CHARING CROSS ROAD
Leicester Square
LONG ACRE
DRURY LANE
Covent Garden
CHARING CROSS STATION
VICTORIA
Westminster
WESTMINSTER BRIDGE
RIVER THAMES
LAMBETH BRIDGE
MILL BANK
ALBERT EMBANKMENT
VAUXHALL BRIDGE
Vauxhall
NINE ELMS LANE
FENTIMAN RD
HARLEYFORD RD.
Oval
Kennington Park
KENNINGTON ROAD
KENNINGTON PARK ROAD
LAMBETH PALACE RD
LAMBETH ROAD
WESTMINSTER BRIDGE RD
YORK ROAD
Lambeth North
WATERLOO STATION
WATERLOO ROAD
WATERLOO BRIDGE
STAMFORD ST.
Temple
EMBANKMENT
Aldwych
STRAND
Somerset House
SOUTHAMPTON ROW
Holborn
HOLBORN
CHANCERY LANE
Chancery Lane
HOLBORN VIA.
FLEET ST.
THEOBALDS RD.
GRAYS INN ROAD
GUILFORD ST
KING'S CROSS ROAD
ROSEBERRY AVENUE
CLERKEN WELL ROAD
FARRINGDON ST.
BLACKFRIARS BRIDGE
Blackfriars
RIVER THAMES
LUDGATE HILL
QUEEN VICTORIA ST.
Mansion House
St Paul's
CHEAPSIDE
ALDERSGATE ST.
GOSWELL ROAD
CITY ROAD
OLD STREET
Old Street
CITY ROAD
Moorgate
MOORGATE
Bank
SOUTHWARK BRIDGE
SOUTHWARK STREET
BLACKFRIARS RD
SOUTH WARK BRIDGE RD
BOROUGH RD.
LONDON RD
ST GEORGE'S RD
Elephant and Castle
NEWINGTON CAUSEWAY
NEW KENT RD
WALWORTH ROAD
BOROUGH HIGH ST.
Borough
GREAT DOVER ST.
LONG LANE
ST. THOMAS ST.
TOOLEY STREET
LONDON BRI. STATION
LONDON BRIDGE
Monument
Monument
LEADEN HALL ST.
FENCHURCH ST.
Tower Hill
TOWER HILL
TOWER BRIDGE
MINORIES
EAST SMITHFIELD
LEMAN ST.
Aldgate
COMMERCIAL ST.
WHITECHAPEL
HOUNDSDITCH
BISHOPS GATE
LIVERPOOL ST. STATION
GREAT EASTERN ST.
HACKNEY ROAD
ABBEY STREET
OLD KENT ROAD
ALBANY ROAD

First opened to the public in 1847, London Zoo now has one of the most valuable and comprehensive collections of wild animals of any zoo in the world. There are over 5000 animals housed here and the majority were actually born in the zoo.
There is a marvellous aviary where one can observe exotic birds flying in natural surroundings also a Moonlight Hall where day and night are reversed and nocturnal animals which are rarely seen can be viewed. There is a large ape and monkey house, special terraces to see wild cats and many, many more attractions.
Admission £3.50 adult, £1.50 child, subject to revision.
Map Ref. 1F

BOATING

London parks offer the best facilities for hiring small sailing dinghies and rowing boats. The two largest parks for this activity are:

The Serpentine Lake
Hyde Park.
Tel: 01-262 3751
Map Ref. 3E

and

Regents Park Lake
Regents Park.
Tel: 01-486 4759
Map Ref. 1F

It is advisable to telephone beforehand to check on weather conditions on the lakes and for times.

MODEL SHOPS

Beatties
112 High Holborn, W.C.1.
Tel: 01-405 6285
Specialists in model railways and model cars. Wonderful selection.
Map Ref. 2I

W & H Models
14 New Cavendish Street, W.1.
Tel: 01-935 8835
Scale models and kits, Landbuilt trains, planes and boats.
Map Ref. 2F

Patrick Models
107 Lillie Road, S.W.6.
Tel: 01-385 9864
Model railways, racing cars and wide variety of kits.
Map Ref. 6C

Hamley's
188 Regent Street, W.1.
Tel: 01-734 3161
A real children's paradise of games and models with every conceivable thing you can think of. Almost impossible to choose from the huge selection.
Map Ref. 2G

TOY SHOPS

Selfridges
Oxford Street, W.1.
Tel: 01-629 1234
Big selection of toys for all ages.
Map Ref. 2F

Mr. Patrick
107 Lillie Road, S.W.6.
Tel: 01-385 9864
This great London toy store stocks many models, games and toys.
Map Ref. 6C

Tridias
44 Monmouth Street, W.C.2.
Traditional toy shop with lots of soft toys, wooden toys and dolls.
Map Ref. 2H

Hamley's
200 Regent Street, W.1.
Tel: 01-734 3161
The six floors of this world famous store are packed with every conceivable toy. A real children's paradise.
Map Ref. 2G

Laffeaty's
345 Kings Road, S.W.3.
Tel: 01-352 2705
General toy shop selling most things for boys and girls of all ages.
Map Ref. 5E

Games Centre
126 Charing Cross Road, W.C.2.
Tel: 01-240 5691
Also in Oxford and Regent Street, W.1.
Over fourteen thousand games and puzzles of all kinds.
Map Ref. 2G

Eric Snooks
32 Lower Courtyard, Covent Garden Piazza, W.C.2.
Good sensible, old fashioned toys as well as very modern ones make this a delightful place for both children and grown-ups.
Map Ref. 3H

James Galt
30 Great Marlborough Street, W.1.
Tel: 01-734 0829
Very good selection, particularly of educational toys.
Map Ref. 2G

The Doll's House
29 Lower Courtyard, Covent Garden Piazza, W.C.2.
Tel: 01-379 7243
This shop specialises in really beautiful craftsman of doll's houses, as well as having a selection of antique ones. Doll's house furniture is also sold.
Map Ref. 3H

The Tree House
237 Kensington High Street, W.8.
Tel: 01-937 7497
A paradise for children with many original toys. Soda fountain.
Map Ref. 4B

HAIRDRESSING

Harrods
Knightsbridge, S.W.1.
Tel: 01-581 2021
Tube: Knightsbridge

There is a special department for children, where stylists take great care to see that children's hair is well cut and easy to manage. A blackboard and Lego help to pass the time.
Map Ref. 4E

Most hairdressers have assistants to do children's hair, therefore it is worthwhile asking, when you book your own appointment, whether you can take your child as well.

INTERESTING PLACES TO GO

Chelsea Pottery
13 Radnor Walk, S.W.3.
Tel: 01-352 1366
Tube: Sloane Square
The pottery often runs classes for children where they can learn to turn a pot, glaze and fire it. Telephone for times and details.
Map Ref. 6E

Geffrye Museum
Kingsland Road, E.2.
Tel: 01-739 8368
Buses: 22, 48, 243.
A paradise for children with its fascinating series of period rooms and

a whole range of activities and classes for children. There is a staff of qualified teachers who are ready to help and instruct. Over sevens only. Telephone for timetable.

Map Ref. 6D

Little Angel Marionette Theatre
Dagmar Passage, Cross Street, E.1.
Tel: 01-226 1787
Tube: Angel.
Puppet theatre which excels in fairy tales. For performance times telephone the theatre, most weekends and holidays.

No Map Ref.

National Gallery
Trafalgar Square, W.C.2.
Tel: 01-839 3321
Tube: Trafalgar Square.
During school holidays the Gallery generally runs a quiz for children. They take a questionnaire and explore the Gallery to find the answers. The questions are often quite hard and need real ingenuity to find the solutions therefore it is better for smaller children to be accompanied.
There is plenty of space for them to draw pictures as well and many of these are then put on show.
Admission Free.
Open: 10.00am-6.00pm, Monday to Saturday.
2.00pm-6.00pm, Sunday.
Closed: Christmas Eve, Christmas Day, Boxing Day, Good Friday, New Years Day and some Bank Holidays.

Map Ref. 3H

Natural History Museum
Cromwell Road, South Kensington, S.W.7.
Tel: 01-589 6323
Tube: South Kensington.
This Museum has a Children's Centre with games, models and microscopes.
Admission Free.
Open: 10.00am-6.00pm, Monday to Saturday.
2.30pm-6.00pm, Sunday.
Closed: Some Public Holidays.

Map Ref. 5C

National Theatre
South Bank, S.E.1.
Tel: 01-633 0880
Tube: Waterloo.
Older children will love the hour-long tour behind the scenes at the National Theatre complex. All the theatres are visited as well as the scenery workshops and paint docks. Telephone for details.

Map Ref. 3I

Madame Tussauds
Marylebone Road, W.1.
Tel: 01-935 6861
Tube: Baker Street.
Madame Tussaud's claim that everyone goes here at least twice in a lifetime — first as a child, second to take a child! Famous for its waxworks and its Chamber of Horrors.

Map Ref. 1F

The Royal Institution
21 Albemarle Street, W.1.
Tel: 01-408 2992
Tube: Green Park.
For strictly serious scientists, the Royal Institution has a Junior Associateship charging a small yearly subscription. The Associate can take two friends on specified days to the Faraday Museum and may use the library and attend special activities. For details telephone the Secretary.
Faraday Museum open Tuesday and Thursday.
Admission: 40p Adults, 20p Children.

Map Ref. 3G

The London Dungeon
34 Tooley Street, S.E.1.
Tel: 01-403 0606
Tube: London Bridge.
A mediaeval horror museum in slimy vaults. Very realistic.
Admission £3.60, Children £1.50.
Map Ref. 4K

Planetarium
Marylebone Road, W.1.
Tel: 01-486 1121
Tube: Baker Street.
A spectacular music and light show which is informative as well as entertaining.
Open: 11.00am-4.00pm.
Map Ref. 1F

Science Museum
South Kensington, S.W.5.
Tel: 01-589 3456
Tube: South Kensington.
This museum has a Children's Gallery — a push-button paradise where children can make things move, and light up.
Map Ref. 5C

Unicorn Theatre
Great Newport Street, W.C.2.
Tel: 01-836 3334
Tube: Leicester Square.
A small theatre specialising in plays for children. Box office will give you times and details.
Map Ref. 3H

Tate Gallery
Embankment, S.W.1.
Tel: 01-821 1313
Tube: Pimlico or Westminster.
The Tate Gallery offers activities for children during school holidays. Telephone for details.
Map Ref. 5H

Kidsline
Tel: 01-222 8070
Manned by Ann Griffiths from 4.00pm to 6.00pm evry weekday, kidsline will give information on entertainment, playcentres and playgrounds and anything else for children.

TOY THEATRES

Pollock's Toy Museum
1 Scala Street, W.1.
Tel: 01-636 3452
Tube: Goodge Street.
Small museum with principally toy theatres, puppets, dolls and folk toys. A shop attached where you can buy toy theatres.
Open: 10.00am-5.00pm, Monday to Saturday.
Small admission fee. Suitable for 4 to 12 year-olds.
Map Ref. 2G

Transport Museum
Covent Garden, W.C.2.
Tel: 01-379 6344
Tube: Covent Garden.
Transport through the ages — London Transport style. A must for the enthusiasts.
Open: 10.00am-6.00pm, Monday-Sunday. Closed Christmas.
Admission: Adults £1.60, Children and OAP's 80p.
Map Ref. 3H

Leisure Centres
Many London boroughs have Leisure Centres for children. For times and places telephone the appropriate borough. Numbers can be found in the telephone directory.

CHILDREN'S RESTAURANTS

Children and restaurants are not necessarily compatible — here is a short list of reasonably-priced ones which serve the food that children like — and which seems to like children!

Chicago Pizza Pie
17 Hanover Square, W.1.
Tel: 01-629 2669
Tube: Oxford Circus.

Deep dish pizzas with generous fillings — even the greediest child finds it hard to get a whole one down! Made freshly, so be prepared for a wait.
Map Ref. 2G

Cranks
8 Marshall Street, W.1.
Tel: 01-437 9431
Tube: Piccadilly.
Vegetarian restaurant with exciting salads, dishes of nut rissoles, small pies and delicious ice creams. Drinks are fun, too, with fresh fruit and yoghurt ones being very popular. Also in Heal's, Tottenham Court Road, W.C.1. and Peter Robinson's, Oxford Circus, W.1.
Map Ref. 3G

Creperie
56 South Molton Street, W.1.
Tel: 01-629 4794
Tube: Bond Street.
Pancakes galore — all the different varieties you can think of, plus sweet ones with cream! You can actually watch your pancake being made.
Map Ref. 2F

Granary
39 Albemarle Street, W.1.
Tel: 01-493 2978
Tube: Green Park.
Offers an amazing selection and delicious cakes. Get there early as it is very popular. Also includes a take-away section if you want to picnic in nearby Green Park.
Map Ref. 3G

Hard Rock
150 Old Park Lane, W.1.
Tel: 01-629 0382
Tube: Hyde Park.
Lovely hamburgers, charcoal-grilled steaks and enormous sandwiches accompanied by loud music. Good ice-creams and sundaes, American-style.
Map Ref. 4F

Old Kentucky Chain
Found all over London with a fast food menu of chips with everything. Adored by children and quite good.

Rock Garden
Covent Garden, W.C.2.
Tel: 01-240 3961
Tube: Covent Garden.
Chili con carne, hamburgers and other American-style food. You can sit out on fine days and watch the world go by. Children love the check table cloths and odd chairs.
Map Ref. 3H

Texas Lone Star Saloon
154 Gloucester Road, S.W.7.
Tel: 01-370 5627

Tube: South Kensington or Gloucester Road.
NEAR SCIENCE MUSEUM
Very good food of the kind that children revel in.
Map Ref. 5F

Staveley's
642 King's Road, S.W.3.
Tel: 01-731 4247
Tube: Sloane Square.
A disco for children operates here at weekends. Food, especially fish and chips, very good.
No Map Ref.

Dingwall's
Camden Lock N.W.1.
Tel: 01-267 4967
Tube: Camden Town
Very good hamburgers, quiche and salad in this unpretentious place which children seem to like.
No Map Ref.

Pappagalli's Pizza Inc.
7-9 Swallow Street, W.1.
Tel: 01-734 5182
Tube: Piccadilly.
Children are made to feel at home and they all like the pizzas which are indeed very good.
Map Ref. 3G

SPORT

See under separate section 'Sport in London'.

Designed by Paul E. Garbutt

Copyright London Transport Executive